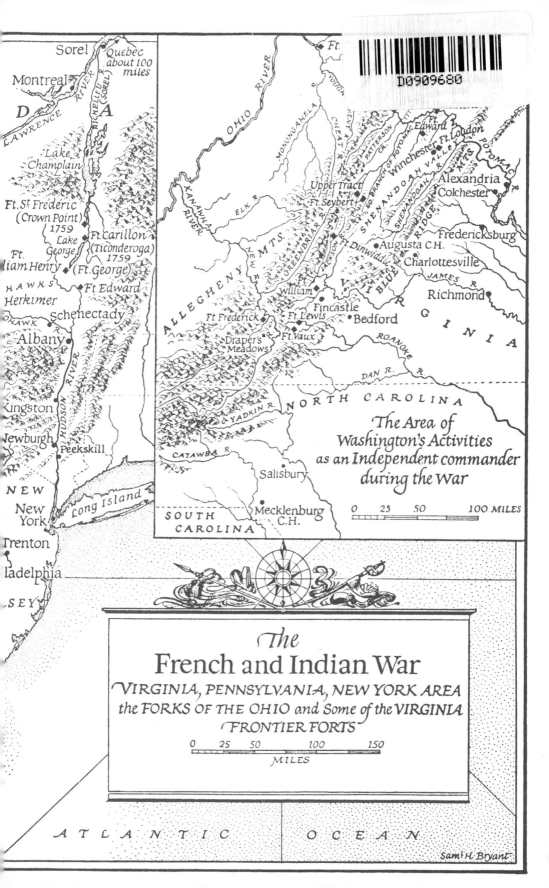

The Area of
Washington's Activities
as an Independent commander
during the War

0   25   50   100 MILES

The
French and Indian War
VIRGINIA, PENNSYLVANIA, NEW YORK AREA
the FORKS OF THE OHIO and Some of the VIRGINIA
FRONTIER FORTS

0   25   50   100   150
MILES

ATLANTIC   OCEAN

Sam¹ H. Bryant

GEORGE WASHINGTON

The Forge of Experience

(1732–1775)

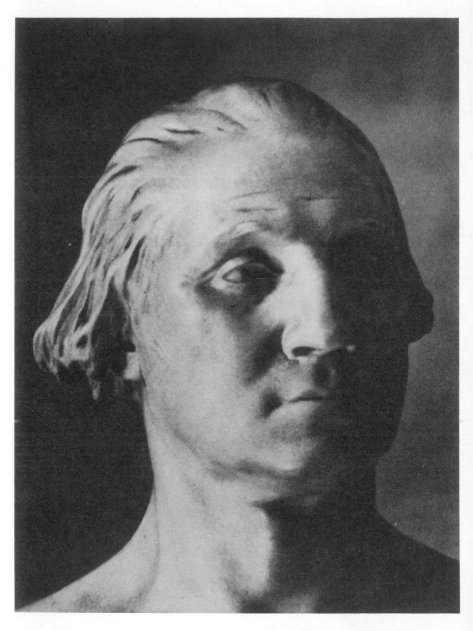

GEORGE WASHINGTON BY JEAN ANTIONE HOUDON (detail).
This version of Houdon's 1784 bust belonged to Thomas Jefferson.
It presents the hero vividly as a virile athletic man. Courtesy of the
Boston Athenaeum. Photograph by H. H. Arnason.

GEORGE WASHINGTON

The Forge of Experience

(1732–1775)

by JAMES THOMAS FLEXNER

with photographs

Little, Brown and Company

BOSTON TORONTO LONDON

A portion of this book first appeared in
American Heritage.

10 9 8 7

MV NY

*Published simultaneously in Canada
by Little, Brown & Company (Canada) Limited*

PRINTED IN THE UNITED STATES OF AMERICA

Contents

Introduction   3

I.   A SELF-MADE MAN

1. Birth of a Hero   9
2. Termagant and Brother   18
3. A Fairfax World   26
4. Surveyor's Wages   34
5. Death and a Beckoning Mission   46

II.   WAR IN THE WILDERNESS

6. Forest Adventure   59
7. Triggering the Seven Years' War   78
8. Defeat and Perhaps Disgrace   93
9. In and Out of the Army   110
10. Nightmare   119
11. Commander in Chief of What   132
12. Hysteria   149
13. Washington Turns to the Crown   169
14. To Death's Door   176
15. Adventures of the Heart   188
16. Wrong Road to Victory   206

III.   TRUE HAPPINESS

17. Domestic Enjoyments   227
18. County Squire   249
19. Children Not His Own   261
20. British Debts versus American Markets   272
21. Eyes West   289

[vii]

CONTENTS

IV.   ROAD TO REVOLUTION

22. Dragon's Teeth   309
23. The Sucking Vortex   324
24. A Dreadful Trust   332

V.   APPENDIXES

A. Washington's Farewell to His Officers, French and In-
    dian War   349
B. Acknowledgments   351
C. Statement Concerning Sources and Objectives   353
D. Source References   361

   Index   379

List of Illustrations

George Washington by Jean Antoine Houdon (detail).   *Frontispiece*

MAP: Major George Washington's Route to and from
The Forks of the Ohio and Fort LeBoeuf *page 58*

(between pages 150 and 151)

Chain, compass, and scale drawn by Washington at fourteen.

Plan of Alexandria drawn by Washington at seventeen.

Portrait of Lawrence Washington.

Portrait of Elizabeth Fauntleroy.

Portrait of Sally Fairfax.

Facsimile of the first page of a letter from George Washington to
Sally Fairfax.

Portrait of Eliza Philipse by John Singleton Copley.

Four Englishmen Who Contributed to Washington's Education:
Thomas, Sixth Lord Fairfax; Lieutenant Governor Robert Dinwiddie of Virginia; Governor William Shirley of Massachusetts;
John Campbell, Fourth Earl of Loudoun and the British Commander in Chief.

Braddock's Defeat by Patrick MacKellar, Senior Engineer with the
British Army.

(between pages 246 and 247)

Portrait of Martha Dandridge Custis by John Wollaston, 1757.

Portrait of John Parke Custis and Martha Parke Custis by John
Wollaston, 1757.

How Mount Vernon Grew.
The house George Washington lived in as a boy.
After an enlargement, 1759, in preparation for his marriage.
The completed mansion.

A Mount Vernon mantlepiece.

Portrait of Martha Dandridge Custis Washington by Charles Willson Peale, 1772.

Washington's stepson, John Parke Custis. A miniature by Charles Willson Peale.

George Washington's fishing tackle.

A gold necklace believed to have been presented to Martha Washington by her husband.

Portrait of George Washington in his French and Indian War uniform, by Charles Willson Peale, 1772.

GEORGE WASHINGTON

The Forge of Experience

(1732–1775)

To all those who have down the years separated from the chaff, and preserved, the truth about George Washington, particularly John C. Fitzpatrick and Douglas Southall Freeman, the Library of Congress and the Mount Vernon Ladies' Association of the Union.

Introduction

THIS VOLUME tells about considerably more than half George Washington's life, the forty-three years that elapsed from his birth to his acceptance, at the outbreak of the American Revolution, of the command of the Continental Army. I have elected to call the book *George Washington: The Forge of Experience*, but it might just as well have been called *The Man Almost Nobody Knows*. The great historian Samuel Eliot Morison has stated that, according to popular attitudes, "Washington is the last person you would ever suspect of having been a young man with all the bright hopes and black despairs to which young men are subject."[1]

The Washington who actually lived has been transmuted in the group memory of his people into an impersonal "Father of Our Country." Here is Sigmund Freud's description of how recurring "infantile phantasies" concerning their own fathers affect biographers: "They obliterate the individual features of their subject's physiognomy; they smooth over the traces of his life's struggles with internal and external resistances, and they tolerate in him no vestige of human weakness and imperfection. Thus, they present us with what is in fact a cold, strange, ideal figure, instead of a human being to whom we might feel ourselves distantly related."[2]

Without the least thought of the American, Freud described exactly the somewhat repellent "marble image" that has displaced, in the nation which to so great an extent owes to him its birth, the true George Washington.

Children, of course, universally resist the conception that their fathers could ever have been anything but old; could have been enamored of girls other than their mothers; could have been swept by irresistible emotions; were once eager, fallible, and confused searchers for a personal role in an uncertain universe. The painter Grant Wood summarizes the matter in relation to Washington. When he illustrated the ridiculous story Parson Weems invented of Washington, his little hatchet, and the cherry tree, Wood put on the neck of the boyish figure who "cannot tell a lie" a jowled, toothless head copied from a Gilbert Stuart portrait of Washington as an exhausted old man.

Parson Weems! Shortly after Washington's death, this canting minister filled with invented goody-goody anecdotes the vacuum created by the unwillingness of Americans to accept the idea that Washington was ever really young. Modern sophisticates, of course, smile at Weems. However, instead of turning to the factual record, they have too often revived the father image in a purer form. Thus, Gilbert Stuart's portraits of the tired, aged Washington—"prematurely grown old" as he put it, "in the service of my country"[3]—remain the favorite effigies of Washington despite the existence of even better works of art that show the leader as a virile man, imbued with both sweetness and animal power.

Although conscientious and able scholars have made almost all the facts available, few Americans have any clear idea of how Washington developed and, indeed, of what kind of man he actually turned out to be. This is a tragedy for Washington's reputation.

Infantile phantasies create an unhuman father, more an object of awe than love. By testimony of his contemporaries one of the most lovable of men, Washington is too often viewed today, by his national children, with a vague, uneasy resentment. The extremely human man who was in his lifetime by far the most popular of living Americans is now, although revered, far from the most popular American hero.

To really love and appreciate one's father, it is necessary to disclose, by banishing the delusions of infantile thinking, the man he really is and was. In this volume, we shall seek the actual man who was the father of our country.

When I undertook this biography of Washington, which will in further volumes carry the hero to the closing of his life, I tried to empty my mind of every preconception that existed about his character and career: I tried to start my study as if I had never before heard the name of Washington. I did not even assume that he had been good and great. My labors have persuaded me that he became one of the noblest and greatest men who ever lived. But he was not born that way. He did not spring from the head of Jove already armored with wisdom and strength. He perfected himself gradually through the exercise of his own will and skill.

George Washington was, of course, born with good material to work on, but the very passion and energy of his nature made it the more difficult to direct. The young man we see in this volume drives fast and swerves again and again off the track—in his dark love for his neighbor's wife, in foolhardy maneuvers during the French and Indian War and unexalted scrambles for promotion—but always he swings back again, further ahead on the road to greatness.

Washington was one of the very few Presidents of the United States whose formal studies had come to an end on the elementary school level. However, he possessed a transcendent ability to learn from living. "Errors," he wrote, "once discovered are more than half amended"; and he added, "Some men will gain as much experience in the course of three or four years as some will in ten or a dozen."[4]

This volume presents the experiences from which George

Washington learned, and tries to show, by his actions and his written thoughts, how he reacted at each stage of his long apprenticeship up to the moment when, formed by the years into a great leader, the American hero unsheathed the revolutionary sword.

I

A Self-Made Man

1

Birth of a Hero

I N 1657, the first Washington landed in Virginia. The Wild West was then on the Atlantic seaboard, and John Washington was a turbulent spirit well suited to so violent a world.

Revolution in England had spun off this adventurer whom birth had destined for gentility. Although George Washington himself was to remain ignorant of the transatlantic background of his family,[1] we know that the immigrant's father, the Reverend Lawrence Washington, had enjoyed a rich living in Essex until the Roundheads expelled him for drunkenness. Whether the misfortune was actually due to drink or, as defending High Churchmen insisted, to doctrine, the effect was the same. At the age of about eleven, John was plummeted from affluence to squalor. He completed his break with the gentlemanly life by going to sea, not in the navy but on a merchant vessel as mate and trader.

The chances of cargo carried him at the age of about twenty-five to Virginia, where he married Anne Pope, daughter of a prosperous father, and decided to stay. Sued by his captain, he accused the captain of having on the voyage over hanged a woman as a witch. However, John did not appear at the murder trial; he was, he explained, too busy baptizing his first son (George Washington's grandfather).

After his first wife died, John married in succession sisters who had been accused before him, when he sat as justice of the peace, one with keeping a bawdy house and the other with being the governor's whore. He transacted legal business, sometimes before courts on which he himself sat; he was a Burgess, a vestryman, a coroner, president of the county court, and a chief military officer who was implicated in the murdering of five Indian ambassadors. Having a passion for acreage, he used a legal trick to pull the soil out from under an Indian village. This earned him the tribal name Caunotaucarius (town-taker), which that long-memoried people were later to apply by inheritance to his great-grandson.

As energetic and able as he was rough and unscrupulous, John re-established the Washingtons in the fierce New World at about the rank they had occupied, before Cromwell, in the Old. He made them the equivalent of an English county family. Although no Washington ever sat in the Virginia equivalent of the House of Lords, the King's Council, they often married above themselves. They continued important enough so that, when they produced a transcendently able scion, no eminence was considered, in that semi-aristocratic society, beyond his rightful reach.[2]

John's son and George's grandfather, Lawrence Washington, was not a man of action but of law. As an attorney, he represented London merchants in Virginia. He married Mildred Warner, daughter of a member of the King's Council, and died in 1698, at the age of thirty-nine, leaving a respectable estate. His second son, Augustine, who was to be George's father, was then three. The child was taken to England by a stepfather. He attended the Appleby School in Westmoreland for some four years before, his mother having died, he was brought back to Virginia.

Tradition tells us that Augustine was called Gus and grew

into a blond giant, fabulously strong but miraculously gentle. Authentic information, to be gleaned almost exclusively from legal records, reveals a nervous businessman, much concerned with land speculation; prone to lawsuits; given increasingly, the larger the reward offered, to hesitation and procrastination. His greatest opportunity came when iron was discovered on some land he had patented near Fredericksburg, and an English partnership, the Principio Company, proved eager to mine it. Agreements, contracts, arguments followed each other in bewildering succession; and in 1729 he made a trip to England, where he drew up a new paper which he denounced as soon as he got home.

During his absence, his first wife had died, leaving three small children, Lawrence, Augustine Jr., and Jane. In 1731, the father remarried. The bride was Mary Ball, who was to be the mother of George Washington.

Her father, Joseph Ball, had come from England as a young man and raised a large family in Virginia. He was a widower of fifty-eight when, to the outrage of his children—they had to be placated with a large part of his estate—he married an illiterate widow, Mary Johnson. From this match, Washington's mother was born. Her father died when she was three, leaving her 400 acres, fifteen cattle, three Negroes, and enough feathers to be made into a bed. Her mother married a third time; this husband also died; the mother followed when Mary was twelve, and the child went to live with George Eskridge, a family connection. Her writings indicate that she had little education. With no parents to tame her and as possessor, due to numerous deaths, of a tidy little estate, she became very self-willed. Although she rode out on a silk plush saddle and possessed fine inherited clothes, she remained unmarried long past the age when Virginia girls were considered old maids. She was a ripe twenty-three when she married Augustine.[3]

[11]

Augustine carried his bride to a house—to be known after a subsequent enlargement as Wakefield—which he had built a few years before near where Pope's Creek empties into the Potomac. This house has disappeared. However, it could not have been very large or very elegant since its construction cost the relatively small sum of 5500 pounds of tobacco.[4]

Eleven months after her marriage, at 10 A.M. on the morning of February 11, 1732,* Mary Washington gave birth to a male baby who was probably large enough to increase her pain, and who may have had on his damp skull wisps of red-brownish hair. Had this event taken place in classical times, surely some prodigy would have been initiated from Olympus: a snake sent down to be strangled by the hero in his cradle, or at least a weird clap of thunder. But Virginia dozed through a midwinter morning. The infant was christened George, probably after his mother's former guardian.[5]

In 1733, George's sister Betty was born, and in 1734, his brother Samuel. When, during 1735, his half sister Jane died, George became the oldest child in the house; his two half brothers were across the ocean, at the English school their father had attended. The boy undoubtedly knew from the first the protection of colored attendants, comforting often, annoying when they would not let him totter over to the shining water of Pope's Creek. But before conscious memory occupied its seat in his brain, the family moved.

Upriver they went, some forty miles as the crow flies, many more as the Potomac wanders, to a tract of some 2500 acres which Augustine had bought from a half sister. It was where Little Hunting Creek ran into the Potomac; it was called Ep-

---

* Since in 1752 a reform of the calendar pushed all dates ahead eleven days, we are not wrong in commemorating Washington's birthday on February 22. This was usually the date celebrated during his lifetime, although some of his Virginia neighbors adhered to the 11th. To save confusion, all dates will from now on be given in this volume, not Old Style but in accord with the present calendar.

sewasson and was to become famous as Mount Vernon. The best archeological evidence tells that on the commanding eminence where George Washington's mansion now stands, Augustine had, in preparation for their coming, erected over an older foundation the substantial but not elegant story and a half farmhouse, the ground floor rooms of which are still embedded in Mount Vernon.[6] Here, while the Negroes built their own cabins, George warmed himself before the fireplaces, set at an angle in the corners of the rooms, that were to warm him to the last day he lived. From the doorway opposite the front door in the central hall, the little boy wandered out onto a high flat bluff beyond which the tight world of woods and fields gave way to grandeur: water more than a mile wide before, stretching on and out to the east and southwest, and beyond low rolling hills that carried their greenery on to where the visible world ended.

The jump north had carried the Washingtons into a sparsely settled region. On some of their own land virgin timber still towered; they had few close neighbors. However, the house's inner population grew. In 1736 John Augustine Washington was born, and in 1737, Charles. The father sailed for England to consult his partners, making a departure exciting for a boy of almost five, and months later a return even more exciting: certainly there were presents.

But more important to George's future than any coming or going of his father was the appearance of a tall, dark, sallow man with a narrow intellectual face, a long straight nose and high nostrils. This was Lawrence, the elder of George's half brothers, home at about twenty from his education in England. George must have listened with fascination to the newcomer's tales of his schoolboy adventures, for everyone expected that, when he was old enough, he too would cross the ocean to the family alma mater, the Appleby School.

To cap its other troubles, the iron mine was showing signs of becoming exhausted: if money were to be made, Augustine must be on the scene. In 1738, he bought 260 acres and leased nearly 300 more on the Rappahannock within easy distance of the mine, and by December had taken his family some thirty miles southeast to Ferry Farm. The Washingtons crowded into a moderate-sized wooden farmhouse with four rooms on the ground floor, two above.

The document most revealing of the Washingtons' way of life at Ferry Farm is an inventory of Augustine's possessions there, made when George was eleven.[7] Crowding is indicated; comfort, but little elegance.

The family pride was described as "plate": one soup spoon, eighteen small spoons, seven teaspoons, a watch, and a sword: total value, £25 10s. The glass was worth £5 12s.: a decanter, a mug, three tumblers, and "sundry saltcellars." The chinaware comprised two tea sets, two bowls, two dishes, nine custard cups, four coffee mugs, and eleven plates, to a total of £3 6s.

The prize possession in the "hall" was a looking glass valued at £2 10s. It flanked or reflected a "screwtore" (i.e., escritoire), two tables, one armchair, eleven leather-bottomed chairs, and a fire set. The parlor contained three beds, an old table, three old chairs, an old desk, a looking glass, a set of window curtains, and a sugar box. In the "hall back room" were a pair of those four-poster beds which, when the curtains were drawn, became little rooms within a room; there were also a chest of drawers, a tea table, four rush-bottomed chairs, two window hangings, a dressing glass, a trunk, and a pair of andirons. The back room contained two more four-posters, a "chest and box," and an old chest of drawers. In the passage were a large and a small table and a couch; in the chamber above the hall, three four-posters and a trunk; in the chamber above the parlor, three old beds, six rugs, and "one large cooler." For the thirteen beds and one couch there were six good pairs of sheets, ten inferior pairs, and

[14]

seventeen pillow cases. The Washingtons were well prepared to entertain at dinner: thirteen tablecloths and thirty-one napkins. There was miscellaneous equipment in the four outbuildings: dairy, loft, storehouse, and kitchen.

Close in front of the house flowed the Rappahannock, much narrower than the Potomac, nervous where the other river had been majestic. Its breadth of a few hundred yards rose and fell fiercely with the tide, plaguing the smaller ocean-going ships that sometimes maneuvered near the bottom of George's lawn. The house was held to the river by a bank that rose steeply to tableland behind it. Down this grade the road to the ferry descended, bringing into the boy's view from the windows horses straining to hold back loaded carts. A horse sometimes fell in a hysteria of neighs. The blowing of a horn across the river to call the ferry presaged travelers soon to be landed near George's dooryard: perhaps a neighbor accompanied by children who were his friends; perhaps a mysterious rider. Here was a lively place, and it was all the livelier because the boy was now old enough to ramble on his own.

George had his social relations with his father's seven able-bodied Negroes, the eight of moderate value, and the five not capable, probably because they were too young or too old, of work. The easterly bank that delayed the rising sun was topped by a flat woodland where he may well have in play fought such Indians as he was in reality to fight. The river offered him fishing and boating and swimming. When he got across it, he could explore Fredericksburg, probably the only town he had yet seen. The most impressive structures were the public tobacco warehouses and a stone prison; the church remained half built because of some dispute that excited his elders. There were a wharf and several quarries, a courthouse, and an untidy sprinkling of small homes (the law said none could be smaller than twenty feet square). At the wharf, he sometimes found drawn up, their sails now furled, English ships he had seen from his front lawn. Undoubtedly he got on board sometimes, stared in stuffy cabins, and asked the unending questions of childhood.

When George was almost eight, his brother Lawrence—England having declared war on Spain—turned warrior, securing one of the captaincies in an American regiment raised as part of the British regular army. How the little boy, who preserved through old age a love of resplendent regalia, must have admired Lawrence's uniform! When autumn leaves tumbled down the steep bank, the brother sailed away for the Caribbean as one of the 400 Virginians who took part in Admiral Vernon's expedition against Cartagena.

At home, baby Mildred was born and died. George's second half brother, Augustine Jr., came back from his English schooling, not in the best of humors since his father had not kept him abroad to study law. George was never close to this Augustine, his immediate senior, nor to the boy next below him, Samuel, who was to prove in manhood incompetent and improvident, an irritating financial drain.[8] George was to remember that John Augustine—Jack—four years his junior, was "the intimate companion of my youth."[9]

George's earliest exercise books,[10] which date from before he reached his teens, reveal that he was receiving some very practical education. He wrote a clear if sprawling childish hand; he was learning arithmetic that served accounting, and also the geometric basis of surveying.

The news that trickled in from the Cartagena expedition was first favorable—the amphibious force had battered its way into the harbor; and then bad—a major British attack on the city had been repulsed with dreadful loss. Anxiety for Lawrence mounted at Ferry Farm. He was unharmed, however, and able to come home to tell his little brother of his admiration for Admiral Vernon. However, he expressed nothing but bitterness for the British regular general who, in his scorn for the Colonial troops, had kept most of them languishing on shipboard to die of disease.[11] Memory of these talks was to come back to George when he too served with British regulars.

Lawrence's homecoming was followed shortly by a catastrophe: on April 12, 1743, the father died. George was eleven.

2

Termagant and Brother

AMONG THE many changes dictated by his father's death was the abandonment of the plan that George Washington would, like his half brothers, go to school across the ocean. Had he sailed, would the history of the United States have been different?

In his later years, Washington opposed sending American youths to Europe to be educated. He argued that they imbibed principles "unfriendly to republican government" and "the rights of man."[1] But when his father died, such considerations meant nothing to George: he only saw that his environment had shrunk like a millpond after the dam breaks. Sixteen years later he wrote of "the longing desire which for many years I have had of visiting" England.[2]

The father left more than 10,000 acres in seven or more tracts and forty-nine slaves, but his estate was divided many ways. Augustine had been enough of an Englishman to believe in at least modified primogeniture: Lawrence got among other bequests Epsewasson, which he was to rechristen Mount Vernon after his beloved admiral, and, with a few small provisos, the iron mine. Next in value were the bequests to Augustine Jr., which included George's birthplace. George's share sounded more impressive than it was: Ferry Farm, which was far from fertile, half of an unimportant tract of 4360 acres, ten slaves, three lots of little value in Fredericksburg, and a small share in the residual estate.[3] That all was to be administered by his mother until he came of age proved disastrous. She was a poor businesswoman and, once she had her hands on anything, she would not relinquish it. Although Augustine had made other provisions for her, George was not to get actual possession of his Ferry Farm inheritance until almost thirty years had passed.[4]

Remarriage was in Virginia the common lot of widows. But Mary Washington did not marry again. Since his two half brothers attended to their own estates, George became at eleven the oldest child in her household, captain, under her demanding eye, of a nursery team containing one younger sister and three brothers. Whenever he could, he went visiting, not only to the homes of his half brothers, but far afield, to distant cousins.[5]

Since Mary Ball Washington was the mother of the father of our country, writers have attributed to her their favorite maternal virtues. However, history does not always draw noble men from noble mothers, preferring sometimes to temper her future heroes in the furnaces of domestic infelicity.

One of George's childhood playmates remembered that of Mrs. Washington "I was ten times more afraid than I ever was of my own parents." She was described in 1777 as "majestic" by an awed male.[6] She was clearly a powerful woman, but all her power was centered on herself. Whatever George attempted that was not in her immediate service, she attempted to stop. Copious evidence reveals that his mounting eminence was to her primarily a source of resentment, as she felt it made him neglect her. It must have taken a strong will to adhere to this attitude as her son's greatness flowered and flowered. Would it not have been so much easier to have climbed on the bandwagon and accepted the plaudits of the crowd? However, although she lived into George's second term as President, she never budged from home to take part in any triumphant moment of his career, and all her comments that have been recorded with the least

[19]

possibility of accuracy show her depreciating her son's achievements.

Nonplussed by this attitude towards their idol, Washington's admirers tried to cast Mary Washington as a Spartan mother who was not enthusiastic because in the elevation of her mind she felt that what George achieved was the least that she expected of her son. Unfortunately, the lady refused to co-operate with such an image. During the Revolution, for instance, she complained so loudly that the commander in chief, who was actually providing for her well, was allowing her to starve that she incited, to his rage and embarrassment, a movement in the Virginia legislature to come to her financial rescue.[7]

The total result seems to have been a spontaneous conspiracy of silence among Washington's contemporaries. It is amazing how rarely the long-lived lady is mentioned in letters, diaries, and memoirs. Only after the passage of years had thoroughly obscured the record did "Mary the Mother Washington" take off towards deification.

The truth about Washington's mother is too important for an understanding of her son to permit the indulgence of any desire to explain it away or gloss it over. Certainly the self-reliance that was one of Washington's greatest strengths was fostered in him, at that very early age when it first manifested itself, by his desire to escape from a home where he was not content. And the passionate love of domesticity which swayed him during his happy marriage, that drive to private enjoyments, so unusual in a world leader, which fruitfully tempered his ambitions in the great world, may well be attributed in part to his final realization of the happy hearth which had in his boyhood been denied him.

While yet a boy, he carefully copied down this prophetic poem entitled "True Happiness": *

---

* The spelling and punctuation of all quotations have been modernized.

"These are the things which once possess'd
Will make a life that's truly bless'd:
A good estate on healthy soil
Not got by vice, nor yet by toil:
Round a warm fire, a pleasant joke,
With chimney ever free from smoke:
A strength entire, a sparkling bowl,
A quiet wife, a quiet soul,
A mind as well as body whole:
Prudent simplicity, constant friends,
A diet which no art commends:
A merry night without much drinking,
A happy thought without much thinking:
Each night by quiet sleep made short,
A will to be but what thou art:
Possess'd of these, all else defy,
And neither wish nor fear to die."[8]

New copybooks indicated a change of instructors but no change in the pragmatic approach. George used the conclusions of Euclid as established rules for geometric constructions without any of the reasoning from the axioms now emphasized. He studied the calendar and geography and the zodiacal configuration of the stars. Problems of surveying concerned him so much that he must already have seen in that art escape from his dependence at home.

Justly the best known of George's authentic childhood activities was his copying out 110 maxims under the title *Rules of Civility and Decent Behavior in Company and Conversation.*[9] This was certainly a labor of love, for in his later years Washington was addicted to coining maxims of his own, which are thickest in his letters of advice to the young. His own maxims are much closer in approach to the *Rules of Civility* than to the

Sunday school forgeries—such as the anecdote of the cherry tree, and his inability to tell a lie—Parson Weems attributed to the then dead hero. Between Weems and the *Rules* rises one of the great divides of history. Weems stands for the Low Church, middle class morality which swept the nineteenth century, but the *Rules* were codified by sixteenth century Jesuits for the worldly guidance of French aristocrats.

Of the *Rules* Washington copied down, only the last three would have appealed particularly to Parson Weems: "108. When you speak of God and his attributes, let it be seriously and with reverence. Honor and obey your natural parents although they be poor. 109. Let your recreations be manful, not sinful. 110. Labor to keep alive in your breast that little spark of celestial fire called conscience."

Telling the truth is nowhere urged, but courteous dissimulation is. As for acting "against the moral rules," that is only forbidden in the presence of inferiors. Nothing is said about obedience to the Deity or getting into heaven: ethical behavior has its reward on this earth as it makes you well thought of in society.

The first forty maxims elaborate on the first one: "Every action done in company ought to be with some sign of respect to those that are present." Examples range from "In the presence of others, sing not to yourself with a humming noise nor drum with your fingers or feet" to "Kill no vermin, as fleas, lice, ticks, etc., in the sight of others." Other sets of rules deal with table manners—"Cleanse not your teeth with the tablecloth"; and clothes—"Keep to the fashion of your equals." In general and specifically in a copious section distinctions are laid down for the ways of acting with inferiors, equals, or superiors: when accompanying a man of "great quality, walk not with him cheek by jowl but somewhat behind him, but yet in such a manner that he may easily speak to you."

There is nowhere the slightest reference to behavior in the

presence of ladies. Nor is there any urging of frugality or diligence at one's labor. Benjamin Franklin's bourgeois good sense,
as in "Early to bed and early to rise / Makes a man healthy,
wealthy, and wise," would be almost as out of place as Weems's
canting. The lessons, which Washington well learned to the
great benefit of his future career, are aimed at that profound
courtesy to one's fellow men that grows from careful attention to
the effects of one's own acts on the feelings of others.

George undoubtedly read what came to hand that he found
interesting, since all his life he sought in books instruction and,
to a lesser degree, pleasure. An early memorandum notes that he
had got in an unspecified volume to "the reign of King John, and
in the *Spectator* read to No. 143."[10]

The title pages of Washington's copybooks are lettered and
spaced for effect; his calligraphy and mathematical diagrams
show conscious artistry as well as care. One of the aspects of
George Washington's character that is least appreciated is his
esthetic urge: from boyhood, he found a delightful connection
between beauty, utility, and clarity.

Washington was to encourage his presumptive biographer,
David Humphreys, to write, in explaining his father's unrealized
desire to send him to England for an education, that youths
brought up in Virginia "were in danger of becoming indolent
and helpless" because they were given "a horse with a servant to
attend them, as soon as they could ride."[11] Whether or not
young George had such a servant, he must have spent much
time on horseback, since he became celebrated for his skill and
grace as a rider. His physical prowess also became stupendous:
surely he engaged in all the rough and energetic sports of
boyhood.

John Adams was to state, "That Washington was not a scholar
was certain. That he was too illiterate, unread, unlearned for his
station and reputation is equally past dispute."[12]

This stricture was to some extent inspired by jealousy of the athletic pragmatist who was not perpetually expounding ideas but to whom, nonetheless, the nation listened in preference to intellectual John Adams. Yet the mature Washington would not have denied the charge. Some of the diffidence which sweetened his use of power was inspired by that "consciousness of a defective education" which he gave as a reason for not putting down on paper his recollections of the Revolution.[13] As the victor in that conflict, he wrote humbly that Virginia's college, William and Mary, "has ever been in my view an object of veneration."[14] The few important public bequests in his will were aimed at providing education for others.

Washington's formal education had come to an end when he was fourteen or fifteen. Only in the mathematical bases for surveying had it carried him beyond what would today be considered the elementary school level. Everything else he came to know he taught himself from experience, conversation, or the printed page. The world was his university, and for a man of George Washington's gifts and temperament it is not a bad one.

Concerning where Washington received what formal training he did have, there are almost as many legends and theories as there are leaves on an elm. Little or no attention has been paid to the two most solid pieces of evidence. Humphreys reports Washington as stating that "his education was principally conducted by a private tutor."[15] This must have referred to the years before his father's death. That he also attended a school (probably after his father's death) is made clear by a letter George Mason wrote him in 1756 which referred to a Sergeant Piper as "my neighbor and your old schoolfellow."[16] Since Mason lived close to Mount Vernon, the implication is strong that at the time indicated George was staying with his brother Lawrence.

As it turned out, Lawrence's installation at Mount Vernon of a bride, Anne Fairfax, had a much greater effect on George's career than any schoolmaster, for Anne belonged to a great English family that lived in a mansion adjoining Mount Vernon. Her kinsman Lord Fairfax, who held a royal grant to a huge slice of Virginia; her father, William Fairfax, who had come from abroad to be Lord Fairfax's agent; and her English-educated brother were to open to George that aristocratic world which had been prophesied to him by the *Rules of Civility*. And after Anne's brother had got married, the future hero fell in love with his neighbor's wife.

3

A Fairfax World

AS HIS brother Lawrence's protégé, George frequented Belvoir, the mansion William Fairfax had built overlooking the Potomac within distant sight of Mount Vernon. The house was described, probably by George himself, as "of brick, two stories high, with four convenient rooms and a large passage on the lower floor; five rooms and a large passage on the second; servant's hall and cellar below. Convenient to it are offices, stables, and a coach house; adjacent is a large and well-furnished garden stored with a great variety of fruits all in good order."[1]

The dining room furnishings were, whenever possible, of mahogany and were worth sixty-two pounds as compared with the six pounds three shillings for the "hall" which served as a dining room at Ferry Farm. The Ferry Farm parlor contained three beds,[2] while the parlor at Belvoir, presided over by a chimney glass worth ten pounds, was exclusively a second sitting room. This was a different way of life: George found its natural inhabitants fascinating. He was as charmed as only a boy whose own domestic life was unhappy could be.

When he stated, as an elderly man, that study abroad endangered young American democrats, did he recall that, without leaving Virginia, he had learned aristocratic mores in the mansion just across Dogue Run? Perhaps it was the most trenchant lesson of his life when as much of this system as he had adopted slipped out from beneath his feet.

That the Fairfaxes had a great influence on the young hero is well known; but the result is commonly misunderstood because writers, eager to find transatlantic sources for Washington's greatness, have attributed to his neighbors everything from being great glories of English society to contributing to the *Spectator*. We shall get a sharper picture if we examine Washington's neighbors one by one.[3]

Washington was to write that among the Fairfaxes he owed the greatest obligations to William.[4] The grizzled master of Belvoir had been destined by his birth in Yorkshire, forty-one years before Washington was born, to what his young disciple was to describe, after the Fairfax spell had passed from him, as "the accursed state of attendance and dependence."[5]

As the younger son of a younger son of the fourth Lord Fairfax, William inherited no considerable estate, but he was prevented by his status from engaging in private employment. He could only make his way through the patronage—or as he put it, the "interest"—of some powerful kinsman. This method put him in the Royal Navy at an early age, but when his patron departed from the command leaving him behind, he felt the despair of a fish gasping helpless on a deck.

Kinsmen eventually came again to his rescue: now he was in the army, and after a while he became chief justice of the Bahamas. In that remote corner of the earth, he took a rebellious step, marrying an English girl whose family was so obscure that his grand relations in England circulated the rumor he had espoused a Negress.

William was soon back in attendance in London anterooms. He had now so schooled himself that, as he wrote apologetically to his mother, he no longer could make any "outward show" of emotion. His motto remained, "I trust in God I shall never procure the disesteem of any relation," and in the end this got him, after a customs appointment in Massachusetts, the position of agent to his cousin, the sixth Lord Fairfax, in Virginia.[6]

Lord Fairfax was the inheritor of a grant made in 1649 by Charles II of more than five million acres between the Potomac and the Rappahannock. The inhabitants of Virginia had always protested, and they were still protesting when William took charge. In this controversy between local control and royal prerogative, Lawrence's marriage to William's daughter deeply committed the Washingtons to the royal side, which, indeed, triumphed: the Fairfaxes were able to muster so much influence with the Crown that during 1745 His Lordship's most extreme claims were confirmed in London.

As the Fairfax representative in Virginia, William had been placed by interest in a position of great power. He could now bring his innate abilities to bear as president of the King's Council. And he saw to it that many of the best land grants he was in a position to bestow moved into his own strongbox.

Adherence to the God of Things-As-They-Are having at last rewarded William Fairfax, he had seemingly buried his old rebellions, but perhaps, in moments of emotion, they reared up again to cast an angry glow over the advice he gave George Washington. That advice was to follow the methods he had himself pursued: an assiduous courting of the great.

In telling the boy that to be a "philosopher" meant to accept and manipulate without repining reality as it presented itself, that to kick against the pricks was to "sicken your mind," William Fairfax introduced George, by way of noble example, to a world from which the lad was eventually to draw strength for revolutionary ends: the ancient Romans.[7] And the old place server impressed on his young disciple the classical conception that the greatest of all achievements was, through honorable deeds, to win the applause of one's countrymen.

William Fairfax came to love George Washington like a son, perhaps because his own son, George William Fairfax, was so unexciting.

George William had, as a boy, gone through shattering experiences. His father had still been struggling with adverse destiny when he sent the six-year-old lad home to be educated. He humbly begged his grand relations for "indulgences to [a] poor West India boy." But the titled Fairfaxes were most concerned with wondering whether the boy would prove really to be a mulatto. When George William met a new grand relation, he was subjected to an undisguised assessment of the fairness of his skin. The boy could rebel or cringe. He cringed.[8]

After fifteen years of subordination in England, George William reached Virginia. His family fortunes there were riding high, but the temperament his previous experiences had shaped did not permit him to enjoy being in the Colonies an important man and a great matrimonial catch. He wrote a hand which in its meticulousness verged on aberration. He dressed and behaved with equally painful care. His strong hooked nose and heavy brows shading eyes placed close together contrasted strangely with the tremulous downcurving of his mouth and the timidity of his entire expression. At twenty-one, he was seven years George Washington's senior, but the boy was so much the more vital that the difference of age seemed to disappear, and they became close friends.

To the American youth, George William expatiated on the glories of English aristocratic life, for he could hope, if the right deaths were accompanied by a suitable lack of births, to become someday, in his own right, Lord Fairfax. This dream softened his memory of the cruelties he had suffered in England. He considered Belvoir, which seemed to Washington so elegant. a "tolerable cottage" in a "wooded world."[9]

In that wooded world, Lawrence Washington was rising on the twin wings of his own abilities and the Fairfax influence: he was amassing land; he sat in the House of Burgesses; and he was adjutant general of the Virginia militia. However, he was worried about George, whose prospects were shrinking as his mother mismanaged Ferry Farm. (George was later to remember how "sensibly" he had felt in those years "the want of money.")[10]

The boy was fourteen and at Ferry Farm when he received from Lawrence a mysterious summons to elude his mother and go to Fredericksburg for a meeting with William Fairfax, who would be passing through. Fairfax handed him a letter from Lawrence stating that Captain Green of a Royal Navy vessel stationed in Virginia had need of a midshipman. The appointment could be got for George, if, as Lawrence urged, George wished it. The boy was taken aback, but, so William reported to Lawrence, he promised to "be steady and thankfully follow your advice as his best friend." Then William produced a second letter, more carefully phrased, which he told George to give to his mother.

There were great scenes at Ferry Farm. Mrs. Washington agreed and then refused, consulted everyone, listened most to those who were opposed, but on one occasion allowed things to get to a point where George, as he told Humphreys, had his "baggage prepared for embarkation. However, the plan was abandoned in consequence of the earnest solicitations" from his mother.[11]

Observing this close escape, the historian stands aghast. Supposing George Washington had become a midshipman in the British navy? Probably he would have been dissatisfied, since, as his maternal uncle, Joseph Ball, pointed out, he lacked the influential patrons necessary if he were to advance in that service.[12] Yet the future rebel would have become at a very early age linked to His Majesty's establishment.

For his part, George was relieved. He never showed any taste for the ocean, traveling, even at greater inconvenience, over-land. But he was already harboring military dreams. He read, certainly in translation, Caesar's *Commentaries,* and for the large sum to an impoverished boy of two shillings sixpence he bought *A Panegyrick to the Memory of Frederick, Late Duke of Schomberg.*[13] Frederick was such a German mercenary com-mander as Washington was eventually to meet in the field.

A great new excitement in George's world was heralded in the summer of 1746 by the arrival at Belvoir from England of three foxhounds. They were the advance guard of an awe-inspiring visit: Lord Fairfax himself planned to cross the ocean and wanted a good pack established before he arrived. The in-habitants of Belvoir put the imported dogs to the local bitches with all the care a violinist lavishes on his Stradivarius, for on His Lordship's humor their continuing prosperity depended.

Thomas Fairfax, sixth Lord Fairfax of Cameron, was the first peer Washington had ever seen. He was short and dumpy. His goggling brown eyes and long, thin, curved nose gave his face a fishlike expression. He has been made over by historical tradi-tion into the very embodiment of British culture: it was he who was supposed to have contributed to the *Spectator.* Actually, His Lordship had two obsessions: a hatred for women and a love of fox hunting.

The nobleman liked to shake under the lad's nose a marriage agreement pages long with his own name engrossed therein and that of the bride clipped out. He complained that after all matters of property had been successfully negotiated, the female had jilted him for a duke. This proved—and he was launched on one of his rants against women, in the course of which he de-scribed in detail "the fatigue he underwent in sitting up for a month together full dressed" when his brother was being married.[14] His idea of a compliment to the ladies of Mount Vernon was to bring to their doorstep his hounds and a fox in a bag so that, without effort, they could watch the kill.[15]

To the fascination of George, who loved fine array, His Lordship's room at Belvoir was crowded with clothespresses: the latest male fashions arrived by standing order from London. But, unless George slipped a brocaded coat over his own shoulders, he never saw how the finery would look if worn, for Lord Fairfax always appeared in soiled hunting clothes. He was kind to the boy who had such a way with horses. But associating with the peer was like associating with a bluff, benevolent bear who might strike out at any time with a lethal paw.

Now the parlor at Belvoir housed daily exercises in "attendance and dependence." The William Fairfax connection, including Lawrence Washington, was eager to hold His Lordship as their guest so that they could ward off other money- and position-hungry relatives. But they were under his eye too. It was, of course, part of the system that when "interest" put a courtier in a position to do so, he would feather his nest, but the question of how sumptuously depended on how he appraised the patriarchal generosity of the patron. That the William Fairfaxes were doing very well for themselves was very clear: how far His Lordship was pleased or displeased was less so. If he frowned, it might be because he was remembering how close he once got to matrimony, or he might be wondering about that valuable bottomland William had patented to his daughter, Anne Washington.

His Lordship could not be questioned, as he blandly did what he pleased. After Lawrence had prepared for him a carefully worded petition, he put it in his pocket, and that was the last anyone heard of it.[16] He would talk sometimes—was it a threat or was it insensitivity?—about a nephew he had in

England, Thomas Bryan Martin, who was so excellent a land agent and might be induced to come to America. And would he not have more sport if he moved permanently to Greenway Court, a hunting lodge he had built over the Blue Ridge Mountains? There were undoubtedly times when George was told inconspicuously to curb his horsemanship so that Lord Fairfax would certainly earn the mask of the fox.*

---

* In 1751, when George was nineteen, Lord Fairfax actually imported Martin and moved permanently to Greenway Court. Although the land office remained at Belvoir for another ten years—George William succeeded his father as manager—the peer, with Martin by his elbow, now usually attended to important (and lucrative) affairs.[17]

4

Surveyor's Wages

AS WASHINGTON grew to young manhood, Virginia civilization existed in stages, a four-step geographic stair. The long-settled plantations, the greatest houses, were in the Tidewater, where the land, going back some seventy-five miles from the ocean, was so flat that the rivers which ran through it pulsed with the rhythm of the sea. Up these lengthy estuaries, ocean-going boats sailed, mobile bits of London that drew up at the planters' wharves, loading tobacco, and unloading goods brought from England in return for the previous year's crop.

Where the land began to rise steeply, there appeared in each river falls that stopped the tide and put an end to navigation by the British traders' ships. Although Tidewater planters might own land beyond the falls, it was usually cultivated by recent immigrants, German or Scotch-Irish. These often still lived in the log cabins built when their farms were first cleared, but the region was no longer frontier. A passing Indian would be an object of curiosity, not terror.

Virginia's frontier was over the Blue Ridge Mountains. Into the Shenandoah Valley settlement was beginning to press. But settlement stopped with the great wall that stood at the far side of the valley: the forbidding heights of the Alleghenies. Over these heights was the great central plain of North America, where Virginia had extensive claims but which its citizens rarely dared even explore.

Washington's youth helped prepare him to be the leader of all Americans by making him familiar with the Virginia versions of long-established settlement, back country, frontier, and wilderness. The only broad aspect of the American environment he did not experience was cities, for the direct trade carried on by the Virginia planters with London made these unnecessary. The Colonial capital, Williamsburg, was a large village.

Although in the Tidewater, both Ferry Farm and Mount Vernon were in its most recently developed western part, close to the falls of their respective rivers. Less than a day's ride from either home carried the young man into the back country. And in 1748, the Fairfax influence, which had been pulling his thoughts and inclinations towards English aristocratic life, doubled on itself by sending Washington to an almost complete opposite: the frontier.

For the moment, he was not to go all the way to the Ohio Valley Wilderness—that was to wait for more desperate times. But when the Fairfaxes hired a surveyor to lay out some of His Lordship's lands in the Shenandoah Valley in farm-size lots, George William Fairfax and his friend George Washington went along.

In Washington's journal of this trip, which is the earliest extended piece of writing we have from his hand, he thus described his first encounter with backwoods lodgings: "We got our supper and was lighted into a room and I, not being as good a woodsman as the rest of my company, stripped myself very orderly and went in to the bed, as they called it, when to my surprise, I found it to be nothing but a little straw matted together, without sheets or anything else, but only one threadbare blanket, with double its weight of vermin, such as lice, fleas, etc., and I was glad to get up, as soon as the light was carried from us. [He does not seem to have wanted to offend the land-lord by leaping from the bed.] I put on my clothes, and lay as my companions [on the floor]."¹

The next day, he and his friends found more civilized lodg-ings: "We cleaned ourselves to get rid of the game we catched the night before. . . . We had a good dinner prepared for us, wine and rum punch in plenty, and a good feather bed with clean sheets, which was a very agreeable regale."²

That George went into no rhapsody as he crossed the Blue Ridge Mountains at the view down into the Shenandoah Valley has been held against his esthetic sense, but it merely showed that he was a true citizen of the mid-eighteenth century—the taste for "picturesque scenery" came later. Beauty struck him correctly for his time in relation to the needs of man, thus: "We went through most beautiful groves of sugar trees and spent the best part of the day admiring the trees and richness of the land."³

His style was not without exaggeration—"the worst road ever trod by man or beast"—but in describing danger to himself, he was laconic: "Last night was a blowing and rainy night. Our straw catch'd fire, that we were laying upon, and was luckily perserved by one of our men awakening when it was in a [blaze]. We ran four lots this day which reached below the stumps."⁴

On another occasion: "We were agreeably surprised at the sight of thirty-odd Indians coming from war with only one scalp. We had some liquor with us, of which we gave them part. It elevating their spirits, put them in the humor of dancing, of whom we had a war dance. Their manner of dancing is as fol-lows, viz., they clear a large circle and make a great fire in the middle. Then seat themselves around it. The speaker makes a grand speech, telling them in what manner they are to dance. After he has finished, the best dancer jumps up as one awakened out of a sleep and runs and jumps about the ring in a most comical manner. He is followed by the rest. Then begin their musicians to play. The music is a pot half [full] of water with a deerskin stretched over it as tight as it can, and a gourd with some shot in it to rattle, and a piece of a horse's tail tied to it to make it look fine. The one keeps rattling and the other drumming all the while the others are dancing."[5]

On the day after the dance, Washington noted, "Nothing remarkable . . . being with the Indians all day." As it eventually turned out, he would have been wise to be more interested in Indian ways, but had he possessed any unpragmatic concern with so primitive a culture he would have been a century ahead of his time. It was his attitude towards the German settlers already on His Lordship's land which revealed that his imaginative sympathies were yet narrow.

For these families—call them squatters or call them pioneers —the appearance of the surveying party was a catastrophe, as it indicated that some distant power, irresistible because legal, was planning to expropriate the farms they had created with their own sweat and heart's blood. However, Washington's comment was that "a great company of people, men, women, and children . . . attended us through the woods as we went, showing their antic tricks. I really think they seemed to be as ignorant a set of people as the Indians. They never speak English, but when spoken to, they speak all Dutch."[6]

During thirty-one days over the mountains in blustery March and early April weather—surveying weather, as you could not sight through your theodolite when leafage blocked the view— George studied the methods of an experienced surveyor and kept the field notes; he swam horses over the South Branch of the Potomac swollen by snow melting in the mountains, and paddled forty miles in a day up the same turbulent water in a canoe through pelting rain; he missed and hit wild turkeys, his prize being a gobbler weighing twenty pounds; he viewed with awe "the famed warm springs" and camped beside them "in the field,"[7] not realizing he would visit there again in the most tragic time of his life; he got lost in the Blue Ridge Mountains for most of a day during which he saw a rattlesnake. One night he camped "in the woods near a wild meadow where was a large stack of hay. After we had pitched our tent and made a very large fire, we pulled out our knapsack in order to recruit ourselves. Every [man] was his own cook, our spits were forked sticks, our plates were a large chip—as for dishes, we have none."[8]

When, after an idyllic feast, the sixteen-year-old boy wandered the wild meadow that some mysterious hand had mowed; looked up at towering mountain ledges on both sides; saw, as if stretched between them, a sky full of stars; and heard the rushing of water near his feet; when he sensed the vastness, the newness, the great power and future prosperity of this land, George Washington gave to the west of the North American continent a part of his heart that he was never to regain.

But he had no intention of joining the German settlers in their ignorant and antic ways. Back home, he wrote, "Memorandum: to have my coat made by the following directions. To be made a frock with a lapel breast," etc., etc., to a total of 152 words. When he set out on a round of visits, he took along, according to a packing list, a razor, nine shirts, six linen handkerchiefs, six bands, four neckcloths, and seven caps.[9]

By 1747, Washington was keeping careful accounts of his cash expenditures, down to the last halfpenny, a habit he was to continue long after he had left financial stringency behind him. The pages show that he gained small sums from his various hosts at loo, Lawrence being the only one in his circle who consistently beat him. However, he earned most of these losses back from Lawrence's wife at whist. He went to a dancing school to the tune of three shillings ninepence. As is often the case with those who have to watch their money, he usually had cash in his pocket: he was continually making small loans to his richer friends and relations.

In the winter of 1748–1749, Lawrence and George William attended the session of the Burgesses at Williamsburg which coincided with the social season. Towards spring, Lawrence came back prematurely with a disturbing cough that might reveal consumption. But George William's return was in an altogether different mood. He brought back as his bride a beauty from the Williamsburg dances, the former Sally Cary.

That Washington fell in love with this wife of his friend and neighbor is proved by uncontrovertible documents. As we shall see, on the eve of his marriage to Martha, he declared in writing his love for Sally, and as an old man who had been separated from Sally by the Atlantic Ocean for more than a quarter of a century, he wrote her that all the events of the Revolution and his presidency had not "been able to eradicate from my mind those happy moments, the happiest of my life, which I have enjoyed in your company."[10]

Sally brought to Belvoir, that provincial outpost of English aristocratic life, the best that Virginia had to offer. The Carys had been leaders in the local aristocracy since the middle of the seventeenth century; her grandfather had been rector of William and Mary; her father had been educated there and at Trinity College, Cambridge. From both sides of his family he had inherited one of the amplest of Virginia fortunes. At Ceelys, his mansion on the James overlooking Hampton Roads, at his town houses in Williamsburg and Hampton, copies of the *London Magazine*, the *Gentleman's Magazine*, and the *Annual Register* arrived regularly from England. He sent for the current books they recommended, continually expanding the library that had come down to him from his father. We know that he had Sally taught French.[11]

Concerning those charms which Washington admitted his inability to resist, our best visual evidence is a photograph of a lost portrait. The image is so crude that we stare half baffled, as we would into a distorting mirror. The artist has tortured the body into such pseudo elegance that about it we can conclude nothing. The neck is long and robust over sloping shoulders. Although the head gives the impression of being narrow, it is rather long and high: there is ample room for clear features. Sally's forehead towers under dark hair parted in the middle. Dark brows arch out like wings over deep-set, large, dark eyes. Following the classical ideal, her nose continues without indentation the line of her forehead; it is narrow but juts out strongly and is terminated with ample nostrils. The chin line is firm, and the chin itself a round ball. That Sally's upper lip is much longer than the lower gives the effect less of a cupid's than an Indian's bow.

As the painter daubed it down, the face is more startling than handsome. We must in our mind's eye imbue it with the "amiable beauty" of which George wrote, with the "mirth, good humor, ease of mind—and what else?" She was a coquette, this long dead lady, full of charming vanities, laughingly yet truly annoyed when other women got more attention from the men than she, given in her relations with George to advances and retreats that left the fledgling hero disturbed and baffled.

Letters written by both Sally and George William Fairfax imply that their marriage was as much dictated by dynastic as personal considerations, and, indeed, had it been otherwise it would have been in that society a prodigy.[12] She could not have helped recognizing instantly the power in her gawky, auburn-haired young neighbor that made her sweet and timorous husband allow himself to be led by the boy. Yet the relationship between Sally and George was probably, when they first got to know each other, no more than playful.

George was sixteen and Sally eighteen, a gap which at those ages looms large. She was a matron and in Virginia terms a mature woman, while he had not yet grown into the man he was to become: "six feet high," as he described himself, "and proportionally made; if anything rather slender than thick for a person of that height, with pretty long arms and thighs."[13] The future hero's attitude towards the opposite sex was still touchingly callow, and he was still, however resentfully, tied to his mother's apron strings, in a rundown farm, full of younger children, which he would undoubtedly have been ashamed to show the elegant Sally. A letter he wrote Lawrence during May 1749 is full of complaints which seem to echo his mother's shrill voice. George adds that, because he lacks the money to buy corn for his horse, he cannot get from Ferry Farm to the dancing assemblies.[14]

That summer George secured, through the interest of the Fairfaxes, his first job: assistant to the surveyor who was, at the order of the General Assembly, laying out a town at the head of Potomac navigation. It was called Alexandria and, being only some dozen miles from Mount Vernon, was to become the metropolis of his continuing world. A formal drawing he made of the survey could almost be framed in this age of abstractions as a work of art, for it shows true esthetic reactions to lettering, spacing, shading. (To his personal drafts of surveys he sometimes added childish pictures: one shows a floppy-winged eagle standing before a flowering shrub.)[15]

George procured an official commission to survey in his own right. After a bout of "ague and fever, which I have had to extremity,"[16] he crossed the Blue Ridge to the Shenandoah Valley. Thence he sent one "Richard" a mixture of copybook elegance and youthful exuberance: "The receipt of your kind

favor of the second this instant afforded me unspeakable pleasure as I am convinced I am still in the memory of so worthy a
friend. . . . I have not slept above three nights or four in a bed
but, after walking a good deal all the day, lay down before the
fire upon a little hay, straw, fodder, or bearskin—whichever is to
be had—with man, wife, and children like a parcel of dogs or
cats, and happy's he that gets the berth nearest the fire. There's
nothing that would make it pass off tolerable but a good reward.
A doubloon a day is my constant gain every day."[17]

To "Dear friend Robin," he wrote that he was staying at Lord
Fairfax's hunting lodge, "where I might, was my heart disen-
gaged, pass my time very pleasantly, as there's a very agreeable
young lady lives in the same house . . . but as that's only
adding fuel to the fire, it makes me the more uneasy for, by often
and unavoidably being in company with her, revives my former
passion for your Low Land Beauty, whereas was I to live more
retired from young women, I might in some measure alleviate
my sorrows by burying that chaste and troublesome passion in
the grave of oblivion or eternal forgetfulness," etc., etc.[18]

The "Low Land Beauty" (who could not possibly have been,
since he discussed her freely, the married Sally Fairfax) has
been so widely identified by tradition that she has more heads
than Cerberus. As northerners play the game of "George Washington Slept Here," so southerners play "My Ancestress Refused
George Washington's Offer of Marriage." Thus is conjured up
the unfortunate image of a boobish lover perpetually proposing
and being perpetually turned down.

It is, however, possible that the teen-age George Washington
was not, for the girls, the life of the parties he attended. He was
extremely masculine, which can inspire more fright than pleasure in young ladies first inclining towards the males. He towered over the girls, certainly not yet as graceful in movement as

he was to become. Although his body was that of an athlete, many witnesses commented that he had the largest hands and feet they had ever seen. And all his life he suffered from a superficial shyness because he was both proud and not quick. His "light greyish blue eyes" under his "hazel brown" hair pondered rather than sparkled, and his speech came slowly because it was the result of thought. We know that in 1757 he was cut out—in a situation, it is true, where he did not greatly care—by "a lady's man" who had "always something to say."[19]

Washington's disabilities would be the greater the lighter the flirtation, and in his teens George seems to have been, like other healthy adolescents, more in love with love than any specific girl. He started an acrostic on the name Frances Alexander: "From your bright sparkling eyes I was undone; / Rays you have more transparent than the sun," and continued on bravely in this vein till he was within four lines and letters of the end. Then he threw the whole matter up, we know not whether because he had become bored with the effort or the charmer.[20]

On another occasion, George produced this piece of adolescent idiocy in the high romantic manner:

"Oh, ye Gods, why should my poor resistless heart
    Stand to oppose thy might and power
    At last surrender to Cupid's feather'd dart
    And now lays bleeding every hour
    For her that's pitiless of my grief and woes
    And will not on me pity take
    I'll sleep amongst my most inveterate foes
    And with gladness with [wish?] to wake.
    In deluding sleepings let my eyelids close
    That in an enraptured dream I may
    In a soft lulling sleep and gentle repose
    Possess those joys denied by day."[21]

That there was always in George Washington a histrionic strain is a fact deep buried in the perpetual snow of his legend. When he came to walk on the world's great stage, again and again, at the exquisitely perfect moment he made the most effective gesture, which was all the more moving because he was not thought of as an actor—and, indeed, he did not so regard himself. He only behaved as came naturally to a temperament deeply responsive to drama. (He was a great lover of the theatre, attending performances at Williamsburg or Alexandria or wherever he was when a lighted curtain parted.)[22]

When George was yet young, his playacting sometimes verged on the ridiculous. Thus he jotted down, "What's the Noblest Passion of the Mind at" and completed the question with two mysterious symbols in cipher. No prying eye would fathom that meaning! Nor would it do much better with:

" 'Twas Perfect Love before
But Now I do adore $\Big\}$ Sd Young M:A:his"[23]

The same little book to which he confided such amorous vaporings contains efficient records of surveys.

A surveyor in the wilderness was much more than the word now implies. He was sworn as a government official because, in those unfrequented areas, it was up to him to see that no fraud was done by making surveys larger or smaller than was stated in the deeds, or by laying out land in manners forbidden by the various restrictive laws. On the other side, he served as his employer's agent. When working on a tract already patented, he was an agricultural planner commissioned to divide a large area in the manner that would earn the most money from rent or sale. Or if he were hired to find the land on which to lay out a patent, his role was that of an explorer: he needed to identify and map that acreage which would prove, after the forest had vanished and roads been built and trade begun, the most valuable. Often his duties as an official and the interests of his clients were in conflicts that it took statesmanship to resolve.

In the spring of 1750 Washington rode again over the mountains, laying out forty-seven tracts and making close to £140 before the leaves grew too thick. Wherever he visited that summer, he took his instruments along, picking up jobs and cash. Before the snow fell, he invested his earnings in 1459 acres on Bullskin Creek, a tributary of the Shenandoah.[24] Thus, with his name on a deed to land beyond the Blue Ridge, Washington wrote himself down as a successful businessman. He was not nineteen years old.

Death and a Beckoning Mission

A S GEORGE WASHINGTON took his first self-reliant
steps to escape from financial stringency and his mother,
there began to fall on him the darker shadow of the deepest
personal tragedy he lived through in all his long life. His brother
Lawrence, his "best friend," was advancing into what might
prove a mortal consumption.

Lawrence had opened to George whatever of the great world
the youth had experienced. With his good humor, his charm, his
not too aggressive stick-to-itiveness, the older brother had fitted
perfectly into the Fairfax world which he had made his own.
Although he could be careless, when his attention was really
caught he reasoned things out in all their complications and
implications much as his brother was to do on a greater stage.
He was fond of remembering the military life he had briefly
known; he talked of horses and hunts and land speculations; he
served as a Burgess and lived the public life of a hospitable
planter; yet his long, sallow face was the face of a dreamer, a
minor poet given to musing and melancholy. Effective yet sweet
and gentle, he inspired in his younger brother passionate devo-
tion.[1]

A trip to England and the well-informed doctors of the Old
World had brought no alleviation of the illness that seemed to

be dragging Lawrence to an early grave. And so, when the summer of 1750 solidified itself in the mountains, the sick man sought a remedy at the other pole of the Washingtons' environment. George accompanied Lawrence to the warm springs across the Blue Ridge (later Berkeley Springs, West Virginia).

The wild meadow in which George had encamped when surveying two years before was now dotted with the crude shelters, the habitable wagons, or the tents of sufferers from many ills. A large hollow surrounded by a screen of pine brush had been scooped out of the sand to hold the bubbling aromatic waters that were assumed to be curative whether drunk or bathed in. When there were any ladies to be served, at a stated time long blasts were blown on a tin horn which was a sign that all gentlemen should keep their distance, leaving the waters to the fair. At night, the talk around the campfires was of ailments and symptoms, sweats and purges.

As George listened to his brother cough, he worried, because the springs "are situated very badly on the east side of a steep mountain and enclosed by hills on all sides, so that the afternoon's sun is hid by four o'clock and the fogs hang over us till nine or ten, which occasion great damps in the mornings, and evenings to be cool."[2]

However, Lawrence must in the end have felt at least somewhat improved, since he took over that fall the presidency of the Ohio Company. This partnership had been formed in 1747 to enrich the proprietors through fur trading and land speculation across the Alleghenies in territory claimed not only by Virginia but also by Pennsylvania and the King of France.

The shareholders were a prosperous and politically powerful cabal that included, in addition to Lawrence Washington, the Fairfaxes; Thomas Lee; Robert Dinwiddie, the Lieutenant Governor of Virginia; and overseas in London, the Duke of Bedford and the great Quaker merchant John Hanbury. They pulled wires so effectively that in 1749 the company secured from the British Crown a grant of half a million acres. However, taking full possession was made contingent on building a fort in the Ohio Valley and establishing at least 200 families there.

The fort was planned to double as a trading post, and the Indians were told that this would bring them prosperity because Virginia would pay so well for furs. However, warning French voices sounded at council fires, and soon the Indians were opposing the Ohio Company on the ground (which was not far from the truth) that the object was rather to steal their land than to trade with them. Therefore, establishing the fort, which was intended for "the Forks of the Ohio" (the present Pittsburgh), was postponed, but the Ohio Company built a warehouse and trading post at Wills Creek, in the Shenandoah Valley on the near side of the Alleghenies. These were matters with which George was soon to be first strenuously and then bloodily engaged.

For the moment, the problems of the Ohio Company gave George an early lesson in religious toleration: German immigrants Lawrence was wooing would not settle in Virginia if they were made subject to a law which taxed all for the support of the Church of England. Lawrence petitioned the Virginia Assembly to change the law. "Restraints on conscience," he wrote, "are cruel," and they were also impolitic, since neighboring colonies with religious freedom became populous while Virginia "increased by slow degrees except [for] Negroes and convicts."[3]

When it became clear that the Virginia Assembly would not budge, Lawrence undertook a maneuver which was then (although his brother George was later to extinguish the possibility by force of arms) common with Colonials who could not get what they wanted from their own governments: he appealed to Parliament to override his local legislature. Young George certainly shared Lawrence's disappointment when Parliament refused to intervene.

In the spring and summer of 1751, George accompanied Lawrence on another trip to the warm springs, practiced surveying with energy and profit, and, on a visit to his mother, left his clothes on the bank as he swam in the Rappahannock, to discover, when he came out, that his pockets had been picked. Two servant girls were arrested; one turned king's witness, and the other was eventually given fifteen lashes on her bare back at the whipping post.[4]

But the overriding development of the summer was that Lawrence was getting worse. Late in September, George sailed with him for Barbados in the hope that a tropical climate would help.

Of this adventure, the nineteen-year-old kept a journal. He relished such poetical phrases as "a fickle and merciless ocean." He took pleasure in nautical jargon, writing "RM: FS and DRFS" (reefed mainsail, foresail, and double-reefed foresail). When great storms swooped down, "the seamen seemed disheartened, confessing they never had seen such weather before." Through "a constant succession of hard winds, squalls of rain, and calms," a sloop kept in sight of them for two days. Finally, so George reports, it raised a signal of distress. But the imperious wind blew Washington's vessel on, leaving the sloop and its human beings to the mystery of the ocean.[5]

After a specialist in Barbados had ruled optimistically on Lawrence's hopes, George went into an ecstasy over the scenery. He was "perfectly rav[ished]" by "the beautiful prospects which on every side presented to our view the fields of cane, corn, fruit trees, etc., in a delightful green."[6]

The brothers were extensively entertained, and George had what was probably his first experience of a pleasure he was forever after to crave: "Was treated with a play ticket to see the Tragedy of George Barnwell acted." Never—not even in his youth—inclined to express an opinion when he did not feel himself competent, Washington continued cautiously: "The character of Barnwell and, several others was said to be well performed. There was music adapted and regularly conducted by Mr.——."[7]

Two days later, George was "strongly attacked with the smallpox." He did not recover till December 12.[8] As he lay very sick attended by a sick brother so very far from home, his anxiety could not have been lightened by the realization that Providence was bringing him a great boon: immunity from the major killer of the American Revolution.

In writings about Washington, certain symbols have become current to show that the authors are not averse to debunking the hero. The first is, of course, persistent reference to the toothaches and false teeth that plagued the hero. The second is to describe his face as pockmarked. Actually, he bore only several very light scars on his nose.[9] In those days, when almost everyone had had smallpox either by infection or vaccination, these were no more noticed than we today note the mark left by modern vaccination on an arm or thigh.

As George completely recovered, Lawrence was getting worse, and his spirits were sinking with his body. He would ride only at dawn. To avoid the heat of a sun a half hour high, George had to rush him back to their lodgings. Behind closed blinds in a stifling sickroom, the sufferer who had once been so jovial filled the shortening breaks between coughing spells by complaining about the climate to his brother. Hour after hour passed, until at last the cool of evening enabled Lawrence to stagger out again, like a wounded bat. The order of the night was conviviality with friends—but Lawrence drew the line at dancing, which, he argued with haunted eyes, frequently produced yellow fever.

Eventually, the brothers had to part. Lawrence would see whether the climate of Bermuda was more salutary than Barbados had proved; George, who had his way to make, needed to return to Virginia. On shipboard, just before he was overcome with seasickness, he wrote a helter-skelter summary of his impressions during two and a half months on the island. The larger part was devoted to agriculture, although he commented that the Governor "seem[s] to keep a proper state" but "by declining much familiarity is not over-zealously beloved."[10]

When George landed in Virginia late in January 1752, he had placed behind him his entire physical experience of any territory outside the future United States. He was never to make another ocean voyage. Never in the writings of the rest of his career is there the smallest glimmer, the least metaphor, to show that he had ever been in the tropics. It had been a sad time, best banished from his memory.

Busily surveying, George earned enough to increase his holdings on Bullskin Creek. However, with spring he suffered from "a violent pleurisy," a frightening hint that he might have caught his brother's tuberculosis.[11]

In May, he wrote William Fauntleroy, a rich Virginian with a marriageable daughter, that he proposed "as soon as I recover my strength to wait on Miss Betsy in hopes of a revocation of the former cruel sentence, and see if I can meet with any alteration in my favor."

At almost sixteen, Betsy Fauntleroy was a petite brunette, whose turned-up nose in a small, round face, whose light brown eyes and smiling lips were those of a high-spirited minx. Her father, who was about to send to London for a six-horse chariot with his coat of arms emblazoned on it, did not envision George Washington riding beside him. George Washington came from a secondary family; his principle inheritance had been a second-rate farm on which his mother seemed a permanent squatter; though he was clearly able and energetic, he seemed, like his brother, sickly. His best recommendation, that he had interest with the Fairfaxes, was not enough. As for George, we have no way of knowing whether he was more smitten by Betsy's charms or her worldly position. Her name never appears again in the Washington papers.[12]

When Lawrence came home, it was to sink down beside his fathers. From his deathbed, "in consideration of love and affection," he gave George three lots in Fredericksburg. From Lawrence's will, George received little more than a remote contingency: if the young man survived Lawrence's wife, and if Lawrence's only child, an infant daughter, died without issue, George was to have Mount Vernon and other nearby lands.[13]

Lawrence's wife, after less than six months of widowhood, remarried. Since she went off with her new husband, Mount Vernon, which George had come to regard as more his home than Ferry Farm, echoed back emptily the sound of his footsteps. But across Dogue Run, the door of Belvoir was open to him, with behind it the welcoming male Fairfaxes and the enchanting Sally.

Years later, Washington commented that "a natural fondness for military parade" was usually a "passion" with young men.[14] While Lawrence was still on his deathbed, George had begun agitating for the dying man's position as adjutant general of Virginia. This was a maneuver completely in the Fairfax tradition: apart from visible intelligence and energy, Washington had no qualifications for the post beyond what claims were allowed inheritance and interest. To bolster up interest, he rode the countryside presenting his compliments and his request to those influential in the Virginia government. It was as strange a situation as if a man who was to be a very great violinist, but had as yet no musical knowledge, were to importune the trustees of an orchestra to appoint him first violin.

Virginia was finally divided into four military districts and George appointed adjutant of the smallest and most distant. Although this carried the title of major and £100 a year, the twenty-year-old was not satisfied. There is no evidence that he visited any of the counties under his care or called any of the musters at which he was supposed to instruct "the officers and soldiers in the use and exercise of arms."[15] Washington was more interested in having his appointment changed to his own district. He was again a petitioner on horseback, and, in 1753, he got the berth he wanted: the adjutancy of the Northern Neck.

George became a member of a newly organized Masonic Lodge in Fredericksburg—he rose rapidly to Master Mason—and continued surveying with energy and profit. In the meanwhile, the main action in his story leaped away from the Potomac and Rappahannock, outward from Virginia into the great international arena where kings collide.

The Ohio Valley had long been an Indian hunting preserve with few permanent residents. However, as Colonial encroachment increased to the northward, Iroquois were staying in the valley, while Delawares and Shawnees, displaced by Pennsylvania farmers, moved across the Alleghenies. When Colonial enterprise followed—not only fur traders but land speculators from Pennsylvania and (primarily the Ohio Company) Virginia —this annoyed the King of France.

England and France were arrayed in opposition over much of the world, each determined to keep the other from becoming, by alliance or annexation, the more powerful. Periods of uneasy peace eventuated in wars that involved many European nations and also colonial possessions like those in America. The War of the Grand Alliance was followed by the War of the Spanish Succession. Then came the War of the Austrian Succession. That conflict had ended in 1748, but the international confrontation continued in what would today be called a cold war.

Having no intention of permitting the English to steal a march on them on the American continent, the French mounted in 1749 an expedition which traveled 2000 miles through the wilderness in thirty-three canoes, burying at the confluence of rivers lead plates on which was stated the French claim to all the land that drained into the Ohio. As the English and French engaged in rivalry for treaties in which the Indians ceded land and promised alliance, rum- or brandy-inspired signatures appeared on documents often contradictory. Some savage skirmishing was encouraged, and then, in 1753, the French began fortifying a route between Lake Erie, which they controlled, and the Ohio system.

Three French forts appeared in what is now Pennsylvania. That at Presque Isle (now Erie) was the anchor on the banks of the lake; Fort Le Boeuf (near the present Waterford) held the other end of the portage to French Creek; and Venango (now Franklin) was an advance post at the meeting of French Creek and the Allegheny River. From there on, it was clear drifting downstream to the confluence of the Allegheny and the Monongahela, "the Forks of the Ohio," where the Ohio Company intended to build their own fort.

As Lieutenant Governor of Virginia (the governorship was a sinecure held by a well-connected absentee), Robert Dinwiddie represented the Crown whose territorial claims were being defied; as a Scotch merchant, who had invested heavily in the Ohio Company, he had more personal reasons for outrage at French claims that would wipe the company out. He wrote to his government in alarm. In October 1753, the answer came. Virginia should build forts on the Ohio and send an emissary to the upper wilderness to see if the French were really on English soil. If they proved to be, the emissary should "require of them peaceably to depart." Should the French refuse, "We," George II wrote over his own signature, "do strictly command and charge you to drive them out by force of arms."[16]

Nothing could have been more satisfactory to adherents of the Crown and to Ohio Company stockholders; but serious local problems remained. The land west of the Alleghenies then seemed to most Americans too far off to be of major concern. Dinwiddie knew that in the past it had been difficult to get the various Colonial Assemblies excited about wilderness wars with France, which they believed expressed royal ambitions rather than Colonial interests and would shed innocent blood to line the pockets of land speculators. In this context, the Governor's own position was a ticklish one. He had never, in his dealings with the Indians, made much distinction between the interests of the Colony and of the Ohio Company; and now he had procured from the Crown orders that the Colony should build the fort the Ohio Company, with which he was financially concerned, had planned. Indeed, whatever the long-range situation, it seemed that the stockholders of that company would reap the immediate advantages from the war the King's orders implied.

Keeping that more popular part of the Assembly, the Burgesses, in ignorance, Dinwiddie laid the royal dispatch before the King's Council, on which sat William Fairfax and other company men. The first necessity was to find the right messenger to carry the royal word through the wilderness: George Washington seemed an ideal choice. He was no outsider who might use his mission to make capital against the company. Furthermore, as "An Old Soldier" wrote in London's *Gentleman's Magazine* to explain the appointment, he was "used to the woods," and "a youth of great sobriety, diligence, and fidelity."[17] According to the official record, Washington volunteered, but he was enabled to do so before even the House of Burgesses knew that the opportunity existed.

In an order dated October 30, Washington was commanded to proceed into the wilderness; to make contact with friendly Indians and find out from them where the French forces had posted themselves; to secure from the Indians a bodyguard and penetrate through the forest to the French. He was surreptitiously to spy out the strength of the French garrisons, forts, and communications; he was subtly to determine France's actual intentions; he was officially to present a letter from Dinwiddie which demanded, in the politest possible language, that the French forces withdraw from English territory.[18]

Thus was a mission of world-shaking implications given to an obscure youth in a provincial corner of the earth. "It was," Washington remembered years later, "deemed by some an extraordinary circumstance that so young and inexperienced a person should have been employed on a negotiation with which subjects of the greatest importance were involved."[19]

II

War in the Wilderness

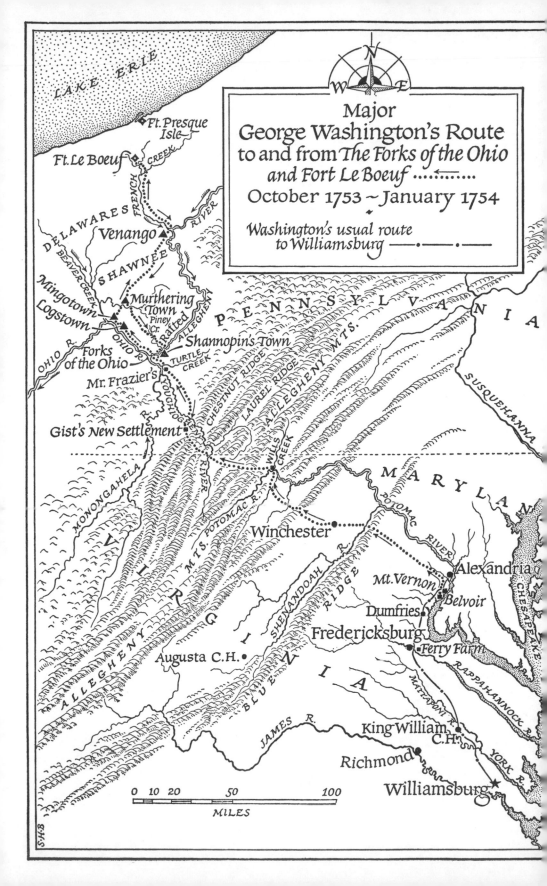

LAKE ERIE

Ft. Presque Isle

Ft. Le Boeuf

FRENCH CREEK

Major
George Washington's Route
to and from *The Forks of the Ohio*
and *Fort Le Boeuf* ⋯⋯←⋯⋯
October 1753 ~ January 1754

Washington's usual route
to Williamsburg —·—·—·—

DELAWARES

Venango

SHAWNEE

ALLEGHENY RIVER

Murthering Town

Piney Cr.

Mingotown

Logstown

Rafted

BEAVER CREEK

OHIO R.

Forks of the Ohio

OHIO R.

Shannopin's Town

TURTLE CREEK

Mr. Frazier's

YOUGHIOGHENY R.

PENNSYLVANIA

CHESTNUT RIDGE

LAUREL RIDGE

ALLEGHENY MTS.

SUSQUEHANNA

Gist's New Settlement

MONONGAHELA

VIRGINIA

WILLS CREEK

POTOMAC R.

MARYLAND

POTOMAC RIVER

ALLEGHENY MTS.

Winchester

SHENANDOAH R.

BLUE RIDGE

Mt. Vernon

Alexandria

Belvoir

CHESAPEAKE

Dumfries

Fredericksburg

Ferry Farm

RAPPAHANNOCK R.

Augusta C.H.

MATTAPONI R.

JAMES R.

King William C.H.

YORK R.

Richmond

Williamsburg

0 10 20   50   100

MILES

S·H·B

CHAPTER

6

Forest Adventure

I T WAS OCTOBER in 1753. At this season Washington had, in past years, brought to a close his surveys in the Shenandoah Valley and gone home. Now, though winter approached, his duty was to leave behind all settlements for that wilderness where the white world shrank to the strength of a sinew and the aim of a firearm; where another order of men, painted and strange, moved with the astounding ease of fish in the ocean. And every step would carry him closer to a European enemy who might fire or suborn secret shots in the forest. George Washington could simply disappear.

He knew none of the languages of those with whom he would deal. To help him negotiate with the white enemy, he selected a Dutchman, Jacob van Braam, who advertised as a French teacher and whose knowledge of that language was at least attested to by the badness of his English. To guide him with the savages and in wilderness travel, Washington had been instructed by Dinwiddie to enlist Christopher Gist. A rough frontiersman, Gist had previously conducted negotiations with the tribes for both Virginia and the Ohio Company. Washington was to discover that, although he seemed "well acquainted with the Indians' manners and customs," he "knows but little of their language."[1] Four "servitors" from the most ignorant class that penetrated across the Alleghenies completed Washington's party. If such a mission seemed, when compared with the French wilderness wizards it was designed to confront, ridiculously inadequate, it was the best inexperienced Virginia could muster—and the young man who was its leader and also its greatest tenderfoot was no ordinary man.

On November 15, Washington's party set out up the steep divide between the Shenandoah and the Ohio valleys, driving before them a flotilla of pack horses loaded with everything they would need for a month in the wilderness. Impeded, as Washington wrote, by "the excessive rains and a vast quantity of snow which had fallen," it took them a full week to reach their first objective, some seventy-five miles as the crow flies.[2]

At last they saw a tiny, smoking spot in the frozen vastness, the cabin of the Indian trader John Frazier, at the confluence of the Monongahela and Turtle Creek. This served as a listening post in the network of rumor that kept the wilderness informed or misinformed. Three tribes of pro-French Indians were said to be out on the warpath against the British; Washington was warned to beware.

The Monongahela being in flood and "quite impassable," Washington left his servitors to bring along the horses, and in a canoe dashed with the current to the Forks of the Ohio. Here, where empires were soon to entangle, there was a great display of meeting waters, but no human sound. Washington spent two days examining the terrain and revising the location for the fort which Virginia, having taken over from the Ohio Company, intended to build. He had seen no fort except one at Barbados, so he based his ideas on common sense, urging the site with "absolute command of both rivers" which was in the next decade to be fortified by his Colony and then France and then the British Crown.[3]

When the horses arrived, they were made to swim across the

Allegheny, and the whole party called, in the greatest style they could muster, on Shingiss, a "king" of the Delawares. The chief (who would eventually join the French) was ceremoniously polite. He agreed to come along to a conference George was calling at the Indian village of Logstown.

Up the banks of the broad Ohio, through land which Washington noted was sometimes "extremely good" and sometimes "bad," they rode till they debouched on a rich meadow, half a mile wide and as long as the eye could reach. To the young planter, it seemed a vision of beauty and opulence. "Between sun-setting and dark," he descried a jutting hill, with a white watercourse tumbling from its brow, that narrowed the valley, and at its feet a ragged conglomeration of Iroquois long houses and squarer Algonquin huts.[4] This was the Indian metropolis of Logstown. He was undoubtedly greeted by a staring of squaws and papooses, a grave deputation of braves. However, he only noted in his journal his disappointment that the Half-King, the most important chief in the neighborhood, was away and had to be summoned.

The next morning, he saw dark shapes moving on the frozen meadow. They proved to be the first enemies the future soldier had ever seen: in his excitement he wrote them down as "four or ten Frenchmen." Under van Braam's questioning, they stated that they had deserted from a detachment of 100 men who had come up from New Orleans to meet a similar group expected down from Canada. (This may have been a tale to frighten the Indians.) They gave information about the impressive number of French forts and garrisons in the wilderness. Washington carefully noted all down, in the process immortalizing van Braam's translation of Illinois as the Black Islands (*isles noires*).[5] Then the "deserters" filed off into the wilderness. History will never know whether or not Washington had entertained the first of the many spies who along the years sought his presence and tried to win his confidence by disclosing not too secret intelligence about the enemy.

When the setting sun threw long purple shadows, the Half-King arrived. The whites, who commonly thought of Indian leaders in monarchical terms, had given him this title because he was a proconsul, sent by the Iroquois legislature, the Onondaga Council, to exert Six Nation authority over the Mingoes, Shawnees, and Delawares who inhabited that part of the Ohio Valley. In his middle fifties an experienced diplomat, the Half-King must have been amused when the young Virginian rushed to him the moment he arrived and asked for a private conference. (Indian courtesy assumed that a traveler was tired and hungry, and thus no business might be discussed until he had eaten and rested.) However, the Half-King did not stand on form, and Washington was soon engaged in an operation which all but the most experienced white men found baffling.

The Half-King had signed, at a council previously held at Logstown, a parchment that, if interpreted in European terms, made him and his suzerainty allies of the English. Thus Washington felt justified in asking through an interpreter what had occurred when the chief had called on the commander of the French fortifications towards which Washington himself was pointed.

The Indian's story began most satisfactorily—he had demanded that the French get off the Indians' land. However, when the Half-King repeated his arguments, his words, though ostensibly still only a report on how he had stood up to the Frenchmen, took on a disturbing double edge which Washington emphasized in his notes with underlinings and capital letters:

"If you had come in a peaceable manner, like our brothers, the *English,* we should not have been against your trading with us, as they do; BUT TO COME, FATHERS, AND BUILD HOUSES UPON

OUR LAND AND TO TAKE IT BY FORCE IS WHAT WE CANNOT SUBMIT
TO." The land belonged to neither the English nor the French,
"but the Great Being above allowed it to be a place of residence
to us, so, Fathers, I desire you to withdraw as I have done [de-
sired of] our brothers the *English*. . . . I lay it down as a trial
for both, to see which will have the greatest regard for it, and
that side we will stand by."

This surely surprised Washington, for the wording of the
Treaty of Logstown seemed to give Indian authorization for the
Ohio Company's ambitions. He must have wondered whether
the escort of warriors on which he would have to rely as he
advanced through an increasingly hostile forest would be as pro-
English as he had been led to suppose.

Now the Half-King was repeating the French commander's
reply to his own speech. He had been threatened; his belt of
wampum had been thrown in his face; the commander had
shouted that the French had power to destroy any English on
the Ohio and all Indians foolish enough to support them.[6]

This was, as Indian diplomacy went, the occasion for Washington to meet bragging with bragging: to say that the English
soldiers were as numerous as leaves on the midsummer trees,
and that the King of France trembled till he shook his long
house whenever he heard the English King's name. But the huge
Major changed the subject. He asked for geographical information.

If George came out of the conference disturbed, he was not
reassured when a group of Indians gathered around him to ask
"very particularly" about some Indians the white men had
imprisoned: "their brothers in the *Carolina* jail."[7]

Washington was glad to have brought his interview with the
Half-King to a close without having the chief ask him to recipro-
cate for the information he had received by stating the nature of
his own mission. The true answer, that he had been deputed to

claim the Ohio Valley for the English, would, of course, have been disastrous—and Washington had no desire to lie. Thus, he had volunteered no information. However honest this may have been, it was far from politic. Nothing annoyed the Indians more than the assumption, only too common among the British, that they could be moved as blind pawns in affairs vitally concerned with their survival. Later, at a crucial moment, the Half-King was to denounce Washington for treating the Indians like slaves.[8]

However, the chief held his peace when on the following morning Washington, in addressing a formal meeting in the Council House, asked that the Indians supply a guard to protect him in delivering a letter "of very great importance to your brothers, the *English,* and I dare say to you, their friends and allies." The Half-King promised the guard, but added that to gather it would take at least three days.

When Washington insisted that his business "required the greatest expedition," the Half-King had a second argument: the French had given him a very special belt of wampum "with the marks of four towns on it"; the return of that belt would be "shaking off all dependence on the French." But, alas, the belt was not at Logstown; certainly it was to the Major's interest to wait till it could be brought so that in his presence the Half-King could throw it at the Frenchmen.[9]

The Major's written instructions had not empowered him to engage in political negotiations,[10] nor did he have the necessary understanding of forest diplomacy. Either because of similiar ignorance, or because he had too much of a servant's mentality to make suggestions, or because his young commander was too impetuous to listen to him, Gist was being of no material help. However, Washington could not resist such an opportunity as the Half-King seemed to be offering him to further such a setback to the French. He agreed to wait.

After he had been suffered to fidget for three days, the Half-King came to his tent with some other sachems and "begged (as they had complied with His Honor the Governor's request in providing men, etc.) to know on what business we were going to the *French*. This was a question I all along expected, and had provided as satisfactory answers to as I could, which allayed their curiosity a little." (That Washington, who is usually so explicit, fails to specify what answers he gave, implies he was not pleased with them.)[11]

The following evening a meeting was held at the Council House from which the Virginians were excluded. Washington heard shouts and was finally notified that "only three of their chiefs, with one of their best hunters, should be our convoy." The Half-King explained that a more formidable group might create danger by alarming the French; "but I," Washington continued, "rather think they could not get their hunters in."

When the party assembled the next morning, Washington was pleased to see that the Half-King was actually bringing along the great belt with four towns on it. However, the other two chiefs, Jeskakake and White Thunder, were also old men. It looked as if only the hunter would be much help in a skirmish.

They traveled for five days along trails well known to the Indians "without anything remarkable happening but a continued series of bad weather."[12] On December 4, Washington saw for the first time a blowing white cloth emblazoned with three fleur-de-lis, the enemy flag rising proud above a fortified house in "an old Indian town," Venango, at the meeting of the Allegheny with French Creek. He ordered the Indians to encamp in the woods (which they meekly did); he strode, with Gist and van Braam at his heels, to the door under the flag. In a moment, he was in the presence of three French officers. The one who looked most like an Indian introduced himself as Captain Joncaire.

If ever Washington stared, he did now, for this man was legend. Philip Thomas Joncaire, Sieur de Chabert, had been raised among the Senecas. He so controlled Indian confidence that his smallest whisper, or so it was said, could lift British scalps all along the frontier from New England to Georgia. How glad Washington was that he had left the Half-King in the woods, rather than exposing him to this diabolical influence! For his own part, Major Washington was glad to accept supper and wine.

In his enchanting role as secret agent, the young Major seemed perpetually to fill his glass but drank little, observing with pleasure that his companions "dosed themselves pretty plentifully with it." When they told him "that it was their absolute design to take possession of the Ohio and by G— they would do it!" he assumed they were drunkenly dropping secrets. Although he had found that the Indians at Logstown, whom the French had threatened, had been loath to back his mission, he did not recognize that a continued barrage of threats was French wilderness policy; they were willing to tip off the British to frighten the tribes.

However, the French officers referred more freely than they might have done had they not been drinking to the string of fortifications which held communication open between Venango and Montreal. Dead sober for all his histrionic gesticulating with his glass, Washington recorded their words on his excellent memory for jotting down as soon as he could get privily to his notes.

Having ascertained that the French commandant to whom his letter was addressed was at Fort Le Boeuf sixty miles up French Creek, Washington wished to hurry off the next morning before Joncaire could meddle with his Indians. But the French agent, after expressing concern "that I did not feel free to bring them in before," sent for the tribesmen. Washington intercepted the

Indians with a warning not to get drunk. So majestically solemn that Washington was reassured, the Half-King stated that he had only accepted the invitation so that he could throw the belt at Joncaire.

After the Indians had filed in, Joncaire put on a long face. He expressed hurt feelings that they "could be so near without coming to visit him." George waited for the Half-King to answer angrily, but the belt remained in the chief's pouch—and what should come through the door but a keg of brandy! In mounting anger which he tried to hide from Joncaire's amused stare Washington saw the liquor go down "so fast that they were soon rendered incapable of the business they came about."

To enjoy, or at least tolerate, the company of drunken Indians was a gift Joncaire had cultivated but Washington had not. The Major retired in mid-party to his tent where, listening to ululations that might well awaken hibernating bears, he resolved that come what may he would carry off his Indians the next morning. But the next morning the Half-King appeared at his tent— Washington was surprised that he seemed sober—and said that a council fire was being lit, at which he intended to return the belt.

Washington hurried to the council with a smiling face. For once, he enjoyed the endless speech aimed at the French which the Half-King had rehearsed many times in his hearing. At last, the chief offered Joncaire the belt. Joncaire refused to receive it, "but desired him to carry it to the fort to the commander."

The following morning, after Gist had argued with the Indians from daybreak to eleven o'clock, the party got under way. During four and a half days they encountered "excessive rains, snows, and bad traveling through many mires and swamps." Then twilight revealed a rectangular enclosure almost completely surrounded by swirling water. There were portholes cut on the log walls for cannon and loopholes for small arms. The portcullis of Fort Le Boeuf rose, and out came some officers bearing an invitation to dinner. Gist noted that the Virginians were received "with a great deal of complaisance."[13]

After they had all slept, Washington arranged with care the travel-crumpled best uniform he had brought through the wilderness. Then he stepped forth as official emissary, through the Governor of Virginia, of George II to Louis XV, through the French commandant, Legardeur de St. Pierre, a knight of the Military Order of St. Louis.

Towards St. Pierre, whom he described as "an elderly gentleman and has much the air of a soldier," Washington comported himself with the courtesy that had been his particular study ever since he had copied down 110 maxims. For his part, St. Pierre "made it my particular care to receive Mr. Washington with a distinction" commensurate with the dignity of Virginia "as well as his own quality and great merit." Wolves might be howling outside, but as far as the participants could achieve it, all was conducted as it might have been at St. James's or Versailles.[14]

When, with Dinwiddie's warning in their hands, the French officers gathered to confer in private, they carried courtesy to the point of cockiness: the Virginia Major was allowed to wander the fort by himself, taking what notes he pleased. As long as the French could control the Indians, they were sure no white army could reach them through the wilderness.

Here is the description Washington surreptitiously wrote of the wilderness fort: "It is almost surrounded by the creek and a small branch of it which forms a kind of island. Four houses compose the sides. The bastions are made of piles driven into the ground, standing more than twelve feet above it and sharp at top; with portholes cut for cannon and loopholes for the small arms to fire through. There are six eight-pound pieces mounted in each bastion; and one piece of four pound, before the gate. In the bastions are a guardhouse, chapel, doctor's lodging, and the commander's private store, round which are laid platforms for the cannon and men to stand on. There are several barracks without [outside] the fort for the soldiers' dwelling, covered some with bark and some with boards, made chiefly of logs. There are also several other houses, such as stables, smith's shop, etc."

Even for professional writers, such a description of a complicated object is difficult to make so coherent and clear. However, Washington's mind was coherent and clear; and he was training himself to be an expert observer.

He stated plainly that his judgment of the size of the garrison—"a hundred exclusive of officers of which there are many" —was merely a guess. To determine with what force the French planned to come downriver in the spring, he ordered some of his companions to count the number of canoes hauled up by the waterways. The tally came to "fifty of birchbark, and 170 of pine; besides many others which were blocked out in readiness to make."[15]

Eventually St. Pierre handed Washington a letter, in which he stated he would transmit Dinwiddie's communication to his general, the Marquis Duquesne, "to whom it better belongs than to me to set forth the evidence and reality of the rights of the King, my master, upon the lands situated along the River Ohio, and to contest the pretensions of the King of Great Britain thereto. . . . As to the summons you send me to retire, I do not think myself obliged to obey it."[16]

Thus, while snow swirled into the rush of frigid wilderness water, in the presence of a young hero yet unknown to history, a gauntlet was thrown that would help plunge European men into the terrible Seven Years' War.

The French offered the Virginia Major two canoes in which to carry the lethal message downstream. "As the snow increased very fast and our horses became daily weaker," he accepted. He sent three of his servitors ahead with the horses. They were to await him, if the rivers froze, at Venango. Otherwise, they should push on to the Forks of the Ohio.[17]

Since it seemed probable that the rivers would actually freeze, forcing land travel through an ice-choked wilderness with diminished horses, Washington must have guessed that his greatest dangers and hardships lay ahead; yet he was not thinking of the journey when he wrote, "I can't say that ever in my life I suffered so much anxiety." St. Pierre had stocked Washington's canoe with liquor and provisions, but the canoe that had been set aside for the Indians remained empty.

Washington had used all the pressure "in my power" to hurry the Half-King into repeating, this time into the correct ears, the speech of defiance he had so often rehearsed into Washington's. But when the Indian proconsul finally held a council with the French, the Virginia Major was excluded. The chief later reported that the Frenchmen had evaded taking the belt, and had promised to live in amicable trade with the tribes. And now the Indians showed no interest in departure!

"I saw," Washington wrote, "that every stratagem which the most fruitful brain could invent was practiced to win the Half-King to their interest, and that leaving him here was giving them the opportunity they aimed at." He lectured the Half-King on his treaty obligations to the British and on the dangers of the brandy pot; he remonstrated to the French; and, although history awaited his message, he refused to budge without the braves.[18]

The young Major had become so absorbed in his tug-of-war with French agents that he forgot that he had not guided the Indians to Fort Le Boeuf: they had guided him. Whatever happened at the moment, when he continued his return journey over the mountains, they would be released from whatever apron strings he had been able to throw over them. They could then return to French hospitality as they pleased.

After holding the Major up for forty-eight hours, the Indians finally "set out off with us."

Washington carefully sent his braves ahead. The river was high and the current so strong that "several times we were like to be staved against rocks." When on the second morning the Virginians caught up with the Indians, there was a lovely smell of roasting meat. Washington's pleasure that those skilled hunters had killed three bears was soon changed to chagrin, as the tribesmen would not move until they had eaten all the meat they could not carry. Night came. A new morning rose to the sizzling of spits and the chumping of jaws; the light revealed the negative effect of the seemingly happy circumstance that the snow had stopped. The water level in the creek was dropping fast. The Indians being too occupied to heed warnings that the canoes would soon be unable to pass, the Virginians set out without them.

"Many times," Washington wrote, "were obliged all hands to get out and remain in the water an half hour or more, getting over the shoals." As the current slowed, the ice that had hugged the shore moved out into midstream. For three days they made desperately slow progress. Then they ground into a solid sheet of ice. They tried to chop a way through till stopped by darkness. The next morning they found a carry "across a neck of land, a quarter of a mile over." As they labored under the weight of canoe and baggage, the Indians reappeared—but no longer alone. Four boatloads of Frenchmen had been added.[19]

The combined party was more populous than friendly. As the Virginians, to keep their canoe from overturning in the shallows, walked beside it, their wet clothes frozen firm as galling armor, some Frenchmen sped by cockily in their canoe. But almost instantly, so Gist wrote, "we had the pleasure of seeing the

French overset, and the brandy and wine floating in the creek." The Virginians "run by them and left them to shift for themselves."[20]

After six days, during which, according to Washington's estimate, they traversed no less than 130 miles of bending stream, they arrived at Venango, where Joncaire embraced his dear Indian friends. But Indian relations seem to have been bumped out of Washington's head when he saw his horses, who were waiting there because his servitors had discovered that the Allegheny was frozen too tight for anything to move by water. The horses were "so weak and feeble" that Washington "doubted much" their ability to carry the supplies needed for a long trip through a glassed-in waste. Pondering this, he hardly heard the Half-King's verbose explanation of why the Indians could not, despite their stupendous loyalty to the Major and the English, leave at once. Determined to proceed at all hazards before his horses weakened further, Washington left the Indians behind after warning them against Joncaire's "flattery."[21]

At some time before they parted, the Half-King had applied to Washington the name Caunotaucarius, "the town-taker." George, who had never taken a town, regarded this as a rhetorical compliment: he did not realize that this title had been earned, almost a century before, by his fierce great-grandfather, John, the settler. That the Indians preserved the title and knew the genealogy that enabled them to reapply it was a demonstration of how accurate and inclusive was that communal memory that took the place of written records. Washington noted in 1786 that the name, "being registered in their manner and communicated to other nations," was always used by the Indians in their transactions with him during the Revolution.[22]

After less than a day's pause at Venango, Washington set out with his fellow Virginians. The drivers of the pack animals "were obliged to ride," but he, Gist, and van Braam gave up their riding horses to spread the load. Washington was now wearing "an Indian walking dress": leather leggings, a knee-length coat belted at the waist, and perhaps moccasins.

The first day, the party managed to cover only five miles. The next brought snow, which piled ever deeper in the narrow trails. "The cold," Washington wrote, "increased very fast." Ice crusts cut the horses' legs. The drivers, "though they were as well clad as they could be, were rendered useless by the frost." The horses moved more and more slowly. After three days, one of which was Christmas, Washington concluded "there is no probability of their [the horses'] getting home in a reasonable time." He himself could move more quickly. He resolved to leave the cavalcade behind.

Gist objected: "I was unwilling he should undertake such a travel, who had never been used to walking before this time." But Washington would not be dissuaded: he and Gist "set out with our packs, like Indians." Washington was to remember that the cold "was scarcely supportable." An unexpected hazard was thirst: snow would burn the mouth and all the small runs were frozen solid. However, they covered eighteen miles. "That night," Gist wrote, "we lodged at an Indian cabin, and the Major was much fatigued."[23]

Washington insisted on setting out the next morning long before dawn. They pushed down the trail to an Indian village called Murthering Town in commemoration of some ancient tragedy forgotten at least by white men. Here they were enthusiastically greeted by a brave whom Gist thought he had seen at Joncaire's on their journey up to the fort. The Indian was full of curiosity about where and why they had left their horses.

To Gist's disapproval, Washington announced a determination of abandoning the trail, which here took a wide loop, and "traveling on the nearest way to forks of Allegheny." He asked the armed Indian to serve as guide. The Indian "seemed very glad. . . . Upon which, we set out, and the Indian took the Major's pack.

"We traveled," Gist continues, "very brisk for eight or ten miles, when the Major's feet grew very sore, and he very weary, and the Indian steered too much northeastwardly. The Major desired to encamp, to which the Indian asked to carry his gun. But he refused that, and then the Indian grew churlish, and pressed us to keep on, telling us there were Ottawa Indians in these woods, and they would scalp us if we lay out; but to go to his cabin, and we should be safe. I thought very ill of the fellow, but did not care to let the Major know I distrusted him. But he soon mistrusted him as much as I."

The Indian said his cabin was within sound of a gunshot, "and steered us more northwardly. We grew uneasy, and then he said two whoops might be heard to his cabin. We went two miles further; then the Major said he would stay at the next water, and we desired the Indian to stop at the next water."

Overhead, towering labyrinths of ice-encrusted branches glowed at their highest reaches dimly with the winter sun, but so little light reached the forest floor that eyes strained in a perpetual gloaming. Eyelids blinked as the three travelers came out into "a clear meadow: it was very light, and snow on the ground." Through this suddenly visible space, the Indian sprinted forward, wheeled at about fifteen paces, and raised his gun. The sharp sound of a shot!

Thus strangely history moves. The bullet, fired by an anonymous savage and aimed for motives unascertainable, speeding in a glade geographers had not found; this little lead pellet, whining through midwinter desolation and loneliness, carried enough insensate venom to change the history of the world. For a second, destiny hung poised. Then Washington shouted, "Are you shot?"

"No," answered Gist.

The Indian ran behind a free-standing white oak and tried to reload his gun, but before he could do so, both Washington and Gist had thrown themselves on him. Gist wanted to kill him. But the future general had never seen a man killed. Although justice and self-preservation both urged, he could not bear to see it now.

"As you will not have him killed," Gist said, still holding down the struggling brave, "we must get him away, and then we must travel all night." He asked the Indian whether the shot had not been an accident, and, when the surprised brave grunted enthusiastic assent, told him to go to his cabin and prepare it for their reception. Released, the culprit went off at a gallop.

Gist followed a short distance and "listened until he was fairly out of the way." Then the two Virginians dashed in an opposite direction, minding nothing but speed. After half an hour, they thought it safe to light a little fire by which they could set their compass. Then they extinguished the fire, "traveled all night, and in the morning we were on the head of Piney Creek."[24]

Washington reasoned from the musket shot that the French had offered the tribes a reward for their scalps: the woods must be full of stealthy hunters! It did not seem safe to sleep. They kept their eyes and ears on the strain as they threaded down along the watercourse towards the Allegheny. As dusk was fading, they saw dinting the snow dim processions of purple shadows. Indian tracks! He and Gist decided to separate and "appointed a place a distance off" where, if all went well, they would meet.

As Washington moved alone through the lethal cold, he listened for a nearby rustle that would mean danger for him, for a distant shot that might mean the death of Gist. Darkness poured down. Surely his heart sounded in his breast as he neared the trysting place. Yes, there was a blacker shadow! Yes, his friend was there! "We encamped, and thought ourselves safe enough to sleep."[25]

On by the side of the creek they slipped the next day, staring ahead to see the Allegheny. Every glow that revealed a clearing ahead seemed a promise. There were many disappointments, and when, at long last, the land really fell away to the river, it was the greatest disappointment of all. That terrible cold had not been cold enough. "We expected," Washington wrote, "to have found the river frozen, but it was not: only about fifty yards from each shore. The ice, I suppose, had broken up above, for it was driving in vast quantities. There was no way of getting over but on a raft."

Having between them only "one poor hatchet," they took turns chopping most of the next day. "Just after sun-setting," they launched the completed raft.

"Before we were halfway over," Washington continued, "we were jammed in the ice, in such a manner that we expected every moment our raft to sink and ourselves to perish. I put out my setting pole to try to stop the raft that the ice might pass by, when the rapidity of the stream threw it [the raft] with such violence against the pole that it jerked me out into ten feet water, but I fortunately saved myself by catching hold of one of the raft logs. Notwithstanding all our efforts, we could not get the raft to either shore; we were obliged, as we were near an island, to quit our raft and make to it."

Only a semi-giant could have escaped from drowning when thus thrown, after suffering so many other hardships, into the ice-encumbered current of a huge, quick, wild river. Washington had been more completely drenched than Gist, but it was the backwoodsman, not the tenderfoot, who had to sit up most of the night rubbing snow on frostbitten toes and fingers. Washington slept fitfully in the bitter cold. Surely he did not dream, as he stirred by the fire, of crossing, at the head of an army, another vast river in which ice smashed against boats.

When he awoke in the dawn's thin light, he certainly gave a cry of joy. The river between the island on which he lay and the far shore had frozen solid. What had been a grinding, murderous hell was now a shining boulevard. Washington and Gist hurried across and were soon in John Frazier's warm trading post.[26]

But there was still much wintry ground to be crossed before he could deliver to Governor Dinwiddie the explosive paper which he had carried so carefully that, despite his ducking, it had not got wet. Waiting at Frazier's for horses, he called on Aliquippa, a "queen" of the Delawares: "I made her a present of a matchcoat and a bottle of rum, which latter was thought much the best present of the two."[27]

On New Year's Day 1754, he started back over the mountains. He was cheered to meet seventeen horses bearing materials for the fort to be built at the Forks of the Ohio, and a day later, "some families going out to settle." On January 7, he reached the comparative civilization of Wills Creek "after as fatiguing a journey as it was possible to conceive."

He spurred on down the Potomac towards Williamsburg and the Governor, but as he approached a familiar mansion, he forgot the eagerness which had made him in the wilderness risk his life to speed his mission. Although he had given in to no need for rest between bouts with nature at her most violent, at Belvoir "I stopped one day to take necessary rest."[28]

If Sally was, as is probable, there, what were her thoughts while her tall admirer told exciting tales of the most important adventure that had been undertaken in her lifetime in her Virginia world? Was this the setting for some of those "thousand tender moments" which George was later wistfully to remember?[29] Hard fact tells us only that, his day of grace over, Washington rode on to Williamsburg, where, insofar as the male Fairfaxes had not warned him, the mixed nature of his reception must have come to him as a surprise.

[77]

7

Triggering the Seven Years' War

T HE PAUNCHY Scotch Governor received the French-man's letter and Washington's report with grim satisfac-tion. This he said, nodding his jowled head for emphasis, would show the General Assembly how wrong they had been to refuse to take any step towards protecting the frontier, preferring to waste their time in trying to keep him, the Governor, from collecting his rightful fee for signing land patents. Dinwiddie would call the House of Burgesses back as quickly as possible. However, the King's Council could meet on the morrow. Washington should then submit a written account of his journey that would reveal France's evil intentions.

Given less than twenty-four hours to "transcribe," as he put it, "from the rough minutes" he had jotted down en route,* Washington mourned that he had "no leisure to consult of a new and proper form."

When Washington was told that Dinwiddie had ordered the

---

* The rough minutes are lost; the quotations in this volume are from the published journal. It appeared in pamphlet form in both Williamsburg and London, and was reprinted, in whole or in part, in various periodicals on both sides of the ocean. Washington used the graphic skills he had acquired as a surveyor to draw, undoubtedly after printed sources, a map of those main geographic features, from the Potomac to Lake Erie, which were relevant to his journey. He marked on it his route, and the location of the various places he had seen. This map Dinwiddie sent in manuscript form to his superiors in London.[1]

narrative to be printed, he added a foreword in which he presaged the methods he was to apply during the Revolution to the assessing of military intelligence. There was nothing, he wrote, to recommend his account "but this: Those things which came under the notice of my own observation, I have been explicit and just in a recital of. Those which I have gathered from report, I have been particularly cautious not to augment, but collected the opinions of the several intelligencers, and selected from the whole the most probable and consistent account."[2]

Firm words for a twenty-one-year-old with an exciting and momentous tale to tell! Indeed, Washington's narrative, if sometimes clumsily and confusedly written, adhered with admirable directness to its function as a record of fact. Those of the Half-King's remarks that were embarrassing to the Ohio Company, particularly his statement that the Indians would support whichever European power did not attempt to establish settlements in the Ohio Valley, were frankly and truthfully reported. However, Washington did skimp the most sensational of his adventures, which we know primarily from Gist's parallel journal. Perhaps because he did not wish to repeat the squeamishness that made him endanger his mission by sparing the miscreant's life, he gives only a brief mention to the murderous Indian from Murthering Town.[3]

Reading the journal today, one is impressed with the greenness of the young man and the cockiness: there is no hint that at any moment he felt he had come up against anything he could not understand and could not handle. Yet he did handle everything. However blunderingly at times, he moved forward with dauntless energy: got where he was supposed to go; delivered his message; came home successfully through stupendous hardships. Taken by itself, the physical vitality displayed was on the level of genius.

Contemporary reactions to Washington's publication gave him a lesson (which he eventually took very much to heart) on how the most honest public act can be discredited if the actor's personal interest is involved. Although the Ohio Company partisans, despite their undoubted wish that he had omitted some of , the Half-King's remarks, cheered Washington's testimony that the French were planning aggression on the Ohio, most others, so Washington complained, considered his story "a fiction and a scheme to promote the interests of a private company."⁴

While controversy raged, Washington had his first experience of being in his own person a political symbol. On his veracity the most cogent arguments for Colonial military action were based: he was the physical embodiment of the war party. And no one could fail to notice him as he walked the streets of Williamsburg for, as he was always to do wherever he went, he towered over his fellow men. Measuring between six feet and six feet three and a half,* weighing close to two hundred pounds, he seemed gigantic in those days when human beings were normally so much smaller than now. It did not detract from the startling nature of his appearance that he moved with the lithe grace of an athlete and that his head which stood so high was crowned, in an environment where most men were brunets, with chestnut hair.⁵

The Virginia Assembly voted Washington £50 "to testify approbation of his proceedings on the journey to the Ohio." He considered this niggardly: "I was employed to go on a journey in the winter (when I believe few or none would have undertaken it), and what did I get by it? My expenses borne."⁶

Dinwiddie was sending out calls for help. The Pennsylvania legislature expressed doubt that the Forks were actually in

---

* In 1763, Washington wrote his tailor that he was six feet tall, but his secretary, Tobias Lear, stated that when prepared for its coffin, his body measured six feet three and a half inches.

British territory. The New York legislature echoed this doubt, although it did promise to help Virginia with £5000. As for the Virginia Assembly, Dinwiddie considered that it showed itself "very much in a republican way of thinking" by forcing him to accept, in return for £10,000 and military preparedness, provisions that clipped his "prerogatives."[7]

After Dinwiddie had authorized an army of 300, the possibility existed that Washington might be rewarded with the command. But, however brisk he was in actual action, the young Major recognized, when there was time for careful thought, his limitations. Concerning the top command, he wrote Richard Corbin, an influential member of the Council, "I must be impartial enough to confess it is a charge too great for my youth and inexperience." But he would like the second post; he believed that, "with my own application and diligent study," he could "in time render myself worthy" of the position if "under a skilled commander or man of sense."[8]

Virginia had been at internal peace too long to boast "a skilled commander"; Dinwiddie appointed "a man of sense," whose military experience consisted in teaching mathematics at William and Mary. Whether Joshua Fry possessed untapped martial powers history was never to discover, for he never caught up with his second in command, Lieutenant Colonel Washington. He was, Washington was to recall, too old and fat to move quickly.[9]

A small Virginia task force engaged in fortifying the Forks was forwarding warnings it daily received from Indians that a huge French war party was on its way down the river. On March 15, 1754, Dinwiddie ordered Washington "to march what soldiers you have enlisted immediately to the Ohio." Fry, it was hoped, would eventually come up with later enlistments. The policy Washington was to follow had been stated in Dinwiddie's previous orders: "You are to act on the defensive, but in case any attempts are made to obstruct the works or interrupt our settlements by any persons whatsoever, you are to restrain all such offenders and in case of resistance to make prisoners of, or kill and destroy them."[10]

To recruit his army and move it across the mountains, Washington needed to handle problems that would have filled a trained commander with despair and rage. Had he been told that he would face the same difficulties throughout his entire military career, he would not have been surprised, since he was too innocent to realize that his situation was a monstrosity limited to primitive armies.

The first difficulty was to get anyone to enlist, and the next was to get money to pay and clothe those who finally did. How many more times was Washington to send authorities the plaint he now first penned: "There are many of them without shoes; others want stockings, some are without shirts"![11] Food and military supplies were equally difficult to secure, and when he at last succeeded, how was he to take them along when he advanced?

Farmers in the Shenandoah Valley, where the army was gathering, were unwilling to rent their wagons to accompany it over the mountains. Washington called on Lord Fairfax, the county lieutenant, for authority to impress vehicles. His Lordship was too busy fox hunting. George then tried to impress illegally—he was not as careful of civilian rights as he was to become—but all except the most decrepit carts and horses were hidden from him. However, he remained energetic and cheerful, and on April 18 ordered what force he had—159 men, some transport, and a few cannon—to set out from Wills Creek for the Forks, almost 200 wilderness miles away.

The troops were still poorly clothed and they lacked tents in a season that was "remarkably cold and wet," yet the men lined up at their young Lieutenant Colonel's orders. By force of personality and by fooling the soldiers into believing they were under military law (the Assembly had passed none), Washington had managed to establish discipline.[12]

Since no road crossed the Alleghenies, Washington's men had to chop a way for the wheeled vehicles, a process too slow for the energetic commander. He rode ahead to ascertain the best route. Anguished calls for reinforcements kept coming in from the Forks, and then there appeared on the trail a little knot of men. Washington recognized the Forks garrison.

The thirty-three effectives had looked over their unfinished walls, so they told him, to see the Allegheny darken with sixty bateaux and three hundred canoes. Out stepped "more than a thousand French," who unloaded eighteen pieces of artillery. What a relief when the commander of this overwhelming force had courteously notified the garrison that if they wanted to go home they would not be molested! Such an offer did not have to be repeated twice.*[13]

Although the strategic Forks were now in the hands of the enemy, the fugitives brought one piece of good news. The Half-King (who had been present) had shouted defiance at the French. He had sent two warriors—they were now staring curiously at Washington—to see if a British army was actually on the way, and also, with a belt of wampum to make it official, a message: the Indians were ready to fall on the French, "waiting only for your assistance. . . . If you do not come to our assistance now, we are entirely undone, and I think we shall never meet again."[14]

Washington called together his few subordinate officers and presided over a council of war. His little army obviously could not displace so powerful a French force, but it seemed clear that Virginia's Indian alliances depended on a brave advance. Fur-

---

* The actual French force (although this Washington did not know) was about 600, four rather than seven times the size of Washington's army.

thermore, Washington felt that inaction would be bad for his soldiers. It was decided to go on to the meeting of Redstone Creek and the Monongahela, about thirty-seven miles from the Forks, "clearing a road broad enough to pass with all our artillery and our baggage, there to await for fresh orders."[15] An Ohio Company storehouse already on the site could be further fortified.

In making this seemingly foolhardy decision, Washington did not count, as he might have done, on the policy the French had just indicated of scaring away, rather than attacking, English forces they caught at a disadvantage. He had not noticed the sequence indicated, although far from clearly, in Dinwiddie's instructions: only if the enemy refused to depart, were they to be attacked. That the courts at Versailles and St. James's had not declared war on each other seemed to the Virginian irrelevant, nor did he realize that, since the Forks had already fallen, a continuance of the uneasy peace was advantageous to Virginia in her state of unpreparedness. He believed (wrongly, so all the documents indicate) that the French had tried to have him and Gist assassinated in the forest. When he now heard that a French scouting party had passed nearby, he regretted that they had escaped before he could annihilate them.[16]

On his own recognizances, Washington notified the governors of Maryland and Pennsylvania of the French advance. The news, he added, "should rouse from the lethargy we have fallen into the heroic spirit of every freeborn Englishman to attest the rights and privileges of our king (if we don't consult the benefit of ourselves)."[17]

In his reply to the Half-King, Washington revealed that in the three months since his last association with that chief he had learned the subterfuges which whites commonly used in Indian relations. Since "our hearts burn with love and affection" for Virginia's Indian allies, he was happy to announce that "a great number of our warriors" with "our great guns" would be in the wilderness immediately "to assist you, whose interest is as dear to us as our lives." He hoped the Half-King would hurry to him for a conference.[18]

Washington believed that he could hold the Ohio Company storehouse unless the French brought heavy cannon down the river; and of this he would certainly hear in time to withdraw. That he might never reach the storehouse did not at first occur to him.

Three weeks after he had written Dinwiddie that he was "destined to the Monongahela," he wrote again to say that his road builders had been able to advance only two to four miles a day. He was much disappointed.[19] Yet what he was achieving was not insignificant. Although the road his men were cutting was no more than a narrow, continuous clearing, with stumps and smaller boulders left in the middle, with only the deepest holes filled in and only the wildest grades a little smoothed, it snaked over the major rise of the Alleghenies, and opened, for the first time in the history of the world, the Ohio Valley to wheeled vehicles.

Finally, Washington was trapped, some twenty miles from his objective, behind the Youghiogheny River that was in flood. Report had it that the French were building at the Forks a formidable fortification—it was called Fort Duquesne—and had received a reinforcement of 800 men. As for his own force, Washington had reduced it. Since the garrison that had surrendered at the Forks had refused to obey his orders, he had sent them back across the mountains lest they undermine discipline.[20]

Waiting for the Youghiogheny River to go down, Washington fumed over an issue he had first met as a boy when his brother Lawrence had sent home from the Cartagena expedition complaints of how the Virginia troops were being upstaged by the soldiers from England. Now, George's pay and that of his fellow officers had been set below that of British regulars in the American service! He could not see, he wrote Dinwiddie angrily, why "the lives of His Majesty's subjects in Virginia should be of less value." Nothing prevented his officers from resigning "but the approaching danger." As for himself, he could only serve with honor by refusing all pay and going on as a volunteer. (He was later reluctantly to take this back, explaining that he needed the money.)[21]

His letter crossed one from the Governor that spoke of great reinforcements on the road. Colonel Fry would soon be there to take command. But, the Youghiogheny having become passable, the Lieutenant Colonel was too eager to wait. He was again on the march when he received a letter from the Half-King which, as it became an important document in the history of the world, deserves to be quoted as the Irish trader and interpreter, John Davison, spelled it, doing his best to reproduce phonetically the brogue he spoke:

"To the forist, his Majestie's Commander offwerses—to hom this may concern:

"On acc't of a french armey to meat Mister Georg Wassionton therfor my Brotheres I deisir you to beawar of them for deisin'd to strik ye forist English they see ten deays since they marchd I cannot tell what nomber the half king and the rest of the chiefs will be with you in five dayes to consel, no more at present but give my serves to my brothers the English."[22]

Washington hurried his troops down the stony side of Laurel Ridge to a wild field called the Great Meadows. Here he found "two natural entrenchments," so close together that the sides could be closed in with wagons to form a hollow square which seemed to his naïve eyes an excellent fort. "By clearing the bushes out of these meadows," he prepared, so he wrote, "a charming field for an encounter." He sent scouting parties out to find the French, and was disappointed when they returned "without having discovered anything."[23]

In the middle of the night, as Washington dozed to whippoor-will and wolf howl, shots! The sentries had fired! He rushed to them: they had seen shadowy figures out there in the dark. Washington's men were now all up and around him under arms. He spaced them behind the ramparts, and everyone stared over, everyone listened. Nothing to see; wolf howl, whippoorwill, and wind in the trees. Finally, dawn. No bodies, upright or prone, became visible in the cleared meadows, but six of Washington's soldiers proved to be missing. It must have been these deserters who had triggered the alarm.

The anticlimax was made up for by the arrival of Gist, who reported that some fifty Frenchmen had passed his nearby house the day before, coming this way. That they had asked for the Half-King was taken by Washington as an excuse for telling "several young Indians who were in our camp that the French wanted to kill the Half-King." This "had its desired effect. Upon the spot they offered to accompany our people against the French."[24]

Washington dispatched about half his force, some seventy-five men, in search of the party Gist had seen. These were still out, when an Indian messenger slipped in to report that the Half-King was encamped with some of his people about six miles away. Furthermore, the chief had come on "the tracks of two men, which he had followed till he was brought thereby to a low, obscure place; that he was of the opinion the whole party of the French was hidden there."[25]

Although Washington feared that this message was a strata-gem of the enemy to take his camp, he could not forbear setting out on the attack. He hid his ammunition, left half his remaining force behind, and with about forty men followed the Indian towards (as he hoped) the Half-King. They went, so he tells us, "in a heavy rain and in a night as dark as pitch, along a path scarce broad enough for one man. We were sometimes fifteen or twenty minutes out of the path before we could come to it again, and we would often strike against each other in the darkness. All night long we continued our route, and the 28th, about sunrise, we arived at the Indian camp."

Washington had last seen the Half-King when he had been unable to pry him away from Joncaire's rum pot, but the chief now expressed eagerness to knock the French on the head.* He had with him a dozen or so braves, only half of whom possessed firearms. "We concluded," Washington wrote, "to attack them together."

Through the fresh forest morning full of sweet odors, with the Indians loping ahead, the party advanced to where the Half-King had seen white men's tracks. As Washington and the others waited, two braves followed the dim marks away into the woods. They were soon back to report that they had seen some thirty Frenchmen "about a half mile from the road in a very obscure place surrounded with rocks."[27]

Indian sources were to tell of a disagreement on strategy between Washington and the Half-King which made the braves resolve to fight separately.[28] Be this as it may, Washington employed, for his first battle, what was to remain through the early years of the Revolution his favorite method of attack: he dispatched several columns along different routes. The Indians were to swing around to the rear; Virginia parties to come in from both the right and left. After the enemy had been thus surrounded, all the attackers were simultaneously to fire.[29]

Leading the right, Washington blundered out on the rim of the hollow in which the French were encamped. He heard

---

* Although he accepted liquor from both sides and put the interest of his own followers first, the Half-King was pro-English. The French, he explained, had "killed, boiled, and eaten his father."[26]

shouts and, looking down, saw some of the enemy gesticulating in his direction, others running to their arms. There was no more point in waiting for the trap to close: he "ordered my company to fire." He was pleased when the fire was echoed from the bluff across the hollow: the Indians were clearly there, although Washington could not see them.

Neither could the French. As soon as they shouldered their firelocks, they concentrated their fire on Washington's exposed company. Their fire seemed so heavy to the tenderfoot commander that he thought it "a most miraculous escape" when only one of the men around him fell dead and no more than two or three sank with wounds. He was to write his brother Jack, "I heard the bullets whistle, and, believe me, there is something charming in the sound."*[30]

The French were going down fast and, indeed, were in their hollow in a desperate situation. After some fifteen minutes, the survivors tried to flee but, finding themselves surrounded, they threw down their arms.

As Washington stepped forward to receive his first surrender, he saw the Indians rushing from their hiding places "to knock the poor, unhappy wounded on the head and bereave them of their scalps."[32] The Half-King was too busy with his own knife to hear Washington's remonstrances. Those French still mobile dashed under the muskets of Washington's soldiers, their voices shrill in a strange tongue and their gestures pleading for protection. The Half-King and some of his braves followed; they demanded with explosive gutturals and with imperious motions of hands already dangling bloody scalps that the Frenchmen be given up to them. As for the enemy officers who were still upright, they were orating in what sounded most strangely like

---

* After this letter had been published in the *London Magazine*, George II commented that the Colonial officer would not consider the sound of bullets charming "if he had been used to hear many."[31]

[89]

indignation. One produced a pouch—perhaps by darting over to a corpse and pulling it from among the bloody clothes—took out some papers, and waved them in Washington's face. Soon a minimum of three interpreters were shouting at Washington translations from French or from Indian.

When the confusion had died down a little, Washington discovered that ten Frenchmen, including the commander, Joseph Coulon, Sieur de Jumonville, had been killed, and that he had twenty-two prisoners. It also became clear that he was being accused of murdering ambassadors. The Frenchmen had carried diplomatic credentials: instructions to find the English, express a desire for peace, but warn them off land belonging to the King of France. Washington was so convinced of the justice of the English claim which he had, on a very similar mission, presented to the French, that this statement of French pretensions seemed to him "so insolent . . . that if two men only had come openly to deliver it, it was [would have been] too great indulgence to have sent them back."[33]

Other passages in the orders to Jumonville Washington had captured instructed the Frenchman to keep his commander informed on British positions and actions. Although Washington had also engaged in spying on his own embassy, he again saw no parallel—and certainly Jumonville's party had been large for a peaceful mission, and they had skulked, not going as Washington had done directly to the enemy commander. Washington assumed that the French had intended to attack if they could to advantage, using their ambassadorial credentials only if faced with a superior force. He wrote Dinwiddie that the Half-King agreed that the diplomatic immunity had been "mere pretense." The chief had added that if the Virginians were "so foolish" as to release the prisoners, who were now demanding just that, the Indians "would never assist us in taking" another Frenchman. As to the claims of the Frenchmen that, "as soon as they had discovered us," they had cried out that they were ambassadors, Washington had heard no intelligible shouts at all.[34]

That, despite all arguments, Washington was not altogether happy with his victory is indicated by the strange manner in which he reported it to Dinwiddie. The letter opened with a long passage—more than a thousand words—in which he continued his complaints because the Virginia officers were being paid less than regulars.[35] Only then did he back into the battle story, which was in total, even with his self-justifications, considerably shorter than the protests.

George II's instruction to Dinwiddie had, although England and France were still officially at peace, envisioned hostilities on the Ohio, but with a proviso designed to keep the onus of aggression from falling on the British: before there was fighting, the enemy should be notified that they were trespassing and given an opportunity to withdraw. Dinwiddie, in his orders to Washington, had hardly gone beyond implying this subtlety. Had he intended it to be observed, he should have underlined it to an inexperienced young Colonial.

Washington's natural turn of mind was direct, cutting through pretensions and subterfuges to bedrock. He had accepted without any hesitations the basic situation of inevitable conflict. By adopting surprise as his tactic, he had fought effectively and in a manner satisfactory to the Indians, but he had precluded the possibility of warning, and had, as it turned out, opened himself, Virginia, and the British Crown to the charge of assassinating an ambassador.

Dinwiddie sent Washington his congratulations, but realized that what came to be known as the Jumonville Affair would stir up diplomatic trouble. In a masterpiece of evasion, he reported to his government that "this little skirmish was by the Half-King and the Indians. We were auxiliaries to them, as my orders to the commander of our forces was to be on the defensive."[36]

Concerning that "little skirmish," Voltaire was to write (exaggerating the ordnance involved), "Such was the complication of political interests that a cannon shot fired in America could give the signal that set Europe in a blaze." Washington had, indeed, shed the first blood in the Seven Years' War, a conflict which, according to Frederick of Prussia, cost the lives of about 853,000 soldiers plus civilians by the hundreds of thousands.[37]

8

Defeat and Perhaps Disgrace

BACK AT HIS camp on the Great Meadows the day after the Jumonville Affair, Washington wrote Dinwiddie, "I shall expect every hour to be attacked, and by unequal numbers, which I must withstand if there are five to one, or else I fear the consequences will be we shall lose the Indians, if we suffer ourselves to be drove back. . . . I doubt not, if you hear I am beaten, but you will at the same [time] hear we have done our duty in fighting as long [as] there was any possibility of hope. . . .

"For my own part I can answer," Washington continued. "I have a constitution hardy enough to encounter and undergo the most severe trials, and, I flatter myself, the resolution to face what any man durst."[1] This was not a boast but a statement of fact. Washington was a physical giant, and, as far as was possible for an intelligent man, he did not know fear. Whether this immunity was altogether an advantage is another matter: it encouraged him to advance into perils which more ordinarily endowed commanders would have evaded.

Washington ordered his men to fix logs upright into the ground, thus finishing in a few days "a small palisaded fort" which he called Fort Necessity. He wrote that inside it, "with my small numbers, I shall not fear the attack of 500 men." However, the Half-King, who had wandered through almost every French fort in inland America, spoke scornfully of "that little thing in the meadow." He tried to persuade the young Virginian that, however conscientiously the surrounding bushes were cut down, the middle of a field was not the perfect spot for a fortification, and that, in any case, a simple wall of palisades was against experienced troops "trifling." But Washington had no intention of accepting the advice of a savage on civilized matters.[2]

Queen Aliquippa (whose heart he had once warmed with a bottle of rum) arrived with twenty-five or more Indian families. When she said they were fleeing French resentment over the Indians' part in the Jumonville Affair, Washington was delighted with this sign of tribal unity with the British. However, he soon noticed that almost all his guests were women and children, and that all had a seemingly magical gift for ingurgitating the food that his men so laboriously carried across the mountains. The Half-King tried to make up for the lack of warriors with great promises: he was sending belts that ordered innumerable tribes to take up the hatchet against the French.

Word came that Fry had died and Washington had been appointed to succeed him as Colonel of the Virginia Regiment. This brought the young man apprehension as well as pleasure. He wrote Dinwiddie that he still "ardently wished" to serve under an experienced officer. He hoped that a new commander in chief who had been appointed, Colonel James Innes, would come quickly to the wilderness.[3] However, Washington was unwilling to have his authority questioned in a manner he felt insulting to himself and to Virginia.

Reinforcements were coming to him across the mountains. About two thirds were additions to his own regiment, but the remaining hundred did not slouch in with the disorderly good humor of the American militia. Wearing regulation uniforms rather than hunting shirts, they marched in files, and at their head appeared an officer who held his back and sword stiffly upright over arrogantly pumping knees. The new arrivals were mostly Colonials, but their "Independent Company" had been incorporated in the regular British establishment and their captain, James Mackay, was a well-born Scot who had received his commission from the Crown. After allowing his men to fall out, Mackay notified Washington that, since any royal commission outranked all Colonial ones, whenever matters involved both the Virginia Regiment and his company, he would give the orders.

Washington replied to Mackay, as he remembered, "with all the politeness that were due to his rank or that I was capable of showing": colonels were colonels and captains were captains, and Virginia was Virginia; it was obviously absurd "for an independent captain to prescribe rules to the Virginia Regiment." Mackay, who was a veteran of Indian warfare on the Georgia frontier (and who George was later to admit was an excellent officer), seems to have been too courteous to point out that Washington's commission was a rapid elevation of an amateur, while he himself had been an officer for eighteen years in an established army. But he did say that Dinwiddie had "not a power to give commissions that will command him." That night, the Virginians and the regulars encamped separately, unable to communicate with each other because neither would accept the parole and countersign established by the other.[4]

Intending to continue his interrupted march to Redstone Creek, Washington had kept some of his men engaged at cutting ahead the slightly smoothed, long, tortuous clearing that served as a road. To his invitation that Mackay's men join in, the Captain replied that regulars did not work on roads without extra pay he was not authorized to give. "We shall part tomorrow!" cried Washington. He would not "suffer" the regulars "to march at their ease whilst our faithful soldiers are laboriously employed."[5]

Mackay and the Indians stayed at Fort Necessity, when Washington started his wagons moving in the wake of his road-building pioneers, groaning towards that faint "pock-pock" of axes to the westward that was the yet whispered chorus of American destiny.

The advance was stopped at Gist's trading station, halfway to Redstone Creek, by the needs of diplomacy with the Indians. Washington, who confessed that "for want of a better acquaintance with their customs, I am often at a loss how to behave,"[6] had been enchanted to be joined by Pennsylvania's skilled Indian agent, George Croghan, and Andrew Montour, a picturesquely painted half-Oneida. They lit a council fire in Washington's camp.

The first arrivals disgorged from the curling wilderness paths were hardly propitious: six Mingoes (Ohio Valley Iroquois) known to be pro-French. They admitted they had been sent as spies, but insisted that they would carry back whatever misinformation suited Washington. Since, according to the rules of Indian diplomacy, they could not be sent away, they were among the some forty braves who attended the council at which Croghan returned a Shawnee who had been imprisoned in South Carolina, and assured the Indians that the English had sent an army for no other purpose than "to put you again in possession of your lands."[7]

To belts of wampum displayed, to ceremonious rhetoric, to ritualistic shouts, to the scent of roasting oxen, to oratory the next day and the next, to the gurgle of rum, the pound of dancing feet, and the rattle of calabashes, to belts of wampum accepted, the council wound its elaborate, orotund, time-consuming way—but from under all the circumlocution there finally emerged the fact that negotiation in this part of the wilderness was officially useless: the issue had been taken out of local hands. The central Iroquois body, the Onondaga Council, had sent through the Ohio Valley a belt ordering their nationals and the Shawnees and Delawares who were their vassals to stay, until further notice, neutral. Although a Delaware chief offered to evade this order in the English interest by "the most subtle measures," persuasion could keep only a handful of Indians in Washington's camp. Even the Half-King returned with his followers to the Great Meadows, where Fort Necessity stood.[8]

Before the Mingoes he regarded as French agents departed, Washington told them in strictest confidence—they should not tell his enemies!—"some stories prepared to amuse [mislead] the French."[9] This was the only fun he had at the congress. Indian affairs looked black, and they soon looked blacker. When he sent to the Great Meadows for the Half-King, that worthy replied that he had "received a blow" and could not come.[10] It seemed increasingly certain that insofar as the Indian violated the neutrality order, it would not be in favor of the British.

Montour and Croghan, Washington was to state, "by vainly boasting of their interest with the Indians, involved the country in a great calamity, by causing dependence to be placed where there was none. . . . Notwithstanding the expresses that the Indians sent to one another," not more than thirty fighting men ever joined his army, "and not more than half of those [were] serviceable upon any occasion."[11]

Furthermore, Croghan, "who was an eyewitness to our wants, yet had the assurance during our suffering to tantalize us and boast of the quantity [of flour] he could furnish as he did of the number of horses he could command."[12] The army suffered from crippling shortages.

It was with trepidation as well as anticipation that George opened dispatches from John Carlyle, the commissary across the mountains. Carlyle was married to George William Fairfax's sister and was thus brother-in-law to the charming Sally, of whom he sometimes wrote news; he doubled as Washington's personal business agent. On the matter of supplying the army, he could offer little more than promises. Thus on June 27, he expressed hopes that he could send in a few days money for the soldiers' back pay, and in a month some flour. He would like to send tools, but would it not be easier for Washington—that is if he had any iron—to have them forged in the wilderness? He was, so Carlyle continued, having difficulty getting the tobacco harvested from Washington's plantations through inspection, as it was "but indifferent." Sally Fairfax was away on a visit, but his own wife had promised to write.[13]

Enclosed in the cover was a letter from Mrs. Carlyle and enclosed in that was another letter which the husband did not know about. Sally Fairfax might be away, but it was from her.[14] This exciting communication Washington destroyed, as he regularly did missives from that fascinating lady, but Mrs. Carlyle's letter remains.

When mail was usually carried by private hands and open to prying eyes, passages that might provoke gossip were commonly phrased with an indirection intended to confuse all but the rightful recipient. In Mrs. Carlyle's letter there is such a passage: "Those pleasing reflections on the hours passed ought to be banished out of your thoughts. You have now a nobler prospect, that of preserving your country from the insults of an enemy, and as God had blessed your first attempt, hope he may continue his blessing, and on your return, who knows, but fortune may have reserved you for some unknown she that may recompense you for all the trials. However, you have my warmest wishes, and may be assured that I am ever your well wisher."[15]

Crisis now struck in the forest. It began as an unintelligible jumble from the mouth of an Indian. Echoed into Washington's ears by an interpreter, this became news that the French at the

Forks had been heavily reinforced. They had boasted to the Indians that they were sending 800 soldiers and 400 braves—three times Washington's total number—against his little army.

The Colonel ordered that the fencing around Gist's storehouse be refashioned into a palisade on which his artillery—nine small swivels—was to be mounted. He called in the detachment that was road building ahead, and summoned Mackay from the Great Meadows. Mackay came; at this moment of great danger, he and Washington seem to have agreed to cooperate without further debate over the top command.

The minutes Washington kept of a council of war specify that he had, to support 400 men, meat and bread for six days, and about twenty-five head of cattle, mostly milk cows, who could not be fed if the enemy besieged and could not be advantageously slaughtered as there was no preservative but a quart of salt. The council reasoned that the French would probably "strive to starve us out by intercepting our convoys." If, on the other hand, the enemy were "so void of knowledge in military affairs as to risk a battle, we must give a total defeat to thrice our number, otherwise be cut to pieces by so prodigious a number of their Indians in our retreat, who are the best people in the world to improve a victory."[16]

The Indians with Washington's army were insisting that it return to the Great Meadows. To this the council agreed, noting that the move would shorten supply lines, get them further from the French, and that Fort Necessity was there.

Since Washington had sent almost all his teams back to the settlements in search of provisions, the men had to pull the guns by hand over what one of his officers dramatically called "the roughest and most hilly" pass in all the Alleghenies.[17] The tempers of the Virginians were not helped when Mackay's regulars refused tug on the ropes. However, Washington managed to assuage the threats of mutiny among his own men. He set an example to his officers by giving up his riding horse to carry munitions—and paid some soldiers privately to carry his baggage on their backs.[18]

It took two to three days to cover some thirteen seemingly perpendicular miles. Food for the march was only parched corn and some beef cooked instantly after the animals were slaughtered. Fortunately for the long, slow, staggering line, there was no war whoop, no musket crack, no ambush.

Everyone had hoped for an abundance of food when they reached Fort Necessity. However, the bins there proved almost empty. From the Indian encampment outside the fort, the Half-King strode over to advise Washington to continue the retreat. The Virginia Colonel replied that his men were too tired to pull the guns any further, and that, in any case, there was "a flying report" that the considerable reinforcements Dinwiddie had long been promising were close.[19] The Half-King returned to the Indian encampment. The Indians picked up their possessions and disappeared into the forest.

Pennsylvania's knowing Indian agent, Conrad Weiser, was to note in his journal that "the Half-King complained very much of the behavior of Colonel Washington to him (though in a very moderate way, saying the Colonel was a good-natured man, but had no experience), saying that he took upon him to command the Indians as his slaves, and would have them every day upon the out scout and attack the enemy by themselves, and that he would by no means take advice from Indians; that he lay at one place from one full moon to the other and made no fortifications at all, but that little thing upon the meadow, where he thought the French would come up to him in open field; that had he taken the Half-King's advice and made such fortifications as the Half-King advised him to, he would certainly have beat the French off"; that the Indians had decamped "because Colonel

Washington would never listen to them, but was always driving them on to fight by his directions."[20]

Washington had insisted that the great risks he had taken were required to preserve the Indian alliance. He had not realized that his tactics were even more foolhardy according to Indian than white strategy. Few Indian nations could muster more than a few hundred warriors. As their military strength depended altogether on their manpower, no chief considered a single brave "expendable": to inflict loss without suffering any was the object of Indian generalship. (This was why their favorite tactic was ambush.) Exposing compatriots to annihilation by a vastly superior enemy seemed to them not only madness but barbarism. If such behavior were to subject Washington to the defeat the Indians foresaw, he might well sink British prestige so low in the forest that to restore it would, if feasible at all, take years.

Washington's army of 400 could by no means all crowd into the palisaded fort which, indeed, could hold little more than the stores and ammunition. A larger area had already been surrounded by an earthen parapet with a ditch behind it. He ordered that this irregular quadrilateral be extended, the longest side to about 160 feet, to include a little brook that would supply water in case of siege. Furthermore, the existing walls should be heightened with logs and more earth. The work went slowly, as more than a quarter of his men were sick, others had to be sent out on scout in place of the vamoosed Indians, and the regulars, by refusing to dig and pile, encouraged some of the Virginians to go on strike, although their own lives seemed to depend on their efforts.

About dawn on July 3, 1754, a scouting party hurried in, supporting a sentry wounded in the heel. They shouted at Washington that "the enemy were within four miles of us, that they were a heavy, numerous body, all naked!"[21] Nakedness did not appear in another report, which stated that 600 Frenchmen were on the march. Washington ordered some of his men to their guns, others to their axes and shovels for a frenzied effort to complete the fort.

Towards nine in the morning, word came that the French were close by.[22] Washington lined his men up outside the parapet. Then, to his pleasure, the French appeared in the open field just as he had expected they would. (They had happened on the fort before they had expected to.) Washington's nine swivels barked, at which "the enemy advanced with shouts and dismal Indian yells." Washington bellowed an order. With one unanimous jump, his men leaped behind the entrenchment; they turned and fired. At this, the enemy broke and disappeared.

Before Washington could congratulate his troops on what seemed an initial advantage, a bullet zinged into the fort and then another. Even after the lead had become a downpour, he could see no enemy, only powder smoke drifting upward from "every little rising, tree, stump, stone, and bush." Virginians in what had been planned as safe positions leaped and fell. The artillerymen were driven from their swivels. Anguished screaming and bellowing signaled that the horses and beef cattle were going down under "the constant galling fire."

Crouching low, Washington shunted his men to spots that seemed to promise protection, but, as soon as they revealed their location by firing over the ramparts, enemy bullets came in among them. Now, as he tried to encourage his men, Washington was slipping on blood. But (the French firearms being in the manner of the times inaccurate) the casualties were episodic—a slumped form here, a man crawling there—and the nightmare was able to drag on for hour after hour with enough Colonials still upright to hold the attackers at musket range.

In the late afternoon, the murderous monotony was changed by what seemed to Washington "the most tremendous rain that can be conceived." Its low position made the fort a catch basin. From one trench after another, the men were dispossessed by rising streams of bloody water. The rain wet the ammunition in the cartouches and firelocks, and poured through the roof of Fort Necessity, rendering useless some of the powder stored there.

A sortie to drive away the attackers was impossible, for few of Washington's men had bayonets—and the French were accompanied by Indians. To sue for peace seems not to have occurred to the young Colonel, and, indeed, as evening came on his men managed to increase the intensity of their fire. Perhaps this was because they had broken into the rum kegs to keep their spirits up. Since they had little else in their stomachs— only tastes of flour and bacon—many reeled as they prepared aggressively to shoot.

Darkness was gathering in when the enemy firing hushed and a clear voice called from the drenched meadow, "*Voulez-vous parler?*" Van Braam translated for Washington. Unable to conceive why a superior force should desire a parley, he suspected deceit: the French clearly wanted to get a man past the walls to spy out those angles which they had not yet reached with their fire. Van Braam shouted a refusal, listened to the returning shout, and told Washington that the French were willing to receive rather than send an emissary. Still puzzled, Washington sent van Braam out under a white flag. It glimmered in the fading light and then disappeared in the driving rain.

In the recess from firing, Washington could freely walk the bloody fort and survey the situation. One third of his men, more than a hundred, were dead, gasping out their lives, or contorted by various wounds. For the survivors, the situation was desperate. Even if through some miracle they succeeded in beating off the French, they could not, since the horses were all ensanguined heaps, retreat without abandoning the guns and wounded. Nor could the troops stay where they were, for noth-ing was left to eat.

Since the French could not help knowing that they were now helpless, Washington could expect only the strictest surrender terms. However, van Braam came back all smiles. Although the French commander, Coulon de Villiers, was a brother of the dead Jumonville, although Washington had held the Frenchmen captured at the Jumonville Affair as prisoners of war, de Villiers was willing to let the Englishmen, if they merely surrendered, go home. Washington was too pleased, too young, too inexperi-enced to wonder why.

In as dry a corner as they could find in the dripping stockade, under a candle that sputtered and was often extinguished, van Braam translated the surrender terms from French penmanship blurred by soaking. Mackay and Washington made some minor objections which sent the interpreter back twice to the enemy commander. In each case, the French agreed to what was urged with surprising alacrity.

At last Washington expressed satisfaction with the terms: although all but one cannon were to be left behind, the English-men were to march out of the fort with the honors of war and were to have the right to repossess their baggage. It seemed a small price that the prisoners captured at the Jumonville Affair should be returned to the French and that, till this was done, two of Washington's captains were to be left as hostages.

In their exhaustion and relief, neither Washington nor any of his fellow officers paid much attention to the preamble de Villiers had attached as an explanation of his lenient terms: "Our intention has never been to trouble the peace and good harmony which reigns between two friendly princes, but only to avenge the assassination which has been done of one of our officers, the bearer of a summons." The word *l'assassinat* was also used later in the document to refer to the Jumonville Affair.[23]

During the battle, Washington had been much impressed by Mackay's skill and bravery: he allowed the regular to sign the capitulation first. Then he inscribed his own name with as little anxiety as Pandora had felt when she opened her box.

After the capitulation had been published, international controversy raged over what seemed to be Washington's double admission that the English had assassinated a French emissary. Washington insisted that van Braam, "a Dutchman little acquainted with the English tongue," had translated the French words as "the death or the loss" of Jumonville.[24] But actually the baleful words were, although they strengthened de Villiers's point, not essential to it. The preamble stated clearly that the English were being released because no state of war existed, and, if no war existed, Jumonville had been wrongfully killed, whether or not Washington admitted that the Frenchman had been assassinated.*

The document signed, the wounded (including a "valuable" colored servant of Washington's who was to die) cared for as well as possible, the Colonel had leisure to worry about his baggage, which he now wished he had left at Wills Creek, as the other officers had done with most of their effects. He did not

---

* The capitulation contained a provision which some historians have interpreted as an agreement that the surrendered troops would not come over the mountains again against the French. Should this be the correct reading of the clumsily drafted document, Washington broke his parole. However, the general tenor of the clause which contains the provision makes more reasonable the conclusion that the prohibition applied only to a detachment which was to be permitted to return briefly to the site of Fort Necessity and reclaim any personal possessions which the garrison might hide there from the Indians.

When Washington and Mackay agreed that the Frenchmen captured at the Jumonville Affair should be released, they exceeded their authority. Those in authority refused to honor the promise.

That Mackay signed his name first denoted a final agreement that he was the higher officer, but public opinion abroad and at home ascribed that position to Washington, probably because his rank sounded higher, his was the more vivid personality, and he remained in the public eye.

really believe he would see it again. To van Braam, who was going away with the French as a hostage, he sold for thirteen pounds his superfine broadcloth coat with silver fringes and his fully laced scarlet waistcoat.[25]

The next morning was the fourth of July. Washington led as his surrendered army came out of the fort with, as had been agreed, "the honors of war." This meant that the drummers beat a march, a flag flew—although not the biggest standard in the fort for that was too heavy for the exhausted men to hold high— and the procession included one small cannon. It was a ragged parade since about seventy wounded had to be helped along or carried on soldiers' backs. Washington's heart must have contracted when what seemed a hundred Indians came running, but they were prevented by the French from further depredations than snatching possessions.[26]

As soon as Washington's force was out of sight of the Great Meadows, they abandoned their single cannon; within three miles the main body encamped, too weary and heartsore to carry the wounded any further. But their Colonel hurried on to Williamsburg to report in the capital of his little world on what had taken place.

The effects of Washington's first campaign on his immediate career in the French and Indian War, and on the long-range development of his character and military skill, were profound. If this has too often been overlooked or misunderstood, it is because the light thrown backward by his later achievements has been allowed to gild over how grievously Washington blundered when, at the age of twenty-two, he was put by his own energy and the default of others into a position of conspicuous and complicated leadership for which, as he himself realized and stated, he was not ready.

Washington had failed on three levels: with the Indians, with the French, and as the functioning commander of an expeditionary force.

Although least understood by most of his English contemporaries at home and abroad (English ignorance of Indian motivation was a French trump card in the wilderness), Washington's failure with the Indians was to prove the most disastrous of all his mistakes. Before what seemed to the braves his idiotic military behavior ended in a defeat that seemed to justify all French boasting, there had been a chance that some of the Ohio tribes could be lured to a continuing British alliance. The testimony of England's few skilled watchers in the forest is summed up by the words of the Indian agent Daniel Claus: "There was never the like seen how quick the nations turned after Colonel Washington's defeat."[27] Ahead loomed years of bloody raids on the frontiers, and the massacre of Braddock's proud army.

On the European diplomatic level, Washington had prejudiced the moral position of the whole British Empire at the eve of a world war. A French poet exclaimed, "The assassination of Jumonville is a monument of perfidy that ought to enrage eternity"; while an English writer stated, in a pamphlet published in both London and Boston, that the articles of capitulation Washington had signed at Fort Necessity "were the most infamous a British subject ever put his hand to."[28]

Like Washington himself, his Virginia compatriots kept their eyes so glued to their own ground that they did not see the European effects of his indiscretions in all their livid colors. However, English officials conscious of foreign policy could not view with favor the provincial who had, however unwittingly, helped the French to tie a firecracker to the British lion's tail.

Militarily, Washington had shown both foolhardiness and ignorance. His marching, without waiting for reinforcements or the experienced commander he craved, into the jaws of what he sometimes realized was certain defeat, showed much more bravery than good judgment. He could, it is true, point to promises broken by many people, from Dinwiddie and the Half-King down to venal cattlemen and obscure Indians who wished to cadge a drink of rum—yet certainly wisdom would have indicated less reliance on hope as a substitute for reality. The French and their Indians could have chopped up his line of march a hundred times, and in its location and design Fort Necessity was a travesty of military engineering. In English military circles, Washington's name became synonymous with the long-assumed incompetence of Colonial military officers. General Lord Albemarle, British Ambassador to France, wrote the Duke of Newcastle, "*Washington* and many *such* may have courage and resolution, but they have no knowledge or experience in our profession. Consequently, there can be no dependence on them."[29]

However, few of Washington's fellow Virginians knew more of military science than he did. That his army had fought so bravely against superior numbers seemed to them the crux of the matter, all the more so because newspapers quoted Washington and Mackay as estimating that out of 900 attackers the enemy had lost, in killed and wounded, 300.*

Whatever the situation in the greater world, Washington had become a hero to his neighbors.

As for the historian, he can, without overlooking Washington's failures, see that the young man promised superlatively well.

---

* The French official figure was two dead and seventeen wounded out of 400 Frenchmen and an undetermined number of Indians. This may be too low, but Washington's estimate was certainly too high.

Washington, after he had lost a battle, was always inclined to accept — whether because of optimism or for purposes of propaganda — exaggerated reports of enemy casualties. In this case, the *Virginia Gazette* stated that he and Mackay had told Dinwiddie, "The number killed and wounded of the enemy is uncertain, but by the information given by some Dutch [Germans] in their service to their countrymen in ours, we learn that it amounted to above 300; and we are induced to believe it must be very considerable, by their being busy all night in burying their dead, and yet many remained next day."[30]

Brashness, greenness, all the concomitants of inexperience may be outgrown, and Washington had exhibited to a superlative degree a quality that is inborn: the ability to lead men. As the war unrolled, the Colonial soldiers, hardly trained at all and members of no continuing establishment, displayed a dismaying tendency to flee from their own shadows. Not in disdain but to show the authorities that they needed to be clothed, Washington had written that his recruits were mostly "those idle, loose persons that are quite destitute of house and home."[31] This was hardly promising material, yet, despite some desertions, his soldiers marched into the howling forests and, although badly supplied and often unpaid, built roads as the regulars sneered, fought a superior force, and died under his orders.

In any case, Washington was now an international figure. As the muse of history notes the name of the twenty-two-year-old already engrossed on her pages, she may well wonder whether this premature appearance will smooth or roughen his future path.

In and Out of the Army

WHEN WASHINGTON reached Williamsburg on July
17, 1754, Dinwiddie received the vanquished warrior
with that bland, impersonal courtesy which in an aristocratic
society signaled the decline of interest. The Governor had,
indeed, decided that the energetic stripling who had twice got
him into hot water was a liability. "The late action with the
French," he wrote his government, "gave me much concern. My
orders to the commanding officer were by no means to attack the
enemy till all the forces were joined." Complaining of a lack of
good officers, Dinwiddie hinted that he himself should be given
the military command.[1]

Washington was ordered to rejoin the remains of his regiment
at Alexandria. He had hardly done so when the Governor and
Council sent further orders: he was to march across the Blue
Ridge for a junction with Colonel Innes, who was then to lead
the combined forces over the Alleghenies.

This indicated a replay of the Fort Necessity campaign. On
that venture, Washington had engaged eagerly, but he was a
quick learner from experience. Now he protested that the Virginia army was too small compared to the French, that it was
not supplied or equipped, and that there was not sixpence in the
military chest. Assurances of food from traders were not to be

trusted, nor were the Governor's promises a substitute for ammunition. Sanguine hopes that the Indians would cooperate were illusory. Under the best of circumstances, any Virginian advance must go slowly, and winter was coming. As for the few soldiers he had in his camp, they had suffered so much from civilian inattention to their needs that the very rumor they had been ordered out again had induced six desertions.[2]

Dinwiddie's reaction to the Colonel's protests revealed that the greatest gift Washington had so far revealed, his ability to lead free men to the very limits of actual oppression, was lost on the English functionary, who believed that common soldiers should be brainwashed into automatons. That the Virginia Regiment was unpaid, naked, and starving seemed to the Governor irrelevant. If men deserted, he wrote Washington, it was due to "the want of proper command."[3]

Poor George could only repeat how his soldiers had been bilked and add that if the death penalty were established for desertion, he might be able to hold his men. He had just been called from church to arrest twenty-five who "were going off in the face of their officers."[4]

Despite all his ranting, Dinwiddie failed to get the army across the mountains. He could not secure assistance from neighboring colonies where the defeat at Fort Necessity was not uncommonly welcomed as the frustration of the Ohio Company's efforts to grab the fur trade. And Virginia's own Assembly, when it met in August, again tweaked the Governor's nose by linking military appropriations with a provision aimed at curtailing his financial perquisites. Dinwiddie vetoed the bill and prorogued the House till October.

And so, as summer moved into autumn, the French remained unmolested in the Ohio Valley. Having leveled Fort Necessity, they strengthened their strong point at the Forks, Fort Duquesne, and the lesser forts that protected their communications.

In early September, Washington's heart was gladdened by a rumor, repeated in a letter from a friend in Williamsburg, that the Virginia Regiment was to be incorporated in the British regular army.[5] To become a regular colonel at the age of twenty-two (something possible in England only for scions of the greatest families) did not seem to the naïve Colonial beyond his possibilities (did he not already command a regiment?). When, however, he journeyed to Williamsburg for the October session of the Assembly, he discovered that his consequence there extended only to the smiles of his friends and the admiring stares of little boys. Great matters were being determined on a level from which he was utterly excluded. Dinwiddie was in private conference with Governor Horatio Sharpe of Maryland and Governor Arthur Dobbs of North Carolina.

Dobbs had come from England on a warship with a promise of £20,000 and 2000 stand of arms. When Washington learned he had brought Sharpe a commission as commander in chief (although only with the rank of lieutenant colonel) of all the King's provincial forces in America, his heart must have sunk. He had just been engaged in a controversy with the Maryland Governor.

Hearing that Sharpe had been publicly criticizing his behavior in the Fort Necessity campaign, George had dispatched a letter of self-justification. In his reply, Sharpe had commented with toplofty graciousness on the "freedom" and "ingenuity" Washington had shown in writing him. Then the Governor, who had served in the British regular army (and had, indeed, a very low opinion of Washington's military skill), wrote that he did not deny that Washington had much to explain away, but added condescendingly that he was "disposed to exculpate" rather than "condemn."[6]

Whatever were George's worst fears, they were soon realized.

In order, so it was said, to remove any conflict over command between regulars and provincials, the Virginia Regiment was to be broken into its component companies; there were to be no higher officers than captain, and these were to be commanded by all regular captains.

Washington was inclined to blame his difficulties on his having been traduced to his superiors by rival officers who resented being commanded by him. However, Dinwiddie stated suavely that the new measures had been ordered from abroad (which was untrue). In any case, rather than accept the demotion from colonel to captain, Washington resigned from the army and galloped angrily away from Williamsburg.[7]

Forcing the Virginia Assembly reluctantly to appropriate £20,000, the three governors planned an immediate attack on Fort Duquesne. Sharpe, as he considered his task of advancing across mountain and through wilderness in approaching winter, concluded that he could use the presence of the young man who knew the problems best. Washington received a letter urging him to accept a company, and promising that Sharpe would, by keeping him on separate assignment, keep him from being commanded by anyone who, in his former rank of colonel, he would have commanded.

Washington's reply is dated from Belvoir, but its style, so turgid with emotion it is sometimes hard to understand, suggests that if any Fairfax head leaned over his shoulder as he wrote, it was sleeker and more feminine than that of his mentor William, who liked to urge him "to enjoy the fruits of that philosophic mind you have already begun to practice."[8]

The suggestion that he keep his colonelcy as a purely honorary title, Washington wrote, "filled me with surprise, for if you think me capable of holding a commission that has neither rank nor emolument annexed to it, you must entertain a very contemptible opinion of my weakness, and believe me more empty than the commission itself." Indeed, rather than accept reduction "to a very low command, . . . I choose to submit [without recompense] to the loss of health which I have, however, already sustained (not to mention that of effects). . . . I shall have," the youth continued, "the consolation of knowing that I have opened the way when the smallness of our numbers exposed us to the attacks of a superior enemy; that I have hitherto stood the heat and brunt of the day, and escaped untouched in a time of extreme danger, and that I have the thanks of my country for the services I have rendered it."

Washington's complaint of "loss of health" seems to have been primarily a rhetorical flourish, since there is no other indication that he was ailing at this time. That he tied his being able to withstand the "heat and brunt of the day" with his having "escaped untouched in a time of extreme danger" implies that the soldier (who was never scratched at any battle) already felt an immunity from bullets that was in some mysterious way connected with his personal identity. By his "country" he meant Virginia, and its thanks had been expressed to him, Mackay, and their soldiers in a resolution of the House of Burgesses. He had replied that they had done no more than their "duty to our country and the best of kings."

"It was," Washington concluded his letter to Sharpe's aide, "to obey the call of honor and the advice of my friends" that he had resigned "and not to gratify any desire to leave the military line. My inclinations are strongly bent to arms."[9]

Seeing no immediate hope of further military service, Washington took a step momentous for the nonmilitary side of his career. His mother clearly intended never to release to him his inheritance at Ferry Farm. However, Mount Vernon was empty, and, Lawrence's daughter having died, he was the heir after the absent widow. From her he rented, for 15,000 pounds of tobacco to be paid annually, the house, the plantation, and the eighteen resident slaves.[10]

The late autumn expedition Sharpe had been commissioned to lead had proved impossible to attempt. However, in February 1755, two months after Washington had seemingly committed himself to agriculture by buying Mount Vernon, there sailed into Hampton Roads, Virginia, a British veteran whose orders were to take Fort Duquesne with not only Colonial forces but also two regular regiments from overseas. Washington called himself to Edward Braddock's attention in a letter congratulating the Major General on his arrival.

Braddock's staff soon discovered that the man who knew the terrain and problems best was ex-Colonel Washington, and in early March there arrived at Mount Vernon a letter from Braddock's top aide, Captain Robert Orme: the General, having been informed that Washington would like to serve, "will be very glad of your company in his family [on his personal staff] by which all inconveniences of that kind [rank] will be obviated. I shall think myself very happy to form an acquaintance with a person so universally esteemed."[11]

Washington's reply curled itself into embarrassed efforts at courtliness: his desire to serve as a volunteer was increased by "the General's great good character." However, he was "not a little biased by selfish and private views. To be plain, sir, I wish for nothing more earnestly than to attain a small degree of knowledge in the military art. . . . But, sir, as I have taken the liberty so far to observe that freely, I shall beg your indulgence yet a little longer"; business affairs "into which I was just entering at no small expense . . . must greatly suffer in my absence." He would call on Braddock as soon as the General reached Alexandria.[12]

From the lawn that was now almost his at Mount Vernon, Washington watched day after day a stirring sight. Up the Potomac came fleets of vessels, more and different sail than he had ever viewed, that were to land at nearby Alexandria all the

European panoply of war. When he rode to that now crowded town, he must have had to make an effort, in his proud role as a former Virginia commander, not to gawk at the cannon larger than he had ever seen, the curiously fitted artillery wagons, the tents so efficient and yet so luxurious, and the two regiments of regulars, hundreds of men in identical dress whose maneuvers were to him a revelation: never in his whole life had he seen so many objects moving with such perfect uniformity. Compared to them, even teams of four matched horses seemed ragged.

When Braddock and his military family arrived, the local gentry flocked to pay their respects: it was surely on a social occasion that Washington first saw the squat, elderly, free-mannered General, who said whatever he thought with a bluntness that the Colonials now considered hearty but were soon to regard as rude. The gentry were delighted when Braddock invited them all to a review of his professional army. This was the grandest day Alexandria had ever seen. Sally Fairfax dressed herself more carefully than ever before, and George was of her company. They both expected her to be the belle of the occasion, but to their common chagrin it was to a Mrs. Wardrope that Braddock paid the most attention.[13]

Washington made an appointment with Braddock and Orme for April 2, to settle his personal part in the campaign. However, just as he was about to set out for Alexandria, in rushed his mother. She had been "alarmed with the report" that he intended to go with Braddock and she had come to stop him.[14]

As later correspondence indicates,[15] nothing he could say about the desire for glory, or his duty to his country and his King, impressed her one jot. She had a basic conviction which she repeated over and over: he was being unfaithful to his duty to her. In addition, she probably expressed a mother's worry about the safety of her child. As the clock struck the quarters, the halves, and then the hours, George realized that Braddock and Orme were waiting, but he did not pull away. He begged his mother to make Mount Vernon her home during his absence, listened and argued while the sun traveled across the heavens.

Although it had been only a week since George had first met the English officers, he had so charmed them and they him that when he wrote Orme explaining why he had missed his appointment, it was without self-consciousness or embarrassment, but in the mood of young males joking with each other. He would, he went on to say, gladly join Braddock's family as a volunteer.[16]

He remained too annoyed with Governor Dinwiddie to notify that British official of his decision. However, he did not wish it to escape the attention of the House of Burgesses which, as the popular branch, often opposed the Governor. To John Robinson, Speaker of the House, to Carter Burwell, chairman of the Military Committee, and also to the influential William Byrd III of Westover, Washington sent parallel letters in which he stated that he was going with Braddock "without expectation of reward or prospect of attaining a command." He was motivated only by "the hope of meriting the love of my country and friendly regard of my acquaintances." Rather than have the virtue of this action overlooked, "I chose to proclaim it myself."

He added that to fit himself out to accompany Braddock involved heavy expenses for which he would never be reimbursed. He had hesitated to ask before, but could he not receive from the government £50 to make up for his personal losses in the Fort Necessity campaign?[17]

When five governors appeared in Alexandria to confer with Braddock, Washington, who was to have a lifelong fascination with city building on the Potomac, saw in the selection of "our little town . . . a happy presage." And when introduced to the dignitaries, he showed a gift for recognizing ability as if by instinct. He was most impressed by the brilliant Governor of

Massachusetts, William Shirley, whose "every word and every action discovers the gentleman and great politician."[18]

George's mother could hardly have been pleased when she learned that her eldest, not satisfied with flying from her to war, had summoned her twenty-year-old third son to manage Mount Vernon in his absence. Jack posted to his brother who, as April ended, set out to join his general at Frederick, Maryland.

10

Nightmare

WHILE HE WAS on the road, riding to join Braddock at Frederick, Washington's mind ran on Sally Fairfax. Pausing at his Bullskin plantation, he wrote a letter to her, urging that she lighten the campaign by corresponding with him. "None of my friends," he wrote, "are able to convey more real delight than you can, to whom I stand indebted for so many obligations."[1]

In his early conversations with Braddock, Washington had warned that the army could not move across the mountains as quickly as had been planned. Now, he found the General willing to admit him a good prophet. Braddock had been promised 200 wagons, 2500 horses, and copious supplies, but rarely did anything appear. He was in a rage.

"The General," the young volunteer wrote of his commander, "by frequent breaches of contract, has lost all degree of patience, and for want of that consideration and moderation which should be used by a man of sense upon these occasions, will, I fear, represent us in a light we little deserve; for, instead of blaming the individuals as he ought, he charges all his disappointments to a public supineness, and looks upon the country, I believe, as void of both honor and honesty. We have frequent disputes on this head, which are maintained with warmth on both sides, especially on his, who is incapable of arguing without it, or giving up any point he asserts, let it be ever so incompatible with reason."[2]

Washington himself wrote, "You may with almost equal success attempt to raise the dead to life again as the force of this country,"[3] but he would not tolerate equivalent criticisms of Virginia from an Englishman.

The General was one of those explosive men who enjoyed an argument: "He uses and requires," Washington wrote, "less ceremony than you can well conceive."[4] As an expert in Braddock's family on frontier conditions, the Virginian acted as an accepted gadfly, who was not too important to be brushed away if his buzzing began to annoy. He tried, so he wrote years later, "to impress the General and the principal officers around him with the necessity of opposing the nature of his defense to the mode of attack which, more than probably, he would experience from the *Canadian* French and their Indians. . . . But so prepossessed were they in favor of *regularity* and *discipline*, and in such absolute contempt were *these people held*, that the admonition was suggested in vain."[5]

Among the some hundred Indians in Braddock's camp, the familiar face of the Half-King was missing. (He had died, insisting all the while that he was being killed by French witchcraft.) Insofar as Washington guided Braddock on Indian relations, he achieved no more with the new chiefs than he had with the old. He had learned that Indians "are easily offended, being thoroughly sensible of their own importance,"[6] but he could not think of them—or pretend that he did—as equal allies. Braddock and the English regulars were, of course, even less disposed to bolster the consequence of savages. A delegation of Iroquois sent from the Mohawk River to size up the General reported, "The great man in Virginia did not seem to love

Indians and made but little account of them." Long before Braddock met the French, his Indians had disappeared.[7]

As he circulated in camp, Washington was pleased that he was forming "an acquaintance which may be serviceable hereafter if I find it worth pushing my fortune in the military way."[8] How he was to push his fortunes he could not, of course, foresee, but he did get to know many men whom he was to meet again in another war. He became, for instance, quite intimate with an officer whom he was to oppose when they were both commanders in chief, with Major Thomas Gage. Less welcome at headquarters than this correctly mannered, legitimate son of a viscount, but nonetheless spotted by Washington as an interesting young man, was an ugly, nearsighted, stocky, aggressive captain who was rumored to be the illegitimate son of a duke. His name was Horatio Gates. Washington also got to know that tall, gesticulating, voluble lieutenant who was usually followed around by dogs, Charles Lee.

The idea had been growing in Washington's mind that rather than fight for the rights of Virginia officers in relation to regulars, he should maneuver himself and his friends into the British regular army. After all, his brother Lawrence had been a regular captain during the Cartagena expedition.

Regular commissions offered rewards beyond immunity from being ordered around by Englishmen of lower rank. Not temporary, as were commissions in Colonial forces, but lifetime appointments, they could serve as bases for careers. Or, if you wished to change professions, your commission could be sold for a substantial sum, which rose with rank. If you were retired because of disability, age, or (as in Lawrence's case) because your regiment had been disbanded, you could count on half pay for life.

Braddock encouraged Washington's interest in the regulars, giving him some ensigns' (second lieutenants') commissions to hand to "the young gentlemen of my acquaintance." For him personally the General could at the moment do nothing since a brevet (temporary) captaincy was—as Washington explained—"the highest grade he has it in his power to bestow." However, Braddock promised that after the successful termination of his campaign, he would use his interest in England to secure for Washington "preferment agreeable to my wishes."[9]

It is significant of the aristocratic way of life that during the several years that Washington engaged in the quest for a regular commission, he never stated exactly what rank he desired. When one stretches out one's hand to gain a gift, however deserved, from privilege, one does not specify, but allows privilege to make its own judgment of largess.

Washington undertook no move towards buying a commission, and, indeed, he could not have afforded any rank he would accept. His refusal of a captaincy from Braddock proves he would have gone no lower than a majority. A majority sold for about £2000 sterling.[10] And Washington seems to have hoped for more than that. In his letters he always equated evenly his Virginia rank with those in the regular army. He had retired as a colonel.

Although Washington was eager to serve George II in his regular army, for Pennsylvania he felt only a Virginian's rivalry. As a result of Benjamin Franklin's success in finding horses and wagons after Virginians had failed, Braddock resolved that, once Duquesne had been taken, a supply road for the garrison should be built directly to Pennsylvania. Washington was outraged. Instead of being "the chosen people," he huffed, the Pennsylvanians "ought rather to be chastised," because of their unwillingness to help him and his fellow Virginians during the Fort Necessity campaign. For the moment, however, Virginia's interests were being well served. The old Ohio Company storehouse at Wills Creek had blossomed into Fort Cumberland—a log stockade 400 feet by 160—and it was from here that Braddock was now building the road that would carry him to the French.

When Braddock ordered his volunteer aide to ride posthaste to the seacoast and bring up £4000 needed by the paymaster, Washington moved so briskly that he wore out his horse, but took a roundabout route that enabled him to spend a night at Mount Vernon and call at Belvoir. Sally Fairfax lent him a horse of her own. She enchanted him by saying that she wished him to inform her of his "safe arrival at camp." But then she dampened the fire by insisting that he might not write her directly. He should send the news through somebody of her acquaintance.[11]

His mission completed, Washington obediently sent the news to others, but in the end he could not resist dispatching a letter directly to his charmer. Her forbidding him to do so, he stated, "I took as a gentle rebuke and polite manner of forbidding me corresponding with you, and conceive this opinion not illy founded when I sifted it thus. I have hitherto found it impracticable to engage one moment of your attention. If I am right in this, I hope you will excuse my present presumption and lay the imputation to lateness at my successful arrival. If, on the contrary, these are fearful apprehensions only, how easy is it to remove my suspicions, enliven my [here Washington, in reading the letter after the Revolution, obliterated a word], and make me happier than the day is long by honoring me with a correspondence which you did once partly promise."[12]

To his mother, Washington wrote, "Honored Madam: I am favored with yours by Mr. Dick, and am sorry it is not in my power to provide you with either a Dutch man or the butter you desire, for we are quite out of the part of the country where either are to be had, as there are few or no inhabitants where we now lie encamped, and butter cannot be had here to supply the wants of the camp. . . . I hope you will spend the chief part of your time at Mount Vernon."[13]

As today's astronauts hope to carry the earth's atmosphere with them to the moon, so the British army was building, to travel on through the wilderness, a narrow, continuous strip of Europe. At first, Washington must have been impressed with what the engineers were doing to the curly clearing his army had cut the year before, how they bridged or filled in gullies, how they reduced the steepness of hills, but it soon became clear that the fine road was advancing only two miles a day.

The Colonial thereupon suggested a partial acceptance of wilderness conditions: all supplies should be loaded on pack horses, only the artillery remaining on wheels. This elicited profanity from Braddock. And soon Washington was no longer able to argue. He was "seized with violent fevers and pains in my head"; as the army advanced, he had to jog along lying prone in one of the wagons he had hoped would be left behind.[14]

Typical of the hundreds of things that went wrong with the advance was that the American horses were proving too small and weak to pull the English artillery wagons. Day after day, while his men sickened with dysentery and he seemed to be thrashing helplessly in a morass of green foliage, Braddock cursed the mean world into which he had been dropped. But on June 16, he faced the fact that, at the rate they were traveling, it would take at least a month to get to Duquesne. He called a council of war and, before it met, asked the private opinion of his Colonial adviser. Washington, so he tells us, presented the plan which the council eventually adopted: chosen troops— 1200 it was decided—should dash ahead with minimum artillery—thirty carriages—and all provisions loaded on horseback. The rest of the army would follow slowly with the wagons and heavy baggage as soon as more horses could be procured.[15]

Washington being "excessively ill," Braddock ordered that he should stay behind with the rear division. This so depressed him that the General promised "in the most solemn manner" to summon him before Duquesne was attacked.[16]

The Virginian staggered from his sickbed to see that fast force disappear quickly: the "prospect . . . conveyed the most infinite delight to me." However, "all my sanguine hopes [were] brought very low when I found that, instead of pushing on with vigor without regarding a little rough road, they were halting to level every mole hill and to erect bridges over every brook." Word came back that in four days they had advanced only twelve miles. "They have had frequent alarms and several men scalped."

As he lay suffering in a stationary camp, his friends on the staff ahead and the British officers around him cursing the Colonials for immobilizing them by a lack of horses, Washington's loneliness and sense of dependence made him write it down as "a great misfortune" when his white servant, John Alton, came down with his sickness and "we did not see each other for several days." He wrote bitterly to his brother Jack, "You may thank my friends for the letters I have received, which has not been one from any mortal since I left Fairfax [County] except yourself and Mr. Dalton."[17]

After a week on his back, George climbed painfully into a cart and jogged ahead to the Great Crossing of the Youghiogheny. He had once been held here by flood waters. Now the waters were low, but he was too sick to proceed. Seventeen days passed before he could again get into a wagon. He rocked painfully by the almost obliterated mounds that had been Fort Necessity, passed the place where he had turned into the woods for the Jumonville Affair, moved on through territory his own little army had been unable to reach, and on July 8, caught up with

Braddock two miles from the Monongahela and twelve from Fort Duquesne.

Washington lay down that night to crisply barked orders in the seeming security of a huge, professionally organized camp. Civilization's arm of war had moved deep into the primeval, blotting out with its own sounds the age-old voices and rustlings of the forest, pushing back the darkness with more campfires than the immemorial inhabitants of the Ohio Valley had ever dreamed.

When Washington arose shakily with the dawn, he discovered that, every time he shook his head or took a heavy step, his body still reacted with pain. However, he could not miss this glorious day during which, he was sure, Fort Duquesne would either surrender or be invested. He tied pillows to his saddle, mounted the horse he had not bestrode for about a month, and cantered painfully up to Braddock and his fellow staff officers, who were surrounding the General.

Washington knew that the army intended, in order to avoid what he called "an ugly defile,"[18] twice to cross the Monongahela. He had heard before dawn advance parties going out under Gage to seize the two fords. Now the main party—some 750 men, with all the vehicles, pack animals, and beef cattle, and most of the artillery—began to move.

Gage had flushed some Indians at the first ford, but they had fled. The banks were not steep, the river low and sluggish. After the army had crossed in style, good news came back from Gage. Although he had seen many Indian tracks at the second ford, he had secured with cannon the high banks that had made the crossing there the most dangerous maneuver the British foresaw for this surely triumphant day.

When at the head of the main force Braddock, with Washington in attendance, reached the second ford, he ordered a halt while he posted pickets to protect the rear as his army crossed, made every preparation and took every precaution that his training indicated. Beside the General, Washington scanned through his glasses the opposite shore. Engineers were smoothing a road up the steep, sandy bank. Beyond all seemed as peaceful as if man had never discovered the valley: a long patch of knobby underbrush and then, along gently rising ground, high foliage in lazy motion.

Finally notified that the incline up the far bank was finished, Braddock gave the command, and in the early afternoon, Washington splashed through the water with the other headquarters' officers as the troops swung into motion behind them. Up the bluff and successfully out, so they congratulated themselves, of the worst trap on their route!

After a pause to let the forces re-form and to send out flankers, Braddock and Washington rode on with the main column, the tracks of Gage's advance guard that stretched before them rolling backwards under their horses' hooves.

A rifle sounded ahead.[19] With incredible speed, the noise amplified into the roar of a heavy engagement, mingled with what Washington called "the unusual whooping and hallooing of the enemy."[20] Braddock halted his column and sent to ascertain what was happening. Then, accompanied by Washington, he led his men forward.

Suddenly the road, a twelve-foot clearing between green ramparts, filled with a red-coated wall—black boots flying below, white faces contorted above—that came at a dead run towards the main army. Among the other officers, Washington swung his sword and shouted commands to halt, "with as much success," he wrote, "as if we had attempted to have stopped the wild bears of the mountains."[21] The fugitives rushed pell-mell into the meticulously drawn-up ranks of the men not yet engaged, shattering all order as the soldiers found themselves wrestling with compatriots to keep from being thrown to the ground.

During the same few moments, the sound of firing came running down both flanks, it seemed as if by magic, since the Indians moved so skillfully from behind one tree to behind the next that no enemy was visible. Bullets filled the air, striking particularly the officers who towered, conspicuous on horseback, as they rode in circles, hitting the men with the flats of their swords. Washington's horse sank under him. He leapt clear, his illness forgotten. As a riderless horse reared by, he caught it and sprang up.

Washington's emotion was rage, rage not at the enemy but at the regular privates who were so "struck with such a deadly panic" that commands could not penetrate to them. It seemed to him that most of the human forms dropping around him "received their shot from our own cowardly English soldiers who gathered themselves into a body, contrary to orders, ten or twelve deep, would then level, fire, and shoot down the men before them."[22]

Clearly the hope lay in the provincials! Washington was pleased to see a group of them "advancing to the right, in loose order, to attack." However, a British officer, his horse stumbling on dead bodies, rode over and ordered the Americans back into the seething, desperate inferno of humanity in the center of the road. Washington assumed that the Briton, "from the unusual appearance of the movement," had mistaken it "for cowardice and a running away."[23]

A strange yank on Washington's coat made him look down: there were bullet gashes in it. He pushed his way to Braddock, whose normally red face was brick colored and whose voice was hoarse from shouting. Having finally caught the distraught General's attention, Washington offered "to head the provincials and engage the enemy in their own way." But this violation of military rules Braddock could not countenance[24]—and he had at last seen a direction in which his army could act. Some enemy had come in view on an eminence on the right. Braddock ordered a charge.

When the men hesitated, the General and the remaining officers tried to inspire them by riding ahead into the underbrush. Still the men did not come. The officers turned, rode back, shouted, and then advanced again. During this maneuver, that came to nothing, Braddock fell wounded from his horse, as did Orme and another of the aides. Washington's second horse faded away from under him, and his hat was carried by a bullet off his head.

His sickness was coming back on him in waves, adding feverishness to nightmare. Yet, as he towered on horseback (he had found a third mount) and saw over the heads of the cowering men hardly another officer still upright, he had a strange sense of "the miraculous care of Providence that protected me beyond all human expectation."[25] Lying on the ground, tended by doctors, Braddock beckoned him over and whispered the permission he had previously refused for the provincials to fight in their own way. But it was now too late: Washington could not in the confusion round up enough living and unwounded men.

"I was," Washington wrote, "the only person then left to distribute the general's orders, which I was scarcely able to do," because of his "weak and feeble condition." And soon there were no orders to distribute: the General had sunk into a coma.[26]

The second in command had been killed, and the two lieutenant colonels were down with wounds. "No person knowing in the disordered state things were, who the senior officer was, and the troops by degrees going off in confusion, without a ray of hope left of further opposition from those that remained," Washington, as he wrote, "placed the general in a small covered cart," and, with the troops who were still awaiting orders, withdrew across the Monongahela. On "a piece of rising ground," he formed the troops "in the best order circumstances would admit."[27]

Braddock came out of his coma, sent Washington on "to halt those who had been earlier in the retreat." Then Braddock ordered his sick aide to ride the forty miles back down the road to the second division and arrange for them to forward provisions and cover his withdrawal.

The memory of his ride so haunted Washington that almost thirty years later he recalled how illness, fatigue, and anxiety had left him "in a manner wholly unfit for the execution of the duty. . . . The shocking scenes which presented themselves in this night march are not to be described. The dead, the dying, the groans, lamentations, and cries along the road of the wounded for help . . . were enough to pierce a heart of adamant, the gloom and horror of which was not a little increased by the impervious darkness occasioned by the close shade of thick woods." After Washington had ridden beyond the range of the last wounded fugitive, silence sank, but the blackness still blocked sight, making it impossible for his pair of guides "to know when they were in or out of the track but by groping on the ground with their hands."[28]

The previous morning Washington had risen from a long illness still so weak that he could hardly mount his horse. He had endured grueling hours of disastrous battle. That through the horrors of the night he kept steadily on, that he managed somehow to traverse the forty dreadful miles is the most startling of proofs that his spirit inhabited a remarkable body.

Arriving at the camp in the course of the morning, Washington found that the news had preceded him and that the soldiers and even the officers there were in the grip of extreme terror. When Colonel Thomas Dunbar, the commander, ordered for no rational reason that the drums beat to arms, many of the men, for no rational reason, took to their heels. Washington probably stayed upright long enough to see some wagonloads of provisions finally move off towards Braddock under strong guard— then his illness overwhelmed him.

Swaying on horseback because the soldiers had refused to carry the dying General's litter, Braddock finally appeared. He proved to have one ruling thought: to get out of the forest. He ordered that everything which could not immediately be moved be destroyed: irreplaceable ammunition detonated, wagons burned, cannon smashed. Then the whole army set out passionately for civilization.

A little beyond the ruins of Fort Necessity, Braddock died. Washington, despite his continuing illness, was still the most active of the aides. It seems to have been his decision to bury the Englishman in the center of the road and then run wagons back and forth over the spot "to guard," as he wrote, "against a savage triumph. . . .

"Thus," he continued, "died a man whose good and bad qualities were intimately blended. He was brave even to a fault, and in regular service would have done honor to his profession. His attachments were warm, his enmities were strong, and, having no disguise about him, both appeared in full force."[29]

Although this George Washington could not realize, he would never again find among English officers another friend equally affectionate and powerful.*

---

* Braddock's orderly, Thomas Bishop, attached himself to Washington. This living memento of Braddock and his defeat served the Virginian, sometimes as valet and personal servant, for more than thirty years.

CHAPTER

11

Commander in Chief of What

SICK, HIS MIND still aflame with the horrors he had experienced, Washington rode by slow and painful stages
through an unbelievably quiet midsummer countryside towards
Mount Vernon. At last he could look southeast across a long
clearing to where the story-and-a-half wooden house smoked
peacefully on its little rise. Then he moved left with the road,
entered familiar groves, and, after a few minutes, came into the
open again close to his front door. Surely, before he entered, he
turned to glance across Dogue Run to where Belvoir beckoned.
But he was too "weak and feeble." With a final push of dying
energy, he made his way upstairs to fall on his bed.[1]

A knock on the door: a letter from William Fairfax. It proved
to contain affectionate congratulations on his return, but George
undoubtedly did not read it until he had perused several times
the postscript. The postscript was in Sally's elegant, upright
hand: "Dear Sir: After thanking heaven for your safe return, I
must accuse you of great unkindness in refusing us the pleasure
of seeing you this night. I do assure you that nothing but our
being satisfied that our company would be disagreeable should
prevent us from trying if our legs would not carry us to Mount

Vernon, but if you will not come to us tomorrow morning very early, we shall be at Mount Vernon."*2

To Sally's signature were added those of other ladies, yet George could not fail to notice that the messege had started out, before (so he could assume) discretion intervened, as a personal one.

Although we do know that Washington bought some water-melons the next day (perhaps to entertain the ladies),3 history does not record what descriptions of his adventures the pale sufferer gave his adored Sally. However, various letters he sent to others state his reactions to Braddock's defeat.

It was only in the account of the battle he wrote years later that he stressed the unwillingness of the British command to fight the Indians in their own way. At the time, he expressed puzzlement: a seemingly invincible force had been annihilated "contrary to all expectation and human probability and even to the common course of things. . . . See the wondrous works of Providence! The uncertainty of human things!"4

He defended the suggestion he had made that a part of the army go rapidly ahead by stating that had a larger force been present, it would only have increased the size of the holocaust. For the British regular officers, he had nothing but praise: they had "behaved with incomparable bravery for which they greatly suffered." His blame centered on the way the regular enlisted men had panicked: their "dastardly behavior . . . exposed all those who were inclined to do their duty to almost certain death." Among those sacrificed to transatlantic cowardice were not only the officers, but also the commonality of the Virginia Regiment, who "behaved like men and died like soldiers."5

---

* Probably because it was a postscript to such a letter as he normally kept, this is the only missive George received from Sally during their emotional years which he did not destroy.

Opinion in the Colonies lumped all the English regulars together as fools, cowards, or worse, insisting that the provincials had been heroes betrayed. As the most conspicuous of these provincials, Washington achieved an acclaim that for the first time passed the boundaries of Virginia.

Gist wrote him from Pennsylvania that he had been praised by Franklin, "and everybody seems willing to venture under your command." In Washington's home Colony a minister wondered from the pulpit whether Providence had not preserved "that heroic youth . . . in so signal a manner" because he was destined for "some important service of his country." Even regulars praised him. "Mr. Washington," his friend Orme wrote, "had two horses shot under him and his clothes shot through in several places, behaving the whole time with the greatest courage and resolution."[6]

However, an official inquiry made by the ranking survivors, Gage and Dunbar, placed much of the blame for the defeat on provincials like Washington. The Americans, the regulars argued, had sewed the seeds of the disastrous panic when they spread the word that if the army "engaged the Indians in the European manner of fighting, they would be beat."[7]

Nonetheless, regulars felt in their bones that Braddock had been defeated by something inexplicable and so terrible that against it what remained of the army was completely helpless. The only hope was to get away from the woods before it was too late! In fine formation, the entire English force marched for Philadelphia. Virginia could protect her own frontiers!

After Braddock's defeat, the British high command on both sides of the ocean turned their attention away from the long arm Canada had stretched down through the wilderness to extend bloody claws towards Virginia's back. The long established North American theater of war between England and France was farther north. Of major strategic areas there were three:

Louisburg, France's naval base on Cape Breton Island, which menaced the New England coast; and two watery passages through the usually mountainous wilderness that separated Canada and New York.

The easier route for invasion either way—Burgoyne was to surrender there during the Revolution—went along the Hudson, traversed alternate paths (one including Lake George) to Lake Champlain, and then navigated the Sorel River to the St. Lawrence between Montreal and the ocean. The second route went from Albany westward along the Mohawk River, and, having passed along Lake Oneida and a series of small waterways, came out on Lake Ontario at Oswego, where the British had built a small fortification. This was from Virginia's point of view the more strategic route, since it presented the possibility of cutting France's supply line between well-settled Canada and all her western strongpoints, including Duquesne.

Governor Shirley and New York's frontier leader William Johnson had urged on Braddock that, instead of marching from Virginia for the Ohio, he concentrate on launching an amphibious operation from Oswego that would, by taking Fort Niagara, stop French movement between Lake Ontario and Lake Erie. Duquesne, it was pointed out, would then droop away like a poison ivy plant severed from its root.

Braddock had been too committed to his own march to change, but he had authorized for that summer of 1755 expeditions on both of the northern inland routes: Shirley was to try for Niagara, Johnson to seal off the French fort at Crown Point on Lake Champlain by building below it, at Ticonderoga, an English fort.

When the wilderness exploded in Braddock's face, these expeditions were still in doubt. Shirley's, indeed, never did get really moving. However, Johnson, although he failed to reach Ticonderoga, defeated a considerable French force in the Battle of Lake George (September 8). He built on the shores of that lake England's northernmost strongpoint, Fort William Henry. The British Crown showed how lavishly it could express gratitude to a triumphant Colonial by making Johnson a baronet.

That George Washington was still startlingly parochial is revealed by his indifference to campaigns fought on his continent outside Virginia. He gave in his military thinking little weight to the fact that action to the northward which involved France's Indian irregulars took pressure off Virginia. The possibility that his Colony might be altogether saved by cutting supply lines several hundred miles away came to him so dimly that in the letters he wrote during his French and Indian War service he made only one mention[8] of that keystone in the French western arch, Fort Niagara.

For Virginia, the immediate problems created by Braddock's defeat centered on the very region in which Washington had first written himself man: the Shenandoah Valley. The only town there was Winchester, which boasted about sixty houses, most of them log cabins, and was close to the passes through the Blue Ridge to greater civilization. Some sixty miles (as the crow flies) southwest, right below the Alleghenies that were now Indian ground, was Fort Cumberland, officially over the line in Maryland, but blocking a pass that led to Virginia.

In the area between Winchester and Fort Cumberland, south to the Carolina line and beyond, small farms (some of which Washington had himself surveyed) were embedded in the forest. These were now subject to hit-and-run Indian raids.

When a homestead became a funeral pyre for the scalpless bodies of its owners, all the settlers in the neighborhood usually fled, carrying back the extreme frontier ever farther eastward. In Tidewater minds there flared the fear that if the enemy reached the Blue Ridge and began coming over, it would touch off a slave revolt.

[136]

The Virginia Assembly voted £40,000 to maintain a regiment of 1000 men and also 200 frontiersmen organized into four companies of rangers.

Rumors that Washington could have the command of all these men incited a letter from his mother the purport of which is clear from his reply: "Honored Madam: If it is in my power to avoid going to the Ohio again, I shall, but if the command is pressed upon me by the general voice of the country, and offered upon such terms as can't be objected against, it would reflect eternal dishonor upon me to refuse it, and that, I am sure, must (or ought to) give you greater cause of uneasiness than my going."[9]

Although Washington expressed privately continuing doubts that he possessed enough experience for the command, in his letters to Williamsburg, he merely stated that he would take no steps himself to procure a post where he would probably "meet with such insurmountable difficulties" that he would "lose what at present constitutes the chief part of my happiness, i.e., the esteem and notice the country had been pleased to honor me with." However, if the post were offered to him, he would not refuse, provided that the command were "honorable," by which he meant if his terms were met.

He had, he explained, "suffered much in my private fortune besides impairing one of the best of constitutions." His statement that he could not continue to lose money in the public service induced the Assembly to give him £300 for his past expenditures, a salary of 30 shillings a day, £100 a year for expenses, and a two per cent commission on all the purchases he made.[10]

When Washington further insisted that, as his honor depended on the result, he wished to select his own officers and buy his own supplies, the Assembly was enchanted to pass the buck to him. Officially or unofficially all the functions of the army were dumped into his willing hands. As it turned out, he appointed his own staff and field officers, contracted for supply, recruited his own soldiers, summoned the militia, etc., etc. No better experience could have been conceived to prepare him for his Revolutionary command.

Dinwiddie had warmed up to Washington, even to the extent of recommending him, in letters to the home government, for "the royal favor." On August 14, 1755, he commissioned George Washington, aged twenty-three, "Colonel of the Virginia Regiment and Commander in Chief of all forces now raised in the defense of His Majesty's Colony." Washington was to "act defensively or offensively" as he thought best.[11]

In high spirits and apparently with restored health, Washington inspected his command, riding to Fort Cumberland and then southwest through the Shenandoah Valley some one hundred and twenty miles to Fort Dinwiddie on Jackson's River in Augusta (now Bath) County. The lurking places for Indians were, of course, innumerable, but the enemy was quiescent. His immediate troubles were in settled Virginia. They involved raising, controlling, and supplying his own army.

The draft act, which offered loopholes to the rich, was being actively opposed by the poor. In Fredericksburg some draftees who had been locked in jail for trying to desert were released by a mob. To Dinwiddie, Washington wrote that strong means for enforcing service and obedience were required, and he was soon threatening to resign unless a military code were adopted that enabled him to combat the "growing insolence of the soldiers, the indolence and inactivity of the officers."[12]

Washington tried to fill in for the lack of a military code by making a stupendous clamor. He growled at his officers that the complaints of their men argued "great remissness in you. . . . You are afraid to do your duty!" His general orders breathed threats. He sent out a detachment to bring some mutineers back in irons, held court-martial on the ringleaders, flogged several severely, and held some under sentence of death. While angrily pointing out to his superiors in Williamsburg that he had "no legal right to inflict punishment of the smallest kind," he hid the fact from his army: "I shall keep these criminals in irons and, if possible, under apprehensions of death until some favorable opportunity may countenance a reprieve."[13]

When the death penalty was finally established for mutiny, desertion, and disobedience, Washington stepped up (if that were possible) his threats—"deserters shall be hanged without mercy"—but he found legal flaws in the enabling act that had escaped even the attorney general, and continued to punish deserters "in the old way of whipping stoutly." It was not until the following year that in a particularly heinous situation Washington agreed to the actual execution of "a most atrocious villain."[14]

Although Washington did not yet draw the broad economic inference, long-range planning for supply was made impossible by Virginia's commercial dependence on England. Since his "country" contained no cities where artisans congregated, manufactured supplies had to be bought in Pennsylvania—and the Pennsylvanians were unwilling to accept the money Virginia was printing. Yet Washington had the tenacity and the energy needed to operate successfully hand-to-mouth. With that unflagging attention to small detail, that willingness to do anything that the service required, which were to do so much towards winning the American Revolution, Washington managed to keep what forces he could get together more or less adequately supplied. "Method and exactness," his fellow veteran "Old Soldier," was to write in the *Gentleman's Magazine*, "are the *forte* of his character." As Freeman said, no man ever worked harder.[15]

The troubles from which he suffered demonstrated the endless ingenuity of the spirit of confusion. To take one example: after his men had been kept waiting for their pay almost past endurance, freshly printed money was sent from Williamsburg, but in such large denominations that one bill had to be given to several soldiers. Only tavern keepers would make change, which threw the whole army into its cups. The money vanished leaving only headaches behind.[16]

Most serious of Washington's problems was his complete lack of those Indian irregulars who were so endlessly useful in wilderness warfare. He stormed at Williamsburg to take steps. He did what he could himself, begging Montour, in a letter that dripped with what he admitted was "flattery," to come and "animate" his Indian friends. In the meanwhile, he did the best he could with the frontiersmen enlisted as rangers.[17]

He had hoped to extend Virginia's frontier across the Alleghenies by building forts beyond the mountains, but he soon discovered that to keep any inhabitants even in the Shenandoah Valley might prove beyond his powers. When 150 Indians invaded and separated into small parties, they cut off all communication between most of his regiment, which was stationed at Fort Cumberland, and the endangered inhabitants. Galloping up from the Tidewater, Washington could not get beyond Winchester. There he found "the greatest hurry and confusion, [caused] by the back inhabitants flocking in, and those of the town removing out."

Exhorting the fleeing families to remain, he announced that he would lead the local militia into the woods to attack. At this, the militia colonel took him aside to whisper that the militia would not gather, "choosing, as they say, to die with their wives and families."

Washington then went to a stable and tried to impress a horse. The owner barred his way. He drew his sword and took the horse. Immediately, he was surrounded by a mob of inhabitants who, wishing to keep their animals for their own personal escapes, offered "to blow out my brains." Washington stared them down and continued to take all "the service requires." In reporting to Dinwiddie on his difficulties, he commented, "To such a pitch has the insolence of the people arrived, by having every point hitherto submitted to them."*18

Washington had not succeeded in mounting an expeditionary force when, in the middle of the night, he was awakened by a messenger who, in his "fatigue and fear," could hardly gasp out in broken sentences that Indians were within twelve miles and all the inhabitants of the region were fleeing. As Washington was arming what volunteers the acute emergency enabled him to raise, in came a second messenger "ten times more terrified than the former." He shouted that the Indians were within four miles "killing and destroying all before them, for that he himself had heard constant firing and the shrieks of the unhappy murdered!"

Grimly, Washington set out with twenty-two rangers and nineteen militiamen. Silently, they crouched ahead through the early morning forest. What was that? Certainly shots and shrieks. However, the shrieks sounded strangely familiar. Washington led his men to where they could peer into the noisy clearing. They saw three men "carousing, firing their pistols, and uttering the most unheard of imprecations"—three drunken Virginia soldiers.

After Washington had had his laugh, he meditated on the serious side of the incident. That the frontiersmen were so

---

* When, several months later, Washington submitted his own candidacy to the inhabitants of the Winchester region (Frederick County), in his first effort to be elected to the House of Burgesses, they demonstrated continuing resentment: he was ignominiously defeated.

He had been unable to run in his home district, Fairfax County, as he would have had to oppose Sally's husband. Instead, he canvassed for his friend. A letter stating that he had been "insulted at the Fairfax election" gives credence to the tradition that one William Payne knocked him down with a stick. Washington, so the story goes, leaped up in a Herculean rage but was restrained from pummeling Payne. A duel was expected. However, when his anger had subsided, Washington sent Payne not a challenge but an apology.19

"alarmed at the most usual and customary cries," showed what panic the very thought Indians created. How, under these circumstances, could actual raids be stopped? The reinforcements that soon reached Winchester from the Tidewater stated that they had hardly been able to push across the Blue Ridge against crowds "flying as if every moment was death."[20]

When Washington's scouts reported that the Indians were gone, he sent out rangers to bury the dead—about seventy inhabitants proved to be killed or missing—and himself posted for Fort Cumberland, where a most distressing situation struck him full in the face.

Sitting there like an Oriental potentate was Captain John Dagworthy. He was New Jersey born and forty-four years old. His tangible command was only thirty Marylanders, and his military experience was practically nil, but he had in his pocket a piece of paper he had secured on a foray to England which somewhat equivocally showed him a captain in the royal service. He coolly walked over to the Virginia commander in chief and began giving him orders.[21]

To such a situation as this, which whipped his temper to a point where it was in danger of getting completely out of control, Washington had only one solution: keep out of the interloper's way until the matter could be rectified. However, he had to stay at Fort Cumberland for a few nerve-racking days, making preparations for the winter.

He ordered the construction and garrisoning of several small forts: ninety-foot bastioned quadrangles. These were to cooperate with Fort Cumberland and Fort Dinwiddie, and also with log cabins forted by the inhabitants of various districts, to pin the settlements down until spring brought new developments. He published an advertisement stating that it would soon be safe for the inhabitants of the Shenandoah Valley to go home.[22]

As soon as he could get away, Washington galloped from

Dagworthy's infuriating presence. He radiated protests against Dagworthy's pretensions. When Dinwiddie seemed to him slow in supporting the Virginia command against such usurpation, he complained to Speaker Robinson. Robinson expressed in reply astonishment that "our governor should suffer us to be made dupes of" by "a petty officer" from Maryland.*[23]

Dinwiddie soon came to recognize a crisis. He notified Governor Shirley of Massachusetts, who had succeeded to the command made vacant by Braddock's death, that Virginia patriotism was so incensed at this intervention from another colony that "the dispute is likely to prevent our forces from doing their duty."* He urged on Shirley that the recurring confusions be finally straightened out by giving Virginia's top officers brevet commissions in the regular army for their local ranks.[25]

Although under this plan Washington would hold his new commission only for the duration of his immediate service, it would be a significant step towards his objective of permanent preferment in the regular establishment. He felt that he had a right to as much. Braddock's former aide, Captain Orme, had written him that if he could not get his commission confirmed in England, "I think Mount Vernon would offer you more happiness."[26]

Counting the days until Shirley's answer would be received, George stayed in Williamsburg, participating in its social season, until mid-November. There were balls and he loved to dance; Sally Fairfax shone in the minuet; and he flirted with some more available charmer whose snuffbox he eventually returned through a friend who wrote him, "I took the liberty of

---

* The situation was complicated by the fact that Fort Cumberland, although primarily garrisoned from Virginia, was, as we have seen, actually just over the boundary in Maryland.

* Fort Cumberland was, indeed, a shambles. Whenever Washington's second in command, Lieutenant Colonel Adam Stephen, gave an order, Captain Dagworthy contradicted it. The Virginia officers were so enraged that they illegally court-martialed one of their number for obeying Dagworthy's orders.[24]

communicating the ecstatic paragraph of your letter: what blushes and confusion it occasioned I shall leave you to guess."[27]

When it became time to return to duty, Washington still stayed away from Fort Cumberland and Dagworthy. He could be more useful, he announced, "riding from place to place, making the proper dispositions, and seeing that all our necessities are forwarded up with dispatch." But even this distant activity was made irritating by the fact that as soon as any supplies reached Cumberland, Dagworthy officiously impounded them.[28]

Week after week, and no reply from Shirley! Finally, Washington wrote Dinwiddie that, unless he were relieved of Dagworthy's presumption, he would resign.[29]

At last, the long-awaited dispatch from Shirley came. But the Massachusetts Governor showed no interest in according the Virginians brevet commissions, and wrote—of all things—that he had entrusted the accommodation of the Dagworthy dispute to Washington's critic Sharpe, the very Marylander who was enraging Virginia by backing Dagworthy.[30]

Nothing could have been more unsatisfactory. The time seemed surely to have come for Washington to carry out his threat of resigning. But first he would see whether by a personal interview he could stir up some interest with Shirley, with whom he had, so he wrote, "a personal acquaintance" which might "add some weight." He asked Dinwiddie for permission to carry to the commander in Boston a petition of the Virginia officers, and urged Robinson to help him get Dinwiddie's leave. The Speaker of the Burgesses replied, "I have at present very little interest at court," but he would do his best. In the end, Dinwiddie agreed, and gave Washington a letter stating that "extremes of resentment" threatened to keep the Virginia Assembly from further support of the war.[31]

As he was preparing to set out for Boston, Washington

learned that the immediate problem had been solved: Shirley had ordered Sharpe to order Dagworthy not to assume any command of the Virginia troops. However the question of commissions in the regular army remained. Washington resolved to proceed with his pilgrimage. And so, early in February 1756, he set out on his first extended trip through civilized America.

The Virginia Colonel took along two servants; his aide, Captain George Mercer, who handled his purse; and Robert Stewart, a dashing captain of the Virginia light horse who was becoming his most intimate friend. All were on horseback. The servants, one tall and one short, were in livery colored to go with the Washington coat of arms which had a white field. The officers wore the uniform George had himself designed for the Virginia Regiment: blue regimentals, "the coat to be faced and cuffed with scarlet and trimmed with silver; a scarlet waistcoat with silver lace; blue breeches; and a silver laced hat." Swords hung from knots ornamented in gold and scarlet, or silver and blue.[32] Bravely arrayed for their own honor and the honor of Virginia, they clattered along the wintry roads they would have to traverse for 1100 miles.

The young warrior, whose name was celebrated throughout the Colonies and known in England and France, saw, a few days before his twenty-fourth birthday, his first extensive city: Philadelphia. The three thousand houses all crowded together, the rush of carts down the centers of the streets and the rush of pedestrians along the edges were exhilarating, not the less so because as he strode in his fine uniform, a head taller than the crowd, he attracted attention, his name was whispered. In taverns he was questioned, subtly or bluntly, but he hid his true mission from the tongue of gossip. His own immediate interest was in the shops: he spent £21 9s at the tailor's, £2 14s at the hatter's; gave £1.7.6 to a jeweler, and £1.9.7 to a saddler. A washerwoman received 16s 11d. Since no sum was paid for lodgings, he must have stayed with a friend.[33]

After four or five days, he advanced to New York City, where he spent his first evening with some good fellows at a "club" in a tavern. Then he lodged with Speaker Robinson's son, the same Beverely Robinson who was one day to play an important part in the treason of Benedict Arnold.[34]

At the moment, Washington found the most interesting thing about Robinson to be his wife's sister, the brunette Eliza Philipse. Although slim, "Polly" was also statuesque; her delicate features were somehow expressive of cool strength; her full mouth was both sensuous and firm. She was beautiful and she was rich, an heiress of one of New York's baronial families.

That Polly was available for matrimony did not escape George, although he was to prove halfhearted in his efforts towards this end. Her notoriously strong will, which undoubtedly contributed to her being single at twenty-six, may have reminded him of the female bondage he had suffered in his childhood—and perhaps another image presided too strongly in his heart.

In any case, George now squired Polly around town, taking her to see, among other things, *Microcosm or the World in Miniature*, a clockwork precursor of modern motion pictures. Less sophisticated about such things than the metropolitan heiress who was two years his senior, the huge Colonel (he went to see the show twice) craned forward in his seat to admire the Roman temple, lavishly embellished with sculpture and painted effects, from which, as music sounded, the front wall vanished to reveal a boxlike stage. Therein the stars circled in tiny courses, while gauze clouds sailed; then the lights brightened and the nine Muses played in concert. Comic relief was supplied by the grotesque mechanical dolls in a carpenter's yard. Finally, as the music crescendoed, walls fell to reveal the greatest marvel of all, the machine itself, "when upwards of 1200 wheels and pinions are in motion at once."[35]

During five days in New York, George also went to a dance, did some shopping, and lost some money at cards.

His party left their horses at New London, and went by water to Newport, where they must have spent a gay evening as Washington paid his host the large sum of four pounds for a broken bowl. He seems to have found a naval vessel to take him to Boston: he tipped "a man-of-war's crew" eleven shillings threepence.

In the Massachusetts capital, he was so far from home connections that he had to stay in a tavern (the chambermaid got £1.2.6). A new tailor's bill was large, and he paid £94.17.1 in inflated Massachusetts currency for silver lace. Governor Shirley and his friends took Washington to town in a card game for a pound and a quarter, and other Yankees added to the Virginian's gambling losses £3.18.9.[36]

When he had first met Shirley, Washington had recognized admiringly a "great politician"; now he found the Governor too much so for his taste. Having expressed surprise that there still was a Dagworthy problem after the orders he had had given, Shirley drew up for Washington a paper stating that Dagworthy was in service not as a regular but a Maryland captain. Although this confirmed that the immediate situation had been righted, it sidetracked Washington's contention that he and his officers should be protected from further such usurpation by being placed in the regular establishment. The Virginia Colonel would still be ranked by any captain authentically a regular.[37]

Furthermore, Shirley had approved the appointment of Sharpe, whose distrust for Washington underlay the Dagworthy controversy, as commander of all forces raised in Maryland, Pennsylvania, South Carolina, and also Virginia. Washington may well have shaken his head in emphatic agreement when he read what Stephen wrote him: that he had undertaken a long journey to receive the treatment "which one is always to expect from persons conversant at the courts of princes."[38]

Back in New York, Washington continued his courting of Polly Philipse, with no more definite result than before. His trip was proving so expensive that he had to borrow ninety-one pounds from Robinson. In Philadelphia, he fell sick, so sick that he hired a nurse, but he remained there only four days.[39] He proceeded to Annapolis, where he conferred with Sharpe.

Washington impressed the Maryland Governor into the surprised admission, "He really seems a gentleman of merit." However, Sharpe so little placated Washington that, when he left the interview, he was "fully resolved to resign my commission."[40]

Looking back as commander in chief of another army, Washington drew a distinction between the Revolution in which he was then engaged, "where the object is neither glory nor extent of territory" and "the usual contests of empire and ambition" in which "the conscience of a soldier has so little share that he may properly insist upon his claims of rank, and extend his pretensions even to punctilio."[41]

12

Hysteria

WASHINGTON could contemplate resigning when he viewed the war as one of "the usual contests of empire and ambition,"[1] but, after he was back in Virginia, he could no longer ignore the fact that axes were reaching out on the frontier for Virginia blood. At Williamsburg where he arrived in March 1756, he was persuaded not to resign.

Instead, the young Colonel wrote Sharpe asking to be appointed his second in command. Forwarding the request to Shirley, Sharpe stated agreeably that "Mr. Washington is much esteemed in Virginia." Shirley replied that there was no provincial he would rather advance, but that all planning awaited on further orders from England.[2]

From his regular army friend and future opponent, Gage, Washington received a letter: "Your continuing to head the Virginia troops . . . when a command you were so justly entitled to was given another . . . is no small instance of your zeal for the public service for which you have been ever remarkable."[3]

Actually, Washington's demotion was purely theoretical. The inclusive army Sharpe was to lead never came into being, and the Virginia Assembly, still breathing fire at the interloper from Maryland, voted that their regiment, having been raised for local defense, had no connection with any outside army. Washington continued to hold the top command in Virginia.

There being no immediate possibility of extirpating the French from Fort Duquesne (which Washington realized would be the only true solution), he tried to push ahead with building defensive forts. If they were no more than a day's march apart and had large enough garrisons, eighty to a hundred men, so that detachments could be sent out to prowl between them, perhaps they could form a wall that would turn back Indian raiding parties. Washington calculated that this plan would require 2000 men.[4] The Assembly voted him 1500, but local officials hesitated to enforce the unjust and unpopular draft laws. By June 25, Washington had received only 346 draftees, and in mid-August his regiment had not climbed to 900 men. He could only build one fort of his presumed chain at a time—and the Indians did not wait.

The Indians, Washington complained, "act in defiance of our smaller parties, while they dexterously avoid our larger. . . . Five hundred Indians have more power to disturb our inhabitants than ten times as many regulars." Their cunning, their vigilance and patience in awaiting an opportunity "are no more to be conceived than they are to be equalled by our people. . . . They will travel from pole to pole, depending on chance and their own dexterity for provisions. . . . Indians are only a match for Indians, and without these, we shall ever fight on unequal terms."[5]

Like his fellow Virginians, Washington had abandoned all hope of prying the Ohio Valley tribes away from the French. However, he ardently espoused a plan for bringing up from the south Cherokees and Catawbas, who were the traditional enemies of those tribes. Reports that warriors were on the way made him twice send forces into the forest to greet them. Twice he was disappointed.

Although Dagworthy's pretensions no longer made Fort Cumberland unbearable to him, Washington did not move his head-

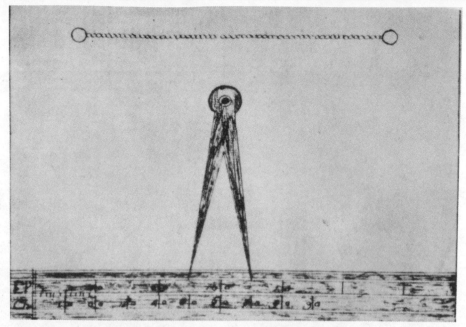

Chain, compass, and scale drawn by Washington
when he was fourteen years old.

Plan drawn by Washington when he was seventeen for the city, then almost nonexistent, that was to become the capital of his local world. Both from *The George
Washington Atlas* (Washington, D.C., 1932).

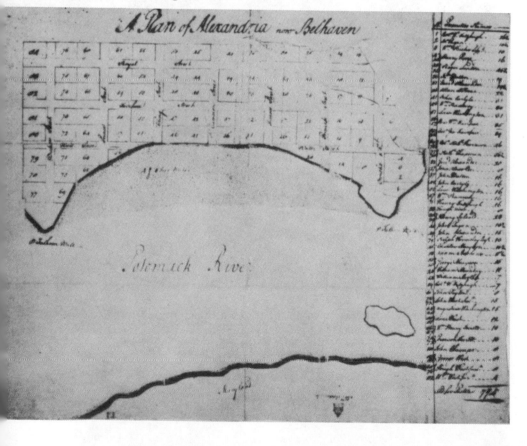

Lawrence Washington, who introduced his much younger and somewhat impoverished half-brother George to the great world, as Virginia knew it. Portrait by a follower of John Wollaston. Courtesy of the Mount Vernon Ladies' Association of the Union.

homas, Sixth Lord Fairfax, the first noble-
an Washington ever knew. His greatest
terests were a love of fox hunting and a
atred of women. Detail of a painting.
ourtesy of the George Washington Ma-
nic National Memorial, Alexandria, Va.

Lieutenant Governor Robert Dinwiddie of
Virginia, who gave Washington his first big
chance, supported and frustrated him, and
in the end departed his enemy. Detail of a
painting. Courtesy of National Portrait Gal-
lery, London.

Governor William Shirley of Massachusetts,
whom Washington found too much of a
"great politician" for his taste. Engraving
by J. McArdell after Thomas Hudson. Courtesy of New York Public Library.

John Campbell, Fourth Earl of Loudoun,
the British Commander in Chief in America
who at one time suspected that Washington
was a spy for the French. From *London
Magazine*, 1757.

FOUR ENGLISHMEN WHO CONTRIBUTED TO WASHINGTON'S EDUCATION

Elizabeth (Betsy) Fauntleroy, to whom Washington proposed when he was twenty, painted by an unknown artist. Courtesy of the George Washington Masonic National Memorial, Alexandria, Va.

Eliza (Polly) Philipse, whom Washington courted when he visited New York at the age of twenty-four. Portrait by John Singleton Copley. Courtesy, Henry Francis du Pont Winterthur Museum.

The first page of a letter George Washington wrote Sally Fairfax, less than four months before his marriage to Martha Custis. Courtesy of the Houghton Library, Harvard University.

Sarah (Sally) Fairfax: This photograph of an extremely crude primitive painting is the only visual record of the beauty, wife of Washington's neighbor and close friend, who was the major love of his young manhood. Courtesy of Mrs. Seymour St. John.

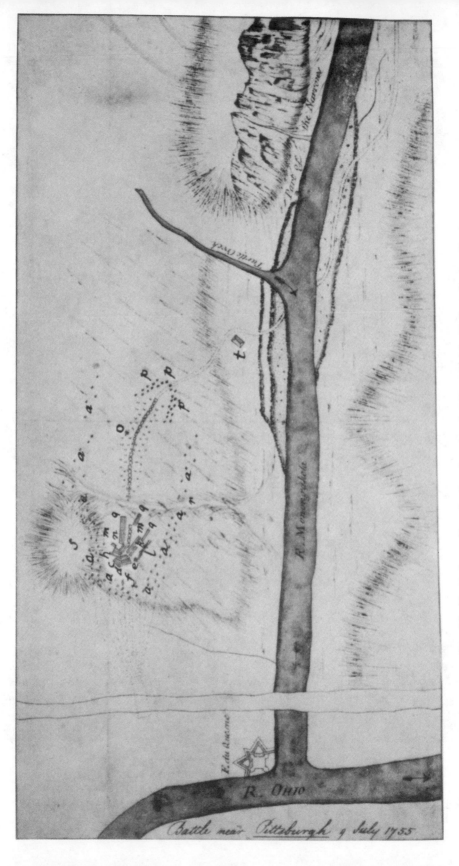

Braddock's Defeat. Detail of a drawing by Patrick MacKellar, Senior Engineer with the army. From the Royal Collection, Windsor Castle, by gracious permission of Her Majesty, Queen Elizabeth II.

quarters from Winchester to that advanced post where most of his regiment was stationed. Since Cumberland was cut off from the settlements at the most crucial moments—when the Indians were out—Washington felt he could be more useful in the securer community which was so close to the pass back through the Blue Ridge that it could serve as a rallying ground for reinforcements and supplies.

In mid-April, Winchester filled with the bloody weeping flotsam of wilderness raids, and Washington's stoicism deserted him completely. "I am too little acquainted, sir," he wrote hysterically to Dinwiddie, "with pathetic language to attempt a description of the people's distresses, though I have a generous soul, sensible of wrongs and swelling for redress. But what can I do? . . . The supplicating tears of the women and moving petitions of the men melt me into such deadly sorrow that I solemnly declare, if I know my own mind, I could offer myself a willing sacrifice to the butchering enemy provided that would contribute to the peoples' ease. . . . If bleeding, dying! would glut their insatiate revenge, I would be a willing offering to savage fury, and die by inches to save a people! I *see* their situation, know their danger, and participate in their sufferings, without having it in my power to give them further relief than uncertain promises."

The rangers and the few soldiers Washington had been supplied for his regiment were marooned in their forts. And as usual the frontiersmen from around Winchester were determined not to leave their families. In "three days' incessant effort," Washington could find only twenty men who would agree to set out in search of Indians.[6]

He sent back across the mountains a call for low country militia, and, in this crisis, they responded by the hundreds. Washington's pleasure in seeing the ragged companies clump in soon changed to alarm. Those who had no guns expressed anger that he could not supply them. Having brought hardly any food, they devoured provisions that it had taken Washington months painstakingly to gather. Discipline they would not accept: when one was released from the guardhouse by his mates, they, for good measure, demolished the building. And if a company could be lined up and inspected, almost no one proved competent to move through a deadly forest.

More militiamen were still appearing when word came from the wilderness that the Indians were going back over the Alleghenies. A council of war decided to hold only 482 out of the some 1175 militiamen who had arrived, and to stop on the far side of the Blue Ridge all further reinforcements. But before the plan could be carried out, in rode another messenger who shouted that the Indians were coming back. At this, hundreds of militia, including many who had been chosen by lot to stay, gathered up whatever government possessions had been issued to them, and vanished into the peaceful night as quickly as if tomahawks were actually waving at their scalps.[7]

Had Washington realized as he wrote Dinwiddie his reactions to his first extensive experience with the militia, how many hundred times over for how many years he was to pen similar passages, perhaps he would have decided never again to lead an army.

In 1756, as in 1776, his object was to persuade the authorities to take the necessary steps so to strengthen the regular force— now the Virginia Regiment, then the Continental Army—that major reliance would be unnecessary on temporary troops called out for emergencies. Such calls, he now pointed out, impeded enlistment for longer terms of service. They required more men and more money, as the militia lost much time marching to and from the front, and were endlessly wasteful of provisions. The militiamen did not serve long enough to be disciplined: "Every *mean* individual has his own crude notions of things and must undertake to direct. If his advice is neglected, he thinks himself slighted, abased, and injured, and, to redress his wrongs, will depart for home."[8]

Back from Williamsburg came admonitory letters. Two were from Washington's mentor William Fairfax. In the first he expressed Dinwiddie's displeasure at Washington's "great uneasiness of mind for not having everything you wish," when Dinwiddie himself was so often disappointed. "Your endeavors in the service of and defense of your country must redound to your honor; therefore, pray don't let any unavoidable interruptions sicken your mind. Your good health and fortune is the toast at every table. Among the Romans such a general acclamation and public regard shown to any of their chieftains was always esteemed a high honor and gratefully accepted."

In his second letter, Fairfax upbraided Washington for complaining about the militia: they had undoubtedly created problems but, having read "Caesar's *Commentaries* and perhaps Quintus Curtius" (the author of a life of Alexander), George must realize that the Roman generals had overcome greater difficulties than he would probably ever have to face. If such greater difficulties should, in fact, "interrupt your quiet, I doubt not but you would bear them with equal magnanimity those heroes remarkably did."[9]

Dinwiddie, in countering Washington's protests, followed no such stoic tack. "I hope," he wrote, "the affairs of the regiment are not in so bad a condition as represented here. The Assembly were greatly inflamed being told that the greatest immoralities and drunkness have been much countenanced, and proper discipline neglected."[10]

Washington's reply was self-defensive. Some of his officers, he knew, had "the seeds of idleness very strongly engrafted in their natures." He had "both by threats and persuasive means endeavored to discountenance gaming, drinking, swearing, and irregularities of every other kind." However, "the unhappy difference about the command which has kept me from Fort Cumberland has consequently kept me from *enforcing* the orders which I never fail to *send*." (It was all Dagworthy's fault.) "If I continue in the service, I shall take care to act with a little more rigor."[11]

Neither this conciliatory attitude nor the implied threat that he might resign stilled the storm which rose to a newspaper article signed "the Virginia Sentinel." The anonymous author attacked Washington's officers as "rank novices, rakes, spendthrifts, and bankrupts," who would abuse common soldiers "in a fit of humor or passion"; who "browbeat and discouraged" the militia "in every noble achievement"; and who gave "the men an example of all manner of debauchery, vice, and idleness when they lie skulking in forts" while the country was being "ravaged in their very neighborhood."[12]

Washington now blamed the agitation on deserters, who told terrible tales to justify their having absconded, and on dissatisfaction inevitable when every frontiersman "expects forces at his own door and is angry to see them at his neighbor's." Feeling stubborn and still sure that he could achieve more by operating out of Winchester, Washington refused to give in to urgings, even from his friend Speaker Robinson, that he "silence the clamor" by moving his headquarters ahead to the front line at Fort Cumberland, so that he could personally supervise both the military activity and the personal behavior of the garrison there.[13]

Instead, Washington warned his subordinates at Fort Cumberland to be more circumspect in the presence of important visitors. He could be jocose about the matter, as when he suggested to Robinson that a minister should be assigned to the regiment so "that we may at least have the show if we are said to want the substance of godliness"*—but he was severely stung.[15]

Young men engaged together on an exciting, dangerous, and patriotic mission, the officers of the Virginia Regiment wore as symbols of fellowship the uniform their Colonel had designed for them—and they did not take kindly to moralistic attacks from paunchy sit-by-the-fires. George himself, huge and muscular, his fists clenched and his face working with anger, sent into scurrying flight one John Baylis who had started to criticize the regiment. From prudent safety, Baylis sent Washington a letter protesting his "putting yourself in a passion" and exhibiting "such a menacing air."[16]

Washington was sometimes able to use the Burgesses as a makeweight against Dinwiddie, but not on this issue which rose from the people rather than the Governor's court. The linking by "the Virginia Sentinel" of alleged debauchery among the officers of the Colony's regular force with alleged browbeating and discouraging of the militia, summarized the broad cultural disturbance that lay behind the charges. Along with their men who had elected them by popular vote, the militia officers belonged to the lower middle class, which followed Puritan mores. However, the gentlemen-officers Washington had appointed to the Virginia Regiment had been nurtured in an older code of behavior, the aristocratic. Whenever during the French and Indian War Colonials from these divergent backgrounds were brought together, conflicts over morality resulted.

In no area was the break between the two systems more sharp than in sexual matters. That Washington's reactions were those of the castle, not the farmyard or the countinghouse, is exemplified by the episode of Captain Peter Hog and his concubine.

---

* Washington continued his campaign to be assigned a minister. A year and a half later he wrote to the then acting governor, John Blair, "Common decency, sir, in a camp calls for the services of a divine . . . although the world be so uncharitable as to think us void of religion and incapable of good instruction."[14]

A Mr. Chew complained to Washington that Hog had lured away one of his white indentured servants and was living with her at Fort Dinwiddie. In an indignant letter to Hog, Washington made no comment on his behaving as young bloods of the upper classes commonly did by keeping a mistress of a lower class. He insisted that the Captain "make immediate restitution" to Chew for the loss of the woman's services. And Hog felt he could defend himself from the charge of having stolen the woman by stating to his Colonel, "She was openly seen in camp. I never intended to conceal her."[17]

In sharp disagreement with Puritan thinking, aristocratic mores did not damn with an all-inclusive taboo free sexual behavior. (A letter from a mutual friend which George's brother Augustine delivered by hand to their brother Lawrence bore a seal that showed "an indecent device, nicely cut, surrounded with the words 'no immodesty.' ")[18] Furthermore, differences of social and economic position were then not only greater than today, but more frankly and practically recognized. Women (to whom so many other careers were closed) were not then considered debauched by becoming the mistresses of their betters: that was, indeed, a recognized method for getting ahead in the world. If the woman were unmarried, she could acquire property and interest that would enable her to make eventually a more advantageous match than she could otherwise have done. If she were married, she could further the advancement of her husband.

This opportunity was by no means grasped only by servant girls. Thus the well-born Boston matron Mrs. Joshua Loring became during the Revolution General Howe's mistress, reigning publicly as "the Sultana of the British army," and, in the process, securing for her husband the lucrative appointment of Commissary of Prisoners.

Captain Hog assured Washington that he intended to free his

doxy by buying up her unexpired time.[19] According to Virginia aristocratic ideas, she was better off with him than she had been as a mere indentured servant to Mr. Chew.

It is nowhere implied in any authentic document that Washington was, after his marriage, unfaithful to Martha.* Yet he was now an unmarried soldier who harbored an unattainable love. Barrack-room conversation in which he participated is certainly echoed by a letter his crony Captain Mercer wrote him from Charleston: "You'll be surprised I have not yet mentioned the fair ones." Alas, the South Carolina girls lacked "those enticing, heaving, throbbing, alluring, plump breasts common with our northern belles."[21]

Washington was in his later years to contrast unfavorably "the giddy rounds of promiscuous pleasure" with "the sequestered walks of connubial life." Was he judging from experience? In 1754, Captain William Peyrouney (a French-born officer with little command of English) wrote him, "I imagine you by this time plunged in the midst of delight heaven can afford, and enchanted by charms even stranger to the Cyprian dame (+ M's Nel)."[22]

Temperamentally opposed to rudeness and vain display, Washington denounced in his orders swearing and obscene language. There is evidence that Washington was himself capable of a very occasional oath.[23] However, the anecdotes of his bursting into stunningly eloquent profanity on various historical occasions seem all to be aprocryphal.

Upbraiding for drunkenness a captain who was also an old friend, Washington urged that "such inconsistent behavior as liquor sometimes prompts you to may be borne by your friends,"

---

* Historical mythology cherishes a letter in which Washington is supposed to have expatiated, when inviting a friend to Mount Vernon, on the charms available in his slave quarters. No reputable scholar has ever seen this letter. The rumor seems to have stemmed from a document the British forged during the Revolution to discredit the American Commander in Chief.[20]

but had no place in a military camp where all should "strive to excel in all laudable emulations." A man who sought self-mastery as passionately as Washington did could not enjoy anything that involved losing control. Although a flood of documents reveal his pleasure in lingering with friends over a convivial bottle, there is no evidence that on any occasion he ever drank too much. As Samuel Eliot Morison says, he believed in drinking like a gentleman, which means as much as you can hold without getting drunk.[24]

A letter to him from Lieutenant Colonel Stephen, describing the 1755 Christmas celebration at Fort Cumberland, reveals how the officers of the Virginia Regiment relaxed: "I had the honor to dine* at the head of twenty-four fine gentlemen yesterday. We had an extremely good dinner, and after drinking the royal healths in a huff and a huzza at every health, we passed an hour in singing and taking a cheerful glass. We then amused ourselves with acting part of a play, and dancing. We parted very affectionately at twelve o'clock, remembering all absent friends."[25]

Although Washington assured Dinwiddie that he discountenanced gambling, he could not really disapprove of this sport of gentlemen which he himself so enjoyed. Repeating to his officers the Governor's orders against the sport, he made it clear that they had not originated with him. However, when he approved the cashiering of a lieutenant who had been so ungentlemanly as to cheat at cards, he used the occasion to admonish his followers against wasting too much time on such "pleasure. . . . As we now have no opportunities to improve from example, let us read." He recommended particularly Humphrey Bland's *Treatise of Military Discipline*, which he had himself ordered from England.[26]

"Discipline," he wrote all his captains, "is the soul of an army.

---

* Dinner hour was at about three P.M.

It makes small number formidable, procures success to the weak, and esteem to all."[27]

"Old Soldier" was to write during the Revolution for publication in England that Washington had not been much liked during his French and Indian War service because he had been "a tolerable strict disciplinarian."[28] This was an exaggeration. Throughout his military career, Washington, it is true, made enemies of those compatriots who would not subordinate their individualism to the necessities of effective command. However, he was extremely popular with the hard core of continuing officers who constituted the backbones of his armies.

"Our colonel," wrote Robert Munford, "is an example of fortitude in either danger or hardships, and by his easy, polite behavior, has gained not only the regard but affection of both officers and soldiers." The officers were welcome at his table, and he saw to it that there was enough wine "to give content." They had "the highest idea of your entertainment and kind manner of your living."[29]

George Washington charmed his officers with that sweetness that was part of his character although it has vanished from his legend. (The adjective most often applied to him by those who knew him as a young man was "amiable.")

He labored to protect his officer corps from incompetents. Although he reluctantly gave in to heavy pressure exerted for two Fairfax sons by his old patron William, he otherwise resisted efforts to have appointments based not on merit but that interest which made the English world go round.[30]

"I shall make it," Washington announced, "the most agreeable part of my duty to study merit, and reward the brave and deserving. I assure you, gentlemen, that partiality shall never bias my conduct, nor shall prejudice injure any, but throughout the whole tenor of my proceedings, I shall endeavor, as far as I am able, to reward and punish without the least diminution."[31]

In practice, however, he tempered justice with benevolence and mercy, as when he urged a commissary not to "distress" a poor man by forcing him to live up to an unfortunate contract that would cost him his "all."[32]

When reporting to his superiors, he usually did not eulogize or blame his subordinates unless he wished what he said to lead specifically to promotion or its opposite. This kept the lines of power within the regiment, leading up to Washington as its head. Captain John Rutherford wrote his colonel that he altogether depended on him for protection, and was "sensible that, as far as justice is on my side, I may depend on your favor."[33]

In his letters to his officers, Washington criticized when he considered that necessary, but rarely included individual praise. From day to day, even in battle, he assumed that each man or detachment would do his best for all, and so, if he phrased a compliment, it was to the regiment as a whole. Pride in the regiment rather than individual pride was what Washington sought to inculcate.

The ambition of all was, as Washington summarized it, to "show our willing obedience to the best of kings" and "by rules of unerring bravery strive to earn his royal favor and a better establishment as a reward for our services."[34]

Washington contended "that we want nothing but commissions from His Majesty to be as regular a corps as any upon this continent." They had in the present war been the first in arms; were enlisted to serve not a few months like the militia but "during the King's or Colony's pleasure"; were "regularly regimented, and trained" and "uniformly clothed, [both] officers and soldiers"; had "done as regular duty for upwards of three years as any regiment in His Majesty's service." Some other officers, he admitted, had much greater seniority, "meaning, I suppose, the length of time they pocketed a commission. I apprehend . . . that there is as equitable a right to expect something for three years hard and bloody service, as for ten spent at St. James' etc., where real service of a field of battle never was seen."

It would be unfair, Washington continued, for such loyal officers as the Virginians to be "dismissed" when with peace the "hard blows and continual dangers" were passed.[35] Clearly George Washington hoped to make a continuing career in His Majesty's army. (Had the King had the gift of prophecy would he not have grappled this young man to his side?)

The Virginia Regiment seemed to Washington all the more important to the Crown when he heard that the fuse he had lighted two years before in the wilderness had finally exploded into formally declared war. The American confrontation had, of course, always been an element in colossal European jockeyings for power. Thus, the Seven Years' War was officially started by England's ally, Frederick of Prussia, who marched, in August 1756, across the Saxon border. England and Prussia became ranged against a most powerful coalition: France, Austria, Sweden, Russia, and Saxony.

As the war escalated elsewhere, it was going badly in British America. Indian raids flashed on every frontier. Although Washington was to claim, on what basis other than rumor and hope it is impossible to tell, that his regiment had kept Virginia's casualties down to half as many as those in other provinces, Virginia was certainly badly hit.

In the one major action of the summer, a French raiding party battered down England's door on the Great Lakes: Fort Oswego was burned to the ground. Although the enemy sailed off again into Lake Ontario, the British regulars who were supposed to keep open the Mohawk River route withdrew in fright to its eastern end. And an intended advance on Ticonderoga was canceled.

However, the British had dispatched across the ocean a regular army general, John Campbell, fourth Earl of Loudoun. Washington remembered how staunchly Braddock, the previous general from overseas, had been his friend. That Loudoun was to hold, in addition to the military command, the honorary governorship of Virginia, made the news of his arrival seem doubly delightful. Surely the high-born Scot would have a special interest in the colony put under his charge!

As he had been trained to do by the Fairfaxes, Washington mobilized "interest" that could be brought to bear on the new general. William Fairfax was, of course, endlessly active, searching out men who knew Loudoun or were certain to meet him. Even Dinwiddie was persuaded once more to back his exasperating but indispensable subordinate. Virginia's Lieutenant Governor repeated the report that Braddock had intended to provide for Washington "handsomely in the regulars." Washington, Dinwiddie continued, "is a person much loved here, and has gone through many hardships." Should Loudoun "promote him in the British establishment, I think he will answer my recommendation."[36]

During mid-September, Washington rode to Mount Vernon to transact some private business. A strangely stiff letter he wrote Sally Fairfax seems to imply that he was keeping away from Belvoir, that his feelings were hurt, and that he was responding to an overture in a prickly manner. His servants, he stated, had given him her message that a seamstress was to be at her house "and that you would, if I sent my linen over, give it to Miss Nancy to make." He was sending a piece of Irish linen, a piece of cambric, and a shirt to measure by. He would like to have somewhat narrower wristbands, ruffles deeper by half an inch and collars by three quarters of an inch. "I am, dear madam, etc. . . ."[37]

As the Indian raids continued almost unchecked, Washington

was smarting from the most violent public attacks he had ever faced, attacks that carried with them implications of cowardice.

Washington was building at Winchester a fort which he hoped to persuade the authorities should replace Fort Cumberland as the main post of the regiment. He was now reporting and making recommendations to Speaker Robinson independently of his reports and recommendations to Dinwiddie, and the Speaker, not unmindful of the fact that Cumberland was legally over the line in Maryland, secured the agreement of a committee of the Burgesses to the change. But Dinwiddie was most concerned by the fact that Cumberland, having been built by Braddock, had been designated a royal fort. He stated angrily that he would rather lose his right hand than abandon any such installation.[38] So the bulk of the Virginia Regiment remained at Cumberland—it was the front line—and Colonel Washington was practically never there.

To worsen matters in the public eye, Washington had made himself very comfortable at Winchester. He had rented a house where he entertained in style; he took fencing lessons to help him pass the time; he rode often to nearby Bullskin Plantation to supervise his private affairs. More and more voices repeated that not only gross immorality among the officers but the bloody disasters of the campaign were all due to the pusillanimity of Colonel Washington, who stayed in comparative safety behind the largest detachment of his army.*

As October approached, Washington decided to inspect the front line, riding several hundred miles south through the Shenandoah Valley to the South Carolina border.

He had got no farther than Augusta Court House when, so he wrote Dinwiddie, he was notified that the Indians were out to

---

* What Washington was now experiencing undoubtedly lay behind the fact that during the Revolution the Commander in Chief was the man in all America who was most consistently in the camp of the Continental Army. Only the most extreme necessity carried him even a day's ride away.

the southward. He called on Colonel David Stewart for his local militia, waited for five days during which five men appeared. It was then whispered to him that sixty miles farther south, on the Roanoke River, there was a Colonel John Buchanan who hated Stewart but who, if appealed to directly, might be able to supply men. Attended only by a captain, Washington galloped down the tightly foliaged road that was like a channel through a shark-infested sea. There were rustlings but no shots. However, Buchanan proved to have no men: all the inhabitants of the area had fled. "It remained only to proceed without men to see the situation of the forts, or return back again."³⁹

As Washington and two companions advanced in a heavy rain, their muskets too wet to fire, they came to where the road began a long S-curve. They were not conscious that their hoofbeats had alerted an ambushed party of hostile Indians who peered out to see them coming around the bend. It seemed to Washington, after he learned what had happened from some white men who had been prisoners with the Indians, another indication of his exhilarating immunity to harm, that the Indians did not lift their muskets. They were awaiting some horsemen coming the other way: two Virginians were to kick their lives out where Washington had just passed untouched.⁴⁰

At a post on Roanoke River, the thirty militiamen who were supposed to be backing up eighteen of Washington's Virginia regulars were unwilling to help build the fort unless given carpenters' pay (which Washington felt he was not authorized to do); so there was no hope of completing the fort before Christmas. When Washington approached another fort, this one altogether manned by militia, he heard firing, and sneaked ahead through the woods expecting to see a siege. He saw the whole garrison outside the stockade, prime targets in the sunlight, shooting at marks. And when, as he advanced up Jackson's

River, he did get an escort of militiamen, they went through the woods "whooping" and "hallooing" at each other; they treated with "derision and contempt" his orders that they go silently and flank themselves with scouts.[41]

However, after three weeks of threading through a hostile wilderness under every circumstance of danger, Washington returned to Winchester without having heard a war whoop or been the target of a single shot.

In letters to his superiors in Williamsburg, the Virginian Commander in Chief had described in harrowing detail the utter disorganization of his command. He thus summarized the situation to Speaker Robinson: "The ruinous state of the frontiers and the vast extent of land we have lost since this time twelve month, must appear incredible to those who are not eyewitnesses to the desolation. [A strip of] upward of fifty miles of a rich and once thickly settled country is now quite deserted and abandoned, from the Maryland to the Carolina lines; great numbers below that, removed through fear . . . and the whole settlement deliberating whether to go or stay."[42]

Washington's reports read less like those of a commander than of an investigating committee about to recommend that commander's removal. This is explained by the way he apportioned the blame for the desperate situation. He spurned with "contempt" all the "calumny and censure that malice and ill-nature" had directed at the Virginia Regiment, and his own activities as its colonel. A little of the blame went to "Maryland and Pennsylvania [for] giving ground so much faster than we did." But most of the blame he placed squarely at the door of the Virginia superiors to whom he was reporting. He accused them of two fatal mistakes: they had not secured the necessary Indian allies; and, by not taking the necessary steps to recruit the Virginia Regiment to full strength and keep it there, they had forced reliance on useless militia, which he lacked the opportunity and power to discipline. In urging the Governor and Council to mend their ways, he was peremptory, addressing them as if they were the subordinates, not he.[43]

Washington was thereupon taught a lesson which, even if he did not learn it at once, undoubtedly influenced his much later behavior to the Continental Congress. Instead of trembling under his criticisms, begging forgiveness and promising to reform, the Governor and Council, for the first time in their relationship with Washington, took the management of the campaign completely out of his hands. They sent him peremptory orders which implied that the blame was his, because he had neglected his duty and avoided danger by refusing to establish his headquarters in the front line. Far from accepting Washington's recommendation that Fort Cumberland be abandoned in favor of the new fort at Winchester (which George had tactfully named Fort Loudoun), they ordered Washington to march himself to Cumberland at the head of most of the garrison he had gathered at Winchester. Dinwiddie added expressions of resentment at Washington's "unmannerly" criticisms.[44]

Washington had responded to much less grievous slaps than this with threats to resign. Now he complained to Robinson, who sympathized but was powerless to help, and comforted himself by buying a puppy to play with. To Dinwiddie, he replied humbly, "I am sorry any expressions in my letters should be deemed unmannerly. I . . . have endeavored to demean myself in that proper respect due to superiors." He insisted that personally he would not mind leaving Winchester—"I am tired of the place, the inhabitants, and the life I lead here"—but removing the hundred men he had been ordered to take with him to Cumberland would leave the fort he was building at Winchester unfinished, the building materials "collected with unspeakable difficulty and expense" open to pillage, and the community unprotected from Indian raids.[45]

Back came another peremptory order: so that he could march with a hundred men to Cumberland yet protect Winchester, he was to pull in the garrisons from all the forts he had built in the countryside. This blow to his strategic conceptions was given a cutting edge by an enclosed quotation from Lord Loudoun that was highly critical of Washington's proposal that Cumberland be abandoned. Thinking in terms of European armies that would not leave behind them a post which could cut their (for them necessary) supply lines, Loudoun did not doubt that strengthening the "advanced" fort was the best way to stop Indian raids. Dinwiddie added his own sarcasm, "It gives me pleasure that going to Fort Cumberland is so agreeable to you, as without doubt it's the proper place for the commanding officer."[46]

Washington obediently ordered the commanders of the little forts to evacuate them, but added comments that breathed angry insubordination: "I heartily commiserate the fate of the poor, unhappy inhabitants left by this means exposed to every incursion of a merciless enemy. . . . You may assure the settlement that this . . . step was taken without my concurrence and knowledge."[47]

In urging Speaker Robinson to find some way by which the Burgesses could cancel the orders sent him by the Governor and Council, Washington brightened the black picture of frontier conditions he had so recently drawn: "The disposition I had made of our small regiment gave general satisfaction to the settlements and content began to appear everywhere." He could not imagine why his arrangements had been vetoed unless villainous calumniators had "perverted" the record for "the worst purposes." However, he would not resign, but would go on in hope of better regulation on the arrival of Lord Loudoun.[48]

To Dinwiddie, he wrote, "Nothing gives me greater uneasiness and concern than that His Lordship should have imbibed prejudices so unfavorable to my character."[49]

A few days before Christmas, Washington moved to Fort Cumberland. He lost small sums at cards and billiards, gave a pound to strolling actors who had miraculously appeared there through winter snows that stopped Indian raids.[50] But his serious attention was directed towards Lord Loudoun. If "interest" with men in power were the way to get ahead in the world, the time to prove it was now.

13

Washington Turns to the Crown

WHEN, EARLIER in that year of 1756, the Indian raids had started up again, Washington had feared that "the murder of poor, innocent babes and helpless families may be laid to my account." Himself helpless to protect the frontier inhabitants, he had wished he could resign before his reputation was ruined. But he had felt he could not resign in the face of "imminent danger"—and now he was sure that his worst fears had been realized.

The Virginia authorities seemed more and more his enemies or helpless to be his friends. Thus, he came increasingly to hope that Lord Loudoun, the Crown's new representative in America, would prove the savior of the Virginia frontier, the Virginia Regiment, and his own career. In anguish of spirit, he wrote Loudoun a long and passionate letter.[1]

Describing Virginia's plight from the outbreak of hostilities to that moment, he blamed every misfortune on stupidity persevered in by Dinwiddie and the Assembly despite the good advice he had himself showered on them. Had they listened to him, the French would not even have been able to create the disastrous situation by taking the Forks and building Fort Duquesne.

When he discussed his first campaign, he glided over the

Jumonville Affair and his defeat at Fort Necessity, insisting rather that the summer of 1754 had been unfortunate because the authorities, by not supplying and paying the troops, had established public attitudes that made recruiting difficult.

Washington retailed at length how the various recruiting and drafting acts were drawn, despite his protests, to defeat their objectives; how the lack of a suitable military code that made punishment almost impossible had conspired with the riffraff put in his army by drafting vagrants and with the inadequacy of clothing and supply (plus the lack of a regular pension system for those who might be maimed by wounds) to allow "mutiny, desertion, and other irregularities" to "creep into the camp." This despite the fact, "I can truly say and confidently assert that no soldiers were ever under better command."

He held forth on the uselessness of the militia and criticized the foolhardiness and misplaced parsimony of the authorities who put reliance on so palsied an arm. However, the Virginia Regiment had, despite all disadvantages, "been very alert in defending the people." Since March, "our troops have engaged in upwards of twenty skirmishes, and we have had near a hundred men killed and wounded." This was more than could be said of the forces in the neighboring Colonies.

Preferring to dwell on his insistence that the only final solution would be to capture Duquesne, Washington, although he had been to a considerable extent its architect, attributed to the Assembly the plan (which Loudoun had scorned) of trying to contain the Indians with a string of forts.* He added more accurately that he had never been supplied enough men to see if the plan would work.

---

* During the Revolution and thereafter, Washington denounced such strategy, pointing out that forts could be "insulted or avoided at the option of" the Indians; that the inhabitants could not be protected because, while the Indians were out, the soldiers were cooped up in the posts; and that when an army is "frittered" into small garrisons and the troops are not frequently relieved, "discipline will always be lax and impositions on the public will prevail."[2]

Washington did not boast to Loudoun, as he might well have done, of how he had discouraged foolhardy Colonial plans to cross the mountains with inadequate armies. Instead, he implied that had his Virginia command been unleashed, they might have effectively attacked in the Ohio Valley, both serving "our country," and "gaining honor to ourselves or reputation to our regiment." This assertion forced him to make a grievance out of the law, which had preserved his autonomy from Sharpe by limiting the regiment to protecting Virginia.

"I must beg leave to add," Washington continued, "my unwearied endeavors are inadequately rewarded. The orders I receive are full of ambiguity. . . . I am answerable for consequences and blamed without the privilege of defense. . . . I have long been satisfied of the impossibility of continuing in this service without loss of honor."

One major reason he was still serving was "the dawn of hope that arose" when he heard of Loudoun's appointment. "Although I had not the honor to be known to your Lordship, your Lordship's name was familiar to my ear, on account of the important services performed to His Majesty in other parts of the world. Do not think, my Lord, that I am going to flatter; notwithstanding I have exalted sentiments of your Lordship's character and respect your rank, it is not my intention to adulate. My nature is open and honest and free from guile!"

The Virginia Regiment had long been "tantalized, nay bid to expect most sanguinely a better establishment." Had Braddock survived, Washington himself would "have met with preferment agreeable to my wishes. . . . I do not know my Lord in what light this short and disinterested relation may be received by your Lordship," but he hoped that "if there be anything in it which appears worthy of redress . . . your Lordship will condescend to point out the way it may be obtained."

That Washington believed that this letter, in which a Colonial

[171]

praised himself and his provincial regiment while blaming everyone else, including royal officials, would help him with a British lord and regular army general, shows that the young man lacked, despite his training under William Fairfax, the necessary turn of mind for a courtier. And as for his attempts to flatter, they were as clumsy as an elephant's attempts to do a deep court curtsey.

Washington enclosed his letter to Loudoun in one to an aide, Captain James Cunningham. For some reason, it seemed to him more suave to address not to the General but to this lesser officer his most audacious proposal: "I am firmly persuaded that 3000 men under good regulation (and surely the three middle colonies could easily raise and support that number) might fortify all the passes between this and the Ohio; take possession of that river; cut the communication between Fort Duquesne and the lakes; and with a middling train of artillery (with proper officers and engineers) make themselves masters of that fortress, which is now become the terror of these Colonies." Regulars, it was implied, would only be needed in the special services, the artillery and engineers. Presumably Colonel Washington would accept the top command.[3]

Loudoun's aide was to acknowledge Washington's letters in polite generalities; he said nothing about any desire of the General to consult with the Colonial. But the Colonial was determined to advise the General. Learning that Loudoun was coming to Philadelphia for a meeting with five governors, Washington asked permission to be in that city.

"I cannot conceive," Dinwiddie replied, "what service you can be of in going there, as the plan concerted will, of course, be communicated to you and the other officers. However, as you seem so earnest to go, I now give you leave."[4]

Washington reached Philadelphia late in February 1757. Since Loudoun had no objection to keeping everybody, including the five governors, waiting, the Virginian's stay stretched to almost six weeks. Had he been in the mood, this could have been a delightful holiday—and certainly no young man ever needed more to relax. He did gamble at cards; he did attend some clubs at taverns and some dancing assemblies; but his purchases in the lovely shops were few;[5] and he lacked the spirit, as a friend pointed out critically, to dash to New York and court Polly Philipse, whom he still vaguely hoped to marry.[6] With passionate attention, he gathered gossip about Loudoun, a most discouraging occupation since the fourth Earl was offending Colonials everywhere by ignoring them.[7]

As bad luck would have it, at this moment, when he needed all the prestige he could muster, there began drifting into the Colonies copies of a book the French had published in 1756 to prove the English the aggressors in the war: *Mémoire Contenant le Précis des Faits, avec leur pièces justificatives pour servir de réponse aux observations envoyées par les ministres d'Angleterre dans les cours de Europe.* A long section (pages 109–147) quoted as evidence a translation into French of what purported to be the journal Washington had kept (and lost) during the Jumonville–Fort Necessity campaign.

The harassed soldier called on a printer who had announced an English edition, was referred to "the little body" (as he put it) who was making the translation, and eventually hired a translator of his own. He was depressed by what the translator produced, felt that his text must have been tampered with, but never sent any corrections to the publishers of either the Philadelphia or the New York editions, both of whom would have been glad to tone down a document that did so little credit to American arms.[8]*

---

* The quotations from Washington's journal in Chapters Seven and Eight of this book are from a retranslation into English of the text as published in the *Mémoire.* That this text is in the main reliable was incontrovertibly demonstrated when Donald H. Kent discovered another copy of the French translation which

Whether or not Loudoun was conscious of the book that revived Washington's worst mistakes, the Earl received other information that made him suspect that the Virginia Colonel was actually a spy for the French.[10] Even after, on discovering that Washington had not black but auburn hair, he realized that the spy must be someone else, he failed to consult the Colonial. To the conferences finally mounted in Philadelphia, the Virginian was not invited. When Washington was at very long last ushered into Loudoun's presence, it was to receive orders.

The elderly Scot, whose supercilious face was weirdly as unlined as the face of a boy, made no effort to put the tall provincial at his ease. Without condescending to communicate what positive plans had been adopted, he stated that there would be no attack that year on Fort Duquesne. Furthermore, South Carolina was considered in more danger than Virginia: 400 Virginia troops were to be sent there. When Washington tried to object or ask for reasons, he was silenced. Having been told that Fort Cumberland was to be preserved but garrisoned from Maryland, he was given, with rigid specifications on the

---

had been sent, in September 1754, by the Marquis Duquesne, Governor of New France, to Hector St. John Crèvecoeur, Commandant of Fort Duquesne. The covering correspondence makes it clear that the Governor was forwarding the document to his field officer as valuable intelligence concerning British actions, attitudes, and plans. For this purpose, the text would certainly be transmitted as accurately as possible. If forged sections were added, this would be done for the propaganda version. But, despite many small variations, the text as published in Paris is in all important particulars the same as the manuscript Duquesne sent to Crèvecoeur.

In his disavowal, Washington stated that he had kept no regular journal, though he had taken "rough minutes of occurrences." He found these in the *Mémoire* text "certainly and strangely metamorphosed, some parts left out . . . and many things added." We can only assume that Washington was voicing an author's usual complaint against a translator, strengthened because his memory of what he had written several years before was vague, and because his "rough minutes" had been smoothed into a more continuous narrative.

The French felt that what Washington had actually written was damning enough. Thus Duquesne wrote Crèvecoeur, "There is nothing more unworthy, lower, or even blacker than the opinions and the way of thinking of this Washington! It would have been a pleasure to read his outrageous journal to him right under his nose."[9]

number of men to be placed in each, a list of five forts to be held by Virginia.

Then, at long last, Loudoun asked a question: what would be the best spot on a certain road for a fort to keep open communication between Winchester, where Washington was to make his headquarters, and Cumberland? Washington started to say that there was a shorter and safer road, but, on seeing Loudoun's face, he answered the question as asked. The only concession he could procure was that if he had any men left after he had established garrisons as ordered, he might place these at his discretion.

As for the Virginian's grievances and all the problems he faced in his Colony, Loudoun could not be made to pay the least attention to them, nor would he listen to Washington's arguments that he and the Virginia Regiment be taken into the regular establishment. Having communicated irrevocable orders, the fourth Earl dismissed George Washington with the cold, bland, impersonal courtesy of an aristocrat dealing with an inferior.[11]

So sternly rebuffed by the British power on which he had placed his hopes, Washington turned again, in despair, to the Lieutenant Governor of Virginia. He sent Dinwiddie a recapitulation, couched in the most emotional terms, of the reasons why he believed that the Virginia Regiment had an absolute right to permanent establishment. Then he added a contention that was to underlie a yet unforeseen revolution: "We can't conceive that being Americans should deprive us of the benefits of British subjects."[12]

CHAPTER

14

To Death's Door

WASHINGTON had received from Loudoun the roughest treatment he had known in his public career. Interest, as he had learned it from the Fairfaxes, had become his enemy— and his conviction that he had amply earned the regular commission he had for so long desired made the blow completely shattering. Since patronage had failed him and merit, it seemed, counted for nothing, Washington could no longer hope for anything permanent: no career in a continuing army, no valuable commission, no half pay if he retired. Instead, his plantations were running down in his absence, and, although he was making a good salary, Dinwiddie was feuding with him over whether he should continue to be allowed more than two servants at the King's expense.[1]

But money was not the most important thing Washington labored for. Rather than accept a paid commission he considered unworthy of his honor, he had accompanied Braddock as an unpaid volunteer. He had then explained that his motive was "the hope of meriting the love of my country and the friendly regard of my acquaintances." Washington subscribed to the stoic conception which he thus phrased in 1781: "The confidence and affections of his fellow citizens is the most valuable and agreeable reward a citizen can achieve."[2]

[176]

This ideal made him highly sensitive—oversensitive his critics tell us—to criticism; and he had experienced to the hilt that his role as commander of an inadequately recruited and supplied army engaged in an impossible task was less conducive to earning praise than blame. He was every day putting his reputation in a balance weighted against it.

Surely the moment had come for him to resign. Yet he did not resign. By serving for so long the frontiersmen of Virginia, he had worn into his brain a feeling of responsibility for them which all his resentments could not eradicate. He resumed his local colonelcy.

Despite all Washington's protests, the draft law the Virginia Assembly passed in April 1757 was even worse than its predecessors, being aimed at militiamen too poor to vote and at the idle who were defined as men "neglecting to labor" for what the magistrates (who were also employers) considered "reasonable wages." Desertions ran over twenty-five per cent.[3]

In desperation Washington ordered a gallows almost forty feet high and had hanged on it two hardened offenders in the presence of as many troops as he could gather. This was a sight he himself hated, and, when even the grisly example failed to stop the flight of desperate men, Washington was driven by pity to pardon a new batch of deserters who had been sentenced to death. "Those poor, unhappy criminals," he explained, had already "undergone no small pain of body and mind in a dark room, closely ironed!"[4]

That summer, the Virginia Regiment never came within several hundred of its authorized strength of 1272 men, and 400 of those he had were marched off by Loudoun's command to South Carolina.

On his return from Philadelphia, Washington had been notified that the years of negotiations with the southern Indians were finally bearing fruit: ninety-five Catawbas were at Win-

[177]

chester. He had galloped off gleefully to greet this first considerable force of Indian allies to appear since the Ohio Valley
tribesmen had left him on the eve of the Fort Necessity defeat.
Soon he added to a letter "an apology for the incoherence of
this. The Indians are all around, teasing and perplexing me for
one thing and another, so that I scarce know what I write."[5]

More Catawbas came in and Cherokees by the score. Some
were carrying goods which, to make up for having received no
presents as they entered Virginia, they had plundered on the
march. They now demanded official gifts to pay them for their
noble support of the British, but Washington, having no Indian
goods, could only feed them well and ask them to wait.

Ritual shouts echoing from several hundred brazen throats
presaged and celebrated the appearance of a Cherokee party
bringing four scalps and two prisoners. They hurried to Washington with their prizes for which they demanded the payment
Virginia had promised. Washington told them that their great
father overseas had appointed Edmund Atkin as his representative to his children, the Indians; Atkin would be there any
moment to see that they were rewarded. Then Washington
rushed off a dispatch to Dinwiddie asking why Atkin had not
appeared. The Indians, he explained, "are the most insolent,
most avaricious, and most dissatisfied wretches I ever had to
deal with." If Atkin were detained, "It will not be in my power
to convince them that it is not mere *hum!* All the rhetoric I can
muster is not likely to detain them more than two or three days."
And, as they sharpened their hatchets, they had not hesitated to
imply that they would use them on the Virginians if they were
cheated. All George had been able to do was to ask them to list
what they wanted, getting "a most extravagant list."[6]

He now had between three and four hundred Indian guests.
He managed to send out eighty with a party of soldiers. They
boasted much of what they would do to the Shawnee towns, but

Washington doubted that his officers could lead them far enough to be of any service.

The next event was that the Catawbas departed in a body. The Cherokees were about to follow, when in rumbled carts with Indian presents. However, Washington did not know how to distribute them, and Atkin was still absent.[7]

On June 2, Atkin arrived and on the 10th Washington wrote, "A person of a readier pen and having more time than myself, might amuse you with the vicissitudes which have happened in the Indian affairs since Mr. Atkin came up. I acknowledge my incompetency, and shall therefore only observe that the Indians have been pleased and displeased oftener than they ought to have been, and that they are gone off."[8]

Atkin had imprisoned some Cherokees and Mingoes he considered spies, forcing Washington to intervene lest other Cherokees fall on the settlers. When he departed, he took with him the interpreter and all the Indian goods, so that the arrival of another group of Cherokees gave Washington "inconceivable trouble."[9]

As the months passed, Washington managed to send a few more mixed parties of Indians and Virginians into the woods. Although they accomplished little, he was convinced that the Cherokees had shown a sincere desire to fight beside the Virginians and that, if adequately rewarded they would "in all human probability" soon change "the desperate situation."[10]

But the situation remained desperate. In mid-September, for instance, France's Indian allies killed ten persons within twelve miles of Winchester, "and notwithstanding I sent a strong detachment from hence to pursue them and ordered the passes of the mountains to be waylaid by commands from other places, yet we were not able to meet with these savages." About two weeks later an Indian party of "not quite a hundred fell upon the inhabitants along the great road between this place and

[179]

Pennsylvania, got fifteen more." From this second raiding party, a detachment of the Virginia Regiment extracted one casualty, bringing Washington a scalp to prove it.[11]

To Dinwiddie, Washington wrote that unless an expedition were undertaken westward the following summer, or a larger defensive force mounted than Virginia could herself maintain, there would hardly be "one soul living on this side of the Blue Ridge the ensuing autumn. . . . I have taken indefatigable pains and found it no easy task to prevail on the bulk of the country to wait the consultations of this winter, and the event of this spring. I do not know on whom this miserable and undone people are to rely for redress. If the Assembly are to give it to them, it is time measures were concerting; if we are to seek it of the commander in chief, it is time our grievances were made known to him."

William Fairfax wrote George that the family at Belvoir hoped "your brave men may keep the enemy far from them, . . . and wishes that all your desires may be fully answered." Some other ladies envisioned for him "that sort of glory which will most endear you to the fair sex." But Dinwiddie grudged giving the Colonel permission to leave Winchester. "I am," Washington complained, "become in a manner an exile. . . . Every person who sees how I am employed will testify that very little recreation falls to my lot."[12]

He tried to cheer himself by making plans for Mount Vernon. He did not know whether his plantations below had produced any tobacco to be shipped, but assumed they had, and therefore asked his London factor to send him in return a marble chimney piece, not to exceed 15 guineas, "a neat landskip," three feet by 21½ inches to use as an overmantel, papier-mâché designs for the ceilings of two rooms, 250 panes of glass, two mahogany tables and a dozen chairs. To double the usefulness of the chairs, he intended to put the removable seats into an old set, which would then be suitable for bedrooms, while the old seats would not, in the dining room, take away too much from the glamor of the new mahogany.[13]

Washington's remunerations as commander and as contractor for supply gave him much Virginia currency to spend. To a friend who had failed in efforts to borrow from "the monied ones," George lent £150. He bought for £350 five hundred acres adjacent to Mount Vernon, and for another £300 slaves to culti- vate the acres.[14]

But preparation for a future as a planter did not assuage the dissatisfaction of the soldier who felt that the career in the British regular army he had earned was being denied him. He engaged with Dinwiddie in such acrimonious skirmishing as he was never to engage in with the Continental Congress.

Although he had from the start of his service suffered from delays in receiving funds for supplies he had bought, when this happened again in June he blamed it on a desire of the Lieu- tenant Governor "to hear that I was involved in trouble." Then, in August, Dinwiddie mildly criticized him for not reporting fully on Indian affairs. Washington answered, "It is with plea- sure I receive reproof when reproof is due, . . . but, on the other hand, it is with concern I remark that my best endeavors lose their reward." Indian affairs were not his province but Atkin's.[15]

Dinwiddie's reply was still temperate, but by now Washing- ton had heard of a rumor said to be circulating in Williamsburg that the frontier scare which had brought out so many militia the year before had been a scheme of Washington's "to cause the Assembly to levy largely both in men and money, and that there was not an Indian in that neighborhood." Convinced that such slanders had turned the Governor against him, he wrote Din- widdie, "That I have foibles, and perhaps many of them, I shall not deny. I should esteem myself, as the world also would, vain and empty were I to arrogate perfection. . . . But this I know, and it is the highest consolation I am capable of feeling, that no man that ever was employed in a public capacity has endeavored to discharge the trust reposed in him with greater honesty and more zeal for the country's interest than I have done; and if there is any person living who can say with justice that I have offered any intentional wrong to the public, I will cheerfully submit to the most ignominious punishment that an injured people ought to inflict. On the other hand, it is hard to have my character arraigned and my actions condemned without a hearing."[16]

Dinwiddie, who had suffered a stroke and was retiring in age and sickness, replied thus: "My conduct to you from the beginning was always friendly, but you know I have great reason to suspect you of ingratitude. . . . I wish my successor may show you as much friendship as I've done."[17]

Dinwiddie's use of the word "ingratitude" smacked of the English system of advancement by "interest." Today we would use the word "insubordination."

The Lieutenant Governor had been, it is true, a far from ideal civilian commander. As Sparks wrote, it was "a foible with him that his zeal outstripped his knowledge and discretion."[18] In raising and supplying armies, he had regarded intention as a substitute for achievement: he had been disgruntled that his colonel did not fight successfully with imaginary forces. He would give detailed orders—often foolish—and then turn inexplicably vague, forcing Washington to use his own discretion although left unsure how far, without rebuke, he might go. Yet, on the whole, Dinwiddie had been Washington's supporter, if only because the official needed the endlessly energetic and resourceful soldier to get anything in the military line done at all.

For his part, Washington had not hesitated publicly to criticize Dinwiddie. He had attacked the policies of the Lieutenant Governor in a letter to Loudoun who was not only Commander in Chief but also, as Governor of Virginia, Dinwiddie's immediate superior. He had consistently intrigued with Speaker Robinson in efforts to have the popular assembly, the House of Burgesses, oppose those decisions of the Governor and Council which he considered to the disadvantage of the Commonwealth. And, in the heat of his passion, he had more than once stated his case more strongly than accurately.[19]

It was probably his later realization that he had behaved in an unwarranted manner which inspired Washington, at a time when the stakes were much higher and his personal prestige much greater, never to encourage or make use of factions in the Continental Congress. But for the moment, he felt no pangs. He wrote Dinwiddie, "I do not know that I ever gave your honor cause to suspect me of ingratitude, a crime I detest," unless "an open, disinterested behavior carries offense. . . . But I have long been convinced that my actions and their motives have been maliciously aggravated." Since Dinwiddie was leaving, he would like to come to Williamsburg and settle some accounts.[20]

Dinwiddie refused him permission. "You have frequently been indulged with leaves of absence. . . . Surely the commanding officer should not be absent when daily alarmed with the enemy's intentions to invade our frontiers, and I think you are in the wrong to ask it. You have no accounts that I know of to settle with me."[21]

And so the bumbling, energetic, avaricious Lieutenant Governor, who had attracted the spotlight of history by giving early opportunities to one of the world's greatest men, sailed for home and history's obscure shades. It seems sad that he could not enjoy the association that would bring him immortality—but it is not easy to get on with a young whirlwind.

For his part, Washington might have been less cantankerous

had his health not been very seriously giving way. During August he had begun to "labor under a bloody flux"—dysentery. However he had gone about his business, ignoring the difficulty as best he could. About November 1, he started to run a fever. On the 7th he was "seized with stitches and violent pleuritic pains." The army physician at Winchester was Edinburgh-trained Dr. James Craik; he bled the Colonel (as he was to do decades later when the former President was deprived of so much blood that he died). On the 8th Craik bled George again twice, but with so little (or much) effect that Washington's "strength and vigor diminished so fast that in a few days he was hardly able to walk."

Craik confessed that "this complication of disorders"—in the bowels and the lungs—greatly perplexed him, "as what is good for him in one respect hurts him in another." To Washington's fellow officers at least, he did not hide the gravity of the situation. A change of air, he told Captain Stewart, and to be kept quiet was "the best chance that now remains for his recovery." There was no time to get Dinwiddie's permission. Washington handed the command over to Stewart and began a painful retreat to Mount Vernon.[22]

The house proved empty except for servants: brother Jack and his wife were away. Across Dogue Run candles lighted the windows of Belvoir and in some comfortable room moved Sally Fairfax. She did not know he was there or even that he was sick. When correspondence between them was forbidden, he had kept her in touch by writing her menfolk. But that autumn William Fairfax had died and her husband, George William, had sailed to England to handle matters of inheritance. She was alone at Belvoir except for some young ladies; he hesitated to communicate with her.

To the Reverend Charles Green in Alexandria, who doubled

as a physician, Washington sent a call for help, adding, "it is painful to me to write." When Green had come and examined him and gone, George finally wrote Sally telling her in laconic terms of his presence and his illness. Green had prescribed "jellies and such kinds of food." Since there was no one at Mount Vernon who could make such things, "I find myself under a necessity of applying to you for a recipe book," and, indeed, for the materials. He needed some hartshorn shavings and hyson tea, and also a bottle or two of Mountain or Canary wine, as Green wished him to drink a glass or two every day mixed with water of gum arabic.[23]

Having vouchsafed us this letter, history slams the door again. We have no way of knowing whether Sally hurried to the bedside of her admirer.

To his scapegrace crony, Stewart, Washington made a pretense of high spirits, joking about—as Stewart recapitulated— "the pompous grimace and formal prescriptions of the learned faculty." But to Craik he complained that he was getting worse. That was not surprising, the doctor answered, as the malady was "of long standing and hath corrupted the whole mass of blood." Craik warned him not to move from bed, adding "the fate of your friends and country are in a manner dependent upon your recovery."[24]

The reiteration in letters he received that his death would be a major loss to his country of Virginia did not supply comfort to keep him from sinking while the dreary winter months dragged slowly by through descending zones of depression. He mulled over and over how all his efforts at securing a commission in the British establishment had failed, and he concluded that "I now have no prospect left of preferment in a military way." As his turns for the better—during one of which he ordered from England a mahogany card table and a dozen packs of cards— proved only the preludes to new pain and debility, he mourned,

[185]

"My constitution is certainly greatly impaired." He set out in January for Williamsburg and better medical attention, but became so ill on the road that he had to return.[25]

Sally did not visit him as often as he wished. In mid-February he received a letter announcing her husband's safe arrival in London and forwarded it to her with this message: "When you are at leisure to favor us with a visit, we shall endeavor to partake as much as possible of the joy you receive on this occasion."[26]

He heard that the report circulated in Williamsburg that he was dead. Some nights he was "in great extremity" and feared he would not live till morning. As the fever mounted he seemed to recognize in himself the symptoms he had watched helplessly as he had stood by his brother's bed. Surely his coughs were echoes of those with which Lawrence had worn out his life in these very rooms. He wrote Colonel John Stanwix, the British officer who was his immediate superior, that he had "now too much reason to apprehend an approaching decay [tuberculosis], being visited with several symptoms of such a disease."

As he had ruined his constitution, "as I now have no prospect left of preferment in a military way, and as I despair of rendering that immediate service which my country may require from the person commanding their troops, I have some thoughts of quitting my command, and retiring from all public business, leaving my post to be filled by some other person more capable of the task, and who may, perhaps, have his endeavors crowned with better success than mine have been."[27]

In early March 1758, Washington managed to drag himself by slow stages to Williamsburg. It was an anxious as well as a painful journey since he expected to receive there from Dr. John Amson, Virginia's leading physician, either his reprieve or his death warrant. The £3.2.6 he paid Amson proved to be the happiest money he had ever spent, for the doctor assured him he had nothing to fear. These words proved miraculous medicine. He had entered Amson's office a very sick man; he emerged well on the road to recovery. No longer aimed at the grave, his thoughts concentrated on matrimony.[28]

15

Adventures of the Heart

WHEN DANIEL PARKE was born in Virginia during 1669, it seems to have been to realize the Biblical prophecy that the sins of the fathers shall be visited onto the children even unto the third or the fourth generation. That he sent money down the years along with the sins increased their lethalness.[1] But after some of his riches had left the family through the remarriage of a granddaughter-in-law, they went to a hero and thus contributed to the birth of the United States.

Daniel Parke inherited not only money but position. A member of the King's Council while still in his twenties, he struck the Governor with a horsewhip. Having married in Virginia and fathered two daughters, he sailed to England, where he sparkled while his Virginia family lived in relative penury. As colonel and aide-de-camp to Marlborough, he carried the news of Blenheim to Queen Anne, who gave him her miniature set in diamonds and £1000. Then he became Governor of the Leeward Islands.

Even if living poorly for the moment, Parke's two daughters were presumptive heiresses to a huge estate. Lucy married Virginia's celebrated patrician William Byrd. Frances (Nancy) married another inheritor of wealth, John Custis.

Custis knew that Nancy was a shrew, but considered the money he expected to inherit through her as a poultice for ravings. However, after Daniel Parke had been assassinated by an outraged mob in the Leeward Islands, a most amazing will came to light. All Parke's property in the Islands was left to an illegitimate family there. Although the Custises were to get most of the estate in England and Virginia, they were to pay the testator's debts. Bills rolled in from England and then the illegitimate heirs insisted that Parke's extensive obligations in the Leeward Islands be paid from the Custis share. John Custis refused, as he put it, "to enrich a kennel of whores and bastards"; he was sued for £6000.[2]

Since, if he lost the suit, John would get little through his shrewish wife, he concluded she was unbearable and arranged to have it cut on his tombstone that he had only lived after she had died.[*] He used the threat to the estate to justify the miserliness which enabled him to keep his two children under his heel. When he failed to hand over the dowry he had agreed should go with his daughter, her husband abandoned her; and, by refusing the marriage settlements custom required, he kept his son, Daniel Parke Custis, from making several suitable matches. As Daniel grew to lonely middle age, the father found a new weapon. He freed a colored boy born on his estate whom he had named after himself, and threatened, whenever his white son did not obey him, to make Jack his sole heir.

Immersed in such difficulties, Daniel failed to fill most of the civic roles that came almost automatically in Virginia to men of his rank. He was thirty-seven when—it was 1749—he made another try at matrimony.

Martha Dandridge, the future Martha Washington, was eighteen. Her family background has been among genealogists a subject for improvisation and argument which emphasizes that

---

[*] The tombstone states that John Custis had died "aged 71 years, and yet lived but seven years, which was the space he kept a bacheller's home at Arlington. . . . This inscription was put on his tomb by his own positive orders."[3]

it was obscure. Her father served sometimes as a county clerk; when he died in 1756 his survivors did not presume to have cut on his tombstone a coat of arms.[4]

That Martha's parents never rose above simple respectability would under normal circumstances have been a bar between her and the wealthy Custises, but the situation was not normal. The Dandridges were in no position to ask that miser, John Custis, for any substantial marriage settlement. This pleased him, although he was never pleased for long. He offered much of his plate and jewelry to a farmer's wife and when she hesitated, he told her, or so she later swore "that unless she would take them he would throw them into the street for anybody to pick up, . . . that he would rather this defendant should have them than any Dandridge's daughter or any Dandridge that wore a head. . . . Mr. Dandridge's daughter," he explained, "was much inferior to his son . . . in point of fortune."[5]

That the match went through was primarily due to Martha's superlative tact: she charmed the dragon with "a prudent speech."[6] This, plus the gift to Jack of a child's horse, saddle, and bridle, secured the approval of John Custis, who made out a new will in the couple's favor, and then died before he could change his mind.

Proving in this marriage fecund, Martha bore in the seven years four children. Two died in infancy, and all commemorated with the middle name Parke the devilish ancestor who had laid the groundwork of family apprehension and wealth.

Since the lawsuit with his illegitimate relations still hung over him, Daniel Custis did not dare touch his property in England, but money poured in so plentifully from his 17,438 Virginia acres that he and his bride lived grandly at White House Plantation on the Pamunkey River. Martha decorated her rooms with furnishings from England and her person with imported finery. When she rode out, she had a choice between her chariot and her chair. During the social season at Williamsburg, she glowed with gentle sweetness at the balls.

Although George could not foresee the time when he would have to dance every set so that all the women present "could get a touch of him,"[7] even in those days he entered the dancing assemblies as a military hero. It is improbable that he did not bend his great height over the tiny hand of little Mrs. Custis (she was hardly five feet tall). She described herself good-humoredly as "a fine, healthy girl." Her hair was dark, her teeth "beautiful," her eyes hazel, her figure probably already agreeably plump.[8] She wore her elegant clothes with a lack of self-consciousness that seemed to make them an actual part of a pretty, simple soul. In the dance she was quick and affable. Above all, she shed on every occasion she attended an infectious gentleness. She put George in a good humor. However, she was a settled matron, who did not flirt or lead a young hero on. His amorous thoughts floated between Sally and young ladies of fortune eligible for marriage.

During July 1757, Daniel Parke Custis died, leaving Martha, who was still only twenty-six, one of the richest unmarried ladies in all Virginia. (Her estate was tentatively appraised at £23,632.[9]) That the charming widow was now available must have obtruded itself into Washington's meditations during his months of illness since, immediately on securing his reprieve from Dr. Amson, he mounted his horse and rode to White House on the Pamunkey.

The young man who, in March 1758, entered Martha's parlor was described by his friend George Mercer as "straight as an Indian, measuring six feet two inches in his stockings and weighing 175 pounds. . . . His frame is padded with well-developed muscles, indicating great strength. His bones and joints are large, as are his hands and feet. He is wide shouldered but has not a deep or round chest; is neat waisted, but is broad across the hips and has rather long legs and arms. His head is well-shaped, though not large, but is gracefully poised on a superb neck. A large and straight rather than a prominent nose; blue gray penetrating eyes which are widely separated and overhung by a heavy brow. His face is long rather than broad, with high round cheek bones, and terminates in a good firm chin. He has a clear though rather colorless pale skin which burns with the sun. A pleasing and benevolent though a commanding countenance, dark brown hair which he wears in a cue. His mouth is large and generally firmly closed, but which from time to time discloses some defective teeth. [He had one pulled the summer before in Winchester.]* His features are regular and placid with all the muscles of his face under perfect control, though flexible and expressive of deep feeling when moved by emotions. In conversation he looks you full in the face, is deliberate, deferential, and engaging. His demeanor at all times composed and dignified. His movements and gestures are graceful, his walk majestic, and he is a splendid horseman."[11]

Martha must have encouraged the intrepid Colonel since when he went back to Williamsburg after spending (one gathers) the night, it was with the understanding that he would soon return. In hardly more than a week, he was back. On each visit, he inundated Martha's servants with largess, giving almost ten times his usual tips.[12] More importantly to be pleased were Martha's two surviving children John and Martha Parke Custis. The two-year-old girl could be cooed at and dangled under the eyes of her adoring mother, and the boy, who was almost four, was undoubtedly impressed with the stranger's uniform and military acclaim. Perhaps he was glad to drill with the Colonel, a tiny figure beside the big one. Washington must have studied

---

* Washington brought "sponge" toothbrushes by the dozen, tinctures of myrrh and other dentifrices, but they did little good. Almost yearly the following passage appeared in his diary with minor variations: "indisposed with an aching tooth and swelled and inflamed gums." The usual solution was extraction.[10]

the extremely chubby children—so a double portrait shows them—with painful attention, since, should his suit succeed, their upbringing would be his responsibility, and he did not take responsibilities lightly.

George seems to have departed without having secured a promise, yet matters had proceeded so far that the final approaches could be made by letter. Certainly, the couple became engaged before they saw each other again. It seems probable that the ring Washington ordered from Philadelphia on May 4—it cost two pounds sixteen shillings—was a wedding ring.[13]

Militarily, the situation was very different from the previous summer. Then Loudoun had demonstrated utter incompetence. He had sailed most of his army away on an expedition against Louisburg that never got within firing distance of the enemy naval base. During his absence, the French and Indians had battered back the British defenses on the Lake Champlain route by capturing Fort William Henry, while a nearby force of English regulars cowered, afraid to advance to the rescue.

However, far away from the American continent, a parliamentary change had elevated to prime minister a man of great abilities. Although William Pitt's name does not appear in Washington's correspondence, he was revolutionizing Britain's war effort and with it the destiny of George Washington.

Loudoun was recalled. For the summer after George met Martha, Pitt had ordered three campaigns in America: one against Louisburg, one against Ticonderoga, and the third— how Washington must have thrilled when he heard the news!— against Fort Duquesne. To command the Ohio Valley attack, Pitt had appointed Brigadier General John Forbes, a fifty-year-old Scot, who may have lacked the lionlike bravery of Braddock but was an expert on military organization.

So bloodily handled in her extremities since Braddock's defeat, Virginia was now in the mood for effective cooperation: she voted militia to garrison the forts and 2000 men to take part in the advance. Washington's Virginia Regiment was to be brought to its full strength of 1000 and there was to be a second regiment over which Washington established, as far as Virginia could give it, titular command.

However, Washington was now in fact one subordinate officer in a major military effort. Forbes's army included, in addition to the some 1600 men Virginia actually raised, 1200 regular Highlanders, about 2700 Pennsylvanians, and other local forces that brought the total to between six and seven thousand.[14] This was by far the largest army with which Washington had served, about three times the size of Braddock's.

Pitt had finally resolved the old conflict over rank by ordering that Colonial officers should command all regulars of inferior grade. Since only a regular colonel could now command him, Washington felt that he could serve without dishonor beside regulars. However, he still suffered from a sense of injustice as is revealed in a letter asking Colonel Stanwix to "mention me in favorable terms to General Forbes." He did not, so he added in phrases that indicated bitter disillusionment with the aristocratic system of patronage, wish the General to consider him "as a person who would depend upon him for further recommendation to military preferment, for I have long conquered such expectations." He merely wished to be "distinguished in some measure from the *common run* of provincial officers, as I understand there will be a motley herd of us."[15]

He was soon notified politely that the General "puts that confidence in your way of thinking which your merit deserves." Forbes, the letter continued, listened to all and then made up his own mind.[16] Hardly an encouraging answer for the man who had been Braddock's aide and trusted adviser!

Early in April, Washington rode off to take command of his regiment at Winchester, opening a campaign that was to bring him more anger and frustration than any other.

In what way and when George broke to Sally the news of his engagement we do not know. However, we do know that as the summer advanced her admirer's approaching marriage was rubbed into her eyes and ears by sights and sounds moving to Belvoir across Dogue Run. George was expanding Mount Vernon to receive his bride.

His decision not to start over again with an altogether new house determined, through its subsequent enlargements, the nature of the private dwelling which was to become, more than any other, a national shrine. Washington's reasons for rebuilding were certainly economy, speed (he was to be married), and (perhaps above all) an instinctive wish not to disturb what he already loved. The same desire to keep his home personal barred him from employing any architect.

The principle change he now made was to raise the roof, inserting a second story into the middle of the old one-and-a-half-story farmhouse. On the ground floor, he preserved intact the old plan: two rooms on each side of a central hallway in a total space thirty-three-feet deep and forty-seven long. He even kept the old-fashioned (and somewhat clumsy) space-saving device of having the fireplaces placed at angles in the corners of the rooms. This sentenced the core of Mount Vernon to being forever cramped. It also prevented the structure from ever being symmetrical, since, although the whole was uniform in depth, the southern half was a few feet longer than the northern.

To this asymmetry, Washington contributed when, wishing a handsomer staircase up to his new second floor, he placed the landing against the front wall in a manner that forced the doorway to go over to one side. This stairway is to modern eyes the star of the rebuilding, very unornate and masculine for the style of the time. The balusters are so simple that they are almost unique.

The exact dates when the structural decorations were installed in the various rooms cannot be determined without tearing into the walls (which would be desecration), but the evidence indicates that George concentrated, when preparing for Martha, on bringing elegance into the West Parlor. It was here he placed the marble chimney piece and the "neat landskip" above it, both of which he had ordered from England. The room was handsomely paneled, the doors flanked with columns and topped with pediments which (with other details) George had conned and simplified from the plates in such English manuals, ubiquitous in Virginia, as Batty Langley's *Builder's and Workman's Treasury of Designs.*

Somehow, perhaps from viewing Mt. Airy, the architect-planned and recently completed seat of John Tayloe, George became interested in rustication with stone blocks—but he had no intention of splurging. He tried to get the same effect on the exterior of Mount Vernon by cutting trenches in horizontal boards to resemble the breaks between blocks, and mixing sand with his paint to make the surface rough. Four outbuildings were connected with the main house in a military manner by palisades surmounting low brick walls.[17]

As his construction supervisor while he was away in the army, Washington used George William Fairfax, who, we may be sure, kept Sally's mind on what was being done for Martha as he burbled daily of stairways and windowpanes and paneling.

At Fort Cumberland, where he was waiting for the advance on Fort Duquesne that seemed eternally delayed, Washington received a letter from Fairfax answering some questions about the rebuilding. His wife, George William continued, had undertaken another set of answers.[18]

Sally's letter, as was his invariable practice, George later destroyed. However, his reply to her, which she seems to have cherished so greatly that discretion could not make her consign it to the flames, makes it clear that she had twitted him about Martha, implying that a desire he had expressed to visit the settlements was not really because he wished, as he asserted, to protest at Williamsburg Forbes's management of the campaign.

Since the meaning, as well as the authenticity (which is irrefutable), of Washington's reply has been the subject of much controversy, the pertinent parts shall be printed here exactly as they appear in the recently rediscovered manuscript.[19] The reader will note how the seemingly weird punctuation in this very personal missive establishes the hesitations and the dramatic pauses of speech.

Camp at Fort Cumberland 12.th Septr 1758–

Dear Madam,

Yesterday I was honourd with your short, but very agreable favour of the first Inst.^{T}. —how joyfully I catch at the happy occasion of renewing a Corrispondance which I feard was disrelished on your part, I leave to time, that never failing Expositor of all things–and to a Monitor equally as faithful in my own Breast to Testifie. –In silence I now express my joy. –Silence which in some cases–I wish the present–speaks more Intelligably than the sweetest Eloquence.—

If you allow that any honour can be derivd from my opposition to our present System of management you destroy the merit of it entirely in me by attributing my anxiety to the annimating prospect of possessing Mrs. Custis. ——When——I need not name it. –guess yourself. –Should not my own Honour and Country's welfare be the excitement? Tis true, I profess myself a Votary of Love–I acknowledge that a Lady is in the Case–and further I confess, that this Lady is known to you. –Yes Madam as well as she is to one who is too sensible of her Charms to deny the Power, whose Influence he feels and must ever Submit to. I feel the force of her amiable beauties in the recollection of a thousand tender passages that I could wish to obliterate, till I am bid to revive them. –but experience alas! sadly reminds me how Impossible this is. –and evinces an Opinion which I have long entertained, that there is a Destiny, which has the Sovereign controul of our Actions–not to be resisted by the strongest efforts of Human Nature.–

You have drawn me my dear Madam, or rather have I drawn myself, into an honest confession of a Simple Fact–misconstrue not my meaning–'tis obvious–doubt in [it?] not, nor expose it, –the World has no business to know the object of my Love, –declared in this manner to–you when I want to conceal it—— One thing above all things in this World I wish to know, and only one person of your Acquaintance can solve me that or guess my meaning. –but adieu to this, till happier times, if I ever shall see them. –the hours at present are melancholy dull. –neither the rugged Toils of War, nor the gentler conflict of A—— B——s [Assembly Balls?] is in my choice. –I dare believe you are as happy as you say–I wish I was happy also–Mirth, good humour, ease of Mind and. ——what else? cannot fail to render you so, and consummate your Wishes. –[. . .]

I cannot easily forgive the unseasonable haste of my last express, if he deprived me thereby of a single word you intended to add. –the time of the present messenger is, as the last ₥ight have been, entirely at your disposal. –I cannot expect to hear from my Friends more than this once, before the Fate of the Expedition will some how or other be determined, I therefore beg to know when you set out for Hampton, & when you expect to Return to Belvoir again–and I should be glad to hear also of your speedy departure, as I shall thereby hope for your return before I get down; the disappointment of seeing [the failure to see] your family would give me much concern.–[. . .]

Be assured that I am D Madam, with the most unfeigned regard,

Yr most Obedient and Most Obligd H^{ble} Serv^{T}
G. Washington

[198]

NB. Many Accidents happening (to use a vulgar saying) between the Cup and the Lip, I choose to make the exchange of Carpets myself–since I find you will not do me the honour to accept mine.

Sally seems to have written a coy reply in which she told of playing the amorous young heroine in an amateur production of Addison's *Cato*. This elicited from George the question, "Do we misunderstand the true meaning of each other's letters? I think it must appear so, though I would fain hope the contrary, as I cannot speak plainer without–But I'll say no more and leave you to guess the rest."

Forbes's expedition, he continued, would probably fail. "I should think my time more agreeable spent, believe me, in playing a part in *Cato* with the company you mention, and myself doubly happy in being the Juba to such a Marcia as you must make." He then launched into some light speculation about the marital intentions of his friends, but did not refer to his own coming marriage or mention Martha.

"One thing more, and then I have done. You ask if I am not tired at the length of your letter? No, Madam, I am not, nor never can be while the lines are an inch asunder to bring you in haste to the end of the paper. You may be tired of mine by this. Adieu, dear Madam, you possibly will hear something of me or from me before we shall meet. . . . Believe me that I am most unalterably, your most obedient and obliged. . . ."[20]

How can these avowals be made to accord with the undoubted fact that George's marriage to Martha proved very happy, supplied, indeed, the greatest strength that came to him from outside his own person during his entire career? Part of the explanation certainly lies in the tendency of both sexes, when on the eve of marriage, to experience a renewed wave of emotion for the old loves that they are abandoning. Towards further insights into Washington's state of mind, clues may be found in his later philosophizing about love.

In 1795 Washington warned a step-granddaughter to beware lest love become for her "an involuntary passion. . . . In the composition of the human frame there is a great deal of inflammable matter, however dormant it may lie for a time, and . . . when the torch is put to it, *that* which is *within you* must burst into a blaze."[21]

To another step-granddaughter he wrote, "Do not then in your contemplation of the marriage state look for perfect felicity before you consent to wed. Nor conceive, from the fine tales the poets and lovers of old have told us of the transports of mutual love, that heaven has taken its abode on earth. Nor do not deceive yourself in supposing that the only means by which these are to be obtained is to drink deep of the cup and revel in an ocean of love. Love is a mighty pretty thing, but, like all other delicious things, it is cloying; and when the first transports of passion begin to subside, which it assuredly will do, and yield, oftentimes too late, to more sober reflections, it serves to evince that love is too dainty a food to live on *alone,* and ought not to be considered further than as a necessary ingredient for that matrimonial happiness which results from a combination of causes: none of which are of greater importance than that the partner should have good sense, a good disposition, a good reputation, and financial means. Such qualifications cannot fail to attract (after marriage) your esteem and regard into which, or into disgust, sooner or later love naturally resolves itself. . . .

"Experience will convince you that there is no truth more certain than that all our enjoyments fall short of our expectations, and to none does it apply with more force than the gratification of the passions."[22]

To what extent did Washington's relations with Sally involve the gratification of the passions? What did he mean when he wrote, "I feel the force of her amiable beauties in the recollection of a thousand tender passages that I could wish to obliterate till I am bid revive them"? Certainly, whatever was their relationship, it did not raise a tremor of scandal that has been caught by history's seismographs.

George remained a favorite of Sally's father-in-law. He became, if anything, even more than before her husband's close friend. So great, indeed, was his intimacy with George William that their mutual admiration for the same woman, which could not have been altogether hidden, seems to have been not a cause of jealousy but a further bond. This would have involved confidence on the husband's part that his wife and his friend would not overstep whatever limits were set up by the dynamics of their three-cornered relationship. Clearly, George William remained convinced that they never overstepped.

George's love for Sally was no quick passion for a stranger. It extended across years and was woven into the existence at Belvoir which had, even before Sally had set foot there, been a shining part of his life.

Long after Sally and her husband had left his world to live in England, after Belvoir had burned down, the triumphant winner of the Revolution visited the ruins. "When I viewed them," he wrote George William, "when I considered that the happiest moments of my life had been spent there, when I could not trace a room in the house (now all rubbish) that did not bring to my mind the recollections of pleasing scenes, I was obliged to fly from them; and came home with painful sensations, and sorrowing for the contrast."[23]

Letters Sally wrote when she was middle-aged and had suffered many troubles reveal a woman of strong mind and high principles, actually such a Roman matron as she had heard her father-in-law praise in his stoic moods.[24] She must always have added to charms of the body charms of the intellect. But it is clear that in her giddier season she had not managed to look consistently down from cold stoic heights on the passionate youth from next door.

Her bridal journey had brought Sally home to a house that was frequented by a young man of genius and male charm whom her husband profoundly admired. However much she might try to deny it to herself, her punctilious and anxious husband must certainly have seemed, in comparison with his powerful junior, a quivery white rabbit.

Twice as George fought to protect Sally and her world from Frenchmen and redskins, George William bustled almost to the point of fighting. In 1755, on hearing that Washington had been given command of the forces of the Colony, he wrote Dinwiddie that he would like "to serve under my valuable friend." He did not go. In 1757 he wrote George that if the militia had not marched the day before, "I believe I should have accompanied them." He never did. And when, in the early winter of 1757 George limped back from frontier service sick as it seemed to death, George William's letters from England showed him in an anguished dither because Lord Fairfax's brother and heir might cross the ocean and appear at Belvoir. "I beseech you," he wrote Sally, to "endeavor to provide the best provision for his nice stomach. . . . I shall endeavor to engage a butler to go over with me at least for one year."[25]

It would have been easier if Sally had possessed children, but these creators of domestic interest were denied her. It would have been easier if her relationship with George had depended on assignations that could with determination and discretion have been avoided. Even in letters to her she had forbidden him to write, he included requests that she give his regards to other members of her household. Did he actually expect her to do so?

Or was he trying to make their correspondence seem normal to prying eyes, to her eyes, normal even in his own?

To George's admiration Sally seems to have reacted with a sometimes desperate coquetry. Almost all of George's communications to her that survive are those of a complaining lover to an imperious beauty who will not write him letters; who wishes him to communicate with her only through a friend; who has banished him temporarily from Belvoir; who is teaching him by experience how impossible it is for him to revive what he has once known. His plaint is always that she is being less kind to him than she was at some previous time. Yet when he withdraws she comes forward, writing him a saucy letter because he does not hurry to Belvoir to tell her of battles; drawing from him, after his engagement to Martha, a passionate avowal which sends her scurrying into renewed evasiveness.

On the question of her own emotions, whether she loved him or not, she kept him on tenterhooks. "One thing," he wrote, "above all things in this world I wish to know." We may be sure that if she did give him an answer in the morning, she managed to reopen the question before night.

Passion for a woman one cannot truly possess can bring no one peace, and certainly George Washington was bothered by the equivocal nature of his love in relation to his benefactors and friends. His love, he wrote its object, strengthened his belief "that there is a destiny which has the sovereign control of our actions, not to be resisted by the strongest efforts of human nature."

Yet, however storm-driven and star-crossed, the young lovers had their triumph. Surely it was no small and easy matter, in a situation so complicated and intimate, involving so many people they admired, and beset with such desperate quicksands, to find and traverse, year after year, a path that made trouble for none but themselves. Here surely was education for a man who was eventually to steer a new nation through history's desperate quicksands!

At the end of his life Washington, who had not seen Sally for twenty-five years, wrote her that none of the great events of his career, "nor all of them together, have been able to eradicate from my mind those happy moments, the happiest of my life, which I have enjoyed in your company."[26] This reflects the normal human tendency to remember excitement as pleasure. All the evidence that survives from the time his love was actually swaying him indicates that it gave him more sorrow than joy. His proposal to Martha was not his first effort to break the chain.

How much of what had happened before her marriage Martha knew, how long the old love bothered George until it was drowned in his firm, consistent happiness with her, no records tell, but it is clear that she and Sally established cordial terms as neighbors. Martha harbored no permanent resentments. Possessed of instincts about human relations that were almost genius, she may have realized that Sally had made a permanent contribution to her continuing happiness. She did not scintillate and keep anyone rocking on waves of uncertainty; there never was a pretty woman who was less of a coquette; she soon became that character from Washington's boyhood poem *True Happiness:* "a quiet wife, a quiet soul." Her husband was to boast that the basis of their relationship was not "enamoured love" but "friendship."[27] Would he have accepted this happiness so wholeheartedly had he not experienced the bleak and slippery shores of illicit passion?

And could not Sally, who spent most of her mature years in England comforting her querulous husband as he suffered through an endless lawsuit with his highborn relations, could she not feel that she had made a contribution to the emerging United States? Her former lover had become the gentlest of history's great captains, one of the heroes of the human race, because he had learned to curb his passions, to keep in chain ambitions that did not serve his fellow men. Had not some of the fire that finally tempered his steel burned as he stood imploringly by her side?

Wrong Road to Victory

A T FIRST THE British high command laid the blame for the angry controversy over roads less on Washington than Virginians in general. And, indeed, it was from outraged officials at Williamsburg that Washington first learned that General Forbes was being persuaded, as he collected supplies in Philadelphia, that he should not revive the now overgrown road Braddock had cut towards Duquesne and the Ohio. The Philadelphians urged a new road that would lead directly to and from Pennsylvania.

If improved and placed in a monopolistic position by British engineers, Braddock's Road would, after peace had been restored, draw the commerce of the Ohio Valley to Virginia. Near the head of navigation for ocean-going vessels, Alexandria would become the great city Washington all his life envisioned on the Potomac and near Mount Vernon.

Since Alexandria was still a hamlet and Virginia herself had to buy from Philadelphia what manufactured goods she did not import from England, Washington could not object to Forbes procuring supplies in Pennsylvania. Nor could he object to using Raystown (now Bedford, Pennsylvania), within easy reach of Philadelphia, as an intermediate staging point. But the idea that instead of then going sideways thirty miles to Fort Cumberland at the head of Braddock's Road, the expedition should advance in a straighter line to Duquesne, he regarded as a villainous attempt of the Pennsylvanians to sacrifice the public good to their own interest. "It has long been the luckless fate of poor Virginia," he mourned, "to fall victim to the views of her crafty neighbors."[1]

Still in Philadelphia, Forbes entrusted to the commander of the advanced posts, Colonel Henry Bouquet, the delicate task of selecting, without offending any colony, the best route. A Swiss who had served in the armies of three other nations before he joined the British, Bouquet had learned to be an expert conciliator. Washington was obviously the most influential Virginian with the army; Bouquet invited Washington to what he hoped would be a soothing conference.

However Washington, having abandoned his ambitions for "preferment," had now no personal motives for conciliating his superiors in the regular army—and, as a Virginian, he was outraged. In the presence of the paunchy, middle-aged Swiss, who looked more like a benevolent businessman than a soldier, the athletic Colonel breathed fire.

Unembarrassedly (as he revealed in a summary he later sent Bouquet), Washington carried the history of Braddock's Road back to the Ohio Company, which had "at considerable expense" opened the communication that way. The road, he continued, had been improved to within six miles of Duquesne. Although Washington had never examined the area over which the alternate road would go, he had been assured by "the most intelligent Indians" that Braddock's was the easiest route to the Ohio. He was confident that the other route would butt against natural obstacles impossible to overcome. And he insisted that, in any case, a new start would so delay everything that the attack would have to be postponed till the next year, which would mean the southern Indians, on whose assistance Washington pinned great hopes, would desert the English and join the French.

Washington scoffed at the main objection raised to Braddock's Road, "that of the waters to pass." He contended that they "very rarely swell so much as to obstruct passage. The Youghiogheny, which is the rapidest and soonest filled, I with a body of troops have crossed after thirty odd days of almost constant rain." (Washington had, it is true, thus crossed the Youghiogheny in the Fort Necessity campaign, but he neglected to state that they had first been immobilized for most of a week.) As for the double fording of the Monongahela which had been the prologue to Braddock's catastrophe, Washington believed it unnecessary: "I cannot conceive the defile" Braddock had thus avoided with such disastrous results "to be so bad as commonly represented."[2]

Bouquet assured Washington that Forbes "several times expressed to me how much he depends on you and your regiment." Then the Swiss labored to induce the Virginian (as he put it) "to yield to the evidence." After the unconvinced and still outraged Colonel had taken his leave, the frustrated conciliator wrote Forbes, "Most of these gentlemen do not know the difference between a party and an army, and find everything easy that agrees with their ideas."[3]

Washington, indeed, felt called upon to try to go over Bouquet's head. To Major Francis Halkett, Forbes's principal aide, he wrote that if Bouquet succeeded in persuading the General to take "a new way to the Ohio . . . all is lost! All is lost, by Heavens!" The Virginian added, "I am uninfluenced by prejudice, having no hopes or fears but for the general good."[4]

Shown the letter, Forbes reasoned that Colonel Washington must be "the leader and adviser" of "a jealousy arising among the Virginians" which had come "to such a length as to be most singularly impertinent." The General wrote Bouquet that such behavior was "a shame for any officer to be concerned in."[5]

When Washington was officially notified that the Pennsylvania road had been decided upon, he wrote loyally, "I wish with all my soul that you may continue to find little difficulty in opening your road." But the issue swelled in his brain until it verged on a pathological obsession. Closing his mind to the extensive preparation necessary before so large and complicated a military machine could move through the wilderness (the very activities at which Forbes most showed his abilities), Washington was soon insisting that had it not been for the disastrous choice of roads, Duquesne would probably already be in British hands.*[6]

Washington's dysentery had returned and he was again identifying in his aching body what might be deadly symptoms of tuberculosis. It was in these weeks that he indiscreetly confided to paper his love for Sally. And from a still stationary post on the near side of the Alleghenies he wrote Speaker Robinson a letter as confused as it was passionate:

"We are still encamped here, very sickly, and quite dispirited at the prospect before us." All hope of glory "is now no more! 'Tis dwindled into ease, sloth, and fatal inactivity, and, in a word, all is lost, if the ways of men in power, like the ways of Providence, are not inscrutable; and why [are] they not? For we who view the actions of great men at so vast a distance can only form conjectures agreeable to the small extent of our

---

* The historical consensus seems to be that Washington was in the wrong. Hon. J. W. Fortesque, in his *History of the British Army*, criticizes Braddock for not having disembarked at Philadelphia and advanced directly for his objective, thus saving distance and time, improving supply and carriage, and making available better forage. Knollenberg points out that, when Washington argued that the distance from Philadelphia to the Ohio was only nineteen miles longer by Braddock's Road, he calculated a route that widely bypassed Forbes's staging point at Raystown. For practical purposes, Forbes's route was forty miles shorter than Braddock's. One was not necessarily more mountainous than the other, and Forbes's route avoided dangerous crossings of both the Youghiogheny and the Monongahela.[7]

knowledge and ignorant of the comprehensive schemes intended, mistake plaguily, in judging by the lump. This may be and yet every f—l [fool] will have his notions, prattle and talk away, and pray, why may not I?"

His notion was that unless his commanders were acting under orders from abroad, "they are d—ps [dupes] or something worse to P—s—v—n [Pennsylvanian] artifice. . . . Nothing now but a miracle can bring this campaign to a happy issue."

Stating that 2000 men had only succeeded in cutting the new road to the foot of the worst barrier, Laurel Ridge, Washington exclaimed, "See, therefore, how our time has been misspent; behold the golden opportunity lost and perhaps never regained. How is it to be accounted for? Can G—l F—s [General Forbes] have orders for this? Impossible. Will then our injured country pass by such abuses? I hope not. Rather let a full representation of the matter go to His Majesty. Let him know how grossly his honor and public money have been prostituted. I wish I was sent immediately home as an aide to some other on this errand. I think without vanity I could set the conduct of this expedition in its true colors, having taken some pains, perhaps more than any other, to dive into the bottom of it."[8]

Washington's reference to England as "home" reveals that his rebellion against his English commanders had not taken forms that lay in the future. And his desire to have the legislature send him on a mission to attack his commander presaged problems he was to face from the other side of the fence during the Revolution when his generals sometimes served also in the Continental Congress. He was now in a similar double position, having just been elected to the House of Burgesses.

The constituency was the region around Winchester where he had been badly defeated three years before. This time he had also suffered from the handicap of not being present—he was trapped at Fort Cumberland—but the officers at Fort Loudoun were extremely active in his behalf, as were various influential Virginians from within the district and, like Sally's husband, from without. Such reports from his campaign manager as, "Will the hatter and his oily spouse show the greatest spirit in the cause," were promising, and, indeed he got the votes of 309 of the 396 voters. A supporter attributed his victory to "your humane and equitable treatment of each individual and your ardent zeal for the common cause." Liquid persuasives were not overlooked by his friends who distributed twenty-eight gallons of rum, fifty of rum punch, thirty-four of wine, forty-six of beer, and two of cider. Far from protesting the bill sent him for this quart and a half per voter, Washington wrote, "I hope no exception were taken to any that voted against me, but that all were alike treated and all had enough. . . . My only fear is that you spent with too sparing a hand."[9]

In his letter to Robinson, Washington had begun by considering the possibility that "comprehensive schemes" he did not understand might explain Forbes's behavior, but had ended by stating that perhaps better than anyone, "I could set the conduct of this expedition in its true colors." As a matter of fact, he did not glimpse at all the large forces that were determining the fate of the campaign and indeed of the entire French war in America.

A hint had been given him when in May he was still mobilizing his regiment at Winchester. He had found there a crowd of Cherokees and other southern Indians that soon augmented to seven hundred. As he was trying, more or less vainly, to send them out against their traditional enemies, the Ohio tribes who had been raiding the Virginia frontier, Forbes's aide Halkett wrote him an appeal to keep the southern Indians from coming towards Pennsylvania, where efforts were being made to wean from the French those very Ohio tribes.[10] However, Washington continued to think in terms of loosing the southern Indians on the Mingoes, Shawnees, and Delawares. He tried to keep the Cherokees from going home, and when they went, dreamed passionately of calling them back.

Washington did not know that, because of British naval action in the Atlantic, the political tide was shifting in the forest. A blockaded Canada was unable to import the necessary Indian goods to keep its fur trade active or to reward warriors. The British agent to the northern Indians, Sir William Johnson, was making use of this situation to bring the Iroquois back to their traditional British loyalty, and the Iroquois were putting pressure on their vassals in the Ohio Valley. From the proprietors of Pennsylvania, Johnson had secured a trump card which he was waiting to play: the agreement to return to the tribes a huge tract in the Ohio Valley which they regretted having, at a drunken orgy, sold. The tribes were being summoned to a great council to be held at Easton, Pennsylvania, in October.

Washington need not have lectured Forbes on the importance of Indian allies: one reason for Forbes's delay in marching was that he was waiting for the Indian negotiations to mature.

In the meanwhile, Forbes was most sympathetic with the idea of having Colonials prepared to fight the Indians in their own manner. Although he could not appreciate what a sacrifice this was for the Virginia Regiment, who had so long drilled and dressed themselves to be like regulars, he gladly accepted Washington's offer to put his men "in Indian dress," i.e., hunting shirts and leggings.

" 'Tis unbecoming dress, I confess, for an officer," Washington mourned; the British did consider the costume "extraordinary"; yet all were pleased to have some forces that could proceed "as light as any Indian in the woods."[11]

That Washington's obsession about roads had not entirely swamped his judgment was shown when Forbes asked his opinion on the possibility of opening Braddock's Road to the extent necessary to serve as a feint that would draw French attention from the advance of the main force down the new road. This, Washington wrote, would be "a thing I should be extreme[ly] fond of" if it could be made practicable, but, since communication could not be established between the roads through the wilderness, a small force on Braddock's Road would be a sacrifice, and staging a large force would create unwarrantable delays.[12]

Deathly ill, Forbes at last advanced towards the frontier in a litter suspended between the rump of one horse and the head of another. After he had reached the camp at Raystown, he called a conference at his lodgings with his colonels, at which he expressed interest in suggestions on how best to avoid a repetition of Braddock's fiasco.

Leaping at the opportunity, Washington sent the general a letter and two drawings. One drawing expressed "my thoughts on a line of march through a country covered with woods" and the other "how that line of march may be formed in an instant into an order of battle." He envisioned "a forced march" of 4000 privates "with field pieces only, unencumbered with wagons."

The Virginian realized that the British troops, trained to fight *en masse* in open fields, could not think for themselves but needed always to be under the orders of an officer. To achieve mobility in the woods, he urged that the army be subdivided from the commands of captains downwards into increasingly smaller units until "every noncommissioned officer will have a party to command under the eye of a subaltern, as the subalterns will have under the direction of a captain, etc." This should be done for the whole force, he believed, but if Forbes felt that would be going too far, it should at least be done for the advanced division.

Washington's battle tactics assumed that "if the necessary precautions are observed" in sending out such flankers as he recommended, the enemy attack "must always be in front." The first division would then "file off to the right and left and take to the trees." The second would penetrate into the woods much farther to the right, trying to get on that flank of the enemy. And to fool the French and Indians, by following "a practice different from anything they have ever yet experienced from us," it would be the "rear-guard division" that would vanish into the forest in a wide arc to the left. The middle of the column, 2500 men, would stand in the road as a reserve, protected by 600 flankers stationed behind trees. Washington included in his sketches six cannon, but could find no use of them. If, however, Forbes had Indians, they should be ordered to go round "unperceived" and fall on the rear of the enemy, who would then be surrounded.[13]

What Forbes thought of all this is not recorded, but we do know that he was feeling in no friendly mood towards Washington and the other Virginia officers. When he summoned them privately to headquarters, it was not to solicit advice but to excoriate them for what he called their "weakness" in declaring "so publicly in favor of one road without their knowing anything of the other." When the provincials had filed out, the General commented that the scolding should "cure them from coming upon this topic again."[14] But he underestimated the stubbornness of Virginia's Colonel.

In mid-October, Loyal Hannon, a strongpoint built by 1500 men on the far side of that formidable obstacle, Laurel Ridge, was ready to receive the main army. Washington led his regiment as part of the general march. For eight days, torrential rains fell, creating washouts and mire, falling horses, stuck wagons and cannon. Every failure that was unfortunate for the cause seemed to vindicate Washington's judgment: his emotions must have been torn.

From Loyal Hannon he wrote Francis Fauquier, Dinwiddie's

successor, who had been egging him on in his opposition to the new road, that it was "indescribably bad. . . . This is a fact nobody here takes upon him to deny! The General and a great part of the troops, etc., being yet behind, and the weather growing very inclement, must, I apprehend, terminate our expedition for this year at this place."*[15]

As Forbes swung painfully after his army on his litter, he heard from the Indian conference at Easton that Sir William Johnson's trump card had worked: the Iroquois had commanded their compatriots and vassals in the Ohio Valley to make peace with the English. The Moravian missionary, Christian Frederick Post, was carrying the news to France's Indian allies encamped in the shadow of Fort Duquesne. But Forbes was far from sure that the effect would be general or quick enough to help the present campaign.

When the general caught up with his army he called a council—Washington attended with the other colonels—to advise him whether he should proceed against Duquesne or merely hold Loyal Hannon as a starting place for the following summer. Three arguments were put forward for advancing: (1) The enemy might be driven from the Ohio. (2) Further Indian raids on the frontier might be prevented. (3) There was a need to justify the expenses of the expedition. Negative arguments were seven: (1) Lack of clothes in approaching winter. (2) Lack of provisions for men and horses. (3) If existing provisions were used up, a winter encampment at Loyal Hannon could not be supplied. (4) Knowledge was lacking of the enemy strength at

---

* Washington's strange inability to raise his eyes from his own backyard is again revealed by his not mentioning in his correspondence an action on the Great Lakes of the greatest importance to his campaign. An English hit-and-run raid, launched from a rebuilt fort at Oswego, had destroyed Fort Frontenac (Kingston, Ontario), a French bastion on the route from Montreal to Fort Niagara and beyond. The British had captured irreplaceable quantities of stores and ammunition intended for Fort Duquesne, and also the entire enemy fleet which kept open those communications on Lake Ontario on which all the French western positions relied.

Duquesne. (5) The danger of losing their cannon. (6) Even if taken, Duquesne could not be held, as the enlistments of most of the Colonials (this did not include Washington's Virginia Regiment) expired on December 1, in nineteen days. (7) A defeat would bring all the Indians, not excepting those who had just made peace at Easton, down on the settlements.

Washington felt vindicated as a prophet of doom when the conference decided as he himself voted: "The risks being so obviously greater than the advantages, there is no doubt as to the sole course that prudence dictates."[16]

The next day Washington's life was put, so he wrote after he had passed through the Revolutionary War, "in as much jeopardy as it had ever been before or since." Scouts rushed into the camp to report that a large enemy reconnaissance party was within three miles. Forbes ordered out 500 of Washington's Virginians, under Lieutenant Colonel Mercer. Listening anxiously in the camp, Washington heard "hot firing." As the sounds seemed to be coming nearer, he concluded that his men were being driven back, and secured Forbes's permission to march with a group of volunteers to the rescue.

After his force had come to within what he judged was half a mile of the firing, the sounds ceased. He sent scouts ahead to find out what was happening and to tell Mercer of his approach. Then he led his own men slowly ahead through thick woods in deepening twilight.

Moving shadows appeared around them under the bare trees; musket fire flashed and banged. Washington's men hurriedly raised their guns and returned the fire. However, in a moment of silence, a voice out there shouting orders came clear to Washington's ears; it was a familiar voice. A face he glimpsed when an opponent clumsily showed himself belonged to the Virginia Regiment!

Washington, as he remembered, ran "between two fires,

knocking up with his sword the presented pieces." Bullets sped around him, killing, before the two ensanguined groups could be made to understand, fourteen men and wounding twenty-six. As he stared down, himself untouched, at the senselessly destroyed bodies of his followers, Washington could get little satisfaction from the fact that his own invulnerability had again been demonstrated.[17]

Out of this unfortunate event came intelligence big with history. Mercer had captured three prisoners: they reported that the French garrison at Duquesne was small, and, more significantly, that the Indian sheds were empty: the Frenchmen's all important Indian allies had departed. If this were true, Forbes wrote, it "gives me great hopes." He decided to assume it was true.[18]

He selected 2500 of the most able-bodied men; they were to carry no tents, only knapsacks and blankets. Provisions and ammunition carts were limited to the minimum, artillery to some light guns. Building the road and leading the march was the task of two companies of artificers and a wide variety of provincials. However cantankerous, Washington was the most experienced of the provincial officers. Accorded for this one maneuver the rank of brigadier general, he was entrusted, under detailed orders, with the command of this advance division.

The Pennsylvanians in Washington's brigade were sent far ahead: they were to pause at a suitable spot and build a redoubt. With his main body, Washington climbed Chestnut Ridge, the last rocky barrier that intervened before the Ohio Valley. After six miles, the road built by Forbes's engineers came to a ragged end. The route ahead was supposed to have been blazed. As his men lounged by their fires, Washington entered the forest to see what the next day's task would be. Through deep leafless webs of black branches, the setting sun cast red light which the snow at his feet reflected up again against the tree trunks. However, the blazes Washington could find were few and unclear. Where ice clung to the rocks in a rapidly flowing stream, he could not determine how it was planned that he get a road across. He wrote Forbes for an engineer.

In the meanwhile, he had to be his own engineer. At dawn the next morning, the forest echoed with ax strokes. Trees crashed, branches were lopped away, trunks were laid side by side: sometimes to bridge streams, sometimes as causeways through marshes. That day they advanced six miles without escaping from the natural entanglements of the Ridge. The next day, the blazed hints gave out altogether. "I have been sadly puzzled," Washington wrote, "for want of a guide." He pressed ahead anyway, on a now generally downward route, and by nightfall his men were bridging Bushy Run.

The cold skies were bright overhead, but even at midday the tangled forest stems to the right and left blocked and bewildered the eyesight. Unable to hold his men together—"a straggling front" was necessary to expeditious cutting—Washington kept flanking parties ever out, but was worried as to what Indians lurked just beyond his flankers: no one knew for sure that the Ohio tribes had been neutralized. Washington complained at having no Indians of his own, and undoubtedly longed for the Catawbas and Cherokees whom the high command he did not trust had discouraged in pursuit of peace with Virginia's red enemies.

When Washington finally reached the camp the Pennsylvanians had been fortifying, he received what seemed desperate news. "I fear," he wrote Forbes, "we have been greatly deceived with regard to the distance from hence to Fort Duquesne." Woodsmen thought they were still thirty miles away. (And only twelve days remained before most of the army would disband!)[19]

Washington now marched ahead with a thousand men to establish another post beyond Turtle Creek and then cut back towards Bouquet's division, which had undertaken the main task of road building. Some Indian tracks were sighted, but there was no gunfire. He was cutting back when the main army appeared.

With Bouquet now in front and Washington in the rear covering the artillery, all advanced. As they came nearer to Duquesne —no one knew exactly how near—Braddock's fate was in every mind. Precautions were doubled and redoubled, even to sending dogs back to Loyal Hannon so there would not be a bark. But the flanking parties on their eternal tours through the woods heard no cracking twigs that a fox did not crack; saw no human footprints in the snow but their own.[20]

On December 24, only six days before disbanding time, the army halted to get its bearings—in exactly what direction and how far away was Duquesne?—when an Indian brought in strange news: he had seen "a very thick smoke . . . extending in the bottom along the Ohio." A few hours later, more news, which Washington thus summarized: "The enemy . . . burned the fort and ran away (by the light of it) at night, going down the Ohio by water, to the number of about five hundred men. . . . The possession of this fort has been a matter of great surprise to the whole army."[21]

It was Christmas morning when Washington rode to the plague spot which had spread the anguish that for the last four years he had labored to eradicate. On the neck of land where, before the fighting had started, he had wished the Ohio Company to build, there stood the smoldering remains of a small square fort, each wall sixteen feet thick and built like a mill dam of squared logs transversely placed: various wrecked outworks were visible. On the other bank of the Allegheny was a large parallelogram with inside it the stacks of thirty burned-out houses. It was a melancholy rather than a savage scene as the smoke rose silently towards the winter heavens—but there were reminders. In the powder magazine that had not been exploded there lay enough scalping knives to fill a good size wagon, and all around the forest there was a scattering of human bones.[22]

Never had destiny dealt a man a greater anticlimax, a success more likely to make him doubt himself. The desolation he saw before him realized what had been his greatest hope during what had seemed an unending time of arduous and discouraging service. Yet the triumph had been accomplished by men he had attacked and mistrusted, men, who refusing his advice and spurning his importunity, had pursued tactics that he was sure would produce disaster.

Supposing he had actually, as he had asked to do, gone to London to agitate against Forbes? What a fool he would have looked had he been complaining in a ministry of Forbes's stupidity "or something worse" when the news came that Duquesne had been triumphantly captured! Yes, Duquesne had been triumphantly captured, but he knew neither how nor why.*

However, the war was by no means over. Canada, the seat of French power on the continent, had been no more than nicked. The Allegheny still flowed from French-held territory to the Forks of the Ohio, and Forbes could do nothing permanent there. Indeed, he had barely enough provisions to stay long enough to hold a treaty with the Delawares who were gathering to express their friendship for the victor. Whatever fort the English would build to protect their conquest would have to wait till the next summer.

A detachment was to spend the frozen season encamped miserably at the Forks. Washington "endeavored to show" Forbes that they should be regulars; the General replied that he

---

* Bouquet attributed the total success of the campaign to Forbes, who took the time to leave nothing to chance; who brought about the treaty with the Ohio tribes, which Bouquet considered "the blow that has knocked the French on the head"; and who refused to yield to Braddock's Road, "which would have been our destruction."[23]

had no royal orders that would justify such an assignment. Under the command of a Pennsylvania officer 200 provincials, including a group from the Virginia Regiment, were left behind, while the English troops marched happily away.

The unfortunate Virginians thus marooned in a frozen waste had, Washington protested, "hardly rags to cover their nakedness."[24] Who could say that they would be sent enough food: England had left Colonials in the lurch before. Who could say that the French would not come down, recapture the Forks, and rebuild Duquesne? Unless precautions were taken—and who could take them better than Colonel Washington?—his comrades might perish from want; the Virginia frontier might soon be again aflame.

Yet these were all contingencies: a major blow had been successfully struck. It would take a new throw of history's dice to change what had happened—a throw that might never come. As long as the existing situation lasted—it might be forever— every Virginia scalp in the Shenandoah and Ohio Valleys could nestle undisturbed on its skull. And Washington, all his efforts to get into the British establishment having failed, regarded himself as solely in "the public service of this colony."[25]

Washington had often before dreamed of retiring from the fight, had threatened to do so, but had stayed on. Now he wrote no angry letters, but let it be known that he intended to resign. His determination was not shaken when the news caused dismay among his officers and incited desertions among his men.[26] The chain of dread responsibility that had held Washington to the service became so weakened that it snapped.

At least one of Washington's closest friends attributed his flight from war and arms to the soft influence of Martha. Although the retiring Colonel must have found reassuring the thought that an agreeable domestic life lay before him, he himself never gave this as a reason for his resignation. Years later, he told Humphreys that he had been forced out of the army by ill health: "his constitution became much impaired, and many symptoms menaced him so seriously with consumption." Certainly, he was far from well, but he was less dangerously ill than he had been a year before. (After he got to Belvoir, he was laid up for only a few weeks.) It is in his correspondence with his officers that we find the explanation, then uppermost in his mind.[27]

His officers—there were twenty-seven signatures—sent him a "humble address." They recalled "the happiness we have enjoyed and the mutual honor we have acquired together. . . . In our earliest infancy, you took us under your tuition, trained us up in the practice of that discipline which alone can constitute good troops. . . . Your steady adherence to impartial justice, your quick discernment and invariable regard to merit . . . first heightened our natural emulation and our desire to excel. . . . Judge then how sensibly we must be affected with the loss of such an excellent commander, such a sincere friend, and so affable a companion! How rare it is to find those amiable qualifications blended together in one man? How great the loss of such a man? Adieu to that superiority which the enemy have granted us over other troops! . . .

"It gives us additional sorrow, when we reflect, to find our unhappy country will receive a loss no less irreparable than ourselves. Where will it meet a man . . . so able to support the military character of Virginia?" They begged him to remain "for another year, and to lead us on to assist in completing the glorious work of extirpating the enemy." They begged to be "led on by the man we know and love."[28]

Washington's reply (which has been recently discovered*) was in effect his farewell to the officers he had served with during the French and Indian War. He wrote with that turgidity

---

* See the complete text in Appendix A.

of style that still accompanied his strong emotions:"It was really the greatest honor of my life to command gentlemen who made me happy in their company and easy in their conduct. . . . That I have for some years (under uncommon difficulties, which few were thoroughly acquainted with), been able to conduct myself so much to your satisfaction, affords the greatest pleasure I am capable of feeling; as I almost despaired of attaining that end—so hard a matter is it to please, when one is acting under disagreeable restraints. . . . Had everything contributed as fully as your obliging endeavors did to render me satisfied, I never should have been otherwise, or have come to know the pangs I have felt at parting with a regiment," for which he had great affection and regard. "This brings on reflections that fill me with grief and I must strive to forget them."

After five arduous years as Virginia's leading soldier, George Washington returned in January 1759 to civilian life with bitterness, resentful of injustice, stung with a sense of unmerited failure. He was not to serve again in any military capacity for seventeen years.

III

True Happiness

CHAPTER

17

Domestic Enjoyments

CONCERNING the marriage ceremony of George Washington and Martha Dandridge Custis nothing is known for certain except that it took place on January 6, 1759.[1] It was probably celebrated either at White House Plantation or the nearby Episcopal Church.

That some disagreement between the newly married couple became a subject of discussion and disapproval among their acquaintance in Williamsburg is shown by a letter which Governor Fauquier sent George a month and a day after the nuptials: "We all wish you and Mrs. Washington as well as you wish each other, in which perhaps you are not now on a par."[2]

The bride had accompanied her husband to Williamsburg for his first session in the Assembly. His fellow Burgesses voted him their thanks for "his faithful services to His Majesty and this Colony, and for his brave and steady behavior from the first encroachments and hostilities of the French and their Indians, to his resignation after the happy reduction of Fort Duquesne." He is said to have risen and bowed and blushed;[3] certainly he was pleased, for it was for such recognition that he had labored; but in his heart he knew that the "happy reduction of Fort Duquesne" had made a fool of him: it had been achieved through methods of which he had loudly disapproved.

Before his first session as a Burgess was over, Washington left Williamsburg to take Martha and his two stepchildren to their future home, which they had not yet seen. As they lumbered northwards in the Custis coach, he wrote ahead in agitation, ordering his manager, John Alton, to get the key to Mount Vernon from Sally's husband:

"You must have the house well cleaned and were you to make fires in the rooms below, it would air them. You must get two of the best bedsteads put up, one in the hall room and the other in the little dining room that used to be, and have beds made on them against we come. You must also get out the chairs and tables and have them very well rubbed and cleaned. The staircase ought also to be polished in order to make it look well. Inquire about in the neighborhood and get some eggs and chicken, and prepare in the best manner for our coming. You need not, however, take out any more of the furniture than the beds, tables, and chairs, in order that they may be well rubbed and cleaned."[4]

George was eager to please, and whatever were Martha's first impressions of the not completed, partially furnished, and only moderately commodious bachelor's nest embedded in its beautiful view, she had the will to say what would most gratify her husband, and the tact to judge what that would be. Despite early disagreements and perhaps even regrets, Martha soon created for George what he had yearned for but not possessed since he was a little child: a happy home.

His mother's final comment on his achievements in the French and Indian War and his bitter resignation was that there had been "no end to my trouble while George was in the army, but he has now given it up."[5] This epitomizes the lack of sympathy or understanding that had made George find Ferry Farm an unhappy place once his father had died.

Like his mother, Martha wished George to stay at her side,

but who would not want his wife so to wish—and she did not scold. As he rode through history's great storms, she kept glowing with the warmth of love a hearth that yearned gently for his return. If she were called to ride out by his side, she might go reluctantly, but she never failed him in the presence of others—not once in forty years!—and she carried everywhere, like a brand from the hearth, those "domestic enjoyments"[6]—it is Washington's phrase—which she shared and made delightful for him.

Although she served her responsibilities so stoutly, Martha was to suffer much from the intervention in her marriage of great affairs. However, she did not seem at the start menaced by such troubles. Her husband had firmly turned his back on the service where he had, as he complained, acted "under disagreeable restraints."[7]

Concerning the decisive campaigns of 1759, during which the British took Ticonderoga, Niagara, and Quebec, Washington wrote, "The scale of fortune in America is turned greatly in our favor, and success is become the boon companion of our fortunate generals." Having twice in one sentence attributed the turn in events to luck rather than military skill, he continued, "I am now, I believe, fixed at this seat with an agreeable consort for life, and hope to find more happiness in retirement than I ever experienced amidst a wide and bustling world."[8]

The capture of Montreal during 1760 completed the conquest of Canada, and brought the war in America to a close. When, more than two years later, the Seven Years War in all its phases ended with a general British victory,* Washington hailed the global tranquillity with a civilian's joy, hoping it would make

---

* According to the terms of the Peace of Paris, England retained her forts, at Gibraltar and on Minorca, which commanded the Mediterranean; received from France, Canada and Nova Scotia and several islands in the West Indies; and laid the basis for her empire in India. Washington and the future United States were to profit during the American Revolution from France's desire for revenge and determination to right the balance of power.

"the trade to this Colony flow in a more easy and regular channel."[9]

John Wollaston's portrait of Martha when she was Mrs. Custis shows an extremely pretty woman. She had a fine forehead; brows forming a wide, low arch over large eyes, which as other portraits also show were slightly slanting; a powerful hooked nose; a strong, rounded chin. This bold, handsome face was especially piquant because it clothed a timid spirit: she stood up to the world less with self-confidence than with courage. Her stature was diminutive; her figure soft, rounded, and very feminine, tapering to delicate extremities. In 1775 she ordered gloves "to fit a small hand and pretty large arm."[10]

To prepare for her wedding, Martha ordered from England "one genteel suit of clothes for myself to be grave but not extravagant and not to be mourning." She wanted enough yellow brocaded grosgrain silk to make a costume, some pink lutestring, a white and a garnet egret, and a long, white necklace. But when it came to a nightgown, she sent back an old one "to be dyed of a fashionable color fit for me to wear, and beg you would have it done better than that I sent you last year."[11]

Since Martha was most concerned with fineness of materials, she commonly ordered stuffs she liked made over, a silk suit, for instance, changed to a sack coat in 1763.[12] Other women often regarded her costumes as plain. This may have been a slight sorrow to her husband, who enjoyed splashy clothes, livery, equipage, but no one ever mistook her plainness for shabbiness. When she was the president's wife, women commented on how she made the befeathered ambassadresses look like popinjays.

After her husband had died, Martha took out of the carefully kept archive at Mount Vernon his letters to her, her letters to him. She burned them.[13] This possessive and overprotective act by a widow who had, during so much of her marriage, been forced to share her husband with an imperious and curious world, left in existence only two authentic letters from him to her. (The most important is quoted in Chapter Twenty-four.) Of her communications to him, we have only a postscript added in 1767 to a report by his estate manager, Lund Washington. Because it is unique, this note deserves to be quoted entire:

My dearest,

It was with very great pleasure I see in your letter that you got safely down. We are all very well at this time, but it is still rainy and wet. I am sorry you will not be at home soon, as I expected you. I had rather my sister would not come up so soon, as May would be a much pleasanter time than April. We wrote to you last post. As I have nothing new to tell you, I must conclude myself.

> Your most affectionate
> Martha Washington.[14]

Although flames licking paper in Martha's hearth consumed forever the most intimate evidence concerning the Washingtons' domesticity,* many other sources of evidence exist.

Usually, the American Revolution marks a great divide in the keeping of papers. Before this world-shaking event, most Colonials considered their affairs of so little interest that, as soon as a document had outlived its practical use, it was thrown away. But after the Revolution, the citizens of the United States felt that every detail concerning themselves was of lasting moment. They jotted journals, scribbled memoirs, piled attics high with correspondence tied in packets.

Before history had dreamed of the Revolution, to a degree prodigious in that place and time, as if some inner voice had

---

* It is an example of how suppression backfires that Martha's act has given rise to rumors, which no evidence substantiates, that she was hiding major rifts in her marriage.

announced to him his destiny, Washington was from the first fascinated with the records of his existence. Who preserves the childish copybooks in which he wrote his first lessons or notes of his boyish expenditures? George Washington did. Beginning in his teens he kept copies of letters, soon, however, omitting those most personal.

Diary notations exist for some three quarters of the days that made up Washington's sixteen years between wars: they fill over 500 printed pages. They are concerned with the physical facts of his life: the weather, where he rode, whom he visited, who came to visit, how he amused himself, illnesses and deaths. The diaries also served as records of his farming and breeding operations. Unlike most journals, they never contain those personal soliloquies in which a man speaks freely to his most intelligent, beloved, and understanding friend—himself.

As if he felt posterity leaning over his shoulder, George, who never wore his heart on his sleeve, kept his notations dry and factual. When he wished to record a matter that was unsuited to the eyes of a stranger, he used a cipher. In 1771 he placed the following letters after the following dates: Feb. 20, S; Mar. 26, A; April 12, a; April 25, a; May 16, M; June 4, A; June 9, A; June 19, A; June 23, A; June 29, A; and July 20, A.[15]

Despite such reticences, existing documents reveal the main features of Washington's married life and also many a detail. We see Martha dangling from her belt the practical symbol of domestic control: a sunburst of keys. Although on a much greater scale, a Virginia plantation was as self-contained as a frontier farm. The housewife had tasks which, if less backbreaking, demanded greater skills. At these Martha was expert. Like any humble farmer's wife, she left outdoors' work to her husband: the smokehouse, the kitchens, the mansion house were her domain. She was particularly expert at hanging and curing meat. ("You know," Washington was to write when he sent Lafayette a

barrel of hams, "Virginia ladies value themselves on the goodness of their bacon.") She saw to collecting ashes for soap and to
the distilling of "a good deal of rose and mint water, etc." Hers
was what George admitted as "the drudgery of ordering and
seeing the table properly covered and things economically
used."[16]

The health, training, and behavior of the household slaves
were, in the first instance, her responsibilities. Like other Virginia ladies, she probably kept a chest of simple medicines in the
bedroom that was also her office. At her feet sat girls engaged in
fine sewing, for craftswomen were not hired but grown on the
estate. She would walk out to supervise what was almost a small
factory, where spinners and seamstresses prepared clothes for all
hands (a seamstress was required to make nine shirts a week
"with shoulder straps and good sewing"). She also decided on
the slaves' privileges: when, for instance, "Old Nanny" was
called to task for raising for her own private benefit "seventy-one
turkeys and other fowls," the slave replied, "Mistress allows
it."[17]

Along with her charms and skills, Martha brought George
substantial wealth. John Parke Custis's property—land, slaves,
cash in Virginia, cash and securities in England—had been
valued at £23,632. One third of this came, with certain restrictions concerning alienation, to George as Martha's husband. The
other two thirds, divided between his stepchildren, was placed
under his administration.[18]

This was, according to the business organization of the time,
an advantage for all parties, since trust officers did not exist and
women were not trained to manage their own affairs. When the
possessions of a widow and her children had to be handled by a
private gentleman, it seemed best to have him deeply involved
as the widow's husband. According to our modern ideas, for him
to become during his lifetime the possessor of her estate was

outrageous—and it did then create abuses*—yet if the husband were, like George, an efficient, loving, and honest man, the arrangement proved excellent for all.

Before his marriage, George (his military reputation aside) had been no more than a minor planter. Martha changed that, and his transformation to another economic sphere was assisted in 1761 by the death of Lawrence's widow, which made him the owner rather than just the renter of Mount Vernon.

Martha had brought to Mount Vernon almost no Custis luxuries except the coach. She and her husband ordered new luxuries from England: clothes, furniture, materials, decorations, rugs, china, glass, candles, spices, sweetmeats, and wine by the butt (150 gallons). The tobacco planter even sent abroad for snuff.

There were thirteen house servants: Breechy the waiter was assisted by Mulatto Jack, the handyman; Doll the cook had a scullion, Beck; Jenny washed, Mima ironed, Betty did fine sewing for Martha, and Moll, who doubled as nurse, did the same for the children. Little Julius waited on Jackie, little Rose on Patsy, Sally on Martha, Bishop on George, and John Alton assisted as a sort of housekeeper and executive officer. Washington also listed as "servants in and about the house" five carpenters, their boy helper, and a weaver.[19]

Martha shone as a hostess. "She possesses," wrote the French traveler Brissot de Warville, "that amenity and manifests that attention to strangers which render hospitality so charming." A Virginia planter's wife could have no more valuable a public quality. In the seven years between 1768 and 1775, the Washingtons entertained about 2000 guests. When George, who spent most of his active hours in the saddle, dismounted at the front

* Some of Washington's most wearing self-imposed tasks between the wars were his charitable efforts to protect the estates of neighboring women from the depredations of men who had married them to steal their money.

door, he commonly found from one to a half dozen unforeseen visitors.[20]

He was described (in 1785) as coming from his farms in a plain blue coat, white cashmere waistcoat, black knee breeches, and black boots. Having courteously greeted his guests, he retired. When he returned he was wearing a clean shirt, plain dark coat, white waistcoat, and white silk stockings. His hair was now neatly powdered. Washington never wore a wig, although he sometimes pinned to the back of his natural hair an artificial cue.[21]

His visitors ranged from total strangers (there was no inn closer than Alexandria) to his most intimate acquaintances; they stayed for a meal or a night or a week. If someone were expected, there was no knowing when he would actually arrive. George would sometimes stare, until the dinner bell rang, from his high bluff down the Potomac waiting to see the right sail.[22]

After severe weather had shut Mount Vernon away from visitors, Martha complained, "I have had a very dull time. . . . The only comfort was that Mr. Washington and the children have had their healths very well." George also found an unfilled dining room "lonesome," strange and melancholy.[23]

However, the Washingtons felt a need to get off by themselves when they so desired. In 1773 and 1774 George doubled the length of Mount Vernon westward from the front door with a three-story addition dedicated to family use. Most of the ground floor was filled with a library. The second floor, which could only be reached by a private stair, contained a large bedroom flanked with dressing rooms. Overhead was another room, probably originally occupied by Martha's son, Jackie Custis.

This solved the problem for the hosts, but the guests overflowed their part of the house. Washington sketched a balancing continuation of the east side of Mount Vernon. It featured an elegant chamber, that could be used as a ball, reception, or dining room, which had so high a ceiling that it almost filled two of the wing's three stories. This was still in the planning stage when he rode off to the Revolutionary War.

Often present at Mount Vernon, often visited at Belvoir, the Fairfaxes remained George's most intimate neighbors. When Martha was ill, Sally rushed round with comfort and presents. When Martha's daughter Patsy died, the Fairfaxes were, with the minister, the only outside guests at the funeral. If at any point this intimacy created strain between the ladies, there is no record of it: the records indicate harmonious friendship.

In 1773, Washington's old friends sailed for England; he promised to supervise their American business. "Mrs. Washington and self," he noted in his diary, "went to Belvoir to see them take shipping."[24] Thus Sally sailed forever out of George's life to become, as we have seen, an altogether satisfying memory.

When visitors to Mount Vernon rode to nearby houses, they often took George and sometimes Martha with them. Occasions of high festivity were the Annapolis Races and the sessions of the Burgesses at Williamsburg, which attracted theatrical companies and waxworks proprietors, and encouraged balls. There were also balls at Alexandria, one of which Washington, to tease his friends who had been the managers, called "The Bread and Butter Ball" because that had been the fare along with "tea and coffee which the drinkers could not distinguish from hot water sweetened."[25]

During 1769, the whole family spent eleven and a half days at Williamsburg. In the social life there, the sexes were so segregated that Jackie, although only fifteen, went to many more parties with George than did Martha. Particularly in the evening the men set out alone.[26]

Washington had quantities of business to shuttle him around his part of Virginia, and everywhere he rode he was entertained.

In the countryside, he stayed in private houses; in town, he spent his evenings with jolly fellows at taverns where they "clubbed"—i.e., shared—the bill. He was always welcome; his popularity was great. A letter he wrote to Burwell Bassett, Martha's brother-in-law, reveals the type of good-natured banter he engaged in with his male friends:

"Dear Sir,

I was favored with your epistle wrote on a certain 25th of July when you ought to have been at church, praying as becomes every good Christian man who has as much to answer for as you have. Strange it is that you will be so blind to truth that the enlightening sounds of the Gospel cannot reach your ear, nor examples awaken you to a sense of goodness. Could you but behold with what religious zeal I hie me to church on every Lord's day, it would do your heart good, and fill it, I hope, with equal fluency. But harkee! I am told you have recently introduced into your family a certain production which you are lost in admiration of, and spend so much time in contemplating the just proportions of its parts, the ease and conveniences with which it abounds, that it is thought you will have little time to animadvert upon the prospects of your crops.

"I say how will this be reconciled to that anguished care and vigilance which is so essentially necessary at a time when our growing prosperity—meaning the tobacco—is assailed by every villainous worm that has had an existence since the days of Noah (how unkind it was of Noah, now I have mentioned his name, to suffer such a brood of vermin to get a berth in the ark), but perhaps you may be as well off as we are—that is have no tobacco for them to eat, and there, I think, we nicked the dogs, as I think to do you if you expect any more."[27]

During the seventeen years between wars, George suffered from one very serious illness. It started with "a violent cold" in May 1761. A few months later, he seemed "very near my last

[237]

gasp. . . . I once thought the grim king would certainly master my utmost efforts, and that I must sink in spite of a noble struggle." He was haunted by the realization that the Washingtons were very short-lived: his father had died at forty-nine, his brother Lawrence at thirty-four.[28]

George sought relief at the warm springs that had been stepping stones on Lawrence's path to the grave, and sent his crony, Captain Stewart, galloping to Philadelphia for the advice of physicians there. They urged that the sufferer come to the city himself for an examination. George also considered crossing the ocean to the doctors in England. However, he stayed in Virginia. He staggered to Williamsburg for a meeting of the Burgesses, but proved too sick to attend. It was only after seven or eight months of serious illness that he began to mend.

When in his usual good health, Washington was so active that it sometimes seemed he was incapable of staying still. Most of his energy went into farming and land speculation, but he had plenty left for amusements.

From a diary entitled "Where and How My Time was Spent,"[29] we discover that in 1768 he hunted foxes on forty-nine days; went to church on fifteen, mostly when he was away from home; paid many visits, attended two balls, three plays, and one horse race; did some duck shooting, and played a quantity of cards.

His "infatuation" with cards brought him a scolding from the Presbyterian Pennsylvanian, Colonel John Armstrong, who wrote that the "game, always unfriendly to society, turns conversation out of doors and curtails our opportunities to mutual good."[30] It was, of course, useless thus to lecture a man who was all his life a gambler, although in the end on the world stage and for the highest stakes. However, Washington's gambling, on any scale, never broke loose from common sense. Once, it is true, he lost £9.14.9 (about $250 in modern money) but, during the three years 1772–1774, his pleasure at cards cost him in the aggregate only £6.3.3. He won £72.2.6 and lost £78.5.9.[31]

Dancing was among Washington's favorite sports. Whatever may have been the case when he had been an adolescent half-swooning over the exquisite existence of femininity, he "relished" balls when a mature man as "so agreeable and innocent an amusement." He enjoyed the physical pleasure of rhythmic movement—the faster the better—once comparing the dance with war as "the gentler conflict." And his eye was sharp for the human comedies involved. Thus he was to write a granddaughter concerning a ball in Georgetown, "Happy, thrice happy for the fair who were assembled on the occasion that there was a man to spare; for had there been seventy-nine ladies and only seventy-eight gentlemen, there might, in the course of the evening, have been some disarray among the caps."[32]

Washington also enjoyed cockfights. He could not resist any spectacle his surroundings offered: he paid to see puppet shows, visited a lioness and a tiger, and gave nine shillings to a showman who brought an elk down the long driveway to Mount Vernon. He was always buying tickets in raffles: for a necklace or an encyclopedia, a carriage, farmland, or a town lot. At boat races, he applauded the winner, on one occasion lending the manager several dozen claret (which were not returned). He had a period when he smoked the "superfine" tobacco he grew on his own plantations in long-stemmed clay pipes which he bought, for himself and his guests, by the gross.[33]

That Washington hunted foxes on forty-nine days in a typical year is the more impressive because all the runs were crowded into the few autumn and winter months when the foliage was not too thick or the farm work too heavy. His diaries are full of laconic descriptions of individual chases, with lists of the participants, invariably all male. Scents were lost and refound; the dogs sometimes took off, despite shouting, after deer; a fox who had successfully leaped into a hollow tree to escape the hounds fell out again dead. Once George and Dr. William Ramsay, coming on the hounds hunting by themselves, gleefully joined in. After a ride of several hours, the fox disappeared into a hole: "When digging it out, it escaped."[34]

As a hunter, George reverted to the passion he had first encountered in Lord Fairfax for breeding hounds. We learn from his diary that Old Harry, the courser with the points he most wanted to reproduce, was so slow in the uptake that when Tipsey became "proud" she was "lined" before Harry noticed by "the little spaniel dog Pompey," and Mopsey had leisure to succumb to the charms of "my water dog Pilot." Both delinquent females were locked up with Old Harry in the hope that their first escapades had come to naught.[35]

Washington's taste in names: for dogs, Tartar, Jupiter, Trueman, Drunkard, Vulcan, Rover; for bitches, Truelove, June, Duchess, Lady, Sweetlips.[36]

The breeding of horses also fascinated him. What stallion covered what mare, even in his neighbor's stables, went down in his journal. He commented that one mare, who had not, would surely never breed, "as I am convinced she had a competent share of Ariel's performances; not content with which, she was often catched in amorous moods with a young horse of mine, notwithstanding my utmost efforts to keep them asunder."[37]

Among the few Custis possessions Washington brought to Mount Vernon was a quantity of books. However, he assigned most of them to his stepson's estate. His accounts do not show him an avid purchaser of reading matter. Yet he gathered enough volumes of his own to justify an order to London for four or five hundred bookplates carrying his coat of arms. His correspondence shows familiarity with such works of the imagination as *Don Quixote, Tristram Shandy,* and *The Tempest,* but his library was strongest in historical works, legal and agricultural manuals. "A knowledge of books," he wrote, "is the basis" upon which knowledge gained from experience "is to be built."[38]

That Washington knew about (and was amused by) the stilted pastoral poetry of the English romantic precursors who were his contemporaries is revealed by the high-spirited glosses he was to pen in describing Mount Vernon to Europeans. When inviting Mme. de Lafayette to America, he asked her whether "the warbling notes of the feathered songsters on our lawns and meads can for a moment make you forget the melody of the opera?" She would find him "in a small villa, with the implements of husbandry and lambkins around me." She would experience "the rustic civility, and you shall taste the simplicity of rural life."[39]

When Washington was called in 1775 from his native acres (like Cincinnatus from the plough) to lead the great American cause, the man, who had been so turbulent during the French and Indian War revealed to a remarkable degree those "Roman virtues" which the eighteenth century conned from Stoic philosophy: lofty patriotism, love of freedom, unselfish service to the state, self-sacrifice, and (above all) self-mastery that excluded all but magnanimous emotions.

Washington could not have imbibed stoicism from any deep study of the classics since he knew no Latin and would, had it been possible, have known less Greek. However, he did own, at the age of seventeen, an outline in English of Seneca's principle dialogues.[40] This Stoic work presaged to a remarkable extent what Washington became. It may well have been recommended to him by William Fairfax, who had found so much comfort among the shocks of the world in remembering how Roman heroes had suffered without repining.

Like William Fairfax, Washington used the word philosophy to connote acceptance of things as they are. Thus in 1785 he wrote Lafayette, who was planning a tour through Germany and

Austria, "As an unobserved spectator, I should like to take a peek at the troops of those monarchs at their maneuverings upon a grand field day, but as it is among the unattainable things, my philosophy shall supply the place of curiosity, and set my mind at ease."[41]

The eighteenth-century English world found its lofty primer to Stoicism in Addison's tragedy, *Cato*, which, so Pope wrote, "calls forth Roman drops from British eyes." Phrases from Cato reverberate through the American Revolution: Patrick Henry was paraphrasing when he cried, "Give me liberty or give me death"; Nathan Hale was paraphrasing when he wished he had more than one life to give for his country; George Washington was paraphrasing when, as he often did, he told unlucky generals that they had done what was more valuable than achieve success, they had deserved it.[42]

We have seen that Washington wrote Sally Fairfax from a military camp that he wished he could play one of the young lovers in an amateur production of *Cato*, "being Juba to such a Marcia as you must make."[43] But it is to the hero of the tragedy, the noble military leader Cato, that writers have liked to compare George Washington. Cato, indeed, resembled Washington at his most elevated and austere, but the American general was a much warmer and gentler man. He happily received repentant mutineers back into the fold rather than sentencing them icily to death as Cato did. Cato would never have sat up, as was Washington's habit, with his staff and guests over the supper table, cracking nuts and jokes hour after hour to shouts of laughter. Washington was Cato turned Virginia country gentleman.

During the mid-eighteenth century, classicism blew through the American air, more constant than the scents of spring or the snows of winter. You did not have to sit in a library to be a classicist. (The uneducated youth, Benjamin West, painted in Lancaster, Pennsylvania, at the age of fourteen, *The Death of*

Socrates.) Everyone from the angry Connecticut apothecary, Benedict Arnold, to George Washington, breathed in classicism. What use they then made of it was a product of their own temperaments.

Washington could have had no serious concern with the philosophical system-building of the Greek Stoic philosophers. However, the Stoic ideal as preached in Rome by Seneca—which, indeed, expresses one aspect of man's universal search for perfection—appealed naturally to him. He would probably have sought it had he never heard of classic times. Yet that "Roman virtues" were so admired, at least outwardly, by his contemporaries, must have helped him break to the saddle the wild horses in his brain. And certainly, the fact that a popular ideal existed with which he could be identified, contributed to the speed with which George Washington became, when again in the public eye, a popular idol.

Washington's religious beliefs mingled Stoicism, which was of all classic philosophies the closest to Christianity, with Christian tenets. As suited a man of his position, he became a vestryman of his local Anglican parish (Truro), a post which carried with it some functions exercised, in colonies where there was no legally established religion, by justices of the peace. However, he was no zealous communicant: organized religion appealed to him primarily (and in these years not very strongly) as a civilizing force within secular society.

Washington was to write Lafayette, "Being no bigot myself to any mode of worship, I am disposed to indulge the professors of Christianity* in the church, that road to heaven which to them shall seem the most direct, plainest, easiest, and least liable to exceptions." Washington never numbered a minister among his

---

* Washington's tolerance was, of course, not limited to the sweep of Christian sects. He wrote concerning securing the services of some immigrants: "If they are good workmen, they may be of Asia, Africa, or Europe. They may be Mohammedans, Jews, or Christian of any sect, or they may be atheists."[44]

intimate correspondents. He never concerned himself with efforts to define God and chart exclusive roads to heaven. About a sermon which had been sent him he wrote, "I presume it is good coming all the way from New Hampshire, but do not vouch for it, not having read a word of it."[45]

Washington could not accept conclusions on the basis of authority or long-standing belief; he was no mystic; he felt he did not know and could never know. In 1773, at a moment of great emotion, when a niece had died as his own stepdaughter had just done, he wrote the newly bereaved father, Burwell Bassett, "The ways of Providence being inscrutable, and the justice of it not to be scanned by the shallow eye of humanity, nor to be counteracted by the utmost efforts of human power and wisdom, resignation, and, as far as the strength of our reason and religion can carry us, a cheerful acquiescence to the Divine Will is what we are to aim."[46]

Despite his lack of doctrine and dogmatism, Washington felt strongly the presence of a higher power which intervened in the affairs of men. However, he shied away (particularly in those earlier years) from using the word God. His favorite term was the one Seneca used, "Providence." That the man whose innate intellectual drive was not analytical but inclusive made no effort to reason out the nature of this force is revealed by the fact, which Freeman points out, that he called Providence interchangeably he, she, and it. "He" could be God; "she" was fate, fortune, perhaps even lady luck; "it" was some inanimate force of nature that science might define. Although he sometimes had difficulty in discovering where in relation to specific events the benignity lay, he never doubted that Providence was benign and would support virtue, that "everything happens for the best."[47]

In 1793 Washington thus summarized the religious philosophy he was evolving during his Mount Vernon years. How happenings would "terminate is known only to the great ruler of events; and confiding in his wisdom and goodness, we may safely trust the issue to him, without perplexing ourselves to seek for that which is beyond human ken, only taking care to perform the parts assigned to us in a way that reason and our own consciences approve of."[48]

George Washington was, like Benjamin Franklin and Thomas Jefferson, a deist.*

On Sundays, Washington was less likely to go to church than to write letters. The reader must have adduced, from the many quotations made in this volume, that Washington had taught himself to write very well. His style was not bookish or colloquial, but oratorical: modeled on the spoken word as refined and cadenced for public delivery. This source of inspiration brought to his sentences rhythm used for effect. Although his prose became turgid when his passions burst from his control, he usually wrote clearly and succinctly, kindling, as the voice would, to restrained emotional flights. He enjoyed writing: with the building of Mount Vernon, it was the main expression of his nature's esthetic side.

To the historian of American art, Mount Vernon presents difficulties. Knowing individuals are not wanting to tell you that it is ugly and, indeed, to any sophisticated eye it seems at first crude. But the longer the time you spend at Mount Vernon, the more your imagination lives in and with the house, the more beautiful it appears.

The application of any accepted rule only deepens the mystery. Any architectural student can point out innumerable clumsy solutions to elementary structural problems—no angle in the building is true—and the way Mount Vernon was designed would seem to forecast certain failure. Washington made no

---

* The reader should be warned that the forgers and mythmakers have been endlessly active in their efforts to attribute to Washington their own religious acts and beliefs. Prayers have been written for him, etc., etc.[49]

serious study of architecture and he evolved his mansion over a period of years without following any initial general plan. Having in the first rebuilding incorporated many features of the simple farmhouse he had inherited, he added on additions one after another. This process included the incidental use of craftsmen when they appeared in the neighborhood: a "stucco worker" was, for instance, let loose in 1775 on the ceilings during Washington's absence.[50]

The amateur architect conned, in the manner usual for Virginia gentlemen, structural details from English builder's manuals. These he usually simplified. He also engaged in audacious acts of esthetic invention.

Washington's method of rusticating Mount Vernon's outside walls by grooving and roughening boards to resemble stone blocks had no parallel in Virginia—no one knows where the idea for this expedient came from—yet it is effective.* And, during the 1780's, in a major burst of practical creative design, he built, to accommodate his many guests as they looked out over his extensive view, a porch which ran the whole length of the house and featured columns rising two stories to join the roof line. This, the first extensive colonnaded two-story porch in Virginia, presaged what became almost the hallmark of Southern pre-Civil War architecture.[51]

The haphazard way Mount Vernon was designed created problems which Washington solved with brilliant pragmatism based on the principles (or lack of them) he enunciated when in 1798 he expressed doubts as to a pediment and parapet that the professional architect, Dr. William Thornton, wished to add to a pair of houses he was having erected in the new national capital. "Rules of architecture," Washington wrote with extreme politeness, "are calculated, I presume, to give symmetry and just

---

* The reader should be reminded that the modern conception of preserving the integrity of materials was unheard of in the eighteenth century.

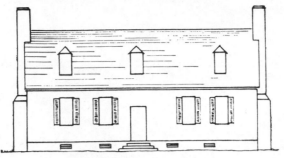

The house George Washington lived in as a boy, and
eventually rented from his brother's widow.

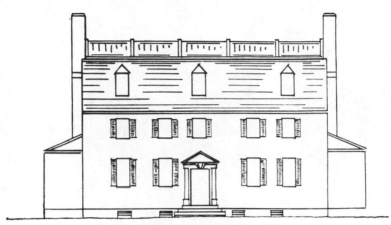

Mount Vernon, after the enlargement made during 1759
in preparation for his marriage to Martha.

The completed mansion. The 1759 house was extended during 1774 to the right,
to supply private living quarters. A similar extension to the left, made in 1776,
was mostly filled by a two story parlor. Washington added the pediment and
cupola after the Revolution.

How Mount Vernon Grew
Courtesy of the Mount Vernon Ladies' Association of the Union.

A family ready-made for George Washington: John Parke Custis and Martha Parke Custis, painted by John Wollaston during 1757, less than two years before they became Washington's stepchildren. Courtesy of Washington and Lee University.

Martha Dandridge Custis, Washington's future wife, painted in 1757 during her first marriage, by John Wollaston. Courtesy of Washington and Lee University.

Mount Vernon: a detail of the west parlor looking much as it did when Washington brought Martha home as a bride. He ordered the "neat landskip, 3 feet by 21½ inches" from London in 1757. The exact date at which Washington's coat of arms was added is not known. Photograph, courtesy of the Mount Vernon Ladies' Association of the Union.

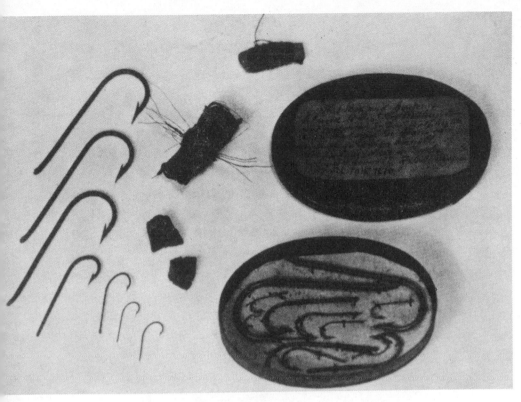

George Washington's fishing tackle presented by him
to his friend Dr. James Craik.

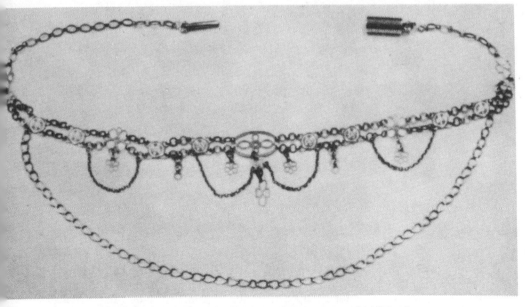

A gold necklace believed to have been presented to Martha
Washington by her husband on their first wedding anniversary.
Both, courtesy of the Mount Vernon Ladies' Association of the Union.

Washington's stepson, John Parke Custis, aged seventeen, whose school principal wrote Washington, "I must confess to you that I never did in my life know a youth so exceedingly indolent or so surprisingly voluptuous. One would suppose nature had intended him for some Asiatic prince." A miniature by Charles Willson Peale, courtesy of the Mount Vernon Ladies' Association of the Union.

Martha Dandridge Custis Washington, painted by Charles Willson Peale at Mount Vernon in 1772, when she was forty-one. Courtesy of the Mount Vernon Ladies' Association of the Union.

George Washington in his French and Indian War uniform, carrying both a sword and a rifle. The gilt, crescent-shaped badge suspended around his neck is a gorget, indicating that he is an officer. This, the only portrait of Washington executed before the Revolution, was done by Charles Willson Peale at Mount Vernon in 1772. Courtesy of Washington and Lee University.

proportion to all the [classical] orders and parts of building in order to please the eye. Small departures from *strict* rules are discoverable only by the skillful architects or by the eye of criticism; while ninety-nine of a hundred, deficient of their knowledge, might be pleased with things not quite orthodox. . . . These ideas, as you will readily perceive, proceed from a person who avows his ignorance of architectural principles and who has no other guide but his eye to direct his choice."[52]

Because he built out the original farmhouse so extensively on the sides, the final structure was extremely shallow for its length. So Washington brought in depth with curved arcades that connected the two extremities to diagonally placed outbuildings, giving the entire complex from the land side the shape of a new moon. From the river side, the porch effectively enhanced width.

The other major problem created by the additions—the danger that a building so long for its height would fail to impress as a unit—Washington handled by adding large decorative elements: a long, low triangular pediment cutting into the roof line on the land side, and a cupola that, rising higher than the exquisitely proportioned chimneys, draws the eye in and upward to a central apex.

A bit here and a bit there, and yet Mount Vernon faces the ages as a single piece, one and indivisible like the union its architect did so much to found. This is not, like George Mason's nearby Gunston Hall, an elegant residence built by a professional for a patron to live in: it is more like a sea creature's shell turned to coral; the plumage of a bird grown to the contours of its own body. Form follows more than function; it follows mind and character. George Washington could be deduced from this building as paleontologists deduce a dinosaur from inanimate bones.

And, equally significant, Mount Vernon seems a natural out-growth of the landscape in which it stands, one with the river and the bluff and the trees. Like his house, the architect be-longed no more to the great world than he belonged to this plot of earth.

18

County Squire

I N THE LETTER which had been his farewell to the officers he had commanded during the French and Indian War, ex-Colonel Washington had made statements that pulled in contradictory ways. He expressed, on one hand, his continuing desire to promote "the reputation and interest" of the Virginia Regiment, and declared, on the other, that "reflections" on his years of service "fill me with grief and I must strive to forget them."[1]

"It is assuredly," Washington was to comment, "better to go laughing than crying through the rough journey of life."[2] Although for a year or two he assumed in the Burgesses his natural role as protector of the Regiment, the time soon arrived when he did not even leave Mount Vernon for sessions in which matters of great moment to Virginia's soldiers were to be decided. After an unfavorable vote, Stewart complained, "We missed your friendly services exceedingly."[3]

Although the French did not bother Virginia again after the fall of Duquesne, Indian troubles continued to ensanguine the frontier. Concerning a 1761–1762 campaign that involved his former colleagues in the Virginia Regiment, Washington wrote, "We live in a state of peaceful tranquillity ourselves, so we are at very little trouble to inquire about the operations against the

Cherokees, who are the only people that disturbs the repose of this great continent."[4] Not even Pontiac's War, which brought back to the Virginia frontier such harrowing scenes as he had once tried vainly to prevent, made him reach for his uniform and his sword.

With passion, with the violence of a continuing explosion, Washington was abandoning "a wide and bustling world"; he was immersing himself in his own neighborhood. As soon as opportunity offered, he moved his constituency from over the Blue Ridge to Fairfax County. He spent between forty and seventy-five pounds at each election. Among his expenses: "fifty-four gallons of strong beer"; "£1.0.0 to John Muir for his fiddler." He usually gave a ball for the voters after the poll, and he was always re-elected.[5]

However, he did not hold onto the Custis townhouse in Williamsburg. He bought in its place a house in the tiny local metropolis of Alexandria. If there were little county business impending, and he had no private business to take him to Williamsburg, he commonly did not ride the 160 miles (a four days' journey) to the sessions of the Burgesses. When in attendance, he sponsored such bills as the one he proposed that would protect the purity of local wells by regulating the raising of local hogs.[6]

That Washington was a poor public speaker is a favorite part of the anti-legend that exists as a reaction to the legend of his perfection; and the conclusion receives backing from the testimony of those who thought of public speaking exclusively in terms of such spread-eagle oratory as Patrick Henry employed. Thus the English traveler, Nicholas Cresswell, wrote that Washington was "always looked on as too bashful and timid for an orator."[7]

Washington revealed his own attitude in advice he gave a nephew during 1787: "Speak seldom, but to important subjects, except such as particularly relate to your constituents, and in the former case make yourself *perfectly* master of the subject. Never exceed a *decent* warmth, and submit your sentiments with diffidence. A dictatorial style, though it may carry conviction, is always accompanied with disgust."[8]

A Virginian thus described Washington as he revealed himself in the Burgesses: "He is a modest man, but sensible, and speaks little—in action cool, like a bishop at his prayers." Jefferson remembered, "I served with General Washington in the legislature of Virginia before the Revolution, and during it with Dr. Franklin in Congress. I never heard either of them speak ten minutes at a time, nor to any but the main point which was to decide the question. They laid their shoulders to the great points, knowing that the little ones would follow of themselves."[9] Until Washington became convinced that there were great points before the Burgesses, he would pay little attention.

Community offices came Washington's way. In addition to being a vestryman of Truro Parish, he became a trustee of the town of Alexandria and justice of the county court. The duties of these posts he often shirked, attending less than half of the thirty-one vestry meetings held between 1763 and 1774, and not appearing at any meeting of the Alexandria trustees until four years after he was elected. He commonly dealt on a more personal basis with the problems of the neighborhood. If an individual asked him for help, he could not, he confessed, refuse "without feeling inexpressable uneasiness."[10]

When, as unpaid commander of the Revolutionary army, Washington was to urge on his estate manager "economy and frugality," he made one exception: "Since neither myself or wife are now in the way to do these good offices . . . let the hospitality of the house with respect to the poor be kept up" by "giving my money in charity to the amount of forty or fifty pounds a year."[11]

[251]

Washington's charitable procedures would horrify a modern social worker. On no more reasoned basis than pity, he tried to alleviate the misfortunes propinquity brought to his notice: a beggar woman with outstretched hand; a debtor truly unable to meet his obligations; a neighbor in need of money or food or seed or business advice; a chance traveler who could use a large meal and a purse slipped in his pocket as he departed. Washington lent a weaver £19 to bring his mother and sister to America—and never was repaid. He offered William Ramsay £25 annually to help him send his son to college on condition that it be not mentioned or regarded as an obligation.[12]

Sanctimonious or self-righteous, George Washington was not. "I have ever laid it down as an established maxim," he wrote, "to believe that every person is (most certainly ought to be) the best judges of what relates to their own interest and concerns."[13] He did not demand good behavior of those he befriended. Thus he went to large expense, when he was already in debt, to help that prince of scapegraces, Captain Thomas Posey.

A veteran of the Forbes campaign, Posey owned the farm immediately west of Mount Vernon, which he called Rover's Delight. Although the name indicated a desire to settle down, Posey was ever ready to postpone labor for a hunt or a frolic or a long session over wine. He was a resource to his more provident, but also convivial neighbor. Small amounts passed continually as loans from pocket to pocket, and then Washington added £254 to make a total debt of £700. Posey was supposed to use the new sum to pay off his other capital debts, but he squandered the money and was soon back for more help. George admonished him but endorsed a note for another £300.

Things got so bad that Posey had to flee the sheriff to Maryland. Washington urged him to sell out and go west "where an enterprising man with very little money may lay the foundation for a noble estate." However, Posey preferred to marry "an old widow woman" who had property, although, as he wrote Washington, she was "as thick as she is high, and gets drunk at least three or four times a week." What made things worse, she "has a valiant spirit when drunk" which reminded Posey of his first wife.

The marriage produced not money but fights in which the Fairfaxes became involved, as the wife fled to them for protection. Washington caught Posey trying to defraud him. He wrote the miscreant angry letter after indignant letter, but did not foreclose the mortgage he held (which would have brought him land next to Mount Vernon he would have loved to have) until the whole matter collapsed into a bankruptcy sale at which Washington at last bought the land, which he made into one of the subdivisions of the Mount Vernon plantation.[14]

Posey became a deadbeat; he spent time in jail, but he remained welcome at Mount Vernon to sleep, eat, drink, and borrow more money. His daughter Milly, who was Patsy's age, huddled under Martha's wing and was still making Mount Vernon her home in 1781. Washington sent Posey's son Lawrence through school (charging the cost to his father's account in a bookkeeping gesture he must have realized was vain). Another son Thomas took Washington's advice about going west, became a colonel at Valley Forge, and Governor of the Indiana Territory. A third son Price kept up a connection with Jacky Custis that enabled him eventually to defraud that incompetent of large sums.[15] It was all part of life in a neighborhood.

Washington was sympathetic with sinners, for he was not himself immune to temptations, nor did he always behave as his conscience would have liked him to do. He recognized that a person's strengths could be the reverse side of his weaknesses; and that in the world, as he and his fellow men had to live in it, virtues were often contradictory.

By the fabrication about the Cherry Tree which established

the legend that Washington could not tell a lie, Parson Weems distorted the record more than he knew. In Washington's pantheon of virtues, truth-telling occupied a place subordinate to such other virtues as charity, compassion, intelligence, bravery, idealism.

If an aging beauty says that she is beginning to look old, the uncompromising truth-teller replies, "I am afraid you are," or is stonily silent. The gentleman reaches for her hand and says, "You never looked lovelier." Washington defined a gentleman as a man who had "too nice a sensibility of the impulses of humanity" to offend.[16]

His ever augmenting exquisite sense of other people's feelings became his greatest asset as a leader. Although in his early years he sometimes stumbled (as in his long self-adulatory screed to Loudoun), by the time he headed the Revolutionary armies, he was awe-inspiringly expert in presenting an argument in the way that would most appeal to the individual addressed. Always the mature Washington preferred persuasion to command, and, as long as he aimed at what he believed was right, he was willing to seek it down different roads. Thus, upon occasion, his letters to different people on the same subject deviate so far that his severest modern critic, Bernhard Knollenberg, has accused him of deceit.[17]

In war, untruth is an essential military weapon. "An enemy," Washington wrote during the Revolution, "is always supposed to be secret as to their real intentions, and may generally be suspected of a view to deceive when they speak openly of them." To discover the facts about the foe while making sure that his spies carried back fictions was a technique of which Washington early realized the importance. As Washington wrote in 1777, "It is our interest, however much our characters may suffer by it, to make small numbers appear large."[18]

During the French and Indian War as in the Revolution, the

weaknesses in his own forces Washington needed most crucially to hide were usually blamable on lack of support from the home front, and Washington quickly learned that the home front was more helpful (as indeed were his own soldiers) when not discouraged. Although he described remediable conditions in frightening diatribes to his superiors, he invariably after a defeat accepted and spread exaggerated reports of enemy casualties. He tended in general to play down bad news and play up good.

Washington was by nature combative. You cannot be a soldier if you hesitate to fight, and you cannot win unless you are willing to use stratagem to catch the enemy at a disadvantage. That some of the qualities which were to make Washington a triumphant military commander spilled over into his behavior as a civilian is not remarkable. However, it is not only remarkable but prodigious, almost unique in history, that he labored so hard (and succeeded so increasingly well) in curbing the aggressive side of his nature when it was not to the advantage of his nation and his neighbors.

The amount of documentation that exists on Washington's life is tremendous, and resentment of the goody-goody image presented by legend has placed beside scholars seeking the whole man a band of determined searchers for flaws. It is amazing that this activity has not turned up more factual information to Washington's discredit. Yet there is some.

We have already seen various occasions when his feet slipped from the path he would have wished to follow. Equivocal considerations concerning his speculations in western land will be examined in Chapter Twenty-one. Two bothersome matters which the documents present will now be recounted so that no man may suspect that the image here presented of Washington's early years has to any degree been achieved by suppression.

In 1761 Washington was opposed for Burgess in Frederick County by his former second-in-command (who was to be one of his major generals and problems during the Revolution) Lieutenant Colonel Adam Stephen. They had once been close friends but had fallen out. Captain Stewart warned Washington that, although "the leaders of all the patrician families remain firm in their resolution of continuing for you," Stephens, by introducing various "strange and chimerical" commercial schemes which he stated would bring prosperity to the county, had "attracted the attention of the plebeians whose unstable minds are agitated by every breath of novelty, whims, and nonsense."[19]

Washington wrote Captain Van Swearingen, "I hope my interest in your neighborhood still stands good, and as I have great reason to believe you can be no friend to a person of Col. Stephen's principles, I hope, and indeed make no doubt, that you will contribute your aid towards shutting him out of the public trust he is seeking. Should Mercer's friends and mine be hurried in at the first of the poll it might be an advantage—but as sheriff I know you cannot appear in this nor would I by any means have you do anything that can give so designing a man as Col. Stephen the least handle."[20]

In 1772 Washington sent some flour to be sold in Barbados, with this admonishment: "I recommend its being lumped off, rather than sold in small parcels for trial, as it was ground out of indifferent wheat, and will, I fear, look better to the eye than it will prove agreeable to the taste, being a little musty."[21]

This document, although completely authentic, is less typical of Washington than the order he gave his manager in 1781 concerning a dispute over land: "Delay not to give him a full measure of justice, because I had rather exceed than fall short."[22]

When cheated, Washington was loud in indignation, all the more so because he knew that he would in probability take no active steps. Concerning a sea captain who had stolen a large consignment of flour and herring, he wrote, "It is not my wish to proceed to any harsh and rigorous measures by which a man just setting out in trade may be injured if there is any possibility of avoiding it." Although in this case he was in the end forced to take legal action, he carried men to court so "very reluctantly" that in 1786 he wrote, "I have had in the course of my life so little to do with law and lawyers that I feel myself extremely awkward in these matters." He could philosophically regard "impositions" as a "tax" that had to be paid "to dishonorable men."[23]

Although he was to be a political revolutionary, Washington did not try to reform the individuals around him. Even as he used what tools existed on his plantation although they might be inadequate, so Washington believed that "we must make . . . the best use of mankind as they are, as we cannot have them as we wish." This is nowhere better exemplified than in a contract he made in 1787 with an alcoholic gardener. Philip Bater agreed that "he will not at anytime suffer himself to be disguised with liquor, except on the times hereafter mentioned." George Washington agreed to give him "four dollars at Christmas with which he may be drunk four days and four nights; two dollars at Easter to effect the same purpose; two dollars also at Whitsuntide, to be drunk two days." On ordinary days, Bater was to have "a dram in the morning, a drink of grog at dinner or at noon."[24]

To tradesmen, Washington was courteous. Thus he wrote James Gildart in 1765, "I wish the chair bottoms may last, as I had a trial of hair once before which were of no durations, and from thence determined to have no more; but perhaps all may not be alike, and these will answer your recommendation of them. If so, they will do exceedingly well."[25]

The paying and earning of wages seemed to Washington a lesser part in the relationship between employer and employee. He notified Thomas Bishop, the servant he had inherited from Braddock, not to expect any increase in wages unless activity justified it. However, "As you have been so long a member of my

[257]

family, it is not my intention to let you want while we both live."[26]

When in 1775 he proffered from the military camp in Cambridge a raise to his estate manager and distant cousin Lund Washington, who was now running Mount Vernon, George felt it necessary to explain, "I do not offer this as any temptation to induce *you* to go more cheerfully in prosecuting *these* schemes of mine. I should do an injustice to you were I not to acknowledge that your conduct has ever appeared to me above everything sordid, but I offer it in consideration of the great charge you have upon your hands."[27]

Should Washington's friends—or even strangers who were friends of friends—ask him for loans, he felt an obligation to comply, and, if he could not, considered it necessary to "acquit myself" in the applicant's "esteem" by explaining why his situation allowed him no other course.

This feeling that a supplicant had, as a general rule, a right to know as much about his own private affairs as was relevant to that man's concerns, elicited from Washington, who was not ordinarily given to self-revelation, suprisingly informative letters, sometimes addressed to individuals with whom he neither had nor wished intimacy. As he once put it, "Although there is no legal obligation upon me to disclose the state of my own finances, and in prudence it might, perhaps, be better to avoid it, yet, sir, as a testimony of my disposition to serve you if I had the means. . . ."[28]

Because his loans to individuals needing help were not business deals, but yet often involved considerable sums of money, Washington was commonly torn as to terms. He did not like to charge interest, and, although self-preservation often dictated insistence on some security, he could rarely bring himself to foreclose. He was happiest when he could write, as in a loan of £302 sterling (about $8000) to Captain Stewart, that it was "to be returned or not as it suited" Stewart's "convenience."* Yet even here he did not comply with Stewart's request that the transaction be omitted from his books, so that if he died his heirs could not collect.[29] Such matters, like all aspects of gentlemanly behavior, depended on sensibility, and were not susceptible of codification.

Dying gentlemen of the neighborhood could not close their eyes in peace until Washington had agreed to serve as executors of their estates. Thus, he found himself writing yet another sick man, "I do not wonder at your solicitude on account of your only son." He had already undertaken the management of so many estates, that this, added to his other affairs, kept him "constantly engaged in writing letters, settling accounts, and negotiating one piece of business or another in behalf of one or other of these concerns, by which means I have really been deprived of every kind of enjoyment, and have almost fully resolved to engage in no fresh matter." Yet, if the father were still determined to make him the guardian of the son, he would not refuse.[30]

As Freeman has pointed out, the more Washington did for his friends and neighbors, the more he felt responsible for them. After he had labored year after year to keep a lady's husband from stealing her estate through every stratagem known to legal chicanery, an observer wrote him that "charity" was common, but that such "steady friendship founded on that principle almost without precedent." Washington had given his word that he would stand by the unfortunate lady, and so he was forever committed. "I do not recollect," he declared in 1786, "that in the course of my life I ever forfeited my word, or broke a promise made to anyone.[31]

The military ambitions George Washington had harbored during the French and Indian War had been for pre-Revolu-

---
* It was returned.

tionary Virginia both novel and strange. It was the patriarchal life which Martha, by her presence and her property, helped him lead that expressed profoundly the cultural preconceptions to which Washington had been raised. He found this neighborhood life so deeply satisfying that the pull of Mount Vernon remained, after the unexpected had placed in his hands the reins of power, an effective counterpoise to fame with all her chariots.

"I have always," Washington wrote, "considered marriage the most interesting event of one's life, the foundation of happiness or misery." How better to spend one's days than in "cultivating the affections of good men, and in the practice of domestic virtues?"[32]

19

Children Not His Own

MARTHA WASHINGTON had been married for three years and was visiting in Westmoreland County with her husband. Her daughter Martha Parke Custis (Patsy), then six, was asleep where the mother could see that she was covered. But she had left John Parke Custis (Jacky), who was seven, at home "for a trial to see how well I could stay without him. . . . If at any time, heard the dogs bark or a noise out, I thought there was a person sent for me. I often fancied he was sick or some accident had happened to him." She decided that "my children's interest" forbade her from accompanying her husband on any more trips unless both children came along.[1]

Jacky was healthy, good-natured, and unenergetic, wearing a self-satisfied smile on his round, soft face with its doe's eyes and trivial chin. Patsy was dark, spindly, and sickly from the start. A stepfather's duty, George wrote, was to be "generous and attentive."[2]

"I conceive," he explained, "there is much greater circumspection to [be observed] by a guardian than a natural parent, who is only accountable to his own conscience," while "any *faux pas* in a guardian, however well meant the action, seldom fails to meet with malicious construction."[3] He hesitated to interfere between the mother and her children. Thus he could influence the upbringing of his stepchildren only so far as he could per-suade Martha—and in this aspect of their communal life alone her loyalties did not urge her into agreement with his wishes.

In any case, George's natural inclination was to be indulgent. He was to write in connection with his stepgrandchildren that he considered "the first rudiments of education" should be "a mere amusement, because it is my desire that the children should not be closely confined."[4]

All his stepchildren's best clothes came from England: for Jacky, for instance, "handsome silver shoe and knee buckles" ordered when he was four; a silver laced hat when he was seven. Patsy received at the age of six "a stiffened coat made of fashionable silk" and "one pair pack thread stays."[5]

Toys, too, were imported. After almost two years of marriage, Washington ordered, "a Tunbridge tea set, three neat Tunbridge toys, a neat book, fashionable tea chest, a bird on bellows, a cuckoo, a turnabout parrot, a grocer's shop, a neat dressed wax baby, an aviary, a Prussian dragoon, a man smoking, and six small books for children." As the children grew older, Jacky sometimes could not think what he wanted; the factor was asked to select from what was newest and best. But Patsy always craved another "doll baby" in the most fashionable clothes. Her feminine accomplishments were prepared for by the order of a spinet.

Each child had a colored body slave, Jacky's being four years his senior and dressed, on formal occasions, in livery "suited to the arms of the Custis family."[6]

When Jacky was seven, his stepfather hired as tutor a Mary-lander, Walter Magowan, who lived at Mount Vernon for eight years, until he went to England to take Holy Orders. His arrival was followed by a requisition sent to London for a terrifying array of Latin books, mostly two copies of each, to be charged, as was one ream of writing paper, equally to Jacky and Patsy.

The same order included "a neat small Bible bound in Turkey and 'Martha Parke Custis' wrote on the inside in gilt letters; a small prayer book, neat and in the same manner."[7]

Patsy was twelve when she first cried out and fell. Eight months later, Washington placed in his diary this grim note: "Joshua Evans, who came last night, put an iron ring on Patsy (for fits)."[8] It did no good, nor did a luxuriously appointed family stay at that old haven of sick Washingtons, Warm Springs.

As the epileptic became a young lady, every effort was made to give her a normal life. Milly Posey stayed at Mount Vernon as a playmate. Fine clothes were unloaded for the sufferer from each London boat: a handsome suit of Brussels lace; a complete set of paste—necklace, earrings, sprig combs, pins and buttons for her stomacher. The peripatetic dancing master, whose presence in each mansion house signaled an overnight party, came several times a year. (Surely, Washington, who so loved to dance, revolved boisterously with the adolescent girls.) When Patsy was sixteen, her parents took her to Williamsburg for the season. On the same day, George bought her there seven pounds' worth of silk and "four boxes of fit drops."[9]

Although she was an heiress, as Patsy entered the nubile years her callers were not suitors but doctors. She was gratified with a music box and a parrot. When she went to Alexandria for the launching of a ship, she was given as pocket money the huge sum of three pounds. Even Martha knew she was dying; the mother turned her eyes on Jacky "as her only hope."[10]

That the doctors did not always approve of the way her mother and stepfather spoiled her, and that she was refractory to contrary advice, can be concluded from a letter from an Annapolis doctor, dated March 21, 1772, urging that Martha press on the girl "regular, moderate exercise, temperate living which she may think abstemious, and her being attentive to keep her body cool and open, which last may I hope be effectively done and agreeably to herself by the use of barley water and light cooling food. Frumenty [a kind of porridge] made of barley or even of wheat would, I think, be very proper food—is agreeable to many and might perhaps be so at times to Miss Custis."[11]

In June 1773 Washington wrote Burwell Bassett, "It is an easier matter to conceive than to describe the distress of this family, especially that of the unhappy parent of our dear Patsy Custis, when I inform you that yesterday removed the sweet innocent girl, entered into a more happy and peaceful abode than any she has met with in the afflicted path she has hitherto trod.

"She rose from dinner about four o'clock in better health and spirits than she had appeared to have been in for sometime; soon after which she was seized with one of her usual fits and expired in it in less than two minutes without uttering a word, a groan, or scarce a sigh. This sudden and unexpected blow, I scarce need to add, has almost reduced my poor wife to the lowest ebb of misery; which is increased by the absence of her son [at school] . . . and want of the balmy consolation of her relations."

Martha's sorrow, George continued, made him wish more than ever that he could persuade her mother "to make this place her entire and absolute home . . . It might suit her well, and be agreeable both to herself and my wife. To me, most assuredly, it would."[12] Mrs. Dandridge did not come.

George's own mother had at last—in 1771, when she was in her early sixties—been persuaded to evacuate Ferry Farm, but there is no evidence that she was invited to join her son at Mount Vernon. She moved into Fredericksburg near her daughter, Mrs. Fielding Lewis. George bought the necessary land for £275 and built thereon a medium sized but elegant house. This was only the beginning of what the maneuver cost him.

Ferry Farm, had, of course, been legally his since his father's death, but he took over with it some nearby property actually his mother's, for which he agreed to pay her an annual rent. He combined all into one plantation, which he tried to set up on a paying basis. That effort was frustrated by Mary Washington, who commandeered "everything she wanted from the plantation for the support of her family, horses, etc."[13] (There is a highly believable tradition in Fredericksburg that the old lady would drink no water but that from a spring on Ferry Farm, where she daily went or sent for a jugful.) George continued to call on his mother as little as he could, and, if he did, he usually found himself out of pocket by some pounds. When he paid her what he owed for rent, he carefully noted in his account book the name of a witness in whose presence it was done.[14]

Washington's stepson was also a problem. Even before his sister had died, Jacky had been too much under Martha's wing. When late in 1768 tutor Magowan went back to England, it took George six months of arguing to get the fourteen-year-old sent off to school. Washington wrote the Reverend Jonathan Boucher, whose private academy in Caroline County, Virginia, was chosen, that the boy would bring with him his personal servant and two horses. The family would "cheerfully pay ten or twelve pounds a year extraordinary to engage your particular care of and a watchful eye to him, as he is a promising boy, the last of his family, and will possess a very large fortune; add to this my anxiety to have him fit for more useful purposes than a horse racer."[15] Probably following a list drawn up by the preceptor, Washington sent to England for more than a hundred books to be charged to Jacky's account.*

---

* These included Cicero's *Works* in twenty volumes; Blackwell's *Sacred Classics* in two; the poems of Thomson and Milton; Hume's *History of England;* works on classical antiquities, Greek, French, logic, arithmetic, and grammar, and a textbook thus finely denoted, "Rolling Method of Studying Belles Lettres." There were no titles that applied to science apart from theology.[16]

The school moved to Annapolis. Almost every time Jacky came home for a vacation, his stepfather had to apologize that the lad reappeared so late, with (as Washington stated in 1770) "his mind a good deal released from study and more than ever turned to dogs, horses, and guns."[17]

As Jacky advanced into his teens, he developed a concern with "dress and equipage" that made Boucher write, "I must confess to you that I never did in my life know a youth so exceedingly indolent or so surprisingly voluptuous. One would suppose nature had intended him for some Asiatic prince." The danger of Jacky's leaping into an unfortunate marriage gave Boucher the opportunity of suggesting that he himself should be paid to accompany the rich lad on the Grand Tour of Europe.[18]

Martha responded with alarm. George admitted that "the more conspicuous the point of view a man is to appear in, the more pains should be taken to enlarge his mind." However, he considered Jacky "by no means ripe enough for a traveling tour. Not that I think his becoming a mere scholar is desirable education for a gentleman," but he was not yet sufficiently proficient in book learning to profit from what he saw.[19]

Jacky, Washington continued, should read more Latin authors. Whether he would gain any advantages in learning Greek, "I do not pretend to judge of"; however, if he were to travel abroad, French (which George did not himself have) was "absolutely necessary." A "gentleman" should be familiar with those eighteenth century approaches to science, natural and moral philosophy.

The stepfather was disturbed that Jacky lacked the mathematical bases for surveying: "nothing can be more essentially necessary to any man possessed of a large landed estate, the bounds or some part or other of which are always in controversy." Furthermore, Jacky should have a greater knowledge of America, "as it is to be expected that every man who travels with a view of observing the laws and customs of other countries should be able to give some description of the situation and government of his own." That Washington (although he himself read both) did not put forward modern history and literature as subjects for formal study was typical of the time. His omission of religion (except in so far as it was included in moral philosophy) was more startling.[20]

The eventual decision was to send Jacky not abroad but to that precursor of Columbia University, King's College, in New York. However, before he could be got off, he became, without consulting his parents, engaged to Eleanor Calvert, the child of an illegitimate son of the fifth Lord Baltimore.

Although prosperous and a member of the Maryland Council, the girl's father admitted to Washington that a match with Mr. Custis far exceeded his most sanguine hopes.[21]

Washington had written him that Jacky owned 15,000 acres of land, much adjoining Williamsburg and none more than forty miles from it; several lots in that city; between two and three hundred Negroes; eight to ten thousand pounds deposited in England; and a right in his mother's dower on her death. Such an estate "ought to entitle him to a handsome portion in a wife. But, as I should never require a child of my own to make a sacrifice of himself to interest, so neither do I think it incumbent on me to recommend it as a guardian."[22]

Washington was more worried about Jacky's studies. Having persuaded Martha to agree, he wrote Calvert that the match would have to be postponed until Jacky had completed his education. "I shall recommend it to the young gentleman, with the warmth that becomes a man of honor . . . to consider himself as much engaged to your daughter as if the indissoluble knot was tied." To Burwell Bassett he admitted that, as Jacky had "discovered much fickleness already," he feared that the youth might change his mind and "injure the young lady," or elope and then wish "to be at liberty again."[23]

Washington escorted the rebellious young man to New York during 1773. Although he had not been that far from home for seventeen years, the reputation of the prosperous Virginia planter and former soldier had traveled more widely than he. During his week in Philadelphia, he was entertained by Lieutenant Governor Richard Penn, with whom he dined twice and breakfasted on the morning of his departure, and by other prominent citizens. He went to a ball and spent an evening at the Jockey Club.

He was accompanied from Philadelphia by that Scotch peer of dubious title, Lord Stirling, who was to be one of his generals in the Revolution. At Burlington, he dined with the Governor of New Jersey, Benjamin Franklin's illegitimate son William, who would make Washington great difficulty as a leading Loyalist. The next night, Washington spent at Lord Stirling's mansion at Basking Ridge, New Jersey. By the time he reached New York, he was so far from home that he had to lodge in a tavern. However, he had friends with whom he dined: James De Lancey, the future commander of Tory cavalry raiders, and his fellow veteran of Braddock's campaign, Thomas Gage, now Lieutenant General and His Majesty's commander in America.[24]

In the urgency of his concern that Jacky continue his education, Washington made requests of the Reverend Miles Cooper which drew from that president of King's College this reply: "As to my turning *private tutor,* as it were, it seems to me so inconsistent with my office . . . that I must beg to be excused." However, Jacky was soon writing home that "there is as much distinction made between me and the other students as can be expected": alone among the undergraduates he dined with the faculty and took part in their recreations.[25]

In the meanwhile, Nellie Calvert was visiting at Mount Vernon. She worked so successfully on Martha's soft heart that George soon found himself cast as a monster opposed to young love. Submitting, as he wrote, to "a kind of necessity," he agreed to Jacky's abandoning his education to get married in February 1774 at the age of nineteen.[26]

Martha's son spent the rest of his short life as a rich idler, almost sinister in his bland, myopic selfishness. To George Washington, John Parke Custis was no substitute for a son of his own.

Since Martha had proved extremely fecund in her previous marriage, bearing four children in seven years, the last shortly before her husband's death, George had every reason to suppose that an exciting announcement would come early in his married life with her. When he began to become uneasy, how much later he concluded that his marriage with Martha was destined to be childless, we have no way of knowing.

However, the documents show Washington refusing to accept the conclusion that, since Martha had borne children to another man, the flaw was in his own physical makeup, and that therefore he was destined, under all circumstances, to remain forever childless. A touching flutter of hope is revealed in his request, after his army had won the independence of the United States, that Congress return him his commission as commander in chief: "It may," he wrote, "serve my *grandchildren* some fifty or a hundred years hence as a theme to ruminate upon, *if they should be* contemplatively disposed."[27]

More specific was a letter he wrote when fifty-four years old asking his nephew, George Augustine Washington, to settle on a part of the Mount Vernon estate. He explained that the nephew could count on inheriting the tract on which he would live unless Washington himself had an heir of the body. That such an heir would appear was, George continued, most unlikely: "If Mrs. Washington should survive me, there is a moral certainty of my dying without issue, and should I be the longest liver, the matter in my opinion is almost as certain, for whilst I retain the reasoning faculties, I shall never marry a girl; and it is not probable that I should have children by a woman of an age suitable to my own, should I be disposed to enter into a second marriage." But in arranging the matter with his nephew, he did not preclude the possibility of his leaving the entire Mount Vernon estate to his own son.*28

For any man to fail to have children is a blow; for so physical a man as Washington it must have been a double blow. Furthermore the private half of his career was dedicated to the creation of the kind of estate Virginians built as the foundation for a great family. Indeed, with only a few public bequests and minor remembrances to friends, Washington eventually left everything he had gathered together to his relations, but in what a discouragingly scattered manner when so many nieces and nephews and stepgrandchildren had an equal, and no one an overwhelming, claim!

In the Revolutionary years Washington's longing for a son expressed itself in tender patronage and friendship extended to a succession of able young men: first Joseph Reed, then Alexander Hamilton, and then permanently to the youth who proved to be so perfect a voluntary son, the Marquis of Lafayette.

Washington's refusal, after the Revolution had been won, even to consider the possibility that he might join the then rulers of all other important nations as a king was (even if this is hard to realize today) the most revolutionary act of his life. Although his decision would undoubtedly have been the same, he would

---

* Because there has been so much written and unwritten gossip on the subject, it should be added that these brief paragraphs summarize everything that is known for certain about Washington's childlessness. There is as little reason (none) to believe that he ever had a child by another woman, as that he was impotent. It seems probable that, despite his natural unwillingness to accept the fact, he was sterile. However, it is possible that Martha suffered some injury during Patsy's birth or thereafter which brought an end to her childbearing.

surely have been torn by conflicting loyalties had he had a son capable of succeeding him. And the very existence of such a son would certainly have increased, as the United States was being born, a dangerous disunity by augmenting the fears which Washington's popularity and power inspired (however unjustly) in some very influential breasts.

Should one believe, as Washington himself did, that a beneficent destiny rules the affairs of men, it would be logical to conclude that—as the old saying goes—Providence kept George Washington from having any children of his own so that he could better be the father of his country.

20

British Debts versus
American Markets

WHEN AT THE age of twenty-seven, Washington, home from the wars and just married, settled down at Mount Vernon, he possessed almost no actual experience as a Tidewater planter. Far from interfering with the profitable Custis operations, he switched his own business in England from the factors he had found for himself* to the Custis factor, Robert Cary & Co.

To Cary, Washington wrote that he intended to use on his own plantations the Custis seeds and methods.[1] However, he regarded this as only as a temporary expedient.

He ordered agricultural books from England, including "a small piece in octavo called *A System of Agriculture or a Speedy Way to Get Rich*." From the more technical of the manuals he copied out with his pen, probably to engrave the contents on his memory, long extracts. But he also engaged in personal experimentation, for he realized that "what is good and profitable husbandry in one country may not be so in another."

---

* The similarity of names had made him first turn to one Richard Washington, who he assumed was a distant cousin and would therefore treat him fairly, but he was soon using other factors as well. None had proved satisfactory.

His carpenters built a huge "box with ten apartments." In each he mixed soil from a designated section of the plantation with horse, cow, or sheep dung, and then planted wheat, oats, or barley all to the same depth, which was "done by a machine made for that purpose. . . . I watered them all equally alike with water that had been standing in a tub about two hours exposed to the sun." He noted the speed with which the grain came up in the various boxes; but he was forced to go to Williamsburg, and found on his return that "the ground was so hard baked by the drying winds . . . that it was difficult to say which numbers looked most thriving."[2]

Washington's use of the experimental method was very modern; but even more so was his recognition that almost all his experiments were inconclusive because there was one all important variable he could not control: the weather. Results in a drenched season were inapplicable to a dry one. Yet he enjoyed his experiments and continued them as long as he lived.

Resolving to initiate wine culture, Washington reasoned that it would be best to eschew "the foreign grape" and find a suitable species that grew naturally in America. "I selected about 2000 cuttings of a kind that does not ripen in Virginia till repeated frosts in the autumn meliorate the grape and deprive the vines of their leaves." He hoped thus to avoid early ripening in the hot American summers and autumns and the "too great fermentation occasioned thereby." However, he was soon forced to ride off to the Revolutionary War. "Had I remained at home," he later wrote a French friend, "I should ere this have perfected the experiment, which was all I had in view."[3]

Empirical observation, man's most ancient tool for acquiring knowledge, he tried to systematize by noting in his diaries the weather, the orders he gave, what every gang or individual did on each farm, and how it all turned out.

Finding his carpenters slow at hewing boards, Washington sat down and watched. He thought out what motions could be eliminated, and then calculated how many board feet one workman should be able to hew in an hour. Carefully, he noted that these statistics served only for poplar; other woods awaited "some future observations."[4]

Whenever he read of a new agricultural machine, he yearned to buy one. However, that it was effective would not be enough. It would have to be, he mourned, so strong it could withstand the ministrations of very unskilled labor, and so simple that, if it did break, it could be mended by a common blacksmith.[5]

In 1760 Washington, being short of horses for the early spring ploughing, put his coach horses into the shafts. The going was so heavy that they had continually to stop, which worried him lest "it should give them a habit of stopping in the chariot." Clearly a lighter instrument was needed: "Peter (my smith) and I made several efforts to make a plough after a new model, partly of my own contriving," but they gave up at sunset. A week later Washington "spent the greatest part of the day in making a new plough" which was "of my own invention." On trial "she answered very well." This emboldened him to attempt further refinements. Now, "she ran very true, but heavy, rather too much for two horses." Thus ended his plough.[6] Washington's approach was that not of a true inventor but of a frontiersman tinkering to solve for the moment a specific difficulty.

Despite all his efforts he did not, in those early years as a planter, make the fundamental observation on which his prospects at Mount Vernon really depended. The soil, as he wrote years later, had "an under stratum of hard clay impervious to water." Moisture "penetrating that far and unable to descend lower," created sogginess and also continually washed away the top soil. What remained was unfertile, so heavy it was difficult to plough, and cut with "injurious and eyesore gullies."[7]

In the division of the Custis estate, Washington had taken the cash "since it best suits my purpose to have money that can be commanded [rather] than money at interest."*⁸ Due to the "terrible management" from which it had suffered while he was fighting, he had found Mount Vernon in a most dilapidated condition. To renovate and enlarge he spent his new prosperity with a lavish hand.¹⁰

He bought about 2000 acres contiguous with Mount Vernon which, in the immemorial manner of Virginia planters, he set up as a semi-separate farm. Called Dogue Run, it had its own overseer who presided over a work force resident in its own "quarter" of one-room cabins. To populate the quarter, Washington invested heavily in more slaves.

In these years before he had in so many ways transcended his environment, Washington accepted the Virginia labor practices to which he had been raised. Although susceptible to personal appeals—a slave who would "by no means consent to leave this neighborhood" was not sent—he regarded his Negroes less as people than property. He did his best to keep them well, having an annual contract with a local doctor and establishing a hospital in a small building near the mansion house; but when a slave died, he noted down the cash value he had lost. Towards this attitude he was undoubtedly helped by the fact that many were new arrivals from Africa, who spoke "very broken and unintelligible English." One had "a small face with cuts down each cheek," and another his teeth "filed sharp."¹¹

However, Washington had no sympathy with Tom who was able enough to be made the master of a work gang, but proved "both a rogue and a runaway." Washington sent him off to be sold in the Indies, writing the captain of the vessel that he should be kept handcuffed till the ship had sailed. "He is exceedingly healthy and strong, and good at the hoe, . . . which gives

---

* As late as 1788, Washington wrote concerning public securities, "I am so little acquainted with matters of this kind that I hardly know the use of them."⁹

me reason to hope he may, with your good management, sell well, if kept clean and trimmed up a little when offered for sale." Washington wished the sales price to be spent on a hogshead of molasses and one of rum, two small pots of sweetmeats, etc., etc.[12] The admirer of Washington who reads this with horrified twentieth century eyes may rest assured that this was then for Washington an unusual if not a unique act, and that the hero's entire attitude soon changed.

Slaves lacking any incentive to make themselves even moderately skilled artisans, and free labor being almost unprocurable in Virginia, Washington bought the time of indentured joiners, bricklayers, gardeners, etc., who had agreed to work for a certain number of years in return for their passage money to America. In addition, he rented some of his acres to sharecroppers who were supposed to pay him in tobacco grown, but were often a liability since he had to get them started with food, horses, tools.

All these matters, added to his belief that a man was "called upon to live up to his rank," ran to so much money that expenses "swallowed up before I knew where I was all the money I got by marriage."[13]

Not that he failed to work hard. Daily he was up before dawn, forever on horseback supervising the plantation factory. In addition to growing tobacco, he had to make the whole operation as far as possible self-sustaining. Pork had to be produced by the thousands of pounds (6632 in 1762), Indian corn raised to feed the Negroes, fish extracted from the Potomac to be eaten fresh by all and salted down in barrels for the hands. Fruit trees were grafted, cider bottled, cereal grains raised for man and beast. Liquor supplied slaves with some incentive; after buying as much as fifty-six gallons at a time, he established his own still, which could in a day change 144 gallons of cider into thirty of applejack.[14] The horses required special care; ditches had to be dug for drainage; fences built after the Colonel had himself surveyed the fields. Leather had to be collected for shoes and lime burned for his brickyard.

An old mill—which he always referred to as "she"—had to be supplied with water to turn the wheels, fed with grain, and propped up, as she was very shaky in storms. Washington's own carpenters erected the farm buildings and kept them in repair; his blacksmith was so busy he needed helpers. The mill and the artisans worked for neighbors. Washington acted as retailer for his tenants, exchanging goods he had sometimes imported from England for tobacco.

Tobacco! That was always the end product. It was cut when ripe, hung in special barns, and when just dry enough put in hogsheads weighing from 660 to 1100 pounds. And then off to England to restore his balance with Cary & Co., and to pay for new purchases.

Washington was soon loud in complaint to Cary because his tobacco was selling for less than his neighbors': "Certain I am no person in Virginia takes more pains to make their tobacco fine than I do, and 'tis hard that I should not be as well rewarded for it."[15]

He kept voluminous accounts in a complication of ledgers, but flaws in his bookkeeping methods grew in seriousness with the size of his affairs. Recording primarily debits and credits for individuals, and also cash outlays, he kept no general record of bills payable and made no adequate distinction between capital and other expenditures. And, although he conscientiously noted such items as "charge Miss Custis with a hairpin mended by C. Turner . . . one shilling," his balances would not come out right. Trying desperately to strike one in December 1769, he remembered a cash payment of £52.16.1½ made in May "and neglected to be charged before." Further cogitation bringing no further enlightenment, he was at last forced to include the following debit: "By cash lost, stolen, or paid away without charging, £143.15.2." He was to warn his stepson that money not invested in land or bonds "will melt like snow before a hot sun, and you will be able to give as little account of the going of it."[16]

Washington had been married hardly more than a year when he felt it necessary to assure Cary: "My own aversion to running in debt will always secure me against a step of this nature, unless a manifest advantage is likely to be the result from it." When in another year Cary notified him that he was overdrawn on their books by £1871, Washington replied that considering the balance to the credit of his stepchildren the estate was still solvent. Then he added to his personal indebtedness a draft for £259, which represented the purchase of more slaves.[17]

Early in 1763 an accounting from Cary was "transmitted to me with the additional aggravation of a hint at the largeness" of what he owed. His reply blamed the debt partly on the "short prices" Cary got for his tobacco, and added, "I shall endeavor to discharge it as fast as I can conveniently." But at this moment Stewart needed a loan to buy a commission in the regular army. Placing the obligations of friendship over those of business, Washington sent Stewart £300 with an apology that he could not spare more and the request that Cary be kept in ignorance of the loan.[18]

Washington somewhat reduced his purchases from England, but try as best he could he could not keep his expenses in Virginia down: friends continued to need help and his way of life had to be kept up, and opportunities kept appearing to improve his plantations. Add to this that his tobacco was worse than usual—some inferior narrow leaves had gotten mixed with the best leaves by accident—and the result was £300 added to his debt.[19]

In January 1764 he wrote Cary that he intended to invest

more advantageously some of the money belonging to his step-children which was to some extent balancing on the firms' books his own indebtedness. The businessman replied with a blast, which in turn elicited from the Virginia gentleman a reply most informative as to his business conceptions.

Washington began with a defense of his own character: "In whatsoever light it may appear to you, it is not less evidently certain that mischances rather than misconduct have been the causes." It was not his fault that for three successive years the weather had been unfavorable to tobacco culture, that Cary had got such poor prices for what he had sent, that some of his own debtors had not paid him. "And, as things have turned out, (and you have such occasion for your money) it is unlucky likewise that I have made some purchases of land and slaves in this country."

It was not in his power to make remittances, "I should add in a manner convenient and agreeable to myself," faster than his crops should furnish the means. However, not desiring that anybody "should suffer in the most trivial instances in my account," he was willing to pay Cary interest on what he owed.

If receiving interest did not satisfy the factors, he would make the sacrifices necessary to discharge the whole debt immediately, "and effectually remove me from all mention of it, for I must confess I did not expect that a correspondent so steady and constant as I have proved, and was willing to have continued to your house while the advantages were in any way reciprocal, would be reminded in the instant it was discovered how necessary it was for him to be expeditious in his payments. Reason and prudence naturally dictates to every man of common sense the thing that is right, and you might have rested assured that so fast as I could make remittances without distressing myself too much, my inclinations would have prompted me to it." Although he had just ordered Cary to send him, however much it cost if it really suited his needs, a machine for grubbing up tree stumps, he stated that he would from now on keep his orders contracted.[20]

Washington clearly felt that a businessman insulted a gentleman by requesting payment unless the businessman were in crucial need of the money. The best security was—or should be—his debtor's sense of what was right and dislike of being hampered by debt. Thus Washington commented in 1778 on how disillusioning it was that some men were so full of "rascality" that "the only way to make them honest is to prevent their being otherwise by tying them firmly to the accomplishment of their contracts."[21]

Washington's use of his wards' assets to cover his own debts outrages modern estate practice, but, on the other hand, a modern estate administrator would feel justified in charging for his services, and would certainly bill the estate for out of pocket expenses.* Washington not only gave his services but actually paid out, according to his own estimate, "some hundreds of pounds." Even if he deprived his stepchildren of interest—a consideration that does not seem to have occurred to him—their loss was much less than their gain. When he discovered that Cary, having established the giving of interest, was paying 4 per cent on the Custis money and charging him 5 per cent, he did not demand that his interest be lowered but that his wards also receive 5 per cent.[23]

As for Robert Cary and Company of London, they had every reason to enjoy the state of their account with George Washing-

---

* The distinction, so sharp in modern ethics, between a man's personal and his business affairs was dim according to the aristocratic mores Washington followed. Thus, during 1758, he saw no conflict in having Lieutenant Charles Smith, who was his military subordinate in command of Fort Loudoun, also supervise his Bullskin plantation. In his official capacity, Smith employed on public business the wagon he was renting out for Washington's private account. On the other hand, Washington often paid from his own pocket for military supplies, in effect advancing money to the state without contract or any payment of interest.[22]

ton, Esq., of Virginia. They made a double profit on his business transactions, first selling his tobacco and then spending the money as his purchasing agent—and he was not present to impose on either transaction fair play. When his debt became heavy, they charged interest and the British currency laws were arranged to make it almost impossible for Virginia planters to pay off such obligations. The fact of the debt made Washington—or so it seemed—Cary's financial serf: they did not have to be moderate or even careful in their dealings with him, however much he complained.

And how he complained! In the hundreds of letters he wrote his English factors it is hard, if not impossible, to find a word of praise for anything they had done. They were, he was sure, selling his tobacco for less than it was worth; and on the matter of purchases, his difficulties were innumerable.

To begin with, what he ordered often did not come at all. There was the tragic moment when, with six-year-old Patsy following him in tears, Washington combed the hold of a ship to find a trunk of goods for her which she had been anticipating for a whole year, and which was listed on the captain's invoice but had not been embarked. (It appeared a year later.) Then there were the goods that were landed on a wrong one of Virginia's rivers, involving Washington in the expense and trouble of finding a coastal vessel to bring them on. Then there were the goods that were tampered with on shipboard—wine was usually half drunk and afterwards watered—or smashed. Then there were the goods that arrived with parts missing, like some ploughs which were "entirely useless and lie upon my hands a dead charge." Then there was that endlessly recurring fact that the goods shipped were, as Washington exclaimed, "mean in quality but not in price, for in this they excel."[24]

Washington suspected that when the British tradespeople heard that goods were being bought for export, they added ten to twenty per cent to the price and pawned off what was least saleable. Although he always asked that he be sent what was most fashionable, he got, he was sure, articles "that could only have been used by our forefathers in the days of yore." In ordering Patsy's spinet, he implored Cary to "bespeak this instrument" as if for himself.[25]

When Washington commissioned fine clothes—"a superfine blue broadcloth coat with silver trimmings"; "a fine scarlet waistcoat full laced"; "one pair crimson velvet breeches"—he sent his measurements across the ocean. However, the clothes that came back fitted so badly that in despair he wondered whether it would not serve better to have the tailor measure some Londoner who was also six feet fall, slender, and with pretty long arms and thighs.[26] Other Virginians certainly had the same difficulties, which conjures up a fascinating vision of parties where everyone was dressed to the nines in intensely elegant clothes that did not fit.

Very annoying were the substitutions made by the factor. Washington, directly on his retirement from the military, had ordered for his parlor mantlepiece busts of six soldiers: Alexander the Great, Julius Caesar, Charles XII of Sweden, and the King of Prussia not to exceed fifteen inches high, and Prince Eugene and the Duke of Marlborough, somewhat smaller. He received a group (four figures) of Aeneas carrying his father out of Troy, and two groups (two figures each) featuring Bacchus and Flora. The factor condescendingly instructed the Colonial in what order the statues should be placed on his mantle.[27]

Seeking to be at all times eminently fair, Washington admitted, in the middle of his complaints, that he did not know what his tobacco should actually bring, what was an equitable price for his purchases, what was truly fashionable. "For want of better knowledge of trade," he was not sure he was correct in asking that some of the savings Cary got in purchasing wholesale be passed on to him. Always he tried to appeal to the better instincts of the factor by pointing out what a loyal correspondent he had been. Typically, he ended a diatribe, "However, gentlemen, I hope to find it otherwise for the time to come."[28]

By 1764 when he had devoted only five full years to tobacco culture for export, George Washington, who was to discard so many traditions, concluded that the traditional Virginia economic pattern was a misfortune. But how to break away was another matter.

Thinking at first still in transatlantic terms, he tried, since Parliament had established a bounty to encourage their culture in the Colonies, hemp and flax—but these proved unsuited to his land. Then he turned his eyes inland, resolving to produce what he could sell locally. Abandoning tobacco which had to be exported—in 1765 he grew very little and in 1766 none—he was soon raising an annual crop of "7,000 bushels of wheat and 10,000 of Indian corn, which was more the staple of the farm."[29]

He sold his wheat by contract to an Alexandria firm, Carlyle and Adam. The senior partner was John Carlyle, husband of George William Fairfax's sister; and in business controversies with this old friend, Washington went far beyond his petulant complaints to his London factors. When Carlyle and his partner explained a breach of contract by stating that, suspecting no design, they had not read the document carefully, George wrote that their argument implied "that you were either two fools or I was a knave employed as your attorney. . . . You are pleased to declare 'you had rather be a thousand pounds in any other gentleman's debt than the trifling sum of a hundred in mine.' This, gentlemen, does not POSITIVELY give me one moment's concern." He had asked only for what was his due, and he really needed the money.[30]

In 1769 Washington's wheat crop was six times that of 1764, and in 1770 even better. In addition, his new method of farming took so much less of everyone's time that he was able to diversify his economic base. By putting in the Potomac more seines and a schooner built by his own men, he enlarged his fisheries, selling shad by the thousand and herring by the hundred thousand. He increased his number of weavers so that they could work for all comers. Beside his old mill which he kept in operation, he erected a commercial mill that began grinding in 1770, cutting out a profit he had formerly paid Carlyle and Adam, and also giving him another service to sell to the neighborhood. An English traveler noted that this mill has "a pair of Cologne and a pair of French stones, and makes as good a flour as I ever saw."[31]

Washington was demonstrating that a Virginia planter could, by self-reliance exercised within the borders of the Colony, reverse the usual balance of trade. Far from going into further debt to England, he was sending surplus cash there. In 1765 he paid Cary interest on £1500. By 1766 he reduced this to £1300, and by 1770 to £1000. He cut down his American purchases of slaves and high priced land to make this possible, and was ordering fewer luxuries from abroad.[32]

The problems Washington faced and conquered at Mount Vernon were in many ways like those he was to face at Valley Forge. He could no more lay off his work force than he could tell his soldiers to go home. "The nature of a Virginia estate," he explained on the very verge of taking command of the Continental army, is "such that without close application it never fails bringing the proprietors into debt annually, as the Negroes must be fed and clothed, taxes paid, etc., etc., whether anything is made or not."[33]

Even as Washington was to urge the Continental Congress and his military commissaries to think far ahead, he had to think ahead on his plantation. Almost all his tools, everything too complicated for his own artisans to make, came from England, and this year's order did not sail up the Potomac till next year.

During the Revolution, the Congress and the commissaries commonly failed him. At Mount Vernon, his English factors often did not deliver what he needed. Whether general or planter, he had to do without, using ingenuity to achieve nonetheless his end.

If the militia were troublesome, his slaves were even more so. Having no hope of changing their lot by their labors, they naturally did as little work as they could get away with. Punishing slackers, Washington believed, "often produces evils which are worse than the disease."[34] The solution was individual justice and effective command. Individual justice meant that no one was made to work harder than his fellows or allowed to work less hard. The sick were treated efficiently and kindly, but those who pretended to be sick were sent back to the fields. Command meant something close to the organization of an army.

The only way to keep the Negroes at their tasks, Washington believed, was to have an overseer always attending to them. If the overseer slept late, so would the slaves; if the overseer slept too hard, the slaves would wear out the plough horses by riding them all night; if the overseer were drunken, the slaves would take every advantage, even to blackmail. The basis of an effective plantation force was efficient subalterns. Washington noted, for instance, that it was bad to have a gang so small that "a man of character" would be unwilling to work beside the men, or so large that complete personal supervision was impossible.

But no more than a military company could a plantation gang operate usefully on its own: everything had to be correlated into a larger whole. This meant a chain of command, from the leader of a gang, to the manager of an individual farm, to various staff officers, and, at last, to the commander in chief, who was Washington himself.

As Washington perfected his organization, he prospered. Yet the many writers who claim that by the Revolution he was the richest man in Virginia (or in all America) are guilty of gross exaggeration. The usually accurate contemporary chronicler, "Old Soldier," stated in 1778—perhaps with exaggeration on the other side—that "there are a hundred men in Virginia who have better estates than Mr. Washington, nay 500."[35]

During his fortieth year, Washington paid quitrents on 12,463 acres. This sounds stupendous, but not a single acre was in the most valuable neighborhoods. Washington, as we have seen, boasted that all the Custis lands were within forty miles of Williamsburg. His own closest lands were almost twice as far away: they were 5518 acres at or near Mount Vernon and 1250 at or near Ferry Farm, all at the far end of the Tidewater. Another 4107 acres were still further west, in the Piedmont, while 2738 (which included Bullskin Plantation) were over the Blue Ridge in the Shenandoah Valley.[36] Our next chapter will show him acquiring huge tracts way out beyond the Alleghenies in the Ohio Valley, but these proved, in the years before the Revolution, an active financial liability.

Washington had inherited from his father ten or more slaves, and an additional eighteen had come with Mount Vernon. Not counting the "dower slaves" who were attached to the Custis estate, he paid taxes in 1760 on forty-nine, in 1765 on seventy-eight, in 1770 on eighty-seven, and in 1775 on one hundred and thirty-five. Since he ceased buying slaves in 1772, this last jump came considerably through natural increase. Births continuing greatly to outnumber deaths in his slave quarters, Washington had by mid-Revolution many more slaves than he could gainfully employ. This plethora reduced his prosperity since by then his principles forbade his selling any slaves without their permission, a permission they refused to give.[37]

Yet we need not drop a tear for an impoverished Washington.* He engaged successfully in large operations, was in no foreseeable danger of being sold out, and could afford, although on a far from unlimited scale, both generosities and luxuries.

When in 1768 the Custis chariot had "run its race," Washington could not foresee replacing an object of such elegance anywhere but in England. He adhered so far to his new economics that he paid the cost—it came to £315.13.6—not in exports or credit but in cash. Yet it was to Cary (who may be considered a father of American independence) he entrusted buying a chariot "in the newest taste . . . to be made of the best seasoned wood, and by a celebrated workman." The latest such importation he had seen, sported, in addition to the customary springs, others "that play in a brass barrel" which seemed to him so useful and ornamental that he hoped to have some too. He preferred green "unless any other color [is] more in vogue." The moulding around the panels was to be lightly gilded; his arms were to be emblazoned on the sides along with any other ornaments "that may not have a heavy or tawdry look." His crest was to be put on a handsome set of harnesses for four horses that would suit either two postillions (men astride the horses) without a coachman, or one postillion with. He added parsimoniously that he would be willing to buy a good chariot second-hand.[39]

Cary sent him, according to the invoice, "a new handsome chariot made of the best materials, handsomely carved" with

---

* After Patsy's death in 1773, her estate, which included upwards of £16,000 in English bonds, was divided evenly between Washington and Jacky. George tried to use his share to liquidate most of his debt to Cary and Company. Although the London factors found "a great deal of formal stuff" with which to hold off any settlement until after the Revolution had exploded, his financial position was greatly improved.[38]

pillars, scrolls, and ribbings, the japanned body green and painted with "gilt, handsome scrolls, ornamented with flowers," etc., etc. The inside was lined with green morocco leather that had been trimmed with Cuffoy lace. The windows sported mahogany Venetian blinds, and the extra springs were there in their brass barrels.[40]

As it came off the boat, the chariot gleamed, a vision of transatlantic elegance elevating provincial America. However, the English builder had not bothered to use for export seasoned wood. Before the chariot had been in use two months, some panels had slipped out of their mouldings and others had split from end to end.[41]

If only Washington had ordered his chariot from Philadelphia, where an American maker would not have despised and cheated his American market!

CHAPTER

21

Eyes West

IN NO OTHER direction did Washington demonstrate such
acquisitiveness as in his quest for the ownership of land.
That he was in his own way a visionary, his contributions to
world changes reveal. However, his visions took tangible form.
Thus the yearning of this childless man for tens of thousands of
acres, many of which could easily prove financial drains
throughout his own lifetime, might well have been an expression
of love, a form of worship for the vast American continent. Not
that he ever expressed in so many words such a conception. Ever
the practical dreamer, he wrote, "Land is the most permanent
estate and the most likely to increase in value."[1]

Remembering that the greatest estates in Virginia had
been created by securing "at very low rates" rich lands, Washington engaged in speculations so uncertain that he characterized them as lotteries.[2] They appealed to the gambler's instinct that was deep in his nature. However, he was not a
gambler who left more than was necessary to chance.

Between the lower James River and Albemarle Sound lay that
tremendous waste of nature, the Dismal Swamp. With some
other prosperous Virginians, Washington concluded that, could
it be drained by a huge ditch that would double as a canal from
Norfolk southwards, not only tolls but tens of thousands of

ideally located acres would reward the entrepreneurs. Display-
ing his typical energy, he agreed in 1763 that he himself would
do the necessary exploring.

That the drowned land was fertile he concluded from the
tangled vegetation which made it almost impossible to move
even when he lay in his canoe flat on his back, pushing overhead
on low branches. However, the wild men familiar with the
region knew a circuitous route that enabled Washington to
penetrate to Drummond Pond, a central lake about three miles
in diameter. Here he could, at last, advance easily. He "paddled
through its whole circuit . . . when it was brimful," in an effort
to find an outlet down which flowed a current that could be
encouraged. He saw nothing but smooth water pressing into
underbrush.

That night he lay on a small rise, and in the morning he
waded through "the weeds, roots, trash, and fallen timber" as far
as he could get—about 500 yards—and to his pleasure discovered that the water was beginning to move perceptibly
towards Albemarle Sound. He recognized that this motion probably took place only at high water, that, in its entirety, the
swamp was discouragingly level, but he hoped that if the imped-
ing vegetation were cleared away there would be enough flow to
free for agriculture some of the higher ground.[3]

Washington thereupon joined with other adventurers in a
successful petition to the Council that they be given the land if
they could improve it. He became one of ten owners who were
each to supply ten Negroes to dig for drainage. However, such
scratching with hoes only nicked the edges of the problem, and
no competent engineer was available in Virginia. The company
(like all such Colonial voluntary associations) had difficulty
keeping alive, but it staggered on through Washington's lifetime: in 1794 he considered it of all his speculations the most
promising. The idea was indeed sound, if visionary at the time.

The canal Washington had foreseen was completed in 1828, and the swamp has been reduced from 2200 to less than 600 square miles.[4]

The opportunity presented by the Dismal Swamp to procure new land near the economic centers was unique. For further speculations, Washington turned his eyes to the Ohio Valley, over which settlement hovered like a thunderhead about to burst, and of which he wrote that "for fertility of soil, pleasantness of clime, and other natural advantages, [it] is equal to any known tract of the universe of the same extent."*[5]

The conception that it would be to the advantage of the commonwealth that small settlers should actually possess the land they improved appealed to Washington no more than modern entrepreneurs are moved by arguments for small neighborhood businesses. He eagerly embraced the Virginia land pattern in which he had been raised and which discouraged little freeholds. He used all the "interest" he could muster to get title to every acre he could possibly secure. "No country ever was or will be settled," he wrote, "without some indulgence."[6]

Indulgence, Washington continued, encouraged the investor to "explore uninhabited wilds," to "waste his time, expose his fortune, nay, life." He saw no conflict between this thought and another which he regarded merely as a spur to activity on his part: "Emigrants are daily and hourly settling on the choice spots, waiting for a favorable opportunity to solicit legal titles on the ground of preoccupancy when the offices shall be opened."[7]

As soon as word reached Virginia in the spring of 1763 that the Treaty of Paris, which brought an official end to the war with France, had confirmed British control of all the territory

---

* This hyperbole reflects the working of Washington's mind when he let himself go into imaginative flights. The noun "universe" is extreme, the phrase "of the same extent" qualifies, and the adjective "known" restores rationality.

east of the Mississippi except New Orleans, Washington became a sharer in a new Mississippi Company which intended to petition the British Crown of 2,500,000 acres.[8] However, Indian troubles known as Pontiac's War had exploded, and, to placate the embattled tribes, the Crown pushed the frontier back in the Colonials' faces by the Proclamation of 1763, which prohibited "for the present and until our future pleasure be known" all settlements beyond the heads of rivers that fell into the Atlantic. This deprived Virginia of the material gains Washington had fought for.[9]

He ordered William Crawford, a surveyor in his employ, to locate for him "valuable lands" in the prohibited area, "for I can never look upon that proclamation in any other light (but this I say among ourselves) than as a temporary expedient to quiet the minds of the Indians which must fall, of course, in a few years, especially when those Indians are [shall be] consenting to our occupying the lands. Any person, therefore, who neglects the present opportunity of hunting out good lands and in some measure marking and distinguishing them for their own (in order to keep others from settling them) will never regain it. . . . I would recommend to you to keep this whole matter a profound secret . . . because I might be censured for the opinion I have given in respect to the King's proclamation, and then, if the scheme I am now proposing to you was known, it might give the alarm to others and, by putting them upon a plan of the same nature (before we could lay a proper foundation for success ourselves) set the different interests aclashing, and probably in the end overturn the whole; all of which may be avoided by silent management and the [operation] snugly carried on by you under the pretence of hunting other game."*[10]

---

* Twenty-four years later, President Washington was to denounce the "diabolical attempts" of "land jobbers who, maugre every principle of justice to the Indians and policy to their country would, for their immediate emolument, strip the Indians of all their territory."[11]

In the fall of 1768 new treaties with the Indians abolished the Proclamation line. The lid having thus blown off, Washington began operating like a man with twenty hands. Nothing had come of the Mississippi Company. A more promising effort to get a huge grant directly from the Crown, the Walpole Company, was primarily a New York and Pennsylvania scheme that menaced Washington's hopes.*

However, there were three preferential positions of which he made use. Most valuable because most exclusive was a promise of 200,000 acres which Dinwiddie had made to the little army that marched across the mountains in the Fort Necessity campaign. Next was a royal proclamation authorizing governors to give land to veterans of the French and Indian War. Third came a grant of land near Fort Pitt to indemnify traders who had lost heavily in Pontiac's War. Washington shared, or so he hoped, naturally in the first two, and he bought into the traders' grant, even as he increased by purchase the extensive rights in the veterans' grants that would presumably come to him as a high officer.

Presumably! It was all a gamble in which one guessed the odds. That the Walpole possibility menaced, that the blanket grant to veterans might be interpreted to apply only to regulars, that the different areas of indulgence seemed likely to overlap, reduced the value of the rights Washington wished to buy. "No man," he wrote truthfully, "can lay off a foot of land and be sure of keeping it."[12]

However, Washington had the determination—which the owners of small rights usually lacked if they did not intend to become themselves frontier settlers—the skill, and the money to explore out the best acres, have them surveyed, and then go all

---

* The claims of the Ohio Company which Lawrence Washington had led were extinguished in return for two shares in the Walpole Company, but this meant nothing to George: although he had served the Ohio Company, he had owned no part of it.

through the legal technicalities and squabbles with rival claimants that were involved in achieving a legal title.

When visiting Williamsburg in May 1769, Washington began his campaign to have Dinwiddie's promise of a land bounty to the Fort Necessity army of 1754 honored:* moving cautiously, he mentioned the matter "in a cursory manner" to Dinwiddie's successor Lord Botetourt. Not till December did he finally present a petition to the Governor and Council, which revealed that he had been interviewing explorers down the Ohio, since he specified as possible locations for the 200,000 acres not only the Monongahela but two more distant tributaries: the Great Kanawha and Sandy Creek.[13]

Washington, who had as a very young man been so unsympathetic to squatters, now wrote Botetourt that it was essential to act quickly before any such appeared on the land the veterans desired: "Unavailing is it to say that these settlements of individuals, illegal in their nature, are not to be respected. To remove them would prove a work of great difficulty; perhaps of equal cruelty, as most of these people are poor, swarming with large families, [and] have sought out these retreats on which perhaps their future prospects in like way wholly depend."[14]

Washington hoped that each claimant under the '54 grant would be allowed to survey his own tract, which would have enabled him to operate altogether on his own. However, in selecting the site at the confluence of the Ohio and the Great Kanawha, the Governor and Council established terms that forced the entire bounty to be found and completely surveyed

---

* Knollenberg argues that since Dinwiddie's proclamation was for the purpose of encouraging men "to enlist," it only applied to what we today call "enlisted men," and that therefore the rich Washington stole from his impoverished former privates all the land he secured under the grant. However, *The Oxford Dictionary on Historical Principles* gives no countenance whatsoever to Knollenberg's narrow, anachronistic definition. To enlist was "to enroll on the list of a military body." The British *Army List*, published annually, was a directory of officers.

before any claimant could get a single acre.[15] In order not to lose his share and the others he was to buy, Washington accepted the total responsibility. He put advertisements in the newspapers to notify everyone in his former army of the opportunity, and arranged for the appointment of Crawford as a special surveyor.

Seventeen sixty-nine was the year that Daniel Boone first crossed the mountains to "the dark and bloody ground" of Kentucky. In October 1770 Washington set out, with his friend and fellow veteran Dr. Craik, to travel the 250 miles down the Ohio from Fort Pitt to the Great Kanawha.

Again he traversed the route where he had fought most of his battles, but memory found no place in his journal. As a land speculator, he wrote of the terrain as if he had never before been on Braddock's Road. Although he mentioned the Great Meadows, he said nothing of Fort Necessity which he had built there. (However, perhaps sentiment as well as interest induced him eventually to acquire this blood-soaked ground.) Of the spot where he had with Braddock seen hundreds of men die, he wrote only that it was too broken and hilly to be of interest to farmers.[16]

At the Forks, where Fort Pitt now stood on the site of Fort Duquesne, Washington lodged in "what is called the town" (Pittsburgh comprised about twenty log cabins). To his party he added Crawford, some other frontiersmen and some Indians.

As the party drifted rapidly down the Ohio in two canoes through swish and gleam, Washington left the steering to others. He stared at the islands and banks to identify the groves of walnut and cherry that signaled "the most luxuriant soil. . . . We see innumerable quantities of turkeys and many deer watering and browsing on the shore side, some of which we killed."[17]

On the second night out, it began to snow. This seemed like a replay of old times, as did the bustle of bad news with which he was received at an Indian village, Mingo Town, (near present Steubenville, Ohio) some seventy-five miles below Pittsburgh. Two traders, Washington was told, had been killed close to Grape Vine Town, another thirty-eight miles down river. As Washington hesitated "whether we should proceed or not," further intelligence reported that only one man had been killed, and he not by tribal action but by some stray murderer. They proceeded.[18]

After another day and a half of drifting they came to where Grape Vine (now Captina) Creek swirled into the Ohio, and saw the cabin supposed to be the scene of the murder. It was an idyllic spot, although the sky lowered. Cautiously they approached the shore, gingerly walked to the house. It was empty. However, there was no indication of violence. So they decided to camp there, sending an Indian and the interpreter to the nearby Indian town to learn the situation. Washington walked up the creek, ascertained that the land continued "fine," returned, slept, and was told the next morning that the casualty had been a boy who had been accidentally drowned.[19]

Back into the canoes, "gliding gently along, nor did we perceive any alteration in the general face of the country, except that the bottoms seemed to be getting a little longer and wider, as the bends of the river grew larger." The sun came out after eight days of rain and snow. On and on, day after day, they drifted with the current through a pristine empire so vast and empty of man that the imagination was staggered.

Even as he admired, Washington kept so careful an account of distance that a reach of river which was, according to his estimate, 113 miles from Fort Pitt, is shown by a modern pilot's chart as 112.[20]

Finally, they reached a place where a small run came in on the east side "through a piece of land that has a very good appearance." On that land was a party of braves in war (or hunting) attire, who beckoned them ashore.[21]

Ashore they came, and the leader of a future revolution was greeted by the leader of a revolution already lost. The Seneca Kyashuta had been more important in Pontiac's Rebellion than Pontiac himself.[22] However, Washington only recognized him as a local potentate and an old acquaintance who had gone with him to the French in 1763, Kyashuta presented Washington with a "quarter of a very fine buffalo." Washington accepted with profuse thanks but a sinking heart: his group would have to remain overnight to cook and eat it, which meant suffering in the evening and again in the morning "the tedious ceremony which the Indians observe in their councilings and speeches."[23]

Washington had been drifting for ten days when at last he glimpsed the Eldorado he sought: a boot-shaped peninsula ten miles wide and bordered on three sides by the Ohio. The Great Kanawha River, which rose in the Alleghenies, flowed at this spot into the Ohio. Nearby were two other rivers: Sandy Creek and the Little Kanawha. The rich bottom land that began here, the Indians told him, ran all the way to the falls of the Great Kanawha, which "must be at least three days' walk across."

"We landed, and after getting a little distance from the river, we came (without any rising) to a pretty lively kind of land grown up with hickory and oaks of different kinds, intermixed with walnut, etc., here and there. We also found many shallow ponds, the sides of which, abounding in grass, invited innumerable quantities of wild fowl among which I saw a couple of birds in size between a swan and a goose, and in color somewhat between the two, being darker than the young swan and of a more sooty color [great blue heron?]. The cry of these was as unusual as the bird itself, as I never heard any noise resembling it before."

To the cry of these unknown visitants from the immensity of

nature, Washington returned to his canoe. The next morning they began an exploration by water and land to find the areas most "rich." Then they made rough surveys, blazing trees to serve as boundary markers. Washington shot three deer and five buffalo, and, as he wandered, he entered into a lifelong love affair with this piece of earth.[24]

So extensive was his continuing passion that he eventually secured title to 30,000 of these acres, 10,000 of which, he wrote, "lie upon the Ohio between the mouths of the two Kanawhas, having a front upon the river of fifteen miles and beautifully bordered by it." The remaining 20,000 extended "up the Great Kanawha for more than forty miles. . . . It is almost superfluous to add that the whole of it is river low-grounds of the first quality."[25]

He foresaw filling the countryside with innumerable tenants: to supply them, he would need "a stage or lodgement" halfway up the river to Fort Pitt. As he paddled back laboriously against high water, he paused opposite the mouth of Pipe Creek and marked for future accurate surveying what came to 587 acres— he called it Round Bottom—of rich low land "a little above a place where the effects of a hurricane appear among the trees."[26]

After an absence of nine weeks and one day, Washington reached Mount Vernon on December 1, 1770. Destiny, carrying him in directions wildly unforeseeable, was to prevent Washington ever seeing his Kanawha lands again; but always that he owned this huge segment of the American future was to him a romantic happiness that combined congruously financial value, utility, and beauty. So endowed with a personal concern with the great West, Washington could never write as Jefferson was to, that whether or not the land across the Alleghenies joined with the Eastern seaboard was of little concern to either part.

Reports of great grants made in England to political favorites became so "very alarming" that when the veterans of '54 convened the following March, only six claimants were represented. These "resolved to proceed at all hazards," and elected Washington manager.[27] To pay the costs, assessments were voted according to the amount of land each claimant would receive— for his right to 15,000 acres Washington should pay £11.5.0. Although he suspected that most of the assessments would not be met, leaving the expense to fall on him, he ordered Crawford to proceed with accurate surveys.

In the fall of 1772 Crawford brought drawings of thirteen tracts to Mount Vernon. In agreeing personally to divide the land among the claimants, Washington accepted a frightening proviso laid down by the "Board" as the Governor and Council were called: if, within a reasonable time, a complaint were made concerning the tracts he had assigned to himself, he was "to give up all interest under his patent and submit to such regulations as the Board may think fit." This danger did not keep Washington from according himself and Dr. Craik much of the best land: after all, they were the only claimants who had undergone the trouble, expense, and risk of making personal explorations.[28]

No objection was raised during the time Washington remained in jeopardy, but subsequently there were murmurings. George Muse, for instance, asserted wrongly that he had not been given his rightful amount of acreage, writing an "impertinent letter" which elicited from Washington a fascinating transcription of his words in a rage:

"As I am not accustomed to receive such from any man, nor would have taken the same language from you personally without letting you feel some marks of my resentment, I would advise you to be cautious in writing me a second of the same tenor; for though I understand you were drunk when you did it, yet give me leave to tell you that drunkenness is no excuse for rudeness; and that, but for your stupidity and sottishness, you might have known by attending to the public gazettes . . . that you had your full quantity of ten thousand acres of land allowed you." He was sorry "I ever engaged in behalf of so ungrateful and dirty a fellow as you are."[29]

When Washington wrote Crawford to ask why certain lands on the Kanawha which he had heard were superior had not been included in the survey, the surveyor replied, to prove that Washington had "received much the best on the whole river," that some claimants who had finally got there to look, had seemed "a good deal chagrined . . . as their front on the river was not over a mile and a half, the most of them, and run back almost five miles, and you in [the] chief of your surveys have all the bottom."[30]

Then there was the complaint of Captain Thomas Waggener who had got little land because he had not paid his assessments, and who was generally convinced he had been cheated. To Waggener's agent, Washington wrote defensively that he had not picked "the surveys that were assigned to me either for the excellency of the land or convenience of situation. If I had, I should have avoided the largest tract I now have (composing a full moiety of my quantum) as every inch of it, from the surveyor's account, is subject to be overflowed."[31]

The surveyor, Crawford, was soon assuring Washington with some vehemence that his land was not in danger of being overflowed, and years later Washington was to state that he had got "the cream of the country."[32]

Knollenberg[33] has found in the Virginia statutes a law, passed in 1712, which forbid tracts more than three times as long as they were deep. In Washington's time, such checks on speculation were commonly most honored in the breach, yet the fact remains that Washington's own description of his Kanawha lands indicates that Crawford assigned him much more river front than the legal proportion admitted.

To criticisms of the advantages he had given himself, Washington replied that "the greater part of the expense attending this business" had fallen on him,* and that "if it had not been for my unremitting attention to every favorable circumstance, not a single acre of land would ever have been obtained."[34]

Concerning the other land bounty in which Washington wished personally to share, the grant offered by the Crown to all veterans of the French and Indian War, there was doubt that it would apply to him, even if it were interpreted to include Colonials. This was because Washington had resigned before the Virginia Regiment was disbanded in 1762. When, early in the proceedings, he urged his brother Charles to buy up rights for him, he insisted that it should only be from soldiers who were sure to participate because they had served to the end. Charles, so he continued, should suggest purchasing "in a joking way, rather than in earnest at first," and buy in his own name "for reasons I shall give you when we meet."[35]

In the end, despite his seeming ineligibility, Washington persuaded the then Virginia Governor, Dunmore, to grant him a colonel's share: 5000 acres. However, since he did not achieve this until 1773, he was able to make little use of these rights before the Revolution intervened.

Once he had divided the '54 grants among the claimants, Washington bothered no further with the interests of the others. He had plenty to do on his own behalf, since, in the final steps towards the possession of his various patents, the large scale of his operations, which had formerly made things easier, became a disadvantage. A man actually on the ground could often whisk the acres away from a distant landlord, and, in any case, final possession rested on his establishing a minimum number of

---

* Washington was reimbursed with additional acres for the disproportionate share he paid out for surveyor and legal fees, but he charged his fellow veterans nothing for his time and leadership, or for his personal expenses in trips to Williamsburg and his voyage of exploration through the wilderness.

settlers on the acres he claimed. That he was one man residing far from the frontier brought Washington many troubles.

Michael Cresap, a frontiersman who was to have the dubious honor of having named for him an Indian war he started with his cruelties, walked on the empty Round Bottom tract to make a counterclaim that interfered with Washington's title as late as 1785.[36]

Using a right bought from Captain Posey, Crawford surveyed for Washington 2813 acres near Fort Pitt in what came to be known as Washington County. To pin the claim down with an appearance of habitation, Washington ordered Crawford to build cabins on the land. One had been built and the carpenter was sleeping in it, when a group of homesteaders descended, scared away the carpenter, and, in building cabins that were truly inhabited, placed one so that it blocked the door of Washington's new empty symbol. "There is no getting them off," Crawford reported, "without by force of arms."[37] This led, after the Revolution, to a lawsuit.

To hold his vast claim in the Kanawha region Washington needed many settlers who would acknowledge his title. He tried to lure tenants with newspaper advertisements. Though he offered farms rent free at first, stipulating only that certain improvements be made, he had no takers, largely because his leases were not perpetual but would expire after "three lives." This meant that a man's great-grandchild would have to hand all the family improvements back to Washington's heirs. Settlers preferred to labor and risk their lives in areas where they could achieve freeholds.[38]

Washington next considered recruiting 200 indentured servants in the Palatinate or Ireland or Scotland or Holland. The scheme proved impractical.[39]

By his fireside at Mount Vernon, he had an inspiration. He rushed off orders to buy all procurable buffalo calves "and make them as gentle as possible." He would nurture tame buffalo herds under the broad Kanawha skies!* But first he would have to get people there.⁴⁰

In 1774 and 1775 he mounted through agents expensive expeditions made up of slaves, servants whose indentures had been purchased on these shores, and hired frontiersmen, all of whom were supposed to float down the Ohio to his Eldorado. But Indian wars flared, and his slaves and servants, who were in the wilderness only because they were forced to be, fled at the merest rumor of scalping drives, dissipating both expeditions.⁴¹ As Washington turned his horse's head and his attention to Massachusetts and the Continental Army, the three year legal term would soon run out, and his Kanawha lands were still uninhabited.

Jacky's one-time tutor Boucher, after he had been forced into exile as a Tory, included in a general diatribe against Washington the charge that the patriot had been "avaricious under the most specious appearance of disinterestedness, particularly eager in engrossing large tracts of land."⁴² We know that as a general rule Washington was not avaricious. However, it cannot be denied that, although in specific cases the moral and legal issues were often confused, from his total activity concerning western land claims there rises the unmistakable impression that in this one aspect of his career he acted as an oversharp businessman. True, he did nothing that was not common practice with speculators in wilderness acres, but he was not usually one to accept the norm of misbehavior. Perhaps he justified himself at the time with the thought that lands which were being distributed as military rewards were his by right because he had fought so long and so bravely. It may, indeed, have been to

---

* The dream of domesticating buffalo never left Washington: a cow was residing at Mount Vernon when he died.

escape similar temptations that he refused all such rewards for his services during the Revolution.

Washington's efforts between the wars to secure for himself a great estate across the mountains fed his old desire to channel the trade of the Ohio Valley down the waterway before his lawn. But his old vision of carts groaning over Braddock's Road faded before a brighter, more extensive vision that was to haunt him for the rest of his life.[43]

In the existing state of technology, boats were by far the most economical way of moving freight, and thus progressive thinkers in all the Colonies foresaw the riches (finally showered on New York some forty-five years later by the Erie Canal) that would come to whatever community most successfully opened water travel into the continent's central plain. The matter was mentioned to Washington in June 1770 by Governor Thomas Johnson of Maryland who asked his support in Virginia for making limited improvements in navigation of the Potomac.

Washington replied that "a partial scheme" would be only "partially attended to." Better to urge making the Potomac the channel of commerce between Great Britain and "a rising empire." The river should be opened to as far above Fort Cumberland as was possible "whence the portage to the waters of the Ohio must commence." Washington admitted himself "a very incompetent judge" of the engineering problems involved, but he was not worried. He always believed that if the matter were important enough, a way would be found.

On the political side, he had practical advice to give: although there was "the strongest speculative proof in the world" that all Virginia and Maryland would benefit, he was sure that the voting of public funds would be opposed in both legislatures as to the interest of Potomac landholders only. Better to get the legislatures to give charters, like those of turnpike roads, to a stock company that would be empowered to charge tolls. Promising to pay back the principal with high interest would attract capital.[44]

Washington's scheme was adopted. He helped steer the charter through the Virginia legislature, finding votes by agreeing to a second charter, to please another area, for similarly developing the James River. Maryland proved a tougher nut to crack, due to the opposition of the Baltimore merchants who feared their trade on the Chesapeake would be cut. The Potomac Canal Company was in abeyance when the Revolution intervened.[45]

When that conflict made further attention to them impossible, Washington's western schemes had been financially nothing but a drain on his estate. Yet they joined with his surveying activities in the then wild Shenandoah Valley, his service in the French and Indian War, and his business troubles with Cary & Co. to swing his eyes away from Europe and into the vast continent, the independence of which he was so passionately to seek.

In 1759 Washington had written of "the longing desire which for many years I have had" of visiting London. In 1760 he had stated, "My indulging myself in a trip to England depends on so many contingencies . . . that I dare not even think of such a gratification than which nothing is more ardently desired."[46] After that George Washington never again expressed any desire to visit the land which he had been trained in childhood to call home.

IV

Road to Revolution

22

Dragon's Teeth

GEORGE WASHINGTON was extending paths that had been walked by his fathers. Like them, he was a figure in a neighborhood; like them, he sought land beyond the receding frontier; like them, he farmed, even if he had moved to new crops and a new economic pattern. He was being more successful than any of his ancestors had been. He was happy to live in this manner, and he intended so to die.

The controversies which, soon after the French and Indian War had ended, the Burgesses engaged in with the government overseas seemed to him continuations of old patterns. Since Virginia's beginning, squabbles had spanned the ocean. The Colonists had picked their sides on specific issues according to their economic interests. When Washington had been young his interests had accorded with royal prerogative. The Fairfax grant, on which the prosperity of his brother Lawrence and his friends at Belvoir had been based, had been a favorite target of believers in colonial autonomy. And the Ohio Company, which had given him his big chance, had been created by the exertion of influence in London.

However, in the first major issue that developed with the peace, Washington's interest was strongly on the home rule side. During the fighting, the Colonists had been permitted to print money to meet their military needs; but in 1763 the English merchants trading with Virginia protested the amount of money circulating there, and in 1764 Parliament overrode the House of Burgesses by forbidding paper emissions. As a result, Virginia, with her adverse balance of trade, became so drained of currency that hardly anyone could pay his debts.

Washington, who hesitated to prosecute correspondents caught in the money squeeze, could not collect what was owed him locally, and he was hampered in his own business activities. These were major reasons that he built up such an adverse balance with Cary & Co. He wrote that the opposition of merchants like Cary to paper money in Virginia "seems to be ill-timed" and, "I suppose, will set the whole country in flames." However, "I will suspend my further opinion of the matter." He was happy to leave handling the issue to those politicians in Williamsburg who were more conversant with such negotiations.[1]

Washington had probably ridden home, in the spring of 1765, from the continuing session of the Burgesses before the news that Parliament had passed the Stamp Act* inspired the Virginia Resolves which were among premonitory guns of the Revolution.[2] The resolves bristled with constitutional arguments. In his correspondence, Washington passed quickly over such arguments, which he noted engrossed "the conversation of the speculative part of the Colonists," to state simply that American liberties were endangered, and then to turn to a bright side: England was cutting off her own nose since "whatsoever contributes to lessen our importations must be hurtful to their manufactures. And the eyes of our people, already beginning to

---

* Do readers have to be reminded that the Stamp Act was objected to as initiating the principle that a tax could be legislated abroad and collected in America by agents of the Crown? It fell primarily on legal and business transactions, which, in retaliation, the Colonials curtailed.

open, will perceive that many luxuries which we lavish our substance to Great Britain for, can well be dispensed with, while the necessities of life are (mostly) to be made within ourselves. This consequently will introduce frugality and a necessary stimulation to industry."[3]

The Stamp Act proved, as Washington had prophesied, a boomerang and was repealed. However, in 1767 Parliament tried again. The Townshend Acts ordered that import duties be collected in America by the Crown and used to make royal officials there independent of Colonial appropriations.

Although Washington knew what was on the agenda and nothing particular seems to have been happening at Mount Vernon, he did not attend the session of the Virginia Assembly that joined other Colonies in violent protests.[4] He was still concerned as a Burgess primarily with County issues.

How far he was outside the inner circle was revealed when, in April 1769, he received from Maryland a sheaf of documents reporting action in Philadelphia and Annapolis on agreements not to import certain goods from England as long as the Townshend duties were in force. He found among the papers a plan for Virginia. Not knowing that it had been drawn up by his neighbor George Mason, he forwarded it to that gentleman for his information.

In a covering letter, he wrote, "At a time when our lordly masters in Great Britain will be satisfied with nothing less than the depreciation of American freedom, it seems highly necessary that something should be done to avert the stroke and maintain the liberty which we have derived from our ancestors; but the manner of doing it to answer the purpose effectively is the point in question.

"That no man should scruple or hesitate a moment to use a-ms [arms] in defense of so valuable a blessing, on which all the good and evil of life depends, is clearly my opinion; yet a-ms, I would beg leave to add, should be the last resource, the dernier resort. Addresses to the throne and remonstrances to parliament we have already, it is said, proved the inefficacy of. How far then their attention to our rights and privileges is to be awakened or alarmed by starving their trade and manufactures remains to be tried."

As for the nonimportation scheme, "I will not take upon me to determine" how far it was practicable. He thought it might be enforced in Virginia "if the gentlemen in their several counties would be at some pains to explain the matter to the people." He "ardently" wished imports could be stopped, less because of any effect that might be created in England, but because that would "emerge the country [Virginia] from the distress it at present labors under," which caused estates to be sold daily for the discharge of debts. He described the happy results he foresaw in a parable:

"The extravagant and expensive man . . . is thereby furnished with a pretext to live within bounds, and embraces it. Prudence dictated economy to him before, but his resolution was too weak to put it in practice, for how can I, *says he*, who have lived in such and such a manner, change my method? I am ashamed to do it; and besides, such an alteration in the system of my living, will create suspicions of a decay in my fortune, and such a thought the world must not harbor. I will e'en continue my course—till at last the course discontinues the estate."

The poor man, Washington continued, would be benefited, if only psychologically, by a reduction in luxury, "because as he judges from comparison, his condition is amended in proportion as it approaches nearer to those above him."[5]

This letter is a major milestone of Washington's road to Revolution. It reveals that, although he had not been publicly active, he was deeply concerned. The mention of arms is the earliest surviving from his pen. Certainly it was typical for the neigh-

borhood patriarch and negligent Burgess to believe that the way
to move opinion was not by ukase from any center, but for "the
gentlemen in the several counties" to explain things to the
people. Equally significant was the entire absence from his letter
of the usual large theoretical arguments.* He preferred to put
forward what he knew from his own experience: that distresses
could be relieved by rebuilding the economy on a local base.
Washington had, indeed, taken a long step towards American
independence in his own fields when he had changed his crop
from tobacco to wheat and corn.

In taking further steps, he was helped by George Mason.
Occupying the next plantation below Belvoir, Mason had long
been a coadjutor with Washington in county leadership. He was
tall but stooped, a valetudinarian, a man not of action but of
books, who had studied the law but never qualified to practice;
a subtle man who hated to leave his jewel-like mansion Gunston
Hall, but rather drew seekers for wisdom there as if he were a
prophet in a cave. Mason asked Washington's help in perfecting
a list of articles Virginians should not import, which opened
between the two men broader discussions. Washington listened
spellbound as Mason expounded philosophical and political
reasoning.

"An innate spirit of freedom," Washington remembered on the
eve of his attendance at the First Continental Congress, "first
told me that the measures which administration hath for some
time been . . . pursuing are repugnant to every principle of
natural justice; whilst much abler heads than my own hath fully
convinced me that it is not only repugnant to natural right, but
subversive of the laws and constitution of Great Britain itself, in

* The historian Henry Steele Commager writes that the Founding Fathers
"thought of little else than politics."[6] From this quite accurate generalization,
Washington was a stunning exception.

the establishment of which some of the best blood in the kingdom hath been spent."[7]

Having with Mason drawn up a list of goods to be proscribed, Washington carried it to Williamsburg for the spring session of the Burgesses. To open that session, the new Governor, Lord Botetourt, inaugurated imported royal pageantry, riding from his palace to the capitol in a resplendent coach behind cream white horses. Washington's reaction was not outrage but pleasure; he later bought the horses.[8]

The Burgesses got things underway, on May 17, 1769, by enacting unanimously "an humble, dutiful, and loyal address" to George III "praying the royal interposition in favor of the violated rights of America." Botetourt thereupon summoned the members to the Council Chamber. Washington trooped upstairs with the others. He heard the Governor read an angry order dissolving the Assembly. With the others, he went downstairs and, after some quick arrangements had been made, along the street to the Raleigh Tavern. There he pulled from his pocket the plan for a nonimportation agreement concerning which he had advised with Mason. After being considered by a committee on which Washington sat, the draft was accepted almost as written.[9]

This was the first even mildly prominent role Washington had played in the Revolutionary cause. He accompanied it by the belated purchase of John Dickinson's inflammatory pamphlet, *Letters from a Farmer in Pennsylvania,* which had been published more than a year before.[10] He also attended a celebration at the Governor's Palace of the Queen's birthnight. Had not the displaced Burgesses toasted "the King, Queen, and Royal Family" at the very illegal meeting from which they had promulgated the nonimportation agreement?

Although Washington had helped draft the agreement, he became so confused in its complications that, when ordering from Cary, he enclosed a copy and placed on the English businessman the responsibility of sending him nothing that was banned. "I am fully determined," he explained, "to adhere religiously to it, and may perhaps have wrote for some things unwittingly."[11]

On his Mount Vernon estate, Washington set his spinners and his weavers and his blacksmiths effectively to work. According to "Old Soldier," being "industrious" and less politically "violent than most of them, he carried the scheme of manufacturing to a greater height than almost any man [in Virginia]."[12]

However, the complicated nonimportation agreement proved unenforceable, all the more so because Virginia was in fact so dependent on imported manufactures. And, as in other Colonies, those patriotic merchants who abided by the stipulations suffered from unfair competition with those who did not. The effort was failing all over the continent, while the British were being conciliatory: they removed the Townshend duties from everything but tea. In 1771, Washington attended a meeting at Williamsburg that withdrew Virginia's restrictions from all untaxed articles. Instantly, he sent off to Cary for clothes for all his family, spices, glass and china, silver spurs.[13]

The Boston massacre, which took place on March 5, 1770, is not mentioned in any of Washington's surviving correspondence. He was trying to keep as calm as possible, approaching a momentous decision with all the deliberation and gravity so important a matter warranted.

For the slowness with which George Washington came to conclusions there was a deep temperamental base and need. He was not an intellectual who could play with a conception for years: turn it round, give voice to it, brighten or dim it according to circumstances. For Washington, the acceptance of a conclusion was taking an almost irrevocable step.

Those unperfected ideas that a more volatile man would

express with the knowledge that he need not act on them and that they could be subsequently withdrawn, were for Washington weights which, in silent cogitation or on private memoranda, he placed on one side or another of a mental scale. He himself described this process as "balancing in my mind and giving the subject the fairest consideration." Only after the fairest consideration pulled the balance irrevocably in one direction, did he state a conclusion to the world. The mercurial Patrick Henry is quoted as stating that Washington's mind "is slow in operation, being little aided by invention or imagination, but sure in conclusion."[14]

That, as the crisis deepened, his innate sense of liberty was receiving from his friends the support of constitutional argument, was for Washington not enough. He needed—which showed the aristocrat was a republican too—to be convinced that "the voice of mankind is with me."[15] And, most important of all at this stage of his trip to rebellion, he required proof that the present controversy with England was basically different from all those that had down the generations preceded it.

Washington, who had himself broken so many leading strings, recognized that a fundamental dichotomy between the Old World and the New existed and would sooner or later raise extremely grievous issues. However, he hoped that the matter could be left "to posterity to determine." He reasoned that such postponement would be possible if the British actions of the moment were nothing more than hasty, ill-considered, and random reactions to individual situations. To accept violent resistance as necessary, he would have to find that America was being subjected to "a regular plan at the expense of law and justice to overthrow our constitutional rights and liberties." This conclusion he hesitated to draw because, as he later wrote, he was at first "unsuspicious of design, and then unwilling to enter into disputes with the mother country."[16]

However, in the spring of 1772 the possibility of what he called "the dernier resort" was rising in his mind. This is revealed by his decision, when finally persuaded to have his portrait painted, to exhume for the occasion, as if to indicate he was a soldier after all, his long unused uniform.

Washington hated to be placed in situations where he felt awkward. "Inclination," he wrote, "having yielded to importunity, I am now under the hands of Mr. Peale, but in so grave, so sullen a mood, and now and then under the influence of Morpheus when some critical strokes are making, that I fancy the skill of this gentleman's pencil will be put to it in describing to the world the manner of a man I am."[17]

The sitter's humorous observation was apt: Charles Willson Peale's 1772 portrait of Washington is one of the least revealing likenesses that excellent artist ever painted.

We get a more vivid picture from Peale's account of how, when he and several other gentlemen were pitching the bar during his stay at Mount Vernon, Washington appeared "and requested to be shown the pegs that marked the bounds of our effort; then smiling, and without putting off his coat, held out his hand for the missile. No sooner did the heavy iron bar feel the grasp of his mighty hand than it lost the power of gravitation and whizzed the air, striking the ground far, very far beyond our utmost limits. We were indeed amazed, as we stood around all stripped to the buff, with short sleeves rolled up, and having thought ourselves very clever fellows, while the Colonel, on retiring, pleasantly observed, 'When you beat my pitch, young gentlemen, I'll try again.' "[18]

With the uniform in which he was painted, Washington undoubtedly harked back to old ambitions—memories and excitements and anxieties—which, indeed, could never have been for long completely out of his mind, if only his unconscious one.

In its strangest aspect, Washington's continuing career was

like a valley watered by two streams which alternated in the sunlight, the one dropping into caverns as the other burst upward. When in the public service, he seemed to ignore his private affairs and his particular corner of earth. When he concerned himself with farming and amassing land, with family, home, and neighborhood, he seemed to have banished what he called "a wide and bustling world." Yet in each situation the other flow continued, if sometimes invisible, always uninterrupted.

"To inveigh against things that are past and unremediable," Washington wrote in 1781, "is unpleasing. . . . We ought not," he continued, "to look back," but then he added, "unless it is to derive useful lessons from past errors, and for the purpose of profiting by dear bought experience."[19]

That Washington regarded experience as the true teacher, kept him from having an intellectual's fear of attacking a problem to which no solution was supplied by reading, theorizing, or precedent. He was not so much afraid of making mistakes, as of failing to recognize them as such: "Errors once discovered," he wrote, "are more than half amended." This attitude enabled him to regard a sense of inadequacy as not a crippling frame of mind, but a salutary one, since it encouraged self-scrutiny. "Diffidence in an officer is a good mark," he wrote during 1777, "because he will always endeavor to bring himself up to what he conceives to be the full line of his duty."[20]

At his resignation as Colonel of the Virginia Regiment, Washington's nerves had been raw and he seemed to have profited little from the experiences through which he had recently passed. But on his eventual return, after his long retirement, to military command, he proved to be in possession of almost all the wisdom that was to be extracted not only from his successes but also from his failures during the French and Indian War.

Writers, knowing that Washington became a very great man,

have been troubled to the point of suppression by aspects of his behavior during his early commands. The interior forces that made Washington a very great man surely caused him to be in retrospect even more troubled. His contributions to the French and Indian War had, it is true, been considerable, enough by themselves to have won George Washington a minor niche in the pantheon of the American past. A lesser man we should have more admired for such achievements; a lesser man would himself have been more pleased with what he had done. When under criticism, Washington had written Dinwiddie, "I should esteem myself, as the world also would, vain and empty, were I to arrogate perfection."[21] In a lesser man, this would have been pomposity; for Washington, it revealed a true desire for perfection.

Washington could recall successes to be analyzed so that they could be repeated, and also thousands of matters, big and small, that signaled fruitful means of amendment. They concerned recruiting, supply, command, tactics, strategy. They concerned the regulars, the militia, the artillery, the engineers. They concerned his relations with his troops, with his colleagues and rivals, with the public, with his superiors both military and civil. They concerned the political aspects of command on every level, and the cooperation (or lack of it) between colonies. They concerned his own behavior, both as an officer and a man.

Abhorring dusky speculations and foggy notions, possessed of a mind that was a searchlight always trying to establish clarity, Washington seems to have had his self-confidence most shaken by the fact that, as his military service drew to a close, he had not understood what was happening. For four years he had labored bloodily to protect the Ohio Valley from the French and the Virginia frontier from the Indians, and then all had been achieved, for some reason he could not comprehend, by men whose strategy he had violently opposed. Certainly Washington's memory of this humiliating ignorance helps explain the caution he now exerted in drawing from his limited view broad conclusions, in seeking, from among cornstalks, leadership in a movement as wide as the continent, involving issues broader than the ocean.

The attack by Rhode Islanders on the British revenue cutter *Gaspeé* outraged the British into threatening to carry the implicated Colonials to England for trial. When the Burgesses, recognizing a precedent most dangerous to American liberty, resolved early in 1773 to establish a committee of correspondence with other colonies for mutual self-defense, Washington voted for the measure, but was not put on the committee, nor did he mention it in his letters. He did, however, as the year advanced, demonstrate practically his disapproval of British customs regulations by engaging in a little smuggling: some goods for Martha were packed in a fish barrel with two rows of Middleton's biscuits at each end.[22]

About New Year's Day 1774 he learned of the Boston Tea Party. Washington expressed disapproval. Such lawless deeds gave the British excuses for ruling with a high hand.[23] However, it was the violence of the British reactions to the Tea Party, known to American history as "the Intolerable Acts," which overcame his last doubts.

The extent of those reactions was still not clear when it became known that the British had ordered the port of Boston closed. Washington voted with the other Burgesses that the day set for the closing should be observed throughout Virginia "as a day of fasting, humiliation, and prayer, devoutly to implore the divine interposition for averting the heavy calamity which threatens destruction to our civil rights and the evils of civil war." The new Governor, Lord Dunmore, responded by dissolving the House. Washington thereupon met with the other members in Raleigh Tavern to denounce the Boston Port Bill, declare common cause with the other colonies, and urge the establishment of a Continental Congress to meet annually.[24]

Bad news continued to stream in: the charter of Massachusetts was to all intents canceled; more troops were being sent to Boston; and the Quebec Act transferred the area between the Ohio and the Mississippi, which Washington had fought for, to the jurisdiction of feudal and Catholic Quebec. Striking even more directly at Washington's concerns, Lord Hillsborough, the Secretary of State, outlawed his claims to thousands of acres by finally ruling that the grants which the Crown had made to veterans of the French and Indian War applied only to regulars.[25]

In a Williamsburg palpitating with premonitions of bloodshed, Washington went to church more often than he had ever done, and also gambled for higher stakes.[26] After he had returned home, Mason brought to Mount Vernon for discussion some resolutions he had drafted. As eventually adopted by the citizens of Fairfax County, the text vigorously denied that "there is an intention in the American Colonies to set up for independent states." Mingled with conciliatory statements and provisions, were statements of common cause with Boston and provisions urging that, if grievances were not redressed, imports be drastically cut and all exports stopped a month later. Since abolishing exports would prevent the paying of debts to England, it was stipulated that Colonial courts would then render no judgments on such debts.

Clause 17 urged that "during our present difficulties and distresses, no slaves ought to be imported, . . . and we take this opportunity of declaring our earnest wishes to see an entire stop forever put to such wicked, cruel, and unnatural trade." Washington's agreement to this is the earliest indication that he was questioning the ethics of Virginia's traditional labor system. He was soon to reveal in a private letter that he saw parallels between the tyranny he feared and the tyranny he imposed: "We must," he wrote, "assert our rights or submit to every imposition that can be heaped upon us, till custom and use shall make us tame and abject slaves as the blacks we rule over with such arbitrary sway."[27]

The paper Washington worked over with Mason eventuated in "the Fairfax Resolutions."[28] With the text as finally approved by a meeting over which he presided, Washington had two disagreements. He was worried about stopping exports because of its essential corollary: "Whilst we are accusing others of injustice, we should be just ourselves, and how can we be, whilst we owe a considerable debt and refuse payment of it to Great Britain?" That this reservation was truly motivated by his sense of honor rather than any lack of militancy is made clear by his opposition to the recommendation that when the new Congress convened, it "draw up and transmit a humble and dutiful petition and remonstrance to His Majesty." Many petitions, Washington pointed out, had already been submitted without effect: "Shall we, after this, whine and cry for relief? . . . I am convinced, as much as I am of my existence, that there is no relief but in their [England's] distress."[29]

Meeting in the fall of 1773, after a poll that gave them a renewed mandate from the people, the Burgesses adopted a program similar to that in the Fairfax Resolutions. They elected seven delegates to the First Continental Congress. Although he had never been on the Committee of Correspondence or even active in the Burgesses, Washington came out in the top three: his ninety-eight votes following closely on the 104 for the speaker Peyton Randolph, and the 100 for Richard Henry Lee. Patrick Henry was next after him with eighty-nine. Young Thomas Jefferson's fifty-one votes were too few.[30]

To George William Fairfax in England Washington wrote a letter which showed that the former soldier was listening with no pleasure to the distant, premonitory clank of arms: "God only knows what is to become of us, threatened as we are with so many hovering evils as hang over us at present, having a cruel and bloodthirsty enemy upon our backs, the Indians, between whom and our frontier inhabitants many skirmishes have happened, and with whom a general war is inevitable, while those from whom we have a right to seek protection are endeavoring by every piece of art and despotism to fix the shackles of slavery upon us." Furthermore, "a cruel frost succeeded by as cruel a drought contributed not a little to our unhappy situation. . . . In short, since the first settlement of this colony, the minds of people in it were never more disturbed or our situation so critical."[31]

However, Washington's hesitations were at an end. The British acts as they followed one another were, he wrote, "self-evident proofs of a fixed and uniform plan to tax us. If we want further proofs, do not all the debates in the House of Commons confirm this? And has not General Gage's conduct since his arrival (in stopping the address of his Council and publishing a proclamation more becoming a Turkish bashaw than an English governor, declaring it treason to associate in any manner by which the commerce of Great Britain is to be affected) exhibited an unexampled testimony of the most despotic system of tyranny that ever was practiced in a free government?"[32]

As long as Parliament's object was to establish tyranny, resistance was essential. It was essential that "our rights [be] clearly ascertained." That much was absolutely incapable of compromise. However, although "I am clearly of opinion that one ought to be drawn, . . . for my own part, I shall not undertake to say where the line between Great Britian and the Colonies should be drawn."[33] George Washington was still happy to leave political subtleties to others.

23

The Sucking Vortex

BEFORE HE RODE off to the First Continental Congress, Washington assisted in a scene symbolic of the death of the past. George William Fairfax and his incomparable Sally had rooted themselves in England. Advertising Belvoir for rent, Washington arranged for an auction of its furnishings. There on the lawn in the autumn, whispered and fingered over by strangers, offered to whomever bid highest against the urgent shouting of routine, were the inanimate companions of many of his saddest, of his happiest, hours. He himself had bought £169 worth, including from Sally's bedroom the bolster and pillows that had so often felt the impress of that dear face.[1]

From September 4 to October 27, 1774, Washington attended the Congress in Philadelphia.[2] Preparing solutions to the main issues was entrusted to two committees: Washington was appointed to neither. John Adams did not list him among the important delegates. The most conspicuous Virginians were Randolph, who was elected chairman, and the two orators, Lee and Henry. Washington spoke rarely. Silas Deane wrote home to Connecticut that he was "a tolerable speaker . . . who speaks very modestly in a cool but determined style and accent."[3]

Washington spent seventeen shillings on political pamphlets and won seven pounds at cards. Socially he was very active. In fifty-three days, he dined at his lodgings only seven times, and in the evenings he usually had a second engagement, often at a tavern. Washington summarized his role in the deliberations as "an attentive observer and witness."[4]

Since the beginning, the organization of British America had been like a cluster of toy balloons that touched but did not merge and was each held in position by an independent string that ran to the hand that held all: Great Britain. Now, for the first time, leaders of all the Colonies were met together to deal with a common crisis. What they eventually decided would probably be less significant than how great a sense of unity they achieved and carried home.

First crack out of the box, the legislative session ran into a question which was almost to wreck the Constitutional Convention twenty years later: should the vote be apportioned by population or by colony? By population would be a step towards mingling the air in the different balloons. This proved too radical. Voting by colony won out. However, a report that Boston was being bombarded created, outside the routine of the sessions, an identical emotion in every breast: all felt, John Adams wrote, as if the capital of their own province was being bombarded. It developed that the British had merely seized the Colony's powder at Charlestown, but the impression remained.[5]

Washington had long been intimate with many Marylanders, had served with some Pennsylvanians in the army and stayed several times before in Philadelphia. But farther south than Virginia (where he had never actually been), or into New Jersey and New York his social tentacles had stretched only very feebly. As for New England, it was, despite his quick, disappointing ride to Boston and Governor Shirley, to him a closed book. Now he joked and drank and gambled and talked seriously with leaders from everywhere. He must have examined with particular attention the delegates from Massachusetts, for they had the reputation of being fire-eaters. Their thinking had, indeed, traveled much further towards independence than Washington's, but they hid this from the tall Virginian so successfully that he denied it to a pro-British correspondent.[6]

Washington was eating fire in his own way. Men in danger of losing "life, liberty, and property," he wrote, would naturally "prepare for their defense. . . . Give me leave to add, as my opinion, that more blood will be spilt upon this occasion, if the ministry are determined to push matters to the extremity, than history has yet furnished in the annals of North America."[7]

Although the mass of delegates (as John Adams wrote) "shudder at the prospect of blood,"[8] all knew it existed. There fizzed around the outskirts of the Congress, particularly in company with New England delegates, a gangling, endlessly voluble, profane, and often unwashed English professional soldier of international experience, now settled in Virginia, who was better described by his Indian name "boiling water" than his legal one, Charles Lee. He was evolving military plans to defeat his former compatriots, and British spies were writing home that if the Americans fought, Lee would command.[9] However, Lee was an extreme radical and in personality a strong, acquired taste. Groups of delegates compared over tavern tables their memories of George Washington's half forgotten military career. During sessions, their eyes dwelt appraisingly on the Virginian who sat there so quietly.

Silas Deane found Washington's countenance somewhat hard, but his air "easy" and "soldierlike." Deane was surprised to find so young looking the soldier who had fought in the French and Indian War from the beginning, had been with Braddock, and "was the means of saving the remains of that unfortunate army." In a doggerel letter home, Dr. Solomon Drowne of Rhode Island wrote:

". . . With manly gait
His faithful steel suspended by his side,
Pass'd W–shi–gt–n along, Virginia's hero."

Drowne added a daydream that the liberties of America could be determined in a single combat between Washington and George III.[10]

Where small freeholds were the agricultural rule and cities flourished, the most prosperous citizens were merchants who thought it a worse evil to interfere with commerce than to accept the dictates of Parliament: in the middle and northern colonies the patriot party did not commonly include the upper class. At a time when everyone gave at least lip service to aristocratic concepts, this disturbed even the patriots themselves. Thus reports that Washington was rich (much richer than he actually was) shed on him a particular glow. His two favorite attributes were combined into a spurious anecdote that was jotted down in several diaries. "Col. Washington," Adams noted, "made the most eloquent speech at the Virginia Convention that was ever made. Says he, 'I will raise one thousand men, subsist them at my own expense, and march, myself at their head, for the relief of Boston.'" Word seeped back to Massachusetts that Washington was "generally beloved."[11]

The meetings, as diverse men and delegations groped for unity, went on and on. A session of the Burgesses becoming imminent, five of the seven Virginia delegates went home. In Virginia, Washington had been most responsive to local interests, putting county before colony. Now that truly large horizons loomed, he reversed his direction from small to big: he and Richard Henry Lee were the two delegates that stayed. Most of the departing members gave their proxies to him, but the radical Henry preferred to trust the radical Lee.[12]

In the end the Congress, now operating with satisfactory unity, set dates for nonimportation and for a later ban on exports; made it clear that all the Colonies would hang together; gave no hint of a willingness to compromise; and indicated strongly that any British resort to force would be met with force. A new session was called for May 10, 1775.

After Washington's return to Mount Vernon, the militia companies of county after county elected him their field officer.[13] That, should hostilities break out, he would be called to command Virginia's forces was clear to all.* But what of the continental top command?

Washington had got to know Charles Lee during the Braddock campaign. Lee was running for commander in chief. When he called at Mount Vernon, Washington lent him fifteen pounds, held him for five days, and listened with respect to this regular officer's tirades on strategy.[15] Although he had been during the French and Indian War so eager for rank, Washington was not making the slightest move towards securing for himself the Continental top command.

Indeed, as 1775 swung into the parade of history, George Washington, whose fame was to be of all fames the greatest beneficiary of what that momentous year saw started, hated the direction of the times. Seventeen years before he had retired from the army, a sick and disillusioned young man, to build a private Elysium, and he had built it much as he had desired. Now all was tottering. His western empire seemed to be fading completely away as Governor Dunmore vindictively threw out all the Kanawha patents on a technicality. And the shortages of cash which British measures had caused were frustrating every move Washington made to protect his property.[16]

He balanced on the brink of a deluge. The leaders (as such he

---

* On January 12, 1775, the Virginia *Gazette* published this quatrain:
  "In spite of Gage's flaming sword
  And Carleton's Canadian troop
  Brave Washington shall give the word,
  And we'll make them howl and whoop."[14]

was certainly cast to be) of an insurrection could expect, if they were unsuccessful, little mercy: should they escape with their lives, surely everything they owned which the British could find would be confiscated. And even if victory were eventually achieved, the local paradise Washington had so lovingly built would probably be destroyed. (Mount Vernon was inflammable and within easy gunshot of waters navigable by the British navy.) "Things," he wrote, "wear a disagreeable aspect, and the minds of men are exceedingly disturbed."[17]

His mind was so disturbed that he suspected George Mason of a cheap trick to cheat him. The two friends had advanced the cost of ammunition for the Fairfax County militia. When Mason began collecting the money to pay for it, Washington accused him of pocketing as his share what could be got from the inhabitants most able and willing to pay, leaving Washington "to scuffle as he could with the rest." Mason wrote indignantly that of course he intended to divide evenly: "It cannot but give me concern that I should be thought capable of such disingenuous conduct."[18]

The flyleaf of Washington's diary for 1775 bears a memorandum: "On the tenth of March, when the cherry buds were a good deal swelled and the white part of them beginning to appear, I grafted the following cherries, viz. . . ." But such fascinations were beginning to fade from him. He drilled militia companies. Charles Lee called again and stayed for five days, talking volubly. Washington conferred with a second British regular settled in Virginia, Horatio Gates. He served on committees of Virginia's now illegal Assembly that sought to put the colony in a posture of defense, and he was elected, this time by the highest vote after President Randolph's, to the Second Continental Congress.[19]

On April 27, Washington was inundated with bad news. From across the Potomac came word that bloody fighting had broken out in Massachusetts at Lexington and Concord. From down river, a horseman reported that marines landed by a royal schooner had broken into the powderhouse in Williamsburg and taken the Colony's powder. And then representatives of militia companies Washington commanded came riding in to report that the men were gathering and only awaited Washington's orders to advance on the royal government at Williamsburg.

From Mount Vernon where dispatches would most quickly reach him, Washington kept a quieting hand on the pulse of affairs. Finally he heard from Randolph that Governor Dunmore had promised to return the powder as soon as he could do so without losing face. "Perfect tranquillity will be speedily restored," the president of the Virginia Assembly continued, unless an unfortunate resort to violence produced incalculable effects. Washington then urged his militia companies to disband. They did so, but other companies led by Patrick Henry actually marched on Williamsburg, forcing Dunmore to pay at once for the powder.[20]

These events elicited from a twenty-five-year-old back country radical named James Madison a comment that cast its reverberations far ahead to the distant future. He praised Henry and criticized Washington as one of the Tidewater gentlemen who had, because their "property will be exposed in case of civil war . . . discovered a pusillanimity little comporting with their professions or the name of Virginian."[21]

Virginia returned to its uneasy peace, but the blood that had been shed at Lexington and Concord did not sink inconspicuously into the New England ground. It cried for more blood. The embattled farmers ringed Boston with ditches and redoubts across which Yankee and British bullets flew.

May 4, 1775, dawned unusually hot, the wind from the south. Under Mount Vernon's high bluff, the broad Potomac sparkled, its surface quicksilver, alive with wind, flow, and tide. Into the mansion house windows from the stableyard there came a jingling as four horses were hitched to the chariot. Martha, who was used to seeing her man off on business, stood beside him in the hall. She reached up, as was her wont, to grasp his coat lapels and pull his face down from its height to hers.[22]

It was like a thousand other occasions, and yet it was different. There was menace in the air, though invisible; menace in their bodies, indefinable until the mind, not directed elsewhere, returned to the thought of impending war. However, it was not this errand that seemed really horrendous, but the next one or the one after that. Washington would ride home again to assume, should necessity require, the Virginia command. That seemed sure—or was it sure? How far did either George or Martha foresee a call that would separate him for long—perhaps forever—from the Mount Vernon they both loved, and from her? He had packed his uniform and was preparing to wear it when the Congress met. Was this to be a symbol of Virginia's spirit? Or was it, even subconsciously, a bid for something else?

The chariot came to the door, its split English panels now replaced with seasoned American wood. Richard Henry Lee, who was going along, got in. Washington got in. The postillion closed the chariot door and mounted on one of the horses. The coachman cracked his whip. The wheels turned, dust rose, and the great adventure had started.[23]

They advanced along roads down which Washington had often passed hardly noticed, but now farmers and townsmen stared anxiously: some took off their hats and cheered. More Virginia delegates joined Washington's cavalcade. About six miles from Philadelphia, they were met by five hundred horsemen. With these clattering beside and behind them, they advanced four miles, and then they heard martial music. Up came a band followed by strutting companies of foot and rifles. The whole formed a parade that moved through the streets of America's greatest metropolis, to shouts—and also frowns.[24]

A Dreadful Trust

"WE HAVE a very full Congress," Washington reported, after a week in Philadelphia, to the Fairfax County patriots, "and I flatter myself that great unanimity will prevail." However, he instantly expressed a doubt: New York, formerly considered a Tory stronghold, was said now to be "zealous" in the patriot cause, "but, as I never entertained a very high opinion of your sudden repentances, I will suspend my opinion till the arrival of the [British] troops there." (Washington, who had served on no committee in the first Congress, had already been appointed on one to advise New York concerning military preparations.)

Massachusetts, so Washington continued, had voted 13,600 men, the other New England governments had levied proportionately, and the British were confined in Boston by about 9000 entrenched Colonials. "It is supposed General Gage will keep close till he receives his reinforcement to consist, our accounts say, of about 2000 men, and to be expected the last of this month. What he will then do, no one can tell."[1]

Although a majority vote would still be divisive if the minority would not come along, unanimity was much more elusive than in the first Congress: the issues had become so much more dangerous. Few wanted war. The ruling hope was that Parliament and the ministry, which represented the British Isles, were acting without the approval of the King, who presided over the whole Empire: surely George III would intervene to protect his loyal American subjects!

Like his colleagues, Washington was torn. He recognized the existence of a state of war: "Unhappy it is . . . that a brother's sword has been sheathed in a brother's breast and that the once happy and peaceful plains of America are either to be drenched with blood or inhabited by slaves. Sad alternative! But can a virtuous man hesitate in the choice?" However, he called Gage's army "the ministerial troops, for," as he explained, "we do not, nor cannot yet prevail upon ourselves, to call them the king's troops."[2]

Congressional policy was to evince loyalty by initiating no hostilities: the Colonials should do no more than defend their rights and possessions where attacked. New York was advised not to oppose the landing of royal troops should the troops come peacefully. Thus the reaction in Philadelphia was horrified shock at the news that Benedict Arnold, a Connecticut officer with a dubious Massachusetts commission, and Ethan Allen, commander of an illegal band originally organized to terrify New York sheriffs, had invaded and captured Fort Ticonderoga, as that royal post slumbered in presumed security. Congress voted to return the fort forthwith to the Crown, and its valuable cannon after "the restoration of the former harmony" which Congress "so ardently wished for."[3]

If only events would stand still—but they would not! All the news from overseas was of more repressive measures. Since Fort Ticonderoga blocked the main invasion route from Canada, the northern colonies were protesting its planned return. And Massachusetts was determined to entangle the whole continent in her present and very active difficulties. She called on Congress to assume "the regulation and general direction" of the New

England army that was blockading the ministerial troops in Boston.[4]

From a purely military point of view, the Massachusetts leaders wished that Charles Lee could be made commander in chief, but they doubted the political wisdom of this, as he could be considered a foreigner. Both Joseph Warren, the president of the Massachusetts Convention, and the influential Elbridge Gerry urged on their delegation in Philadelphia the choice of (in Gerry's phrase) "the beloved Colonel Washington."[5]

John Adams, who was the leader of the Massachusetts delegation, wrote his wife, "Colonel Washington appears at Congress in uniform, and by his great experience and abilities in military matters is of much service to us." (He was, indeed, serving on all military committees.) Then New England's master politician added a passage that prophesied trouble for whoever should be made commander in chief: "Oh, that I were a soldier. I will be! I am reading military books."[6]

The more the matter was considered, the more Washington seemed the obvious choice. The only other native officer with equivalent experience, Connecticut's Israel Putnam, was, at fifty-seven, generally considered too elderly. This left as a principal contender against Washington the existing commander in Cambridge, Artemas Ward of Massachusetts. Charles Lee characterized Ward as "a fat old gentleman who had been a popular churchwarden," and, despite the promptings of local prejudice, many Massachusetts leaders doubted Ward's competence.[7]

Had Ward been Marlborough, his appointment would have been impolitic since there was rife in Congress the fear that (as a Connecticut delegate described it) "an enterprising eastern New England general, proving successful, might with his victorious army give law to the southern or western gentry."*[8] Suspicion

---

* To the modern reader, this may seem a ridiculous fantasy. Washington's contemporaries did not know the subsequent history of the United States, but they did know the history of ancient Rome.

of New England grew as one went southward and, Virginia being the largest southern colony, it had seemed wise to make the Virginian Randolph president of both Congresses. A commander in chief from the same colony was equally indicated. Then, what a gift of Providence it was that Virginia's leading military officer was not only able, but inspired confidence and even love!

Washington bought "five books—military." As he saw the arm of fate swinging in his direction, he felt, so he later recalled, "the utmost diffidence from a consciousness that it required greater abilities and more experience than I possessed to conduct a great military machine embarrassed as I knew ours must be by a variety of complex circumstance: as it were, but little more than a mere chaos."[9]

"It was known that . . . the expense in comparison with our circumstances as Colonists must be enormous, the struggle protracted, dubious, and severe. It was known that the resources of Britain were, in a manner, inexhaustible, that her fleets covered the ocean, and that her troops had harvested laurels in every quarter of the globe. Not then organized as a nation, or known as a people upon the earth, we had no preparation. Money, the nerve of war, was wanting. The sword was to be forged on the anvil of necessity. . . ."[10]

"If we had a secret resource of a nature unknown to the enemy," Washington continued long after the event had been decided, "it was in the unconquerable resolution of our citizens, the conscious rectitude of our cause, and a confident trust that we should not be foresaken by heaven."[11] How far was this resource known to Washington in 1775?

The very deliberation with which he had taken his stand had deepened Washington's conviction that the cause was just. It was, therefore, as far as the human eye could scan, worthy of the immediate support of heaven—but he recognized that Providence often acted in a manner which transcended human scrutiny. As for "the unconquerable resolution of our citizens," that was dubious. Congress was far from resolute. Washington might well ride into the battlefield and then, looking back over his shoulder, find that his fellow Colonials had changed their minds about following him.

Seeking comfort, his mind turned to the Kanawha paradise that had so long haunted his memory and dreams. If defeated, he could retire there, and, with a small band of still faithful followers, fight off for years the vengeful Briton.*[12]

Although he was to find them infinitely useful, Washington's memories of his experiences in the French and Indian War now increased his hesitations. When sounded out by leaders of Congress, he never, as he remembered, "assumed the character of a military genius and the officer of experience." A Connecticut representative, who was badly in need of reassurance, mourned that he was "too modest."[13]

"No desire or insinuation of mine," Washington was to write, drew the command his way. Indeed, he seems actively to have tried to avoid the command, inducing his friend and fellow Virginia delegate, Isaac Pemberton, to argue publicly for Ward.[14]

On June 14 Congress finally took a short step in a momentous direction: it voted to raise on the Pennsylvania, Maryland, and Virginia frontiers six companies to be armed with the weapons that were exclusive to those regions: rifles. Although nothing more was said about command than that these troops should report to whoever was in charge in Massachusetts, the riflemen were to be paid not by any individual state but by Congress

---

* The vision is a fascinating one: George Washington, not the beloved master of Mount Vernon, not the august President of the United States, but the buckskinned leader of a band of noble outlaws, the very hero of a favorite eighteenth century romantic dream. Who can doubt that there were in his character and experience potentialities that would have made him effective (if not content) in this role?

and were to be enlisted in "the American Continental Army." Washington was made head of a committee to draw up regulations for that still nonexistent army.[15]

Also on June 14 a Virginia delegate wrote "Colonel Washington has been pressed to take the supreme command . . . and, I believe, will accept the appointment, though with much reluctance, he being deeply impressed with the importance of that honorable trust and diffident of his own (superior) abilities."[16]

The most detailed account of the events leading up to Washington's selection was written down by the immensely able, little pouter pigeon of a man, John Adams, twenty-seven years later. It suffers from the usual failing of old men's memoirs: a tendency to hog the leading role. However, Adams was always an extreme egotist. While the Revolution was actually in progress, he acted as if he had himself created Washington and had therefore a special right and duty to supervise him as he thought best.

Efforts (so the elderly Adams recalled) to secure agreement on involving all the thirteen colonies in the fighting had been moving with such slowness that he was afraid the army in Cambridge would collapse before help came. He believed that the fear in Congress of a New England general was being fomented by a cabal who wanted Washington. However, the group was so strong that nothing could be done without them, particularly as the New England delegations could not agree on anyone else.

"Canvassing this subject out of doors," Adams discovered that several members of the Virginia delegation were "very cool about the appointment of Washington, and particularly Mr. Pendleton was very clear and full against." (There is an unexplained contradiction between this statement and Adams's previous contention that the cabal for Washington was too strong to be opposed.) In any case, John Adams told his cousin and fellow

Massachusetts delegate, Samuel Adams, that coupling Washington's nomination with a motion to adopt the army in New England was the best way to compel the hesitant legislators "to declare themselves for or against something."

Adams, so he continued, rose in Congress* to move that the army be adopted and a general appointed: "Though this was not the proper time to nominate a general, yet as I had reason to believe this was a point of the greatest difficulty, I had no hesitation to declare that I had but one gentleman in mind for that important command, and that was a gentleman from Virginia." Adams saw a "sudden and sinking change of countenance" in the face of the presiding officer, John Hancock, who wanted the appointment for himself, and at the same time heard a stirring behind him as Washington, who was sitting near the door, started from the room.

John Adams, so he remembered, continued for some time, describing Washington in glowing terms. Samuel Adams seconded the motion, and then there was a long discussion in which a strong argument was made for Ward, because the army was all from New England, and had, under Ward, "proved themselves able to imprison the British army in Boston. . . .

"The subject was postponed to a future day. In the meantime, pains were taken out of doors to obtain unanimity, and the voices were generally so clearly in favor of Washington that dissentient members were persuaded to withdraw their opposition."[17]

Adams's memory failed to bring back (when he wrote his memoir he was desperately jealous of Washington's fame) what the record makes clear: to elect Washington was so much more popular a move than to adopt the army that any specific mention of the adoption (which would be implied by the election)

---

* There is no record of this, but it could have been at a meeting of the Committee of the Whole, where no minutes were kept.

was excluded from the bill that passed Congress on June 15, 1775.

Washington, who knew what was likely to take place, stayed away. Probably he sat alone in his lodgings. His name, so Adams believed, was put in nomination by Thomas Johnson of Maryland. The official minute reads: "Resolved that a general be appointed to command all the continental forces raised or to be raised for the defense of American liberty. That 500 dollars a month be allowed for his pay and expenses. The Congress then proceeded to the choice of a general by ballot, when George Washington, Esq., was unanimously elected."[18]

In all history no general had ever been more strangely and momentously commissioned. Far from stepping to the head of a constituted force, the commander in chief was the only man (no rifleman having yet been enlisted) actually to be enrolled in the Continental Army. Not by any direct vote or broad decision had Congress brought the thirteen Colonies into the war then being waged in New England, but by the act of elevating Washington. There was no nation to fight for: the Declaration of Independence lay more than a year in the future. There was, except for intangibles—grievances and resented atrocities—only Washington.

This was officially recognized when, a few days later, the members of Congress voted that, having unanimously chosen Washington, "this Congress doth now declare that they will maintain and assist him and adhere to him, the said George Washington, Esq., with their lives and fortunes in the same cause."[19] Thus, from the first moment of his command, Washington was more than a military leader: he was the eagle, the standard, the flag, the living symbol of the cause.

John Adams, who was to resent and fear this, already felt it in his bones, and was for the time being jubilant. He hoped that Massachusetts would treat "the modest and virtuous, the amiable, generous, and brave" George Washington as "is due to one of the most important characters in the world. The liberties of America depend upon him in a great degree."[20]

As for Washington, his election was one of the few events in his life—the discovery of Benedict Arnold's treason was to be another—which so dismayed him that he became temporarily incapable of action. (It was natural that a man so ardent and so determined to keep control should clamp on the brakes when his emotions were wheeling frighteningly free.) Despite the danger that Martha would hear first from someone else, he could not bear to notify his wife. It would be a terrible letter to write, since it was "bidding adieu to my family and home to which I never expected to return if the smiles of heaven should prove unpropitious."[21]

Although too personal to have been composed by another, his official statement of acceptance is written in Pemberton's hand.[22] We can only adduce that Washington sat frozen over the paper, until his friend said (in effect), "You dictate and I'll put it down."[*]

On June 16 Washington, solemn in his uniform, reappeared in Congress. Addressing him, President Randolph finally stated what had been implied but not stated in the motion that had eventuated in his election: Congress had assumed control "of the forces raised and to be raised in the defense of American liberty." Then Randolph rhetorically asked Washington whether he would accept the "supreme command."

Washington rose in his seat. He did not advance to the rostrum. He stood in his place, and took a piece of paper from his pocket, and read as follows:

"Mr. President: Though I am truly sensible of the high honor

---

[*] That Pemberton was at this very moment Washington's confidant makes clear that his agitation against Washington's election had been a friendly effort to get his fellow Virginian off the hook.

done me in this appointment, yet I feel great distress from a consciousness that my abilities and military experience may not be equal to the extensive and important trust. However, as the Congress desire it, I will enter upon the momentous duty, and exert every power I possess in their service, and for support of the glorious cause. I beg they will accept my most cordial thanks for this distinguished testimony of their approbation.

"But, lest some unlucky event should happen, unfavorable to my reputation, I beg it may be remembered, by every gentleman in this room, that I, this day, declare with the utmost sincerity, I do not think myself equal to the command I am honored with.

"As to pay, sir, I beg leave to assure the Congress that, as no pecuniary consideration could have tempted me to accept this arduous employment at the expense of my domestic ease and happiness, I do not wish to make any profit from it. I will keep an exact account of my expenses. Those, I doubt not, they will discharge, and that is all I desire."[23]

With no rhetoric, no peroration, George Washington sat down.

Thus, as he stepped into the lead of a major advance in the political progression of mankind, George Washington exemplified immemorial social conceptions. This is not the speech of a king who awes from a distance, or of a "protector" who waves a mailed fist, or of a warrior trying to inspirit troops who were strangers with a foretaste of the strength of his leadership. This is not the speech of a newly elected politician seeking to impress an electorate that has smiled today but might turn on him tomorrow. Although he refers to the cause as "glorious," he does not, as orators do, call on God for its support. He does not boast but confesses inadequacy. He does not promise victory, mentioning rather the possibility of "some unlucky event."

Addressing the Congress and through them the continent and the whole western world, Washington spoke as a neighborhood patriarch would to men who knew him well and who had gathered to ask, at a moment of crisis, that he lead them. Of course, he would do what they wished. However, they had a right to know, so that they could calculate on it, exactly how incompetent he considered himself. And, being his friends, they would be concerned with his personal emotions: his "distress," his fear for his reputation. Thus, as if still at Mount Vernon among his Fairfax County neighbors, Washington bared his heart to the hearts of the multitudes. Since his motives were pure, he was sure he would not lose but gain in their respect. As it turned out, he gained their love.

The specific masterstroke of Washington's speech also stemmed naturally from the Virginia world he had inherited and made for himself. In only one situation in his life had he received a salary—as a soldier in the French and Indian War—and then he had wished that he could afford to refuse it. His economic outlook was that of a landowner who paid salaries but did not receive them, who served others for nothing, who managed his own affairs by balancing income against outlay. All he now asked of Congress was that by promising him his expenses they assure him he would not lose in their service.

Financially, the distinction proved to be only a bookkeeping one, as he received in expenses what he would have received in salary. However, his refusal to accept the stipend they would have demanded dramatized in the minds of the world's money-grubbers what was actually the case: Washington was seeking nothing for himself. Thus, John Adams wrote, "His views are noble and disinterested. He declared, when he accepted the mighty trust, that he would lay before us an exact account of his expenses and not accept a shilling of pay."[24]

Whether or not Hancock had been disappointed, he now exclaimed of Washington, "He is a fine man." Connecticut's Eliphalet Dyer, it is true, grumbled a little that New Englanders had been passed over—"I don't believe as to his military or real service he knows more than some of ours"—but Dyer recognized the expediency of commissioning a southerner, and went on, "He seems discreet and virtuous, no harum-scarum, ranting, swearing fellow, but sober, steady, and calm. His modesty will induce him, I dare say, to take and order every step with the best advice possible to be obtained in the army." Silas Deane raised a shout that has never died, "Let your youth look up to this man as a pattern to form themselves by!"[25]

Three days after his election, two days after his acceptance, Washington finally communicated with Martha: "My Dearest: I am now set down to write you on a subject which fills me with inexpressible concern, and this concern is greatly aggravated and increased when I reflect upon the uneasiness I know it will cause you. It has been determined in Congress that the whole army raised for the defense of the American cause shall be put under my care, and that it is necessary for me to proceed immediately to Boston to take upon me the command of it.

"You may believe me, my dear Patsy, when I assure you, in the most solemn manner, that, so far from seeking this appointment, I have used every endeavor in my power to avoid it, not only from my unwillingness to part with you and the family, but from a consciousness of its being a trust too great for my capacity, and that I should enjoy more real happiness in one month with you at home than I have the most distant prospect of finding abroad, if my stay were to be seven times seven years. But as it has been a kind of destiny that has thrown me upon this service, I shall hope that my undertaking it is designed to answer some good purpose. You might and, I suppose, did perceive from the tenor of my letters that I was apprehensive I could not avoid this appointment, as I did not pretend to intimate when I should return. That was the case. It was utterly out of my power to refuse this appointment, without exposing my character to such censures as would have reflected dishonor on myself and given pain to my friends. This, I am sure, could not, and ought not, to be pleasing to you, and must have lessened me considerably in my own esteem. I shall rely, therefore, confidently on that Providence which has heretofore preserved and been bountiful to me, not doubting but that I shall return safe to you in the fall."

He begged Martha to "summon your whole fortitude and pass your time as agreeably as possible. Nothing will give me so much sincere satisfaction as to hear this, and to hear it from your own pen. . . . My earnest and ardent desire is that you will pursue any plan that is most likely to produce content, and a tolerable degree of tranquillity, as it must add greatly to my uneasy feelings to hear that you are dissatisfied or complaining at what I really could not avoid. . . .

"I am, with the most unfeigned regard, my dear Patsy, your affectionate, George Washington.

"P.S. Since writing the above, I have received your letter of the 15th and have got two suits of what I was told was the prettiest muslin. I wish it may please you. . . ."[26]

To his stepson, he wrote, "My great concern upon this occasion is the thought of leaving your mother under the uneasiness I fear this affair will throw her into. I therefore hope and expect, and indeed have no doubt, of your using every means in your power to keep up her spirits."[27]

There is something pitiful in the hero, as he rides away to immortality, imploring his wife not to write him complaining letters lest it depress him too much. George Washington was far from happy at what destiny was opening up to him. "I can answer for but three things," he wrote Burwell Bassett, "a firm belief in the justice of our cause, close attention in the prosecution of it, and the strictest integrity. If these cannot supply the place of ability and experience, the cause will suffer, and more than probable my character along with it. . . . I am now embarked on a tempestuous ocean, from, whence, perhaps, no friendly harbor is to be found."[28]

V

Appendixes

Appendix A

WASHINGTON'S FAREWELL TO HIS OFFICERS,
FRENCH AND INDIAN WAR

To Captain Robert Stewart and Gentlemen Officers of the Virginia Regiment.

My Dear Gentlemen.

If I had words that could express the deep sense I entertain of your most obliging & affectionate address to me, I should endeavour to shew you that *gratitude* is not the smallest engredient of a character you have been pleased to celebrate; rather, give me leave to add, as the effect of your partiality & politeness, than of my deserving.

That I have for some years (under uncommon difficulties, which few were thoroughly acquainted with) been able to conduct myself so much to your satisfaction, affords the greatest pleasure I am capable of feeling; as I almost despared of attaining that end — so hard a matter is it to please, when one is acting under disagreeable restraints! But your having, nevertheless, so fully, so affectionately & so publicly declared your approbation of my conduct during my command of the Virginia Troops, I must esteem an honor that will constitute the greatest happiness of my life, and afford in my latest hours the most pleasing reflections. — I had nothing to boast, but a steady honesty — this I made the invariable rule of my actions; and I find my reward in it.

I am bound, Gentlemen, in honor, by inclination & by every affectionate tye to promote the reputation & interest of a Corps I was once a member of; though the Fates have disjoined me from it now, I beseech you to command, with equal confidence & a greater degree of freedom than ever, my best services. Your Address is in the hands of the Governor, and will be presented by him to the Council. I hope (but cannot ascertain it) that matters may be settled agreeable to your wishes. On me, depend for my best endeavours to accomplish this end.

I should dwell longer on this subject, and be more particular in my answer, did your address lye before me. Permit me then to conclude with the following acknowledgments: first, that I always thought it, as it really was, the greatest honor of my life to command Gentlemen, who made me happy in their company & easy by their conduct secondly, that had every thing contributed as fully as your obliging endeavours did to render me satisfied, I never should have been otherwise, or have had cause to know the pangs I have felt at parting with a Regiment, that has shared my toils, and experienced every hardship & danger, which I have encountered. But this brings on reflections that fill me with grief & I must strive to forget them; in thanking you, Gentlemen, with uncommon sincerity & true affection for the honor you have done me — for if I have acquired any reputation, it is from you I derive it. I thank you also for the love and regard you have all along shewn me. It is in this I am rewarded. It is herein I glory. And lastly I must thank you for your kind wishes. To assure you, that I feel every generous return of mutual regard — that I wish you every honor as a collective Body & every felicity in your private Characters, is, Gentlemen, I hope unnecessary — Shew me how I can demonstrate it, and you never shall find me otherwise than

Your Most obedient,

New Kent County)   most obliged and
10th Janry 1759)   most affectionate

G° Washington.

Manuscript in the collection of the Rosenbach Library, Philadelphia.

Appendix B

ACKNOWLEDGMENTS

I have been assisted in the preparation of this book by a grant from the American Philosophical Society.

The New-York Historical Society—Frederick B. Adams, President, and Dr. James J. Heslin, Director — has placed at my disposal the superb facilities of its library. Every member of the library staff has helped me on many occasions. I am particularly grateful to Miss Shirley Beresford, Reference Librarian. I also wish to thank Miss Geraldine Beard, Arthur J. Breton, Arthur B. Carlson, Thomas J. Dunnings, Jr., Miss Nila J. Evans, Miss Betty J. Ezequelle, James Gregory, Miss Nancy Hale, Wilmer R. Leech, and Miss Rachel A. Minick.

With all other Americans who cherish our national past, I owe a debt to the Mount Vernon Ladies' Association of the Union for the grace and efficiency with which they preserve and make available Washington's home. I have been hospitably received and aided by Charles C. Wall, Resident Director, Miss Christine Meadows, Curator, Frank E. Morse, Librarian, and other members of the staff.

Among the many libraries that also have helped me, I am grateful to that of the Century Association, the Free Library of Cornwall, Connecticut, the Frick Art Reference Library, the Library of Congress, the New York Public Library, and the New York Society Library.

My wife, Beatrice Hudson Flexner, has given me valuable criticisms and Orville Prescott inspired the title of this volume. Miss Patricia J. Billfaldt has deciphered my almost illegible manuscript to create the kind of copy that makes printers purr. She also made friendly and perceptive suggestions.

I owe debts of gratitude to Edward P. Alexander, H. H. Arnason, Julian P. Boyd, Edward Buckmaster, Mrs. Leslie Cheek, Jr., Leon

Edel, Raymond B. Fosdick, Mr. and Mrs. Louis C. Jones, Bernhard Knollenberg, Walter Macomber, Dumas Malone, David C. Mearns, Henry Allen Moe, Francis S. Ronalds, Marvin Ross, Mrs. Seymour St. John, Charles Coleman Sellers, Arthur B. Tourtellot, Arnold Whitridge, and Alan D. Williams.

My daughter, Helen Hudson Flexner, labored bravely beside me on the index.

Appendix C

STATEMENT CONCERNING SOURCES AND OBJECTIVES

In 1787, George Washington noted in his diary (III, 161) that he had ascertained the number of grains there were in a bushel of various grasses, his highest figure being 13,410,000 for a bushel of timothy. The vision of the man already considered one of the greatest in the world counting and counting tiny objects into the millions is an awe-inspiring one — but, of course, he did not do it that way. He enumerated how many seeds there were in a small fraction of a bushel, and then multiplied.

Washington's example inspired me to estimate how many cards denoting publications about him there are in the catalogue of the New York Public Library. I counted seventy-seven to an inch, and then measured the number of inches: thirty-seven and a half. The result: 2997. And that total, of course, includes only a few of the tens of thousands of publications that refer to Washington without being primarily concerned with him.

This proliferation is the greatest problem which the biographer of Washington must face. For the riot of volumes — new ones perpetually springing up on the rotting remains of the old — has, like a tropical jungle, obscured with legend and special pleading the true George Washington.

The biographer must clear the fields before he can hope to plough. Fortunately, this can be done to a considerable extent by an act of will. For my part, I resolved to ignore all secondary sources (with one major exception) until I had mastered the original documents.

By far the most important sources for my study are Washington's own writings. His personal file of documents — diaries, financial accounts, letters written and received, and so forth to about 75,000 folios — is at the Library of Congress. The complete archive has just been published by the Library in twenty-four reels of microfilm with a printed index: *Presidential Papers Microfilm: George Washington Papers* (Washington, D.C., 1965).

With such exceptions as juvenilia, drafts of surveys, some random notebooks, bits and pieces, almost the entire Washington archive in the Library of Congress, as it refers to the period covered by this volume, has been brought out in more accessible form than microfilm. A glance at the specific references below will reveal my great debt to four publications: the *Writings* of Washington in thirty-nine volumes (Washington, D.C., 1931–1944) and the *Diaries* in four (Boston & N.Y., 1925), both edited by John C. Fitzpatrick; letters written to Washington between 1752 and 1775, edited in five volumes by Stanislaus Murray Hamilton (Boston & N.Y., 1898–1902); and a facsimile in three volumes of the account book Washington called *Ledger A* (Boston, 1922).

Fitzpatrick's two publications also include materials found outside the Library of Congress. They comprise, indeed, an almost faultless compendium of all writings by the mature Washington of any importance that had come to light in time to be printed by November 1940.

Mention should be made of two editions of Washington's writings that preceded Fitzpatrick: Jared Sparks' twelve volumes (Boston, 1834–1837) and Worthington Chauncey Ford's fourteen (N.Y. & London, 1889–1893).

As is notorious, Sparks was not above "improving" the texts he published. However, he had access to some material subsequently lost, and he was a very perceptive historian, whose footnotes and appendices are often of value.

Ford's texts, although accurately transcribed, are in significant contrast with Fitzpatrick's. After Washington had returned to Mount Vernon in 1783, he assigned the task of copying his pre-Revolutionary papers to his nephew Robert Lewis, and, in preparation for this, amended his early prose with interlined corrections. Ford printed the amended texts, while Fitzpatrick, by reading beneath the scratch-outs and comparing the letter-book drafts with the copies actually sent (when available), returned as far as possible to the original wording.

Documents discovered since Fitzpatrick are, as is shown in the source references to those I have quoted, published in a variety of places and are scattered through various collections. The most important repositories for unpublished materials that fall within the scope of this volume which I have found are the Morristown (New Jersey) Historical Library; Mount Vernon; and the Rosenbach Foundation, Philadelphia. Mount Vernon also possesses an invaluable archive of photographed and typed copies of manuscript material in other collections.

Among the unused materials I had the good fortune to find, the most important are David Humphreys's unfinished manuscript, "The Life of General Washington," with accompanying papers (Rosenbach Foundation). That the manuscript existed has long been known since Fitzpatrick published (*Writings*, XXIX, 36–50) an undated list of corrections Washington sent Humphreys, each correction being headed by a number which obviously referred to a passage in a lost text. However, in the absence of the text, the historian could only guess at the relevance of Washington's comments.

On July 25, 1785, Washington wrote Humphreys (Fitzpatrick, *Writings*, XXVIII, 203–204). that he was unwilling himself to compose an account of his experiences. In urging Humphreys to undertake the task, Washington continued, "I should with great pleasure not only give you the perusal of all my papers, but any oral information of circumstances, which cannot be obtained from the former, that my memory will furnish; and I can with great truth add that my house would not only be at your service during the period of your preparing this work, but (and without an unmeaning compliment I say it) I should be exceedingly happy if you would make it your home. You might have an apartment to yourself, in which you could command your own time." Humphreys stayed at Mount Vernon from July 24 to August 28, 1786 (Fitzpatrick, *Diaries*, III, 97–108).

The manuscript kindly made available to me by the Rosenbach Foundation, contains, in addition to the numbers correlated to Washington's written suggestions, expansions and other corrections in Washington's hand, and passages that are clearly notations of Washington's oral communications. Washington so rarely engaged in autobiography that the lengthy (although incoherent) text, which also contains Humphreys's own testimony concerning Washington's private life, is extremely valuable to the record.

Humphreys carried off and kept with his own manuscripts one of the most important single documents connected with Washington's French and Indian War service. This is the letter to Captain Stewart and others which is in effect Washington's farewell to those who were his officers during his first war. The kindness of the Rosenbach Foundation has enabled me to print this document as Appendix A.

After Humphreys's, the most valuable contemporary account of Washington's early years is *Particulars of the Life and Character of General Washington*, signed "An Old Soldier." Obviously by a fellow veteran of the French and Indian War who was familiar with Washington and his affairs, the brief but informative essay was brought out in London in 1778. With other biographical notes gleaned from various contemporary publications, it has been conveniently reprinted in William S. Baker's *Early Sketches of George Washington* (Phila., 1894), 47–55.

Various compendia of official documents and the writings of individuals with whom Washington was associated are cited in the source references.

The one secondary source of which I made great use while doing my basic research was Douglas Southall Freeman's monumental *George Washington,* of which the first two volumes and most of the third — 1420 closely printed pages — deal with the material covered in this book. Freeman's work is as close to being a primary source as such a labor can be, since it is a stupendous example of what is called a "scientific" biography: an effort to assemble evidence with as little subjective emphasis and running interpretation as is humanly possible.

The able general of a foundation-supported research team, Freeman surveyed a vast range of original sources: his reference notes have served me as divining rods day after day. In the ascertaining and statement of fact, he was awe-inspiringly accurate, and I have learned to rely heavily on his judgment concerning the authenticity of anecdotes and materials. However, my objective has been quite different from his. Since he sought historical meaning in Washington's writings and was much less concerned with the character of the writer, he practically never quoted Washington, preferring to tell in his own words what a letter meant. And in selecting material for discussion, he was only secondarily interested in the revelations of personality that are of basic importance to my labors.

Although I have tried to be as accurate in the materials from which I have drawn conclusions as any scientific biographer, my primary purpose has not been to expand and authenticate the factual record. (Such an effort would be superfluous after Freeman.) I have wished rather to elucidate the interrelations of history and character that created one of the world's greatest and most admirable careers.

It was originally my intention to keep my biography down to one volume. However, as I penetrated into the subject, I concluded that the reason there has never been a truly effective one volume *Washington* is that the task is impossible. His life was so long and active, concerned with so much of importance and so much of fascination, that to cover it in a few hundred pages forces either emphasis on some aspects to the arbitrary exclusion of others, or the reliance of the author on sparkling (he hopes) summaries as substitutes for convincing narrative.

Taking my cue from Washington's successor, Lincoln, who said that a man's feet should be long enough to reach the ground, I intend to write a three volume life. The second will deal with Washington's career in the Revolution and his subsequent retirement at Mount Vernon. The third will begin with the Constitutional Convention and continue through the presidency to his last years and death.

Only after I had completed my basic research on Washington's entire life, did I begin the first draft of this volume. And only after the first draft was well on paper, did I start my systematic consultation of secondary sources other than Freeman. To list all I have examined would be no more than a demonstration of industry, useless to the reader. The need in Washington bibliography is not for longer lists but shorter ones. Thus, I shall discuss only those biographies of Washington which were in some way epoch making or from which I received active assistance. Most of those mentioned are cited again in Appendix D with reference to specific parts of my text.

Book length publication got off, within a few years of the hero's death, to a two-pronged start. On one hand, there was John Marshall's solid, factual, five volume *The Life of George Washington* (London, 1804–1807), which was a precursor of Freeman's later work. On the other hand, the persuasive fictionalizer Mason Locke (Parson) Weems began about 1800 publishing his *The Life of George Washington, with Curious Anecdotes Equally Honorable to Himself and Exemplary to His Young Countrymen.* Continually expanding his text with new imaginings (the cherry tree story appeared in the fifth edition, 1806), Weems founded what might be called the Sunday School Tract tradition in Washington biography.

Throughout the nineteenth century, the Sunday School Tract tradition proved as fecund as the wives of a thousand poor parsons. I shall make no effort to follow here its teeming spawn.

In 1826, Washington's stepgrandson, George Washington Parke Custis, began the slow and random publication of articles concerned with Washington and his family. Many of these were gathered, after Custis's death, into a pamphlet entitled *Recollections and Private Memoirs, Compiled from the Files of the National Intelligencer* (Washington, D.C., 1859). This work was edited and expanded with other Custis writings, with a biography of him by his daughter, and "explanatory notes" by Benson J. Lossing, to form the edition of Custis's *Recollections and Memoirs* (New York, 1860) that is commonly known.

The Custis material presents the biographer of Washington with knotty problems. From the death of his own father in 1782 to Washington's death in 1799, from the ages of one to eighteen, Custis had lived at Mount Vernon as a sort of son to his stepgrandfather. Surely, he had accurate information to communicate. However, he wrote of many things he had not experienced (such as his highly suspect account of George's meeting with Martha), and he was seriously infected by the Sunday School Tract bug. He even produced an "I cannot tell a lie" anecdote in rivalry with Weems, this one featuring a horse, not a cherry tree, and the mother, not the father. If a widely circulated dubious anecdote does not go back to Weems, it may well go back to Custis. Yet there are in his text many matters that have the ring of truth, either because they are made probable by irrefutable sources or because they emerge incongruously from the goody-goody treacle.

In 1837, Jared Sparks published as the first volume of his *Writings of Washington* a competent factual biography. Some years later came Washington Irving's five volume *George Washington* (New York, 1855–1859). Although this is one of the author's least effective works, it adheres to the record.

We shall now skip over hundreds of books to come to one that is a historical prodigy: in 1896, Woodrow Wilson published in New York his one volume *George Washington*. I read the work, brought out only six years before Wilson became president of Princeton and only eighteen before he became President of the United States, with mounting incredulity, for its fatuous romanticism puts it less in the documentary than the Sunday School Tract tradition.

Seven years in advance of Wilson's book, his future opponent concerning the League of Nations, Henry Cabot Lodge, brought out as part of the American Statesman series a two volume *George Washington* (Boston and New York, 1889). However one may feel about their future globe-shaking controversy, it is impossible to deny that in the George Washington lists, Lodge did better than Wilson. His book is eloquently rather than fancily written, sound rather than vaporous.

Eighteen hundred and ninety-six produced, in addition to the unfortunate Wilson biography, one of the best books ever written about Washington. Worthington Chauncey Ford, whose edition of Washington's *Writings* is discussed above, had a brilliant literary brother whom he undoubtedly helped in the preparation of Paul Leicester Ford's *The True George Washington* (Philadelphia, 1896). Although the essay form — individual chapters on "Relations with the Fair Sex," "Tastes and Amusements," etc.—prevented the author from making adequate distinctions between Washington's behavior at various points in his career, this was the first book to show Washington as a true human being. Paul Leicester Ford's restoration of the marble image back to flesh and blood shocked his contemporaries. However, his admiration for a living Washington glows happily down the pages.

The muckrakers came later. Their bible, which was amazingly influential on a generation of readers,* was W. E. Woodward's *George Washington: The Image and The Man* (New York, 1926). Woodward and his followers were no more than shadows cast by Parson Weems. The discovery that the founding fathers had not in fact been characters from Sunday School homilies amazed them and sent them scurrying gleefully to an equally inaccurate opposite extreme. They would digress from strictures against Washington's morality (based on discredited evidence) to leering descriptions of the New England custom of bundling.* Woodward wrote a dashing prose style but muddied the Washington record.

The first volume of Rupert Hughes's *George Washington* appeared in the same year with Woodward. After publishing three volumes (New York, 1926–1930), Hughes abandoned the work, although he had only carried his protagonist to the victory at Yorktown. He showed his membership in the muckraking generation by enthusiastic digressions on such matters as the drinking habits of Virginia parsons, and he suffered from the fact that Fitzpatrick's edition of Washington's *Writings* had not yet appeared. However, he ranged widely to give a perceptive picture of Washington's development as a man. I owe many valuable realizations to Rupert Hughes.

On the 200th anniversary of Washington's birth, Samuel Eliot Morison delivered an address which was published as *The Young George Washington* (Cambridge, Mass., 1932) and has been reprinted without the explanatory notes in Morison's *By Land and By Sea* (New York, 1953). This short essay is abrim with fascinating perceptions about Washington's development.

The great editor of Washington's *Writings*, John C. Fitzpatrick also prepared a biography of him: *George Washington Himself* (Indianapolis, Ind., 1933). The then blooming activities of the muck-

---

* When I was conversing with Bertrand Russell in London several years ago, he gave me the true muckraker's line: Washington was a dishonest lecher who only fought the Revolution because he wanted to evade his rightful debts to British merchants.

* Actually, the young couples who were put in bed together so they would not freeze, were (even if a board were not interposed down the center of the bed) wrapped individually in blankets that it would take time to get out of and back in. The door was left open and the family was home. There was much less opportunity here than in the hayloft during a pause in the milking.

rakers made Fitzpatrick oversensitive to possible criticisms of his hero's behavior, but this is a good book. It was particularly valuable to me in relation to Washington's childhood education.

Freeman's monumental seven volumes appeared between 1948 and 1957.

In 1958, Marcus Cunliffe, an English professor of American history, published in Boston *George Washington, Man and Monument.* This short book combines an excellent summary of Washington's career with interpretation that is provocative.

Among contemporary Washington scholars, Bernhard Knollenberg is the iconoclast. He can be counted on to search out flaws in Washington's behavior, to come to the defense of anyone—be it Governor Dinwiddie or Washington's mother or General Gates—with whom the hero disagreed. Among Knollenberg's various books, the one most relevant here is *George Washington: The Virginia Period* (Durham, N.C., 1964). At its most original, this volume excoriates Washington's behavior in connection with land grants to veterans (see my Chapter Twenty-one). Although there is some fire behind his smoke, it seems to me that Knollenberg went much too far, reverting, as a former lawyer, from the balanced historian to an attorney for the prosecution.

Appendix D

The following abbreviations of sources most often cited will be employed below:

AOS: An Old Soldier, "Particulars of the Life and Character of General Washington," reprinted from *Gentleman's Magazine* (London, August 1778) in Baker, William S., *Early Sketches of George Washington* (Philadelphia, 1894), 47–55

F: Freeman, Douglas Southall, *George Washington, A Biography*, completed by J. A. Carroll and M. W. Ashworth, 7 vols. (New York, 1948–1957)

F, W: Ford, Worthington Chauncey, editor, *The Writings of George Washington*, 14 vols. (New York and London, 1889–1893)

H: Hamilton, Stanislaus Murray, *Letters to Washington and Accompanying Papers*, 5 vols. (Boston and New York, 1898–1902)

Hugh: Hughes, Rupert, *George Washington*, 3 vols. (New York, 1926–1930)

Hump: Humphreys, David, "The Life of General Washington," recently discovered manuscript, Rosenbach Foundation, Philadelphia

GW: Fitzpatrick, John C., editor, *The Writings of George Washington*, 39 vols. (Washington, D.C., 1931–1944)

GW, D: Fitzpatrick, John C., editor, *George Washington's Diaries*, 4 vols. (Boston and New York, 1925)

GW, LA: *Ledger A of George Washington*, facsimile of the originals in the Library of Congress, 3 vols. (Boston, 1922)

S, W: Sparks, Jared, editor, *The Writings of George Washington*, 12 vols. (Boston, 1834–1837)

Complete short titles of other publications will accompany the first citations. Subsequently, as succinct a citation as clarity permits will be followed by such a notation as *"op. cit.* (Chap. 1)." This means that the complete title will be found among the source references to Chapter One.

When a title is repeated in the notes to one chapter, I have in the later references stated it as simply as possible omitting, as superfluous, the form *"op. cit."*

FOREWORD

1. Morison, Samuel Eliot, *The Young Man Washington* (Cambridge, Mass., 1932), 8.
2. Freud, Sigmund, *The Standard Edition of the Complete Works* (London, 1957), XI, 130.
3. GW, XXX, 299.
4. GW, XXI, 181, XXII, 353.

CHAPTER ONE

1. Hugh, I, 496.
2. WASHINGTON'S ANCESTRY: F, I, 15–47, 527–534; Ford, Worthington C., *The Washington Family* (New York, 1893); GW, XXXII, 11, 26–33, 272, XXXV, 281; Hayden, Horace E., *Virginia Genealogies* (Wilkes-Barre, Pa., 1891), 44–144; Hoppin, Charles A., *The Washington Ancestry*, 3 vols. (Greenfield, Ohio, 1932).
3. F, I, 43–46; Hayden, 43–82.
4. F, I, 94.
5. GEORGE'S CHILDHOOD: F, I, 48–72; Fitzpatrick, John C., *George Washington Himself* (Indianapolis, Ind., 1933), 19–35; Hugh, I, 1–38; Washington, George, Early Copybooks in Library of Congress (Reel I, Washington Papers microfilm).
6. Wall, Charles C., "Notes on the Early History of Mount Vernon," *William and Mary College Quar. Hist. Mag.*, 3d Ser., II (1945), 173 ff.
7. [Washington, Augustine], An inventory of the estate of Captain Augustine Washington in King George County, July 1, 1743, MS. in Clerk's Office, King George County, King George, Virginia; photostat at Mount Vernon.
8. GW, XXVI, 41, XXXIII, 504.
9. GW, XXIX, 209.
10. Library of Congress (Reel I, Washington Papers microfilm).
11. *Mag. Am. Hist.*, II (1878), 436; *Virginia Mag. of Hist. and Biog.*, XXX (1922), 1–20.

CHAPTER TWO

1. GW, XXXIV, 59n–60n; Washington, George, *The Last Will and Testament of . . .* , ed. John C. Fitzpatrick (Mount Vernon, Va., 1939), 7.
2. GW, II, 336–337.
3. F, I, 73 ff.
4. See Chapter 21.
5. Washington, *Will*, 17.
6. Custis, George Washington Parke, *Recollections and Private Memoirs of Washington*, with explanatory notes by Benson J. Lossing (Philadelphia, 1861), 131; Watson, Elkanah, *Men and Times of the Revolution* (New York, 1857), 43.
7. Custis, 125–150; GW, XXI, 341–342, XXVI, 43.
8. Fitzpatrick, *Himself, op. cit.* (Chap. I), 30.

9. Moore, Charles, editor, *George Washington's Rules of Civility and Decent Behavior* (Boston and New York, 1926).
10. Fitzpatrick, *Himself*, 28.
11. Hump.
12. Cunliffe, Marcus, *George Washington, Man and Monument* (Boston, 1958), 31.
13. GW, XXVIII, 203.
14. GW, XXIII, 276.
15. Hump.
16. H, I, 277.

CHAPTER THREE

1. Conway, Moncure Daniel, *Barons of the Potomack and the Rappahannock* (New York, 1892), 216–217.
2. Washington, Augustine, Inventory, *op. cit.* (Chap. 1).
3. FAIRFAX FAMILY: Burnaby, Andrew, *Travels Through North America* (New York, 1904), 131, 197–206; Cary, Wilson Miles, *Sally Cary* (New York, 1916); Conway, *Barons;* Harrison, Fairfax, *The Proprietors of the Northern Neck* (Richmond, Va., 1926); Harrison, Fairfax, *Virginia Land Grants* (Richmond, Va., 1926); Neill, Edward D., *The Fairfaxes of England and America* (Albany, N.Y., 1868).
4. GW, I, 129.
5. CW, III, 247.
6. Neill, 67–70.
7. H, I, 38, 232, 256.
8. Cary, 50; Neill, 74–75.
9. Neill, 133.
10. GW, XXX, 36.
11. Conway, 238–240; GW, XXIX, 36; Hump.
12. F, I, 198–199.
13. Fitzpatrick, *Himself, op. cit.* (Chap. 1), 34; H, I, 29.
14. Burnaby, 200.
15. Conway, 245.
16. Conway, 262.
17. Burnaby, 202; Harrison, *Land Grants*, 114.

CHAPTER FOUR

1. GW, *D*, I, 5.
2. GW, *D*, I, 6.
3. GW, *D*, I, 4.
4. GW, *D*, I, 9.
5. GW, *D*, I, 7.
6. GW, *D*, I, 9–10.
7. GW, *D*, I, 6.
8. GW, *D*, I, 11.
9. Conway, Moncure Daniel, *George Washington and Mount Vernon* (Brooklyn, N.Y., 1889), XL; F, I, 229; F, W, I, 8–9.
10. GW, XXXVI, 262; George Washington to Sally Fairfax (9/12/1758), Houghton Library, Harvard University.
11. Cary, *Sally, op. cit.* (Chap. 3); F, I, 230; Hugh, I, 338.
12. Cary, *Sally*, 23, 46.
13. GW, II, 395–396.
14. GW, I, 13–14.
15. F, I, 221; *George Washington Atlas* (Washington, D.C., 1932), pls. 16–24.

16. GW, I, 18.
17. GW, I, 17.
18. GW, I, 15–16.
19. Custis, *Recollections, op. cit.* (Chap. 2), 527; H, II, 140.
20. GW, I, 19.
21. GW, I, 19.
22. Ford, Paul Leicester, *Washington and the Theatre* (New York, 1899).
23. Fitzpatrick, *Himself, op. cit.* (Chap. 1), 44.
24. F, I, 235–236.

CHAPTER FIVE

1. Conway, *Barons, op. cit.* (Chap. 3), passim; F, I, 76.
2. GW, II, 365.
3. F, I, 245; S, W, II, 481.
4. Hugh, I, 56–57.
5. GW, *D*, I, 19.
6. GW, *D*, I, 22.
7. GW, *D*, I, 25.
8. GW, *D*, I, 25.
9. William Williams, *Portrait of Washington*, Alexandria Lodge, A.F. & A.M., No. 22, Alexandria, Virginia.
10. GW, *D*, I, 27.
11. GW, I, 22.
12. GW, I, 22; *Virginia Mag. of Hist. and Biog.*, XIII (1924), 128–129.
13. F, I, 264.
14. GW, XXVI, 389.
15. F, I, 268.
16. F, I, 275.
17. AOS, 48.
18. GW, I, 309; S, W, II, 428–429.
19. Hump.

CHAPTER SIX

1. GW, II, 41.
2. GW, *D*, I, 44.
3. GW, *D*, I, 44.
4. GW, *D*, I, 45.
5. GW, *D*, I, 46–47.
6. GW, *D*, I, 47–49.
7. GW, *D*, I, 50.
8. F, *W*, I, 124.
9. GW, *D*, I, 50–53.
10. S, *W*, II, 428–429.
11. GW, *D*, I, 52.
12. GW, *D*, I, 54.
13. Gist, Christopher, *Journals*, ed. William M. Darlington (Pittsburgh, Pa., 1893), 83; GW, *D*, I, 55–58.
14. F, I, 325; *GW, D*, I, 58.
15. GW, *D*, I, 59–60.
16. F, I, 325.
17. GW, *D*, I, 59–60.
18. GW, *D*, I, 61.
19. GW, *D*, I, 62.
20. Gist, 84.

21. GW, *D*, I, 63.
22. GW, XXIX, 37.
23. Gist, 84; GW, I, 91; GW, *D*, I, 63.
24. Gist, 84–86; GW, *D*, I, 64.
25. Gist, 86.
26. GW, *D*, I, 65.
27. GW, *D*, I, 66.
28. GW, *D*, I, 67.
29. George Washington to Sally Fairfax (9/21/1758), Houghton Library, Harvard University.

CHAPTER SEVEN

1. Ford, Worthington Chauncey, "Washington's Map of the Ohio," *Massachusetts Hist. Soc. Proc.*, LXI (1927–1928), 71–79.
2. GW, *D*, I, 41.
3. GW, *D*, I, 64.
4. GW, II, 7.
5. Lock of George Washington's hair at Mount Vernon; F, W, XIV, 252; GW, II, 395–396, XXXVI, 290; *Pennsylvania Mag. of Hist. and Biog.*, XXVI (1912), 508.
6. GW, I, 56.
7. Dinwiddie, Robert, *The Official Records of . . . in the Collections of the Virginia Historical Society*, 2 vols. (Richmond, Va., 1933–1934), I, 100, 161.
8. GW, I, 34.
9. Hump.
10. Dinwiddie, I, 59, 106–107.
11. GW, I, 32.
12. GW, II, 8, 12.
13. GW, *D*, I, 75.
14. GW, *D*, I, 76.
15. GW, *D*, I, 77.
16. GW, I, 49.
17. GW, *D*, I, 44.
18. GW, *D*, I, 79.
19. GW, I, 41.
20. GW, I, 48.
21. GW, I, 49, 61, 63.
22. F, W, I, 69–70.
23. GW, I, 54; GW, *D*, I, 85.
24. GW, *D*, I, 86.
25. GW, *D*, I, 87.
26. Ambler, Charles Henry, *George Washington and the West* (Chapel Hill, N.C., 1936), 67.
27. GW, I, 64.
28. F, *W*, I, 124.
29. JUMONVILLE AFFAIR: Ambler, 67–68, 71; F, I, 370–376; F, W, I, 122–124; Leduc, Gilbert, *Washington and "The Murder of Jumonville"* (Boston, 1943); Moreau, Jacop Nicolas, comp., *Mémoire Contenant le Précis des Faits, avec leur Pièces Justificatives* (Paris, 1756), 104–156; *Pennsylvania Mag. of Hist. and Biog.*, XVIII (1894), 44–47; S, W, II, 122–124; GW, I, 63–66, 69–70, 73; GW, *D*, I, 86–89.
30. GW, I, 66, 70.
31. *London Magazine*, XIII (1754), 370–371; F, I, 70n–71n.
32. GW, I, 73.

33. GW, I, 65.
34. GW, *D*, I, 89.
35. GW, I, 59–63.
36. Dinwiddie, I, 186, 206.
37. F, III, 89; Parkman, Francis, *Montcalm and Wolfe* (Boston, 1903), I, 1.

CHAPTER EIGHT

1. GW, I, 60, 67.
2. F, *W*, I, 124; GW, I, 73.
3. Dinwiddie, *Papers, op. cit.* (Chap. 7), I, 186; GW, I, 74.
4. GW, I, 81–82.
5. GW, I, 83.
6. GW, I, 72.
7. GW, *D*, I, 95.
8. GW, *D*, I, 100.
9. GW, *D*, I, 99.
10. GW, *D*, I, 101.
11. GW, I, 92.
12. GW, I, 95.
13. H, I, 4–8.
14. GW, I, 137.
15. H, I, 9–10.
16. H, I, 16–18.
17. F, I, 400.
18. Ambler, *Washington, op. cit.* (Chap. 7), 214.
19. Ambler, 215.
20. F, *W*, I, 124.
21. Ambler, 215.
22. FORT NECESSITY BATTLE: Ambler, 73–91, 211–221; F, I, 400–411; F, W, I, 119–124; GW, XXIX, 40; Marshall, John, *Life of George Washington,* rev. ed. (Philadelphia, 1832), notes pp. 11–12; Moreau, *Mémoire, op. cit.* (Chap. 7), 104–156; *Pennsylvania Mag. of Hist. and Biog.,* XVIII (1894), 47–50; S, W, II, 456–464.
23. F, *W*, I, 121.
24. S, *W*, II, 464.
25. F, I, 410; GW, I, 113, 115.
26. Marshall, notes pp. 11–12; GW, XXIX, 40.
27. Flexner, James Thomas, *Mohawk Baronet* (New York, 1959), 121–122.
28. Huske, John, *Present State of North America* (London and Boston, 1755), quoted in Wroth, Lawrence C., *An American Bookshelf, 1755* (Philadelphia, 1934), 40–41; Leduc, *Jumonville, op. cit.* (Chap. 7), 196–214; Thomas, Antoine Leonard, "Jumonville Poème," in *Poésies Diverses* (Paris, 1763).
29. Knollenberg, Bernhard, *George Washington, The Virginia Period* (Durham, N.C., 1964), 29.
30. *Virginia Gazette,* July, 19, 1754, 2–3.
31. GW, I, 32.

CHAPTER NINE

1. Dinwiddie, *Papers, op. cit.* (Chap. 7), I, 255, 281.
2. GW, I, 89–95.
3. Dinwiddie, I, 268.
4. GW, I, 97.
5. H, I, 39.
6. H, I, 51–53.

7. F, I, 440–441; GW, I, 106.
8. H, I, 38.
9. GW, I, 104–107.
10. Indenture between George Washington and George Lee and his wife (12/17/1754), photostat at Mount Vernon.
11. F, II, 13.
12. GW, I, 107.
13. GW, I, 122.
14. GW, I, 109.
15. Mary Washington to Joseph Ball (7/26/1759), Historical Society of Pennsylvania.
16. GW, I, 109.
17. F, II, 27; GW, I, 112–116.
18. GW, I, 116.

CHAPTER TEN

1. GW, I, 117.
2. GW, I, 133.
3. Hugh, I, 208; GW, I, 129.
4. GW, I, 120.
5. GW, XXIX, 41–42.
6. GW, II, 173.
7. Flexner, *Mohawk, op. cit.* (Chap. 8), 131.
8. GW, I, 124.
9. GW, II, 18, XXIX, 41.
10. Knollenberg, *Virginia, op. cit.* (Chap. 8), 160; Pargellis, Stanley M., *Lord Loudoun in North America* (New Haven, Conn., 1933), 308n.
11. GW, I, 129, 134.
12. GW, I, 137–138.
13. GW, I, 135–136.
14. GW, I, 141.
15. GW, I, 143.
16. GW, I, 145–146.
17. GW, I, 145.
18. GW, XXIX, 42.
19. BRADDOCK'S DEFEAT: Braddock, Edward, *Journal of the March of . . . Towards Fort Duquesne,* ed. Carson I. A. Ritchie [London, 1962]; GW, I, 149–159, XXIX, 42–44; Pargellis, Stanley M., *Military Affairs in North America, 1748–1765* (New York, 1936); Sargent, Winthrop, *The History of an Expedition against Fort Duquesne in 1755* (Philadelphia, 1855).
20. GW, XXIX, 42.
21. GW, I, 149.
22. GW, I, 149–150.
23. GW, XXIX, 43.
24. GW, XXIX, 43.
25. GW, I, 152.
26. GW, I, 152.
27. GW, XXIX, 43.
28. GW, XXIX, 44.
29. GW, XXIX, 45.

CHAPTER ELEVEN

1. GW, I, 153.
2. H, I, 74.
3. Fitzpatrick, *Himself, op. cit.* (Chap. 1), 81.

[367]

4. GW, I, 155.
5. GW, I, 149.
6. GW, I, 153n; H, I, 110; Sharpe, Horatio, *Correspondence,* ed. William Hand Browne (Baltimore, Md., 1888), I, 253.
7. F, II, 92.
8. GW, I, 527.
9. GW, I, 159.
10. F, II, 113; GW, I, 156–157, 162–163.
11. Dinwiddie, *Records, op. cit.* (Chap. 7), II, 184, 191.
12. GW, I, 202.
13. Hugh, I, 312; GW, II, 1.
14. GW, I, 264, 294, 296, 358–359, 385.
15. AOS, 51.
16. Fitzpatrick, *Himself,* 86.
17. GW, I, 197–198, 206.
18. GW, I, 200–201.
19. F, II, 145–147; H, I, 158.
20. GW, I, 203–206.
21. F, II, 133–135.
22. GW, I, 208–209, 222–223, 230.
23. H, I, 151.
24. H, I, 144–145, 188–189.
25. GW, I, 129n.
26. H, I, 125.
27. H, I, 178.
28. GW, I, 251.
29. GW, I, 289–290.
30. Dinwiddie, II, 261, 311, 329–330; Shirley, William, *Correspondence,* ed. Charles Henry Lincoln (New York, 1912), II, 372n.
31. H, I, 171–176, 181; GW, I, 294.
32. GW, I, 176, 254–255.
33. GW, I, 298–299; *GW, LA,* I, 26–28.
34. F, II, 160; H, II, 140–141.
35. Gottesman, Rita Susswein, *The Arts and Crafts in New York, 1726–1776* (New York, 1938), 385–386; GW, I, 298.
36. GW, I, 298–299.
37. GW, I, 116, 297n; Shirley, II, 412.
38. H, I, 203.
39. GW, *LA,* I, 28.
40. GW, I, 310; Sharpe, I, 389.
41. GW, III, 359.

CHAPTER TWELVE

1. GW, III, 352.
2. Sharpe, *Correspondence, op. cit.* (Chap. 21), I, 389, 416.
3. H, I, 253.
4. GW, I, 332.
5. GW, I, 305.
6. GW, I, 324–325.
7. F, II, 188; GW, I, 369–370.
8. GW, I, 493.
9. H, I, 231–232, 256.
10. H, I, 213.
11. GW, I, 317.
12. F, II, 209–210.

13. GW, I, 462–463, 465.
14. GW, II, 177–178.
15. GW, I, 382, 505.
16. H, II, 258.
17. GW, I, 260; H, I, 184.
18. Conway, *Barons, op. cit.* (Chap. 3), 259.
19. H, I, 185.
20. Fitzpatrick, John C., *The George Washington Scandals* (Alexandria, Va., 1929).
21. H, II, 174–175.
22. GW, XXVIII, 514; H, II, 39.
23. Morison, *Young, op. cit.* (Foreword), 9.
24. GW, I, 291–292; Morison, 16.
25. Hugh, I, 335.
26. GW, I, 254, 271, 295; H, I, 172.
27. Fitzpatrick, *Himself, op. cit.* (Chap. 1), 102.
28. AOS, 49–50.
29. Bland, Theodorick, *Bland Papers* (Petersburg, Va., 1840), I, 10; H, III, 293.
30. F, II, 371; H, I, 256, 265.
31. GW, I, 271.
32. GW, I, 245.
33. H, II, 340.
34. GW, I, 447.
35. George Washington to Dinwiddie (3/10/1757), Sulgrave Manor, Northamptonshire, England; copy at Mount Vernon.
36. GW, I, 387n.
37. GW, I, 473.
38. H, I, 350.
39. GW, I, 477–481.
40. GW, XXIX, 46–47.
41. GW, I, 492.
42. GW, I, 505.
43. GW, I, 497.
44. H, II, 2–5.
45. GW, I, 508, 511, 514.
46. H, II, 17–20.
47. GW, I, 521.
48. GW, I, 527–529.
49. GW, I, 525.
50. GW, *LA*, I, 32–33.

CHAPTER THIRTEEN

1. GW, II, 6–20.
2. GW, XXXII, 126, XXXVII, 366.
3. GW, II, 5.
4. H, II, 45.
5. GW, *LA*, I, 33–34.
6. H, I, 201.
7. H, II, 140–141.
8. GW, *LA*, I, 34; Marshall, *Washington, op. cit.* (Chap. 8), notes pp. 11–12; S, W, II, 463.
9. Kent, Donald H., "Contrecour's Copy of George Washington's Journal," *Pennsylvania Mag. of Hist. and Biog.*, XIX (1952), 1–32.
10. F, II, 238–240.

11. GW, II, 23, 32; H, II, 31–33.
12. George Washington to Dinwiddie (3/10/1757), Sulgrave Manor, Northamptonshire, England; copy at Mount Vernon.

CHAPTER FOURTEEN

1. GW, II, 61–62; H, II, 63.
2. GW, XXI, 337.
3. GW, II, 97, 118; H, II, 66n.
4. GW, II, 122.
5. GW, II, 25.
6. GW, II, 36–37; *Pennsylvania Archives* (Philadelphia, 1853), III, 175–181.
7. GW, II, 38, 40.
8. GW, II, 53.
9. GW, II, 97–98, 114–115, 140.
10. GW, II, 157.
11. GW, II, 144–145.
12. GW, II, 22, 128, 151; H, II, 99, 126, 131.
13. F, II, 265; GW, II, 23.
14. F, II, 264; H, II, 164.
15. GW, II, 53, 122–123; H, II, 170.
16. GW, II, 133; H, II, 182.
17. Dinwiddie, *Records, op. cit.* (Chap. 7), II, 703.
18. S, W, I, 58.
19. Knollenberg, Bernhard, "Review of Freeman's Volumes I and II," *William and Mary College Quar. Hist. Mag.*, 3d Ser., VI (1949), 111–121.
20. GW, II, 141–142.
21. H, II, 216.
22. H, II, 231, 242.
23. GW, II, 159, XXXVII, 479.
24. H, II, 243, 246–247.
25. GW, II, 162, 166–167.
26. GW, XXXVII, 480.
27. GW, II, 166–167.
28. F, II, 278, GW, *LA*, I, 38.

CHAPTER FIFTEEN

1. CUSTIS FAMILY: Custis, *Recollections, op. cit.* (Chap. 2), 13–19; F, II, 278–302.
2. F, II, 288.
3. Custis, 17.
4. Cary, Wilson Miles, "The Dandridges of Virginia," *William and Mary College Quar. Hist. Mag.*, 1st Ser., V (1896–1897), 30 ff.; F, II, 292–293.
5. F, II, 296–297.
6. Custis, 20.
7. GW, XXVII, 286n.
8. Adams, Abigail, "New Letter of . . . ," *Proc. American Antiquarian Soc.*, LV (1947), 125; F, III, 56n.
9. F, II, 300.
10. Fitzpatrick, *Himself, op. cit.* (Chap. 1), 73; Ford, Paul Leicester, *The True George Washington* (Philadelphia, 1898), 57.
11. F, III, 6.
12. GW, *LA*, I, 38.
13. *Pennsylvania Mag. of Hist. and Biog.*, LXVI (1932), 115.
14. GW, II, 210n.
15. GW, II, 173.

16. H, II, 330.
17. Information from Walter Macomber, consulting architect to Mount Vernon, Charles C. Wall, resident director, and various members of his staff. There is a great need for a detailed published study of Mount Vernon.
18. H, III, 67.
19. In Houghton Library, Harvard University.
20. GW, II, 292–294.
21. GW, XXXIV, 92.
22. GW, XXXIII, 501.
23. GW, XXVIII, 83.
24. Cary, Sally, *op. cit.* (Chap. 3), 45–52.
25. H, I, 249–250; Neill, *Fairfaxes, op. cit.* (Chap. 3), 80–81, 95–96.
26. GW, XXXVI, 263.
27. F, VII, 449; Fitzpatrick, *Himself,* 30.

CHAPTER SIXTEEN

1. GW, II, 278.
2. GW, II, 246–247, 253–260.
3. Bouquet, Henry, *Papers,* ed. S. K. Stevens, Donald H. Kent, and Autumn L. Leonard (Harrisburg, Pa., 1951), II, 268, 277–278, 291.
4. GW, II, 260–261.
5. Forbes, John, *Writings,* ed. Alfred Proctor James (Menasha, Wisc., 1938), 171–173.
6. GW, II, 268, 275.
7. Forbes, II, 270–271; Fortesque, Hon. J. W., *A History of the British Army* (London, 1899), II, 270–271; Knollenberg, *Virginia, op. cit.* (Chap. 8), 65–66.
8. GW, II, 276–278.
9. F, II, 320; GW, II, 251; H, II, 374, 389.
10. H, II, 285.
11. GW, II, 229; H, II, 354, 361.
12. GW, II, 269.
13. GW, II, 295–298.
14. Forbes, 219.
15. GW, II, 300.
16. Bouquet, II, 600–601.
17. GW, XXIX, 47–48.
18. Forbes, 255.
19. GW, II, 301–307.
20. F, II, 362–363.
21. Bouquet, II, 610; GW, II, 308.
22. Bouquet, II, 612–614; *Maryland Hist. Mag.,* IV (1909), 274–275.
23. Bouquet, II, 611.
24. GW, II, 314.
25. GW, II, 397.
26. H, III, 138–142.
27. GW, XXIX, 48–49; H, III, 151; Hump.
28. H, III, 143–146.

CHAPTER SEVENTEEN

1. GW, XXXII, 29.
2. H, III, 154.
3. F, III, 6.
4. GW, II, 318–319.

5. Mary Washington to Joseph Ball (7/26/1759), Historical Society of Pennsylvania.
6. GW, XXVII, 129.
7. See Appendix A.
8. GW, II, 337.
9. GW, II, 395.
10. GW, III, 141.
11. F, II, 302, III, 11.
12. GW, II, 395.
13. GW, I, xix.
14. Mount Vernon Ladies' Association, *Annual Report for 1959*, 40.
15. Hugh, II, 75.
16. GW, XXVIII, 258, 457, XXXII, 459.
17. GW, XXXII, 277; H, IV, 145.
18. F, II, 300.
19. F, III, 22; Thane, Elswyth, *Potomac Squire* (New York, 1963), 47.
20. Brissot de Warville, J. P., *New Travels in the United States of America* (London, 1797), I, 369–370; Cunliffe, *op. cit.* (Chap. 2), 66.
21. Hunter, Robert, Jr., *Diary* (San Marino, California, 1943), 143; Lund Washington to George Washington (10/5/1775), Mount Vernon.
22. GW, II, 401.
23. Martha Washington to Mrs. Bassett (4/6/1762), Mount Vernon; GW, *D*, I, 114.
24. GW, *D*, II, 116–118.
25. GW, *D*, I, 126.
26. GW, *D*, I, 351 ff.
27. George Washington to Burwell Bassett (8/28/1762), copy at Mount Vernon.
28. GW, II, 371; *William and Mary College Quar. Hist. Mag.*, 2d Ser., XXII (1942), 222.
29. GW, *D*, I, 245–303.
30. H, III, 305–306.
31. Ford, *True, op. cit.* (Chap. 15), 199; GW, *D*, I, 246n.
32. George Washington to Sally Fairfax (9/21/1758), Houghton Library, Harvard University; GW, XXXIV, 91, XXXVII, 425n.
33. George Washington to Capt. Van Swearington (5/15/1761), Mount Vernon; Fitzpatrick, *Himself, op. cit.* (Chap. 1), 145–146; Ford, *True*, 202.
34. GW, *D*, I, 284.
35. GW, *D*, I, 293, 297.
36. GW, *D*, I, 271, 289.
37. GW, II, 386.
38. GW, III, 50–51, XXIV, 143, XXVIII, 15, 284; *Virginia Mag. of Hist. and Biog.*, VII (1909), 404–412.
39. GW, XXVII, 385, XXVIII, 418.
40. Griffin, Appleton P. C., and Lane, William Coolidge, *A Catalogue of the Washington Collection in the Boston Athenaeum, with . . . an Inventory of Washington's Books drawn up by the Appraisers of his Estate* (Boston, 1897), 179; L'Estrange, Sir Roger, *Seneca's Morals by Way of Abstract, to which is added A Discourse under the Title of an After-Thought* (London, 1746).
41. GW, XXVIII, 209–210.
42. Addison, Joseph, *Cato* I.ii; II.iv; IV.iv.
43. George Washington to Sally Fairfax (9/21/1758), Houghton Library, Harvard University.
44. GW, XXVII, 367.
45. GW, XXIX, 259, XXXI, 253.

46. GW, III, 133.
47. GW, X, 237, XXVIII, 421, XXXIII, 383.
48. GW, XXXII, 398.
49. For an excellent discussion, see Boller, Paul F., *George Washington and Religion* (Dallas, 1963).
50. Lund Washington to George Washington (11/12/1775), Mount Vernon.
51. See Note 7, Chap. 15.
52. GW, XXXVII, 78–79.

CHAPTER EIGHTEEN

1. Appendix A.
2. GW, XXVIII, 516.
3. H, III, 232.
4. GW, II, 371.
5. Ford, *True, op. cit.* (Chap. 15), 298.
6. Alexander, Edward P., "Washington in Williamsburg," *Washington Association of New Jersey Reports* (1956), 14; F, III, 58.
7. Hugh, II, 213.
8. GW, XXIX, 313, 324.
9. *Virginia Mag. of Hist. and Biog.*, XV (1908), 356; Van Doren, Carl, *Benjamin Franklin* (New York, 1938), 529.
10. GW, III, 262; Knollenberg, *Virginia, op. cit.* (Chap. 8), 188.
11. GW, IV, 115.
12. F, III, 377; GW, II, 499.
13. GW, II, 377.
14. GW, II, 458, 476; GW, *LA*, I, 14, 92, II, 168; Thane, *Squire, op. cit.* (Chap. 17), 79.
15. GW, II, 476, 505 ff.; Thane, 78–83, 193.
16. GW, VIII, 21.
17. Knollenberg, "Review," *op. cit.* (Chap. 14), 111–121.
18. GW, VII, 198, XIII, 102.
19. H, II, 202.
20. American Art Assn., *Illus. Cat. of Washington Holograph MSS . . . to be sold . . . May 3rd and 4th, 1923* (New York, 1923), No. 342; GW, II, 359, gives the last word as "trouble" not "handle," which quite changes the meaning.
21. GW, III, 98.
22. GW, XXI, 385.
23. GW, III, 105, XXIX, 11–12, 62.
24. GW, IV, 179, XXIX, 207.
25. GW, II, 433.
26. GW, XIV, 362.
27. GW, IV, 114–115.
28. GW, XXIX, 137.
29. GW, XXXVII, 494; Knollenberg, *Virginia*, 117.
30. GW, III, 262–263.
31. GW, XXIX, 18; H, IV, 398.
32. GW, XXVII, 288, XXVIII, 152.

CHAPTER NINETEEN

1. Wharton, Anne Hollingsworth, *Martha Washington* (New York, 1896), 56–57.
2. GW, XXVII, 158.
3. GW, III, 44.
4. GW, XXVIII, 128.

[373]

5. GW, II, 334–335, 369–370.
6. Fitzpatrick, *Himself, op. cit.* (Chap. 1), 122; GW, II, 370.
7. GW, II, 371.
8. GW, *D*, I, 313.
9. F, III, 270; GW, III, 23; GW, *D*, II, 63, 86–87.
10. GW, III, 52.
11. John Johnson to Martha Washington (3/21/1772), Mount Vernon.
12. GW, III, 138.
13. GW, XXX, 401.
14. F, III, 595–598.
15. GW, II, 486–488.
16. GW, II, 515–517.
17. GW, III, 35.
18. H, IV, 42.
19. GW, III, 48–52.
20. GW, III, 36–37.
21. H, IV, 188–189.
22. GW, III, 131.
23. GW, III, 129–131.
24. GW, *D*, II, 111–113.
25. H, IV, 8, 233.
26. GW, III, 167–168.
27. GW, XXVII, 312.
28. GW, XXIX, 29.

CHAPTER TWENTY

1. GW, I, 253, II, 330.
2. GW, XXIX, 388; GW, *D*, I, 153–158; Hugh, II, 107.
3. GW, XXVII, 54–55.
4. GW, D, I, 122.
5. GW, II, 413–414.
6. GW, *D*, I, 136, 140, 142, 149, 152.
7. GW, XXXVI, 240.
8. GW, II, 347.
9. GW, XXIX, 430.
10. GW, II, 397.
11. F, III, 168n; GW, III, 53, 177, 398n; GW, *D*, I, 118n.
12. GW, II, 437.
13. GW, II, 397, XXV, 227.
14. F, III, 116.
15. GW, II, 357.
16. F, III, 60–61; GW, XI, 447; Haworth, Paul Leland, *George Washington, Country Gentleman* (Indianapolis, Ind., 1945), 15; Hugh, II, 57.
17. GW, II, 349, 362–364.
18. GW, II, 393, 396–398.
19. GW, II, 405.
20. GW, II, 413–417.
21. GW, XIII, 408.
22. F, II, 317; H, III, 115.
23. GW, II, 461–462, V, 28.
24. GW, II, 348, 380, 405, 419.
25. GW, II, 250, 370.
26. Ford, *True, op. cit.* (Chap. 15), 186–187; GW, II, 352, 395.
27. GW, II, 333–334.
28. GW, II, 379, III, 59.

29. GW, II, 430–432, 445–451, XXIX, 49.
30. GW, II, 444–453.
31. Cresswell, Nicholas, *Journal, 1774–1777* (New York, 1924), 27.
32. GW, *LA*, II, 192, III, 284.
33. GW, III, 285.
34. GW, XXXIII, 12.
35. AOS, 48.
36. Hugh, II, 117.
37. Ford, *True*, 138–139; Lund Washington to George Washington (4/8/1778), Mount Vernon.
38. GW, III, 164–165, V, 30.
39. GW, II, 488–489.
40. GW, II, 489n–490n.
41. GW, XXXVII, 493.

CHAPTER TWENTY-ONE

1. GW, X, 414.
2. GW, II, 459.
3. GW, XXVII, 377–381; GW, *D*, I, 188–194.
4. F, III, 93–95, 102–103; GW, XXXIII, 379.
5. GW, XXI, 182.
6. GW, III, 68.
7. GW, III, 86.
8. F, III, 96; GW, *LA*, II, 167, 169.
9. Flexner, *Mohawk, op. cit.* (Chap. 8), 261–262.
10. GW, II, 467–471.
11. GW, *D*, IV, 196.
12. GW, III, 2.
13. Knollenberg, *Virginia, op. cit.* (Chap. 8), 91–100, 135–137, 182–186, 194–195.
14. GW, II, 530.
15. GW, III, 66.
16. GW, *D*, I, 407–410.
17. GW, III, 31; GW, *D*, I, 418.
18. GW, *D*, I, 412–415.
19. GW, *D*, I, 417.
20. Fitzpatrick, *Himself, op. cit.* (Chap. 1), 143; GW, *D*, I, 418.
21. GW, *D*, I, 423.
22. Flexner, *Mohawk*, 243–245.
23. GW, *D*, I, 423–424.
24. GW, *D*, I, 426–427.
25. GW, XXVII, 353.
26. GW, III, 153–154; GW, *D*, I, 417.
27. GW, III, 121.
28. Knollenberg, *Virginia*, 95.
29. GW, III, 179.
30. H, IV, 275.
31. GW, III, 124.
32. GW, XXXIII, 407; H, IV, 274.
33. Knollenberg, *Virginia*, 185.
34. GW, III, 124, XXVI, 251.
35. GW, III, 2–3.
36. GW, III, 153–154, XXVIII, 155–156.
37. GW, XXVIII, 112 ff.; H, IV, 293.
38. GW, III, 144–146, XXXVII, 502–503.

39. GW, III, 187–200.
40. Fitzpatrick, *Himself,* 142; GW, III, 261.
41. GW, III, 199 ff., 498–499, XXVII, 361–362.
42. Baker, William S., *Early Sketches of George Washington* (Philadelphia, 1894), 32.
43. Nute, Grace L., "Washington and the Potomac," *American Hist. Rev.,* XXVIII (1922–1923), 497–519, 705–722.
44. GW, III, 17–21.
45. GW, XXVII, 374.
46. GW, II, 336–337, 345.

CHAPTER TWENTY-TWO

1. GW, II, 399–400; H, III, 288–289.
2. F, III, 130–131.
3. GW, II, 425–426.
4. F, III, 197.
5. GW, II, 500–504.
6. *New York Times Book Review,* 12/27/1964.
7. GW, III, 240–241.
8. F, III, 269–270; GW, D, II, 19n.
9. F, III, 219–224.
10. GW, D, I, 325n.
11. GW, II, 511–512.
12. AOS, 50; Hugh, II, 213.
13. F, III, 275–277; GW, III, 60–61.
14. Ford, *True, op. cit.* (Chap. 15), 83; GW, XI, 476.
15. GW, III, 234.
16. GW, III, 231, 241–242.
17. GW, III, 83–84.
18. Custis, *Recollections, op. cit.* (Chap. 2), 519.
19. GW, XXI, 378.
20. GW, VII, 471, XXI, 181.
21. GW, II, 133.
22. GW, III, 168–169, H, IV, 272.
23. GW, III, 224.
24. F, III, 350–354.
25. GW, XXXVII, 506.
26. F, III, 358; GW, D, II, 152–153.
27. GW, III, 242.
28. Rowland, Kate Mason, *The Life of George Mason* (New York, 1892), I, 418–427.
29. GW, III, 229, 232–233.
30. F, III, 370.
31. GW, III, 224–225.
32. GW, III, 232.
33. GW, III, 242.

CHAPTER TWENTY-THREE

1. Conway, *Barons, op. cit.* (Chap. 3), 215–221; F, III, 371.
2. GW, D, II, 162–169.
3. Burnett, Edmund C., *Letters of Members of the Continental Congress* (Washington, D.C., 1921), I, 28.
4. F, III, 377; GW, XXVII, 58.
5. Adams, John, *Familiar Letters of . . . and his wife, Abigail Adams* (New York, 1876), 31.

6. GW, III, 244–246.
7. GW, III, 246.
8. Burnett, I, 60.
9. *London Chronicle*, April 27, 1775, quoted in Willard, Margaret Wheeler, *Letters on the American Revolution, 1774–1775* (Boston and New York, 1925), 42.
10. Burnett, I, 28; *Pennsylvania Mag. of Hist. and Biog.*, V (1881), 110–111.
11. Austin, James T., *The Life of Elbridge Gerry* (Boston, 1828), I, 79; Burnett, I, 2, 28.
12. F, III, 389.
13. GW, III, 276n.
14. F, W, II, 457n.
15. GW, D, II, 181.
16. GW, III, 280–283; H, V, 158.
17. GW, III, 268.
18. H, V, 109–112.
19. F, III, 405; GW, D, II, 179, 191–192, 194.
20. F, III, 410 ff.; GW, D, II, 193; H, V, 162–165.
21. Madison, James, *Papers* (Chicago, 1962), I, 144–145.
22. Custis, *Recollections, op. cit.* (Chap. 2), 41.
23. F, III, 418.
24. F, III, 418–420.

CHAPTER TWENTY-FOUR

1. GW, XXXVII, 511.
2. GW, III, 291–292.
3. *Journals of the Continental Congress* (Washington, D.C., 1905), II, 56.
4. F, III, 429.
5. Austin, *Gerry, op. cit.* (Chap. 23), 79; F, W, II, 478n.
6. Adams, *Familiar, op cit.* (Chap. 23), 59.
7. F, W, II, 480n; Moore, George H., *Treason of Major General Charles Lee* (New York, 1860), 27.
8. Burnett, *Letters, op. cit.* (Chap. 23), I, 128.
9. GW, XVI, 9; GW, D, II, 198.
10. GW, XXX, 297.
11. GW, XXX, 296.
12. GW, IV, 359.
13. Burnett, I, 128; GW, XVI, 8.
14. F, III, 434; GW, III, 297.
15. *Journals of the Continental Congress*, II, 89–90.
16. Burnett, I, 124.
17. Adams, John, *Diary and Autobiography*, ed. L. H. Butterfield (Cambridge, Mass., 1961), 321 ff.
18. *Journals of the Continental Congress*, II, 91.
19. *Journals of the Continental Congress*, II, 97.
20. Burnett, I, 130–131.
21. GW, XXVIII, 472–473.
22. GW, III, 293n.
23. *Journals of the Continental Congress*, II, 92.
24. F, W, II, 481.
25. Burnett, I, 128, 135; Deane, Silas, *Papers* (New York, 1877), I, 59.
26. F, III, 452–454.
27. GW, III, 295.
28. GW, III, 296–297.

Index

ADAMS, FREDERICK B., 351
Adams, John, 23–24, 324–327, 334, 337–340, 342
Adams, Samuel, 337–338
Addison, Joseph, 242
Aeneas, 286
Albany, N.Y., 135
Albemarle, General Lord, 108
Albemarle Sound, 289–291
Alexander, Edward P., 351
Alexander, Francis, 42
Alexander the Great, 282
Alexandria, Va., 41, 110, 115–118, 184, 206, 235, 263, 283
Algonquins, 61
Aliquippa, 77, 93
Allegheny River, 61–62, 65, 73, 76–77, 183, 220
Allen, Ethan, 333
Alton, John, 125, 228, 234
American Philosophical Society, 351
Amson, John, 186, 191
"An Old Soldier," 55, 139, 159, 286, 315, 355–356
Anglican Church, 227, 243, 251, 262
Annapolis, Md., 148, 236, 263, 266, 311
Anne, Queen, 188
Annual Register, 39
Appleby School, 10, 12–13, 16, 18
Arlington, Va., 189n
Armstrong, John, 238
Arnold, Benedict, 146, 333, 340
Atheists, 243n
Atkin, Edmund, 178–179, 181
Augusta Court House, Va., 163
Austria, 161

BAHAMAS, 27
Baker, William S., 356
Ball, Joseph, 11, 30–31
Ball, Mary. See Washington, Mary Ball
Baltimore, Fifth Lord, 267
Baltimore, Md., 305
Barbados, 49–51, 60, 256
Basking Ridge, N.J., 268
Bassett, Burwell, 237, 244, 264, 267–268, 344–345

Bassett, Mrs. Burwell, 231
Bater, Philip, 257
Bath County, Va., 138
Baylis, John, 155
Beard, Geraldine, 351
Beck, 234
Bedford, Duke of, 47
Bedford, Penna, 206
Belvoir, 26, 30–32, 39, 52, 77, 113, 123, 132, 162, 184, 198, 201–203, 222, 236, 324
Beresford, Shirley, 351
Berkeley Springs (Warm Springs), W. Va., 38, 49, 238, 263
Bermuda, 50
Betty, 234
Billfaldt, Patricia J., 351
Bishop, Thomas, 131n, 234, 257–258
Blackwell's Sacred Classics, 265n
Blair, John, 155n
Bland, Humphrey, 158
Boone, Daniel, 295
Boston, Mass., 147–148, 320–321, 324, 327, 330, 332ff
Boston Massacre, 315
Boston Port Bill, 320
Boston Tea Party, 320
Botetourt, Lord, 294–295, 314
Boucher, Jonathan, 265–267, 303
Bouquet, Henry, 207–209, 218, 220n
Boyd, Julian P., 351
Braddock, Edward, 107, 114–131, 133–135, 143, 162–163, 171, 176, 193–194, 208, 209n, 326, 328
Braddock's Road, 206–217, 222
Breechy, 234
Breton, Arthur J., 351
Buchanan, John, 164
Buckmaster, Edward, 351
Buffalo, Washington wishes to breed, 303
Bullskin Plantation, 45, 51, 163, 280n, 286
Bundling, 359
Burgoyne, John, 135
Burwell, Carter, 117
Bushy Run, 218

[381]

Byrd, William, 188
Byrd, Mrs. William, 188
Byrd, William III, 117

CAESAR, 31, 153, 286
Calvert, Eleanor. *See* Custis, Mrs. John
  Parke
Cambridge, Mass., 258
Canada, 220, 229n, 333
Canals, 304–305
Cape Breton Island, 135
Captina Creek, 296
Carleton, Guy, 328n
Carlson, Arthur B., 351
Carlyle, John, 97–98, 283
Carlyle, Mrs. John, 97–98
Carlyle & Adam, 283–284
Caroline County, Va., 265
Cartagena Expedition, 16–17, 85–86,
  121
Cary, Robert & Co., 272, 277–284, 287,
  310, 314–315
Cary, Sally. *See* Fairfax, Sally
Catawbas, 150, 177–179, 218
Cato, 199, 242
Caunotaucarius, 10, 72
Ceelys, 39
Century Association, 351
Charles II of Sweden, 282
Charleston, S.C., 157
Charlestown, Mass., 324
Cheek, Mrs. Leslie, Jr., 351
Cherokees, 150, 178–179, 211, 218, 250
Chestnut Ridge, 217–218
Chew, Mr., 156–157
Cicero, 265n
Classicism, 28–29, 31, 153, 176–177,
  241–243
Claus, Daniel, 107
Columbia University, 267
Commager, Henry Steele, 313n
Committees of Correspondence, 320,
  322
Concord, Battle of, 330
Connecticut, 333–334, 342
Constitutional Convention, 325
Continental Army, 336ff
Continental Congresses, called, 321;
  First, 322, 324–328; Second, 329,
  332–345; during Revolution, 166,
  181, 269
Cooper, Miles, 268
Corbin, Richard, 81
Cornwall, Conn., Free Library, 351

Craik, James, 184–185, 295, 299
Crawford, William, 292, 295, 299–300
Cresap, Michael, 302
Creswell, Nicholas, 250
Crèvecoeur, Hector St. John, 174n
Croghan, George, 96–97
Cromwell, Oliver, 10
Crown Point, 135
Cumberland, Fort, 122–123, 136, 138,
  140, 142–144, 150–151, 154, 158,
  163, 166–167, 174, 196–197, 206,
  210, 304
Cunliffe, Marcus, 360
Cunningham, James, 172
Curtius, Quintus, 153
Custis, Daniel Parke, 189–191
Custis, George Washington Parke, 357–
  358
Custis, Jack, 189–190
Custis, John, 188–190
Custis, Mrs. John, 188–189
Custis, John Parke, 190, 192–193, 228,
  233–236, 240, 253, 261–269, 278–
  280
Custis, Mrs. John Parke, 267–269
Custis, Martha Dandridge. *See* Wash-
  ington, Martha
Custis, Martha Parke, 190, 192–193,
  228, 233–236, 244, 253, 261–264,
  277–282, 287n
Custis Estate, 228, 233–234, 240, 250,
  286
"Cyprian dame," 157

DAGWORTHY, JOHN, 142–144, 147, 154
Dalton, Mr., 125
Dandridge, Martha. *See* Washington,
  Martha
Dandridge, Mrs., 264
Davison, John, 86
Deane, Silas, 324, 326, 343
Death of Socrates, 242–243
Deism, 245
De Lancey, James, 268
Delawares, 53, 61–62, 77, 97, 212, 220
Dick, Mr., 123
Dickinson, John, 314
Dinwiddie, Fort, 138, 156
Dinwiddie, Robert, 47, 54–56, 68–69,
  77–78, 80–82, 84–85, 90–91, 93–95,
  108, 110–113, 117, 138, 151–155,
  158, 162–163, 166–167, 169, 172,
  178, 180–183, 202, 293–294, 319,
  349, 360

Dismal Swamp, 289–291
Dobbs, Arthur, 112
Doll, 234
Don Quixote, 240
Drowne, Soloman, 326–327
Drummond Pond, 290
Dunbar, Thomas, 130–131, 134
Dunmore, John Murray, 301, 320, 328, 330
Dunnings, Thomas J., Jr., 351
Duquesne, Fort, 85, 111–113, 115, 124–126, 150, 169–170, 172, 174, 193, 196, 206–207, 209, 215–222, 227, 295
Duquesne, Marquis, 69, 174n
Dyer, Eliphalet, 342–343

EASTON, PENNA., 212, 215–216
Edel, Leon, 351–352
Episcopal Church. *See* Anglican Church
Epsewasson, 11–12, 18. *See also* Mount Vernon
Erie, Penna., 54
Erie Canal, 304
Eskridge, George, 11–12
Euclid, 21
Eugene, Prince, 282
Evans, Nila J., 351
Ezequelle, Betty J., 351

FAIRFAX, ANNE. *See* Washington, Mrs. Lawrence
Fairfax, Fourth Lord, 27
Fairfax, George William, 25, 29–32, 35, 39–40, 97–98, 141n, 184, 186, 196, 201–202, 211, 228, 236, 283, 322, 324
Fairfax, Sally, 5, 25, 39–41, 52, 77, 98, 113, 116, 119, 123, 132–133, 141n, 143, 162, 184–186, 195–205, 234, 236, 242, 324
Fairfax, Sixth Lord, 25, 28, 31–33, 35, 41, 82, 240, 309
Fairfax, William, 25–30, 32, 55, 113, 132, 153, 159, 162, 173, 180, 184, 201, 241
Fairfax County, Va., 125, 141n, 250, 332, 342
Fairfax County militia, 329
Fairfax Resolutions, 321–322
Faquier, Francis, 214–215, 227
Fauntleroy, Betsy, 51–52
Fauntleroy, William, 51–52

Ferry Farm, 14–19, 27, 30, 35, 41, 52, 114, 228, 264–265, 286
Fitzpatrick, John C., 354, 359–360
Flexner, Beatrice Hudson, 351
Flexner, Helen Hudson, 352
Forbes, John, 193–194, 197, 199, 206–220, 252
Ford, Paul Leicester, 358–359
Ford, Worthington Chauncey, 354, 358
Forks of the Ohio, 54, 60, 71, 77, 80–81, 83–85, 99, 220–221. *See also* Duquesne, Fort
Fortesque, J. W., 209n
Forts. *See specific names*
Fosdick, Raymond B., 352
Franklin, Benjamin, 23, 134, 245, 251
Franklin, Penna., 54
Franklin, William, 268
Frazier, John, 60, 77
Frederick, Maryland, 119
Frederick County, Va., 141n, 255
Frederick of Prussia, 92, 161, 282
Fredericksburg, Va., 11, 15–16, 19, 30, 52–53, 138, 264–265
Freeman Douglas Southall 259, 356–357, 360
French and Indian War, causes, 47, 54–77; Washington fires first shots, 78–110; rest of 1754, 110–115; Braddock's campaign, 114–135; rest of 1755, 136–148; 1756 campaign, 149–172; 1757 campaign, 172–184; 1758 campaign, 193–194, 197, 199, 206–220; 1759 campaign, 229; 1760 campaign, 229; peace, 229n, 291
Freud, Sigmund, 3
Frick Art Reference Library, 351
Frontenac, Fort, 215n
Fry, Joshua, 80, 86, 93

GAGE, THOMAS, 121, 126–127, 134, 149, 268, 322, 328n, 332
Gaspée, 320
Gates, Horatio, 121, 329, 360
Gentleman's Magazine, 39, 139
George II, 54, 89n, 91, 160, 210
George III, 314, 326, 333
Georgetown, Va., 238
Georgia, 95
Germany, 31
Gerry, Elbridge, 334
Gibraltar, 229n
Gildart, James, 257

Gist, Christopher, 59, 64, 67–68, 71–77, 79, 84, 87, 96, 99, 134
Grape Vine Town, 296
Great Meadows, 86–87, 93–97, 99–109
Greek, 241, 265–266
Green, Captain, 30
Green, Charles, 184–185
Greenway Court, 32, 41
Gregory, James, 351
Gunston Hall, 247, 313

HALE, NANCY, 351
Hale, Nathan, 242
Half-King, 61–67, 70–72, 79–80, 83–91, 94–95, 97, 100–101, 108, 120
Halkett, Francis, 208, 211
Hamilton, Alexander, 270
Hamilton, Stanislaus Murray, 354
Hampton, 198
Hampton Roads, 115
Hanbury, John, 47
Hancock, John, 338, 342–343
Henry, Patrick, 242, 250, 316, 322, 330
Heslin, James J., 351
Heron, Great Blue, 297
Hillsborough, Lord, 321
Hog, Peter, 155–157
Holland, 303
Howe, William, 156
Hughes, Rupert, 359
Hume, David, 265n
Humphreys, David, 24, 30, 123, 222, 355

ILLINOIS, 61
Independence, 321, 325, 339
India, 229
Indiana Territory, 253
Indians, 36–37, 48, 53–55, 59–67, 70–75, 77, 79–80, 83–91, 93–94, 96–97, 99–100, 102, 106–107, 120–121, 126–129, 138, 140–142, 150–152, 161–162, 167, 177–181, 193, 207–208, 211–220, 249–250, 292–293, 295–297, 303, 322
Inflation, 309–310
Innes, James, 94, 110
Intolerable Acts, 320
Ireland, 303
Iroquois, 53, 61–62, 96, 120–121, 212, 215
Irving, Washington, 358

JACKSON'S RIVER, 138, 164–165
James River, 39, 289, 305

Jefferson, Thomas, 245, 251, 298, 322
Jenny, 234
Jeskakake, 65
Jesuits, 21
Jews, 243n
Jockey Club, Phila., 268
John, King, 23
Johnson, Mary, 11
Johnson, Thomas, 304, 339
Johnson, Sir William, 135–136, 212, 215
Joncaire, Philip Thomas, 66–67, 72–73, 88
Jones, Mr. and Mrs. Louis C., 352
Julius, 234
Jumonville Affair, 87–93, 104–106, 125, 169–170, 173–174
Jumonville, Joseph C., 90, 104, 106

KANAWHA, GREAT, 294–295, 297–298
Kanawha, Little, 297–298
Kanawha land grants, 294–303, 328, 336
Kent, Donald H., 173n–174n
Kentucky, 295
King's College, 266, 268
Kingston, Ontario, 215n
Knollenberg, Bernhard, 209n, 254, 294n, 300, 352, 360
Kyashuta, 297

LAFAYETTE, MARQUIS DE, 232–233, 241–243, 270
Lafayette, Mme. de, 241
Lake Champlain, 135, 193
Lake Erie, 54, 135
Lake George, 135
Lake George, Battle of, 136
Lake Oneida, 135
Lake Ontario, 135, 161, 215n
Lancaster, Penna., 242–243
Langley, Batty, 196
Latin, 241, 262, 266
Laurel Ridge, 86, 210
Le Boeuf, Fort, 54, 66–71
Lee, Charles, 121, 326, 328–329, 334
Lee, Richard Henry, 322, 324, 327, 331
Lee, Thomas, 47
Leech, Wilmer R., 351
Leeward Islands, 188–189
Lewis, Mrs. Fielding, 12, 264
Lewis, Robert, 354
Lewisburg, 135, 139
Lexington, Battle of, 330

Library of Congress, 351, 353–354
Lincoln, Abraham, 357
Lodge, Henry Cabot, 358
Logstown, 61–65
Logstown, Treaty of, 62–63
London, 78, 305, 309
London Magazine, 39, 89n
Loring, Mrs. Joshua, 156
Lossing, Benson J., 357
Loudoun, Fort, 210, 280n. *See also* Winchester, Va.
Loudoun, Fourth Earl, 162, 167–177, 180, 183, 193, 254
Low Land Beauty, 41
Loyal Hannon, 214–215, 218

MACKAY, JAMES, 94–95, 99, 104–105, 108, 114
Macomber, Walter, 352
Madison, James, 330
Magowan, Walter, 262, 265
Malone, Dumas, 352
Marlborough, Duke of, 188, 282
Marshall, John, 357
Martin, Thomas Bryan, 33
Maryland, 84, 112, 142–144, 147–149, 163, 165, 174, 252, 267, 304–305, 311, 324, 336, 339
Mason, George, 25, 247, 311–314, 321, 329
Masons, 53
Massachusetts, 28, 118, 324–325, 329–330, 332ff
Massachusetts Charter, 320
Massachusetts Convention, 334
Meadows, Christine, 351
Mearns, David C., 352
Mémoire Contenant le Précis des Faits, 173–174
Mercer, George, 145, 157, 191–192, 216–217, 256
Microcosm or the World in Miniature, 146–147
Mima, 234
Mingo Town, 296
Mingoes, 62, 96–97, 179, 213
Minick, Rachel A., 351
"Ministerial troops," 333
Mississippi Company, 292–293
Moe, Henry Allen, 352
Mohammedans, 243n
Mohawk River, 135, 161
Moll, 234

Monongahela, 60, 85, 126–127, 130, 208, 294
Montour, Andrew, 96–97, 140
Montreal, 66, 135, 215n
Moravians, 215
Morison, Samuel Eliot, 3, 158, 359
Morristown, N.J., Historical Library, 354
Morse, Frank E., 351
Mount Vernon, during Washington's early years, 12–14, 18–19, 24–26, 32–35, 41, 52; rented during French and Indian War, 114–117, 123–124, 132, 143, 162, 180, 184–186; between conflicts, 228–288, 298–299, 311, 315, 321; Washington inherits, 234; time of Continental Congress, 324, 328–331; during Revolution, 246, 251, 258, 329; after Revolution, 354; Washington wills estate, 269–270; restoration and library, 354–355; land and slaves added, 181, 233, 253, 275, 286–287; architectural quality, 245–249; described in pastoral terms, 240; furnishings, 180–181, 185, 196, 199, 257, 282, 324; rebuildings, 195–196, 235–236; soil, 272
Mount Vernon Ladies Association of the Union, 351
Muckrakers, 359
Muir, John, 250
Mulatto Jack, 234
Murthering Town, 63, 79
Muse, George, 299

NECESSITY, FORT, 86–87, 93–97, 99–112, 125, 131, 169–170, 173–174, 208, 293
Negroes, 13, 15, 18, 27, 29, 48, 105, 114, 117, 267, 275–276, 285–287, 290, 321–322
New England army, fear of, 333–335, 337
New Hampshire, 244
New Jersey, 142, 268, 324
New London, 147
New York City, 145–146, 148, 173, 267–268
New York Colony, 81, 293, 324, 332–334
New-York Historical Society, 351
New York Public Library, 351, 353
New York Society Library, 351

Newcastle, Duke of, 108
Newport, 147
Niagara, Fort, 135–136, 215n, 229
Noah, 237
Nonimportation agreements, 311–315, 321, 327–328
Norfolk, Va., 289
North Carolina, 112, 136
Nova Scotia, 229n

OHIO COMPANY, 47, 54–56, 59, 79–80, 84–85, 111, 122, 207, 219, 293n, 309
Ohio Valley, 34–35, 47–48, 53–134, 170–173, 193–194, 206–220, 292–304, 309, 321, 328, 336, 360
"Old Soldier." *See* "An Old Soldier"
Oneidas, 96
Onondaga Council, 62
Orme, Robert, 115–117, 129, 134, 143
Oswego, Fort, 135, 161, 215n
Ottawas, 74

PALATINES, 303
Pamunkey River, 190–191
Paris, Peace of, 229n, 291–292
Parke, Daniel, 188–190
Parke, Frances. *See* Custis, Mrs. William
Parke, Lucy. *See* Byrd, Mrs. William
Parliament, 48, 310–311, 322, 327, 332–333
Payne, William, 141n
Peale, Charles Willson, 317
Pemberton, Isaac, 336–337, 340
Penn, Richard, 268
Pennsylvania, 100, 122, 139, 147, 165, 180, 206, 209–212, 217, 220, 293, 324, 336. *See also* Philadelphia
Peter, a smith, 274
Peyrouney, William, 157
Philadelphia, 145–146, 148, 172–175, 193, 206, 209n, 238, 288, 311, 324–328, 332–345
Phillipse, Eliza (Polly), 146–148, 173
Piper, Sergeant, 24
Pitt, Fort, 293, 295–296, 298. *See also* Forks of the Ohio and Duquesne, Fort
Pitt, William, 193–194
Pittsburgh, 295
Pontiac's War, 222, 250, 293, 297
Pope, Alexander, 242
Pope's Creek, 12

Posey, Lawrence, 253
Posey, Milly, 253, 262
Posey, Price, 253
Posey, Thomas, 252–253
Post, Christian F., 215
Potomac, 12–13, 15, 26, 115, 117, 206, 284, 304–305
Prescott, Orville, 351
Presidential Papers Microfilm: George Washington Papers, 353
Presque Isle, Fort, 54
Principio Company, 11, 13–14, 18
Proclamation of 1763, 292
Prussia, 161
Putman, Israel, 334

QUEBEC, 229
Quebec Act, 320

RALEIGH TAVERN, WILLIAMSBURG, 314, 320–321
Ramsay, William, 240, 252
Randolph, Peyton, 322, 324, 329–330, 334, 340
Rappahannock, 15–16, 49
Raystown, Penna., 206, 209n, 213
Redstone Creek, 84, 96
Reed, Joseph, 270
Rhode Island, 320, 326
Roanoke, 164
Robinson, Beverley, 146, 148
Robinson, John, 117, 143–144, 154, 164, 166–167, 183, 209–211
Rome, 334n
Ronalds, Francis S., 352
Rose, 234
Rosenbach Foundation, 350, 354–355
Ross, Marvin, 352
Round Bottom, 298, 302
Royal Navy, 27, 30–31
Rules of Civility, 21–23, 25
Russell, Bertram, 359n
Russia, 161
Rutherford, John, 160

ST. JOHN, MRS. SEYMOUR, 352
St. Lawrence River, 135
St. Pierre, Legardeur de, 68–70
Sandy Creek, 294, 297
Saxony, 161
Schomberg, Frederick, Duke of, 31
Scotland, 303
Sellers, Charles Coleman, 352

Senecas, 66, 241, 244, 297
Seven Years' War, 92, 161, 193, 211, 229, 291. *See also* French and Indian War
Sharpe, Horatio, 112–115, 144–145, 148–149, 171
Shawnees, 53, 62, 96–97, 179, 212
Shenandoah Valley, 34, 36–38, 41–42, 45, 47, 60, 82, 136–144, 149–172, 174–184, 194, 196, 206, 209, 211, 221
Shingiss, 61
Shirley, William, 118, 135, 143–144, 147–149, 324
Slaves. *See* Negroes
Smallpox, 50
Smith, Charles, 280n
Sorel River, 135
South Carolina, 63, 96, 147, 157, 163, 174, 177
Spain, 16
Sparks, Jared, 182, 354, 358
Spectator, The, 23, 27, 31
Stamp Act, 310–311
Stanwix, John, 186, 194
Stephen, Adam, 143n, 148, 158, 255–256
Steubenville, Ohio, 296
Stewart, David, 164
Stewart, Robert, 145, 184–185, 238, 249, 256, 258–259, 278, 355
Stirling, Lord, 268
Stoic philosophy, 176, 201–202, 241–242
Stuart, Gilbert, 4
Sweden, 161
System of Agriculture or a Speedy Way to Get Rich, 272

Tempest, The, 240
Thomson, James, 265n
Thornton, Dr. William, 246
Ticonderoga, 135, 161, 193, 229, 333
Tom, a runaway, 275–276
Tourtellot, Arthur B., 352
Townshend Acts, 311, 315
Tragedy of George Barnwell, 49–50
Trinity College, Cambridge, 39
Tristram Shandy, 241
True Happiness, 21
Truro Parish, 243, 251
Tunbridge, 262
Turner, C., 277

Van Braam, Jacob, 59, 61, 72, 103–106
Van Swearingen, Captain, 256
Venango, 54, 65–67, 70, 72
Vernon, Admiral, 16
Villiers, Coulon de, 104–105
Virginia Assembly, 48, 80–81, 111–113, 137, 144, 149–150, 153, 169, 180–181, 314. *See also* Virginia House of Burgesses and Virginia King's Council
Virginia Convention, 329
Virginia Gazette, 180n, 328n
Virginia House of Burgesses, 30, 39, 46, 55, 78, 114, 117, 141n, 144, 155, 163, 167, 183, 210–211, 227–228, 236, 309–311, 314, 320–322, 327
Virginia King's Council, 10, 28, 55, 78, 81, 110, 166, 188, 290, 294–295, 299, 349
"Virginia Sentinel," 154–155
Voltaire, 92

Waggener, Thomas, 300
Wakefield, 12
Wall, Charles C., 351
Walpole Company, 293
War of the Austrian Succession, 53
War of the Grand Alliance, 53
War of the Spanish Succession, 53
Ward, Artemas, 334, 336, 338
Wardrope, Mrs., 116
Warm Springs. *See* Berkeley Springs
Warner, Mildred, 10
Warren, Joseph, 334
Warville, Brissot de, 234
Washington, Augustine (father), 10–18, 238
Washington, Augustine (half-brother), 11, 16, 18–19, 156
Washington, Betty (sister). *See* Lewis, Mrs. Fielding
Washington, Charles (brother), 13, 301
Washington, George
    CHRONOLOGICAL EVENTS: ancestry, 9–12; childhood, 12–17, 228; education, 5–6, 16, 18, 21–24, 26–27, 35, 232, 241; youth, 18–45, 232; surveyor, 16, 21, 35, 37, 41, 44–45, 53, 266, 277; love for Sally Fairfax, 5, 25, 39–41, 52, 77, 98, 113, 116, 123, 132–133, 141n, 143, 162, 184, 195–205, 236, 242, 324; almost enters navy, 30–31; first western trip, 35–

38; illnesses, 41, 50–51, 114, 124–132, 138, 184–186, 209, 222, 237–238; before wilderness mission, 46–56; trip to Barbados, 49–51; militia major, 52–53; mason, 53; wilderness mission, 56–80, 84; Jumonville affair, 80–93, 104–106, 125, 169–170, 173–174; Fort Necessity campaign, 93–112, 117, 169–170, 173–174, 208, 293; resigns, 110–115; Braddock's campaign, 107, 115–131, 132–135, 143, 162–163, 171, 176, 193–194, 208, 209n, 326, 328; rest of 1755 campaign, 136–145; trip to Massachusetts, 145–148; 1756 campaign, 149–172; 1757 campaign, 172–184; Philadelphia trip, 172–175; courts Martha, 186–193, 195–201, 204–205, 221, 358; 1758 campaign, 193–194, 197, 199, 206–223, 249, 280n, 319, 349–350; married, 227; life based at Mount Vernon, 20–21, 157, 228–288, 343; stepfather, 192–193, 228, 233–236, 240, 261–269, 278–280; childless, 269–271; Dismal Swamp speculation, 289–291; speculation in Ohio lands, 286, 291–304, 309, 321, 328, 336, 360; exploration on Ohio, 295–298, 301n; promotes Potomac Canal, 304–305; portrait painted, 317; road to Revolution, 309–345; First Continental Congress, 322, 324–328; between Congresses, 328–331; Second Continental Congress, 329, 332–345; during Revolution, 148, 163n, 181, 210, 229, 242, 251, 258, 268, 270–271, 285–286, 304, 337; after Revolution, 292n, 355, 358

AMUSEMENTS: athletics, 23, 317; cards and gambling, 38, 147, 158, 167, 173, 185, 238–239, 289, 321, 324; cockfights, 239; dancing, 38–39, 41, 147, 158, 173, 191, 198, 235–236, 238–239, 250, 263, 268; entertaining, 159, 163, 234–236, 242, 252; fencing, 163; fine clothes, 32, 38, 106, 145–147, 162, 235, 282; hunting and dog breeding, 31–34, 166, 238–249, 252; races, 236, 238–239; raffles, 239; riding and horse breeding, 23, 192, 240, 314; shooting, 238; snuff and smoking, 234, 239; taverns, 146–147, 173, 236–237, 268, 325; theatres and other shows, 44,

49–50, 146–147, 158, 167, 199, 236, 238–239; visiting, 236–237, 268

ATTITUDES TOWARDS: American west, 37, 252, 289, 298; charity, 251; classical culture, 28–29, 31, 153, 176–177, 241–243; drinking, 153, 157–159, 211, 236, 257; education, 18, 23–24, 252–253, 262, 266–267; England, 13–19, 26–33, 48, 86, 148, 160–161, 175, 210, 238, 288, 305, 309ff; gambling, 153; inventing, 274; keeping word, 259; land grant policy, 37, 291–292, 294, 302; manufacturing, 139; marriage, 200, 261, 267, 270, 343; reforming individuals, 252, 257; sexual behavior, 153, 155–157, 200, 267–268; slavery, 275–276, 286–287, 303, 321–322; swearing, 153, 157; travel, 51, 266–267; truth telling, 252–255; Virginia patriotism, 148–149, 221

BUSINESS CONSIDERATIONS: accounts, 277–278, 354; assets, 234, 286, 327; borrower and lender, 181, 252–253; 258–259, 275, 277–280, 328; business concepts, 206, 230, 257, 280n; Custis estate, 228, 233–234, 240, 250, 272, 274–277, 287n; estate industries, 234, 252, 275–277, 284, 315; exporter, 256; fisheries, 276, 284; handles friends' estates, 236, 259; mills, 277, 284; relations with employees, 257–258, 342; relations with English factors, 180–181, 196, 234, 262–263, 265n, 272, 274, 277–283, 287–288, 310, 314–315; relations with tradesmen, debtors, creditors, etc., 253, 256–257, 283; smuggling, 320; stock companies, 290, 304–305; turns to local trade, 282–284

DOCUMENTATION: 3–5, 230–232, 353–377

LANDOWNER: aquisitions of land, 45, 51, 114, 181, 234, 238–239, 253, 264–265, 275, 284, 286, 289–304; breeder, 232, 303; experimenter, 272–274; farmer, 98, 176, 180, 232, 237–238, 240, 265, 272–280, 282–286, 313, 322, 329, 353

MILITARY: cartographer, 78; clothing troops, 82, 111, 170, 215, 221; discipline, 83, 111, 138, 152, 158–159; engineer, 83, 85, 95, 217–218;

enlistment and drafts, 82, 138, 140–141, 150–151, 170, 177, 182, 216, 319; fooling the enemy, 254–255; forts, 93–94, 101, 142, 150, 170; headquarters controversy, 142–143, 150–151, 154, 163; Indians, 37, 64, 67, 70–71, 83–84, 87, 93, 100–101, 107–109, 120, 140, 150, 178–179, 207–208, 211–212, 218; intelligence and spying, 61–63, 66, 68–69; 79, 215–216; leadership, 109, 111, 139, 155, 160; military chest, 139–140, 170, 181; military vs. civilian rights, 82, 140–141, 319; militia, 138, 151–155, 164–166, 170, 177, 285, 319; officer appointments, 138, 159; officers' behavior, 153–159, 163; pensions, 170; propaganda, 108n, 255; provincials vs. British regulars, 16–17, 85–86, 95–96, 99, 101, 142–144; punishments, 111, 138–139, 159–160, 170, 177; reading manuals, 81, 158; road controversy, 206–217, 222; strategy and tactics, 83–85, 88, 93, 99–101, 110–111, 120, 124, 128, 133–134, 136, 140, 142, 150, 170–171, 180, 208, 211–216, 220, 227, 319; supplies, 82, 111, 138, 139, 170, 182, 209, 215, 221, 280n, 319; transport, 82, 209; uniforms, 16, 145, 155, 212, 316, 330; Washington's commissions, 52–53, 55–56, 81, 94, 137–138, 149; Washington's desire for regular commission, 112, 121–122, 138, 143, 145, 147–149, 160–162, 171, 175–176, 181, 185–186, 194, 207, 221; Washington's military attitudes during peace, 229–230, 249–250; Washington's pay, 52, 80, 117, 137, 176, 181, 339, 341–342; Washington's relationship with officers, 155, 158–160, 222–223, 349–350; Washington's resignations and threats to resign, 112–114, 144, 148–149, 166–167, 169, 177, 186, 221–223, 229, 249, 349–350

PERSONAL: appearance, 41, 50, 80, 145, 174, 191–192, 282; artistic urge, 23, 36, 41, 49, 195–196, 245–249, 282; character, 3–6, 24, 44, 49–50, 79, 91, 114, 137, 141n, 159, 176–177, 181–182, 205, 216, 222, 253–255, 283, 291n, 299–300, 303–304, 315–319, 335–336, 340–341, 343; coat of arms, 145; experience teaches, 5–6, 318–320; humor, 236–238, 242, 317; relationship with ladies in general, 41–44, 98, 143–144, 157, 173, 270n; neighborhood leader, 249–260, 312–313, 341–342; orator, 245, 250–251, 324; reading, 23, 31, 81, 158, 235, 239, 240–241, 266, 314, 324, 335; religion, 22, 48, 154–155, 209, 227, 237–238, 243–245, 251, 262, 266, 321, 335–336, 341, 344; teeth, 50, 192; writer, 21, 36, 41–44, 69, 179, 197, 222–223, 232, 245, 291n

POLITICAL CONSIDERATIONS: during youth, 52–53; during French and Indian War, 117–118, 143–144, 147, 155, 167, 171–172, 182, 319; road to revolution, 309–345; Continental Congresses, 321–322, 324–329, 332–345; Burgess, 141n, 210–211, 227–228, 236, 238, 249–251, 255–256, 305, 310–311, 314, 320–322; diplomacy, 91, 107; Justice of the County Court, 251; opposes independence, 321, 325; rivalry with other colonies, 122–123, 142n, 143–144, 147, 149, 163, 171, 206–216, 293–311; sense of responsibility for neighbors, 148–149, 176–177, 234n, 259; trustee of Alexandria, 251; vestryman, 243, 251

Washington, George Augustine (nephew), 269–270
Washington, Jane (half-sister), 11–12
Washington, John (great-grandfather) 9–10, 72
Washington, John Augustine (brother), 13, 16, 89, 118, 125
Washington, Rev. Lawrence (great-great-grandfather), 9
Washington, Lawrence (grandfather), 9–10
Washington, Lawrence (half-brother), 11, 13, 15–19, 24–26, 30, 38–39, 41, 46–52, 85–86, 121, 156, 186, 238, 293n
Washington, Mrs. Lawrence (sister-in-law), 24–25, 32, 38, 52, 114, 234
Washington, Lund (cousin), 231, 258
Washington, Martha, ancestry, 189–190; Custis marriage, 190–191, 230, 269; Custis estate, 228, 233–234, 240, 250; courted by Washington, 191–193, 195–201, 204–205, 221, 358; Washington marriage in general, 157,

199–200, 205, 227–237, 253, 259–260, 331; relation with Sally Fairfax, 204–205, 236; burns correspondence with Washington, 230–231; only surviving letter to Washington, 230–231; no children by Washington, 269–271; after Washington elected commander-in-chief, 340, 343–344

Appearance, 190, 230; character, 190, 205; style of dressing, 230, 234, 344; housewife, 232–233; hostess, 234–235; mother, 261–269; visiting, 236, 261

Washington, Mary Ball (mother), 11–12, 19–20, 30, 41, 46, 48, 114, 116–118, 123–124, 137, 228, 264–265, 272, 358, 360–361

Washington, Mildred (sister), 16

Washington, Samuel (brother), 12, 16

Washington County, Penna., 302

Waterford, Penna., 54

Weems, Mason Locke (Parson), 4, 21–22, 100–101, 254, 357–359

West, Benjamin, 242–243

West Indies, 275–276

White House Plantation, 190–191, 227

White Thunder, 65

Whittredge, Arnold, 352

William and Mary College, 24, 39, 81

William Henry, Fort, 136, 193

Williams, Alan D., 352

Williamsburg, Va., 35, 39, 44, 77–78, 80, 110, 112–113, 143–144, 181, 186–187, 191–192, 227–228, 236, 238, 250, 263, 267, 294, 301n, 314, 320–321, 330

Will's Creek, 48, 77, 82, 105, 122. *See also* Cumberland, Fort

Wilson, Woodrow, 358

Winchester, Va., 136, 140–142, 151–152, 154, 163, 166–167, 175, 177–180, 192, 194, 210–211

Wine culture, 273

Wollaston, John, 230

Wood, Grant, 4

Woodward, W. E., 359

YOUGHIOGHENY RIVER, 85–86, 125, 208